For Reference

Not to be taken from this room

DATE			

Theory and History of Literature
Edited by Wlad Godzich and Jochen Schulte-Sasse

For other books in the series, see p. 265.

Oral Poetry:
An Introduction

Paul Zumthor

Translation by Kathryn Murphy-Judy
Foreword by Walter J. Ong

Theory and History of Literature, Volume 70

University of Minnesota Press, Minneapolis

Originally published as *Introduction à la poésie orale*, copyright ©
1983 by Éditions du Seuil, Paris.

**The University of Minnesota Press gratefully acknowledges
translation assistance provided for this book by the French Ministry
of Culture.**

Published by the University of Minnesota Press
2037 University Avenue Southeast, Minneapolis MN 55414.
Printed in the United States of America.

Library of Congress Cataloging-in-Publication Data

Zumthor, Paul
   [Introduction à la poésie orale English]
   Oral poetry : an introduction / Paul Zumthor : translation by
Kathryn Murphy-Judy : foreword by Walter J. Ong.
      p.   cm. — (Theory and history of literature : v. 70)
   Translation of: Introduction à la poésie orale. Paris : Editions
du Seuil, c1983.
   Bibliography: p.
   Includes index.
   ISBN 0-8166-1724-4.
   ISBN 0-8166-1725-2 (pbk.)
   1. Oral interpretation of poetry. 2. Oral tradition. 3. Oral-
formulaic analysis. 4. Narration (Rhetoric) 5. Poetry—History and
criticism. I. Title II. Series.
PN4151.Z8513   1990   89-22717
801'.951—dc20   CIP

Contents

Part II. The Forms

Part III. The Performance

Part IV. Roles and Functions

Foreword
Walter J. Ong

Only in the past few decades have we discovered the difference between the managing of thought and expression in primary oral cultures (cultures with no knowledge of writing at all) and in cultures that have deeply interiorized literacy. Earlier studies of verbal art forms had concentrated on texts. Recent discoveries concerning the thought forms and the modes of expression of oral cultures have revolutionized our understanding not only of orality but also of what literature itself is and of the dependency on literacy of thought forms that we have taken for granted in literate cultures as "natural."

Paul Zumthor's work here belongs in the new tradition studying orality-literacy contrasts. It deepens our understanding tremendously. The basic question Zumthor undertakes to answer is whether there is a specific oral poetics or "poeticity." To answer this question, he examines not merely oral verbalization but a much wider and deeper matter, the nature and uses of voice as such. As he says, we have no history of voice. Voice and language are distinct objects for the anthropologist. But voice without language (a shout, voice-control exercises) has a certain impotence, and so does language without voice, writing. The culmination of voice is not merely any use of language, but song.

Focusing on voice and song, and all the things to which voice and song relate, and ransacking all available sources, this book moves in a direction totally opposite to much current critical speculation, which, the author declares, in concentrating on "text" has not only failed to refocus our long text-bound horizons but "blurred the picture all the more by reinscribing the long-standing tendency to sacralize the letter in a burlesque of our mental processes." Zumthor considers texts, of course, but he considers them—and all of human life—not merely in terms of sound but specifically of voice, evoking eventually all the ancient magic associated with voice and its connection with the center of human existence. In all this he is fully aware of the work of structuralism and deconstruction, with which he does not butt heads but whose shortcomings he undertakes to compensate for.

Song comes from music and from grammar, but more from music. It is a privileged signifying practice, touching the fully subjective in us, where symbol, culture, and natural powers merge. In speech, the speaker tends to blend into the circumstances. In song, the self "claims for itself the totality of its space." Bodily (muscular) and psychic powers merge. One thinks of Wallace Stevens's poem "The Idea of Order at Key West": "She sang beyond the genius of the sea / But it was she and not the sea we heard. / For she was the maker of the song she sang. / She was the single artificer of the world / In which she sang." Zumthor's book could be construed as a vastly learned expansion and explication of the deepest message in Stevens's lyric.

Zumthor casts his net very wide—chronologically, geographically, sociologically, psychologically, and aesthetically—and does so with consummate skill. He moves from ancient Greece and other early cultures through intervening cultures to every part of the modern world—Africa, India, East Asia, both Americas, Australia, Europe, and all the rest—circumstantially reviewing the use of voice and attendant practices, such as dance (part of the orality of poetry, and generally if not always at least vaguely erotic) and gesture (which is extraordinarily powerful but "never exact"—keen, offhand perceptions such as this illuminate Zumthor's entire book). He discusses the relationship of epic song to political organization (cultures with strong central control tend to have epics more than do other cultures, etc.). Aristotle's idea of the epic was too abstract and schematic: song is always rooted, and in many soils. Zumthor discusses the silence beyond language and voice, and evokes archaic times when (presumably) language and music were one, comparing those times to our own age, which he styles as "broken apart by the corruption of writing."

He is not in the least nostalgic, however, and by no means repudiates writing but only points out some of its problems. The modern world asserts itself strongly and in detail throughout this book, which moves easily from an aside about Granny Riddle in Arkansas in 1970 to an in-depth discussion of jazz and rock music, where score, lyrics, and singing itself are often the work of the same person. Zumthor celebrates with great enthusiasm the fact that Afro-American music is the only music that has today caught the ear of all five continents and unifies all five. It has Africanized the world—a music that communicates rather than simply pleases, although it pleases, too, and, like other song, forces the present to make some sense.

Especially when using the guitar, Afro-American music reintroduces the almost magical feeling once always evoked by voice everywhere. (The Tupi of Brazil would not eat a captive singer, believing that he belonged to another world.) This unification of the world by song was possible because song is, in its own way, the fully universal art.

Hermeneutics or interpretation preoccupies students of the humanities today, and Zumthor moves into the hermeneutic field by pointing out that in song the interpreter is the singer, "the individual whose voice and gestures are perceived during performance by sight and sound." Gesture re-creates sacred space-time. The interpreter does not, however, work alone, but in conjunction with his or her auditors: out of the interplay between the two the full meaning of the song emerges. Moreover, the styles of interaction vary greatly from culture to culture, as Zumthor shows in detail, depending on such things as the organization of a village or a brotherhood or a family, and on individual personalities. Everything is in action at once in this oral hermeneutic of song, a hermeneutic that consists of the interplay of interpreter (the singer) and audience. To understand anything of what is going on here, you have to understand and be engaged by everything — which is the way hermeneutics should be and can never be if we restrict its target to the text. In these perspectives, the song fully appropriated means everything, the text alone nothing. The song incorporates all of life. The text simply lies there, waiting for voice.

Yet there are many kinds of mixtures of vocality and textuality in songs, and Zumthor treats these too, in vast detail. He is no simplifier, with a magic line to divide the two modes, oral and inscribed. Paradox often rules their mixture. When opera was created, he states, the Orphic myth ruled it (in Peri's *Euridice* [1600], in Monteverdi's *Orfeo* [1607]), yet, although conceived of by the humanist tradition as the highest form of song, opera came into being when print and the visual were triumphing and actually put a damper on the values of voice. Among endless other details the author handles is the not infrequent blindness of many singers (he does not forget Milton and Milton's literary orality), refrain-listening compared to silent listening, and song in which nature is one of the interlocutors.

Zumthor also discusses the various dominance patterns of music and poetic text. In some music the text is assertive, in other music — from traditional to modern rock — the syllables may at times be scarcely articulated. Voice is not to be identified with the primitive. He traces in Europe and the United States down to present times the presence of wandering singers such as Woody Guthrie. Radio and television have had effects on voice: radio identifies with folklore, altering little the external form of oral poetry. The radio of the Solomon Islands broadcasts indigenous songs and tales a quarter of an hour each week, and similar practices are found in Brazil, Cameroon, Senegal, and Somalia. Television also preserves oral poetry, but it lacks the tactility associated with the direct presence of performer and audience. An earlier way of communicating over distances has been the African "talking drums." Because they work not in code but as imitations of the human voice, Zumthor treats them, too. They transmit news, but their more profound function is "to claim a consciousness and to arouse its voice."

As in all matters so humanly profound as voice, there are always paradoxes. Voice unifies, and yet the history of the voiced word is tied up with the history of polemic, as in Western rhetoric. (Zumthor does not treat rhetoric directly, for he is concerned specifically with poetry as such.) Voice leads at times to division and scandals, for song often expresses a desire for transgression in order to defuse with a lesser evil the act of transgression itself: hence traditions of songs calculated to defuse scatalogical or sexual or religious taboos.

The present work is truly a trailblazer in its linkage of voice not merely with social structures but chiefly with the depths of subjectivity, intersubjectivity, and the person, where the physical and psychic merge. Oral poetics cannot be grasped in depth without this deeper understanding of voice. Voice emerges from the womb of silence, but, unlike the body, returns always to the womb. One ascribes to it material qualities such as tone, timbre, volume, pitch, and range, but it is also an archetypal psychic symbol. It is essential for language, but extends beyond language to the direct, inarticulate expression of emotion. It is tied in with bodily rhythms, sheer energy. It connects with states of trance. It is archaic, yet as up-to-date today as ever, combining freely and creatively with the most advanced technologies. These tantalizing subjects and many more are explicated and classified in detail in this remarkable book. The book is itself an academic song about voice such as we have never heard before.

Oral Poetry

Chapter 1
The Presence of Voice

It may seem ludicrous to *write* a book about voice, all the more so when that book was inspired by another: in this case, Ruth Finnegan's *Oral Poetry, Its Nature, Significance, and Social Context* (1977) rounded out the following year by *Oral Poetry: An Anthology*. Reading her work I was able to crystallize a rather far-ranging corpus of research begun nearly ten years before.

Finnegan put the final strokes to a half century of research into the world of oral poetic traditions. Her attempt at synthesis finds its grounding in the post-1940, Anglo-American school of Chadwick, Bowra, Lord, and their German followers, for example, Bausinger. For Finnegan and her colleagues, unlike the majority of French scholars given to formalism or history, anthropology and literary studies seem to converge at a certain point.

Finnegan uses a set of diverse external classifications to group her descriptions of facts and situations: she refuses to theorize. Furthermore she emphasizes poetic forms that are connected either directly or indirectly to ancient traditions and preindustrial cultures and thereby has set up a framework that must be modified if not completely dismantled. For me, then, questions that I once asked myself within the confines of medieval studies now call for a series of theoretical responses no less than a razing of cultural barriers. A general poetics of orality is lacking, one that will act as a forum for individual inquiries and offer functional notions applicable to the phenomenon of the transmission of poetry by voice and memory, to the exclusion of all other media.

A fundamental question underpins this poetics: is there a specific oral poeticity? I aim here to do no more than outline a tentative answer. Rather than analyze individual and concrete texts I have looked at characteristics that define text reception in the total absence of written intervention. In each chapter, I have had to force myself to be conscious of what the human voice is and what it implies: the incongruity between the universe of signs and the overdetermined limits of matter, the silhouette of a barely discernible groundwork of memories, the rupture of logics, and the ripened bursting of the seam between being and life. Still, we must strive therein to make sense of history in the face of uncontrolled elation.

The integration of a primordial symbolism and phonation is most evident in the use of language: it is also there that all poetry takes root. For researchers, voice and language are distinct anthropological objects. But a voice without language (a shout, voice-control exercises) is not distinct enough to convey the complexity of the forces of desire animating it. The same impotence affects language without voice, that is, writing. Thus, our voices demand language and at the same time enjoy an almost perfect freedom of use vis-à-vis language. It culminates in song.

No one would think to deny the important role that oral traditions have played in the history of humankind: archaic civilizations and a good many cultures still marginal today have maintained themselves solely or principally by means of these traditions. It is difficult for us to conceive of them in nonhistorical terms and especially to convince ourselves that our own culture is thoroughly imbued with and quite dependent on them. It is no different for the orality of poetry. It is readily accepted for African or Native American ethnic groups; yet, we have a hard time recognizing the presence of a very lively, oral poetry in our own midst. One example among many others: according to an article in *Le Matin* on April 10, 1981, every year in France ten thousand songs are contracted to three thousand professional singers who produce hundreds of records. In spite of the eloquence of such figures, most literary scholars continue to ignore them.

Long ago our passion for the spoken word died out. It was progressively eliminated from our "basic personality," the matrix of our character traits. It is a story often told. Thanks to a long-standing aesthetic prejudice, all artistic language production is identified with writing: whence the difficulty we have in recognizing the validity of that which is not written. We have so refined the techniques of these arts that our aesthetic sensitivity spontaneously rejects the apparent immediacy of the vocal apparatus. Criticism during the 1960s and 1970s on the nature and functioning of "the text" failed to take sight of the new horizons but managed to blur the scene all the more by resuscitating the long-standing tendency to sacralize the letter and produced a travesty of our mental processes.

It is strange that, among all the institutionalized disciplines, there is not yet a science of voice. Let us hope that one is forthcoming. (Bologna 1981 [a one-hundred-page manuscript kindly lent me by the author] is moving in this direction.) Such a science would provide a theoretical base for the study of oral poetry where at present there is none. It would include vocal linguistics, anthropology, and history in addition to physics and physiology. Sound is the most subtle and most malleable element of the concrete world. Has it not provided, does it not still provide, the space of initial contact between the universe and intelligibility — for both humankind and the individual as they both develop? Nonetheless, voice is the desire to say what you mean as much as a desire to exist. As the locus of an absence that changes into presence when used, voice modulates cosmic impulses that cut across us, collecting some of their signals: an infinite resonance that makes all matter sing . . . as is evident in the many legends about bewitched plants and rocks that once upon a time were friendly.

Before all differentiation, as an unutterability suited to clothing itself in language, voice is a *thing*: its material qualities—tone, timbre, volume, register— can be described and custom has assigned to each a symbolic value: in European melodrama, the tenor is given the role of the persecuted, righteous man; the soprano portrays idealized femininity; the bass characterizes either wisdom or madness. The Japanese have played on these nuances most subtly. From the ancient Romans to the creators of Chinese opera, from Native Americans to Pygmies, many cultures valorize them and attempt to codify them within a system. Between animal and human societies, only the latter hear their own voice as an *object* emerging out of the multiplicity of noises: around this voice the social bond is strengthened and solidified; meanwhile poetry takes form.

Voice lodges in the silence of the body, as the body does in the womb. But unlike the body, voice returns to its matrix, immediately and constantly erasing itself as speech and sound. It speaks such that the echo of this prepartum desert resonates in its hollow, whence life and peace, death and madness arise. Voice breathes creation. Its name is spirit: Hebrew *ruach*, Greek *pneuma* but also *psyche*, Latin *animus* as well as certain Bantu terms. In the Bible, the breath of Yahweh engenders the universe as it engenders Christ. It is identified with sacrificial smoke. These analogies are maintained in the esoteric imagery of the Middle Ages. Tristani (1978) has disclosed the existence of an erogenous respiratory phase in the development of the individual, one independent of the classical psychoanalytic oral phase. In it a specific libidinal phase takes root, and afterward the phonic oral erogeneity of speech is articulated.

Freud's case studies of Dora, Schweber, Little Hans, the Wolfman, and the Ratman (*Standard Edition*, vols. 7, 10, 11, 17) or Jung's archetypes and the collective unconscious (pp. 89-95 and *passim*), and even recent studies by Rosolato, Thomatis, and Vasse could be cited here. There is no doubt that voice constitutes an archetypal form in the human unconscious: a primordial and creative image, both an energy and a configuration of features that predetermine, activate, and structure our first experiences, feelings, and thoughts. It is not at all a mythical content, but a *facultas*—the symbolic possibility open to representation, constituting through the ages a cultural heritage transmitted (and betrayed) with, in, and through language and other human coding systems. The image of voice reaches deep into a region of lived experience where it escapes conceptual formulas and where prescience alone operates: a secret, gender-defined existence with implications of such complexity that it exceeds all particular manifestations. As Jung stated, it "makes something reverberate in us that tells us that we truly are no longer alone."

This dense backdrop of potential and interactive meanings distinguishes voice from sight, another bodily emanation associated with voice in myth as well as in performance. Whatever may be the expressive and symbolic power of sight, it lacks the concrete solidity of voice, of the tactile sensation and urgency of breath. Unlike speech, it is unable to use a simultaneously absent and present object to reset games of desire, constantly to recast the game of desire in an object that is at once both absent and present in the sound of words.

This is why language without voice is unthinkable. Nonvocal systems of communication (such as whistling in the Pyrenees and the Caucasus) are often called language but only in the figurative sense. I will use the word "speech" (*parole*) here for vocalized language, language that is realized phonically in voice.

Yet voice exceeds speech. It is, in Vasse's terms, that which de-sign(ate)s the subject by language. It "cries in the desert of nonbeing [*le desêtre*]." Voice does not convey language: language is ferried across in voice leaving nothing in its wake. Perhaps in the furthest recesses of our minds, voice exercises a protective function: it preserves a subject threatened by language and slows the loss of substance that would permit perfect communication. Voice *speaks itself* at the very moment it speaks; in and of itself, it is pure exigency. Using voice procures a delight, an outpouring of joy. Voice constantly aspires to rebirth within the flow of language that is both disclosed by voice and feeds on it.

Intense emotions arouse voice, though rarely language. Murmurs and cries are intimately tied to elemental dynamisms. A baby's first cry, children shouting at play, or the scream unleashed by a devastating loss or an unspeakable joy, the war cry (which with all its might aspires to the status of song): full Voice, denial of any and all redundancy, explosion of being in the direction of lost origins, a time of voice without speech.

In fact, in voice, speech is uttered as recall, rehearsal of an initial contact, at the dawn of all life. The trace lives in us, half-erased, like the figure of a promise. Brought forth from this gulf "between the transparency of the abyss and the materiality of words" as Vasse describes it, voice lets an "unlimited resonance beyond itself" be heard. What it leaves us — anterior and interior to the word it carries — is a question about beginnings: about that timeless moment when sexes, generations, love and hate were One.

Each syllable is breath, beating to the rhythm of the heart; the energy of breathing teamed with the optimism of matter converts a question into an announcement, memory into prophecy; it dissimulates the marks of what has been lost and what irremediably affects language (*langage*) and time. That is why voice is speechless speech, a purified, vocal thread tenuously relating us to the Unique: what the first theologians of language, in the sixteenth century, named the *word* (*le verbe*), Husserl's "phenomenological voice," close to the "body of voice"; voice that is consciousness; voice that words come to inhabit, but which in truth neither speaks nor thinks (it simply works, "in order to say nothing," petrifying phonemes); and voice for which spoken discourse serves as a raison d'être after the fact.

So it is that a purely oral idiom, like that of archaic civilizations and even our own childhood, has definitively marked our linguistic behavior. It is marked by the preservation of what Michel de Certeau calls this "glossalia disseminated in verbal outbursts." Such markings persist into our technological universe and even our "adulthood" and underlie all attempts at language by virtue of a profound corporeal trace. Producing desire at the same time as produced by it, vocal sound creates discourse without any programming by preconceived intentions or predetermined content. It continually digresses except when a false orality pretends to verbalize writing.

A body is there, one that speaks: the body is represented by a voice emanating from within; it is the most supple and least restricted part of the body because it goes beyond the body by its variable and playful acoustics. The archetypal image of a vocal body belongs to the "anthropological sources of the imaginary" defined by Durand. Thus Western mythologies ascribe a beguiling or terrifying role to any awesome, incorporeal voice: the Hellenic Echo, the voices of ghosts, the fountains, earth, clouds, and others cited in Sebillot's folklore. Its fascination reverberates in the voice of the beggar in Marguerite Duras's film *India Song*. Other cultures have codified the connection between body and voice seemingly in order to protect it and use it. They dictate who speaks under what conditions and in what posture, or they classify the social role of the speaker aurally. In 1980 one of my students from Upper Volta [Burkina Faso] assured me that in his ethnic group, confidential matters are discussed while reclining, serious words are spoken seated, but what is said standing is of no importance.

Such is the paradox of voice. It constitutes an event in the world of sound just as bodily movement does in the visual and tactile world. And yet, to a certain degree, it escapes full, sensorial comprehension. In the world of matter, it presents a sort of mysterious incongruity (see Ong 1967, pp. 111–36; Gaspar, p. 23; Husson, pp. 60–75; Schilder, pp. 205–11; Bernard 1976, chapter 5, and 1980, pp. 55–58; Rondeleux, pp. 48–52). For this reason voice provides information about the body producing it: more than a look or a facial expression, one is betrayed by one's own voice. More than a look or an expression, voice is sexual; it embodies rather than conveys an erotic message.

Speech production (*énonciation de la parole*) thereby assumes value as a symbolic act in and of itself: by virtue of voice, it is exhibition and gift, aggression, conquest, and the hope for an audience. As a exteriorized interiority, freed of any need physically to invade the object of its desire, vocalized sound goes from interior to interior, connecting two existences without recourse to mediation.

Values attached thus to the biological existence of voice are simultaneously so concretized in linguistic and in mythico-religious consciousness that it is difficult to distinguish the two. Nevertheless, the values stay there, unappropriated, moving, rich in ambiguous connotations, sometimes contradictory, sometimes focused on a small number of indecipherable structures. It would be easy to make an inventory of recurrent elements in mythologies and in artistic iconography that elaborate such structures. Fragmentary images would relate to the incorporation of primitive power and to the organs that produce it; voice (*la voix*) and its tracks (*ses voies*), a deep throat leading to the guts and innermost reaches; the emblematic mouth; the passage leading out of the body. Speech—both the expression of an idea and its discharge—is that in and through which every articulation becomes metaphoric.

Though Latin etymologically links the word "mouth" (*os, oris*) to the idea of "origins," this "orifice" is as much an entrance as an exit. Every source relates to voice, issuing forth from the mouth, whether an exile or a homecoming. The mouth, however, does not involve vocality alone: food gets absorbed into the body through it. It repeats the erotic image of lips sucking at the breast. The mouth is a locus of nourishment and love; it is a sexual organ in the ambivalence of speech. Whence derives the extensive symbolic field surrounding mastication. It has two tracks, one good, one bad: one eats but one also vomits, just as one defecates. From the "mouth of hell" on the medieval stage, a demoniac world spews onto our own. Gluttony is just the other side of a lively gourmandism: the ogre's other face is Gargantua. The gnashing maw of the ravenous dragon is the other face of the gently yawning mouth of mythical Cocagne. There is also the woman with the *vagina dentata* in Native American folktales from Labrador. These contradictions and oppositions culminate in the esoteric figure of the self-devouring *ouroboros*. Moreover, in the biblical tradition, the snake's discourse initiates "original" sin. Speech depends on instinct for its preservation; self-preservation is self-nourishment. Voice repeatedly articulates an instinctual drive toward language production that elsewhere unites self-preservation and eroticism.

The live voice of "oral" communication highlights two aspects of the body. One can be said to "drink in" the words of another, a speaker can "swallow" his words. Although these lexical markers are minimal, they are nonetheless indelible. Eating up one's interlocutor—incorporating him—bespeaks the totemic repast, the eucharist, cannibalism. The Egyptian hieroglyph for "mouth" designates the power of creation; the mouth in the *Upanishads* denotes total consciousness; the Bible associates it with fire—be it purifying or destructive.

Lips spread to let a word pass much as the primitive egg breaks open. In the teratological phantasms of medieval and baroque art, the monstrous mouth is symbolic of the horror of a degenerate body.

Meaning circulates between the sound-producing organ, the sound emanating from it, and the speech thus produced (at the heart of these mythic configurations). Any of the three elements is, at any given moment, a possible substitute for the other two (see Thompson, index, *mouth, voice*; Chevalier and Gheerbrant, vol. 1, pp. 225–26; Lascaux, pp. 390–94). In the Christian tradition where Christ is the Word, speech is valorized. African and Asiatic traditions, on the other hand, take into consideration the form of the voice attributing the same transforming or curative power to its timbre, its loudness, and its fluency. The African king speaks little and never raises his voice: the griot explains aloud, if he must, what has been said to his people; any shouting is female. The same still holds true today in Japan for giving commands.

According to a Bantu sage, the flow of voice is one with the flow of water, blood, and semen. Yet it can also be associated with the rhythm of laughter, another power. The archaic motif of prophetic laughter was preserved the legend of Merlin well into the thirteenth century in the West. Revelatory voice arises from a burst of laughter and cannot be dissociated from it. In the end, the meaning of the words no longer matters: voice alone, in its obvious mastery of itself, suffices to seduce (like that of Circe so vaunted by Homer for its tones and warmth or that of the Sirens). It suffices to calm a nervous animal or an infant (*in-fans*, one who does not speak) still outside language.

Because voice can be defined only in terms of relationships, separations, or articulations between subject and object, between One and the Other, it cannot be objectified and thus remains enigmatic, nonspecular. It summons, constitutes, and imprints on the subject the mark of alterity. Voice ruptures a closure, frees its producer from a limitation it has revealed. Voice is the instigating force of its own order: once vocalized, every object assumes at least a partially symbolic status for the subject. The listener listens, in the silence of the self, to this voice that comes from elsewhere; lets the sound waves resonate; and, all judgment suspended, gathers together their modifications. This attention becomes the listener's place outside language, outside the body, all in the space of a single listening.

Voice is a game, a vocalic rhythm antecedent to a preestablished, measurable space and time. It is "meaning" (*sens*) only insofar as this word designates direction and process [*sens* also means "direction," where one is proceeding — Trans.]. Voice is found symbolically "placed" within the individual at birth. From then on, voice signifies an opening up and an issuing forth (in opposition to the closure of the umbilicus, as Vasse would have it). Later, upon entering historical circumstances, the child "hears" the warmth and freedom of the maternal voice or the protective austerity of paternal law. It is an equivocal experience: the iconoclasm of order and reason juxtaposed with the imagined presence of the maternal signified (*signifié maternel*). But the doubling of meaning goes further back to where the infant in utero floated in the living Word, perceiving voices and, so they say, bass tones better than sharp ones, an acoustic advantage for the father. But the mother's voice is heard in the intimate contact of the two bodies, common warmth, and soothing pulsations. Here the rhythms of future words are born in a communication made of modulated feelings, of "uterine music." That "music" when played for a newborn immediately brings on sleep and for an autistic child brings on a healthy remission (as in the therapy of Tomatis) (Kristeva 1974, pp. 23–24; Rosolato 1968, pp. 294–99, and 1978; Tomatis 1975, pp. 37–48, 56–76, 117–20, and 1978, pp. 65-80).

As prenatal nothingness grows more and more distant and as the sense of the body as instrument takes form, voice for the sake of another freedom eventually serves language. The symbolic invades the imaginary. In any event, the memory persists of a fundamental chicanery, the trace of anteriority the pure effect of sensory deprivation that each cry, each utterance seems in an illusory way to be able to fulfill. Here, so I think, we approach the origins of all oral poetry.

Part I
Poetic Orality

Chapter 2
Defining the Field

For more than a century and a half, the study of oral culture has been left to the experts—ethnologists, sociologists, folklorists, and linguists. The latter labor under a particular bias. Together, however, they have amassed a considerable body of observations, which in and of themselves are for the most part incontrovertible, and yet subsequent interpretations are often incompatible if not contradictory.

Such research and polemics have taken place at the margins of the public domain. At the same time literary criticism has either ignored or disdained the field. This isolation has resulted in manifold variations of highly technical doctrines but also has established an imprecise lexicon for the study of oral poetry, a vocabulary laden with stratifications left over from romanticism, positivism, and their residues (Finnegan 1977, pp. 30–46; Bausinger, pp. 9–64; Zumthor 1979).

Even today the terms "folklore" and "popular culture" harbor certain presuppositions from which the study of oral culture has not yet managed to free itself. Despite their imprecision, the terms of orality will be redefined here to include latencies all the while superseding them.

The term "*folklore*," coined in 1846 by W. J. Thoms from the *folk*, or people, and their *lore*, or knowledge, referred to a set of customs; still it allowed the sense of *Volksgeist, Volkspoesie, Volkslied* (spirit, poetry, folk song) to pass into English and later into French. Once formulated by Grimm and Herder (1775–1815), these ideas remained current in German thinking until 1870, albeit somewhat tempered or distorted by the idea of *Naturpoesie*. Grimm's "Nature Poetry" was an anonymous, traditional, "simple," "authentic" poetry, one therefore opposed to the art of a "literate" culture. It remains a secondary formulation despite any hypostasizing.

For the remaining years of the twentieth century, folklore assumes a double meaning: on the one hand it refers to a vague and unscientific concept of little value to ethnologists; on the other hand it gets revalued by regionalist movements and tourism. Then again, scholars who use it do so with an understanding of the term that limits it to language acts (*faits de langage*, for Jakobson and Bogatyrev in their famous essay) or to a variety of behaviors and activities. For this reason, Leach's dictionary in 1949 listed no fewer than thirty-three definitions of folklore (Leach; Du Berger 1973, pp. 18–65; Edmonson, pp. 109–55; Jakobson 1973, pp. 59–72).

The current trend is to accord this word enormous latitude: the sociological perspective of a "situational folklore," essentially a process of communication (Paredes and Baumann, pp. 3–15; Paredes 1971, pp. 21–52, 165–73; Dorson, pp. 7–45; Ben-Amos 1974, pp. 295–97). However repetitive and stable the folkloric object or some of its component parts may appear, its status as an object of tradition is merely accidental and not essential.

These definitional characteristics apply to all oral poetry. The methodological perspective of contemporary folklorists may well serve its study to the extent that they attempt to overcome the opposition between "what emerges and what is reproduced, between the extant, the attainable and the possible" (Hymes 1973, p. 1). Our task is to free ourselves from a postulate attached to the very idea of folklore: that of a difference in time, in space, or in cultural configurations, a postulate so deeply rooted in our perceptions that the historical movement by which a social structure or a form of discourse progressively loses currency is deemed a "folklorization"!

The same ambiguity obtains for the adjective "popular," when invoked with terms such as "culture," "literature," and especially, "song." Where it adheres to a notion of appropriation and property, the word "popular" loses all conceptual value: rather than a quality, it designates a point of view, one particularly embroiled in the world in which we live. Using it, do I allude to a mode of transmission of cultural discourse? To some remnant of archaic features that more or less reflect an ethnic character? To the class of people who leave such traditions? Or to supposedly specific forms of reasoning, speech, conduct (Alatorre, p. xxi; Biglioni, pp. 13–15)?

None of these interpretations is completely satisfactory; as a group, however, they hark back to an undeniable, albeit shifting, reality. In most societies, once they have reached the stage of statehood in their evolutionary process, the existence of a bipolarity engendering tensions between the hegemonic culture and various subcultures becomes evident. These subcultures exercise a strong historical function—that of a dream of disalienation, of reconciling person to person, person to world. They give meaning and value to daily life—by no means, however, to identify them with current concepts of "popular traditions," today's museological artefacts. These tensions, obvious since antiquity in the West, became so focused beginning in the eighteenth century that they brought about a complete divorce between the dominant class and the others in the areas of general knowledge, attitudes, taste, the art of living, and rhetorics. Burke recently wrote an entire book considering these very questions in which he describes the shunting and eventual scuttling of European "popular cultures" between the sixteenth and nineteenth centuries, that is, during the Age of the Book (Burke; Poujol and Labourie; Bouvier).

No history of oral poetry can ignore this facet of its reality. And yet nothing authorizes the identification of *popular* and *oral*. As early an author as Montaigne could gloss "popular poetry" as "purely natural," opposed to that poetry that is "perfect as befitting art." In 1854, the bulletin of the "Committee for Language, History, and Arts in France" spoke of a poetry spontaneously born out of the heart of the masses, an anonymous poetry, "to the exclusion of works that have a recognized author and that the people have made their own in adopting them" (*Essais*, I, chapter 54, p. 300; Laforte 1976, p. 2; Roy 1981, pp. 286–87).

By emphasizing the social connotation, we find ourselves back in the realm of the folklorizing prejudice. In the name of clarity, Menendez Pidal proposed a distinction based on the mode of distribution. He defined compositions of recent date as "popular poetry" when dispersed to a broad sector of the public for a more or less brief period of time during which the form would remain mostly unchanged. "Traditional poetry," then, would refer to those pieces not only received but also digested by a vast public through a continuous and lengthy process of re-creation and variation (Menendez Pidal 1968, I, pp. 45–47; Finnegan 1976, p. 82).

Menendez Pidal was considering only a sung poetry that implicitly he set in a class by itself—the same poetry that since the fifteenth-century *Arts of the Second Rhetoric* had been labeled "rural rhymes." Songs are, in fact, the least recognized subgroup of "popular poetry." The criteria tend to slip away whenever a definition is attempted. Most frequently it is anonymity that may be construed dynamically. A song becomes "popular" when its source is forgotten. For this, however, we have to distinguish several degrees of "popularity." It has been written that a song is "popular" when the public at a modern festival sings it in chorus, or when, as with protest songs, intense participation bespeaks a deep commitment to its message. Davenson in a book on traditional French songs has taken the stand of the spectator: there is "popular" song only because there exist scholarly individuals who, treating it as something foreign, insist on studying it or taking an institutional interest in it. Hence, the notion indicates no definable reality although it continues to develop and be modified as time goes on (Wurm, p. 65; Clouzet 1975, p. 24; Davenson, pp. 22–27).

Today these distinctions no longer satisfy many researchers. In North America, this dissatisfaction manifests itself in the prevailing opinion that within a given class of texts (though not defined as such) the "folkloric" is the object of an oral tradition and the "popular" is conveyed by mechanical media. Another group may treat "oral literature" as a subclass of "popular literature" whereas still another group may refuse to connect these two categories or may restrict (disregarding the fact that it begs the question) the label "primitive" to any "purely" oral poetry (Dorson, pp. 2–5; Dundes, p. 13; Mouralis, pp. 37–39; Finnegan 1977, p. 232, and 1976, pp. 41–47; Coffin and Cohen, pp. xiii–iv).

The most disturbing elements in such discussions derive from the implicit or explicit recourse to an irrelevant opposition: the separation of "literary" and nonliterary or, in other words, the sociological from the aesthetic. What is meant here by "literary" is the full resonance of connotations developed over the past two centuries in reference to an *Institution*, to a system of specialized, ethnocentric, and culturally imperialistic values. Until sometime around 1900, in scholarly discourse, all non-European literature was relegated to the status of folklore. Conversely, the nineteenth-century discovery of folklore and what were called, tellingly, oral literatures flew in the face of the Institution at the very moment that Literature undertook its quest for identity, assembling for its purposes philosophy, history, and linguistics and positing an unexceptionable "literary absolute."

Such antecedents cannot simply be dismissed, although nothing in the multiple forms of today's oral poetry admits a definition dependent on the notion of literature. In Europe and in North America there are abundant examples of "folkloric" texts with obvious literary origins, ones transmitted as much by written media as by voice. In 1909, Hoffmann de Fallersleben counted one thousand seven hundred out of ten thousand popular German songs that had demonstrably literary origins. The situation is comparable in Russia and in France (Laforte 1976, pp. 114–15, 65–74; Warner, p. 101; Davenson, pp. 45, 66, 265–66). The question, then, is: are they "Literature" or are they not?

On the French scene, the question becomes: how many poems in Paris of the 1950s, written and edited in a "literary" fashion and then put to music, have become a common corpus and part of the collective consciousness? For French grammar school children of my generation, were not the fables of La Fontaine turned into a type of oral poetry par excellence? *Le Vieux Chalet* ("The Old Chalet"), a sort of lively popular refrain, was written in the thirties by Joseph Bovet, a fact that has not precluded a journalist talking to Davenson from referring to it, in all sincerity, as an "old song of the fifteenth century." There is nothing new here: since the fifteenth century everybody in Florence sings verses from *The Divine Comedy*. Even in the eighteenth century Venetian gondoliers would sing octaves from Tasso.

Nevertheless, we can still ask how many poems and short stories have been borrowed from some popular tradition? Davenson has studied the route taken by several French songs, going from the literary to the popular, then back to the literary. The rich European tradition of Christmas carols from the fifteenth to the nineteenth century demonstrates the inextricable mixing of the literary and the nonliterary in a jumble with the oral and the written (Davenson, pp. 52–54; Poueigh, pp. 248–52). Amateur scholars collected early "popular" songs from the fifteenth and sixteenth centuries. They then bestowed certain literary marks on this material, which later reverted to the peasant tradition. Whence derive the extremist theories of academicians like Meier who during the early part of this century asserted that popular art is nothing but "degenerate culture."

These hasty characterizations, these attempts at classification devoid of interpretive value, expose the shared presupposition that oral poetry is something *alien* whereas what is written *belongs* to scholars. For the ethnologist, it is alien in space and time; for the sociologist of urban folklore, it is qualitatively alien. The common feature that, within a limited context, justifies joining "oral" and "popular" as qualifiers curiously remains hidden. Fictional discourses destined for public consumption (i.e., "literary" in a broad, sociological sense) separate into layers gradated by the distance of the producer of the text from its consumer. This distance (its importance for the typology of cultures is emphasized by Zolkiewsky, p. 14) varies according to several parameters: the spatiotemporal dimension of the gap between the parties concerned; the complexity of the means of transmission; and the economic investment required. Balkan ballads still disseminated orally by village singers, on this scale, are found to be closer to serial novels than to the elitist literature of the avant-garde.

A poetics cannot, however, be founded on considerations of this type. Rather than a point of departure difficult to perceive as anything but "alien," let us start from forms of orality that are uncontestably *ours* such as those transmitted by record or radio. We just might discover inductively some suitable principles of analysis (by means of various transformations) for studying all aspects of oral poetry, even those furthest removed from our daily life.

It is not productive to think about orality in a negative fashion, by contrasting it with writing. Orality does not mean illiteracy, nor should it be perceived as a lack, stripped of the values inherent to voice and of all positive social functions. Because it is impossible for us to picture a purely oral society from the inside (supposing that one ever existed!), we imagine that orality exists only as a remnant, a throwback from a former time, from an originary moment. Such thinking among those who study oral forms of poetry often leads to corollary, albeit unspoken, stereotypes of "primitives" (Ong 1967, pp. 19–20; Finnegan 1977, pp. 23–24).

The entire economy of epistemological lines of questioning cannot be set up at the preliminary phase of this study. Scattered about we can find the bases of a methodology that addresses the incomparable aspects of the oral transmission of poetry. Only by intentionally culling these disparate bases could they be consolidated, but then the very genesis of the project—the cold distance of academic writing—would be disallowed. The term "writing," particularly in phenomenological parlance for the past twenty-five years, is equivocal. Writing does not go without saying—it is not self-evident. But voice—is it a given? By no means do we need to rehash the debate opened some fifteen years ago by Derrida and to hypostasize an original Voice (Derrida 1974, pp. 69–71, and 1978, pp. 200–201 and 203). No doubt our voices carry the trace of some "archiwriting"; but the trace may be considered "inscribed" in another manner in this discourse, one all the less temporal as it has been rooted in the body and is open to memory alone. Insofar as it is a locus and means of articulation of phonemes, voice (that carrier of language in a tradition of thought that considers it and valorizes it within this single function) is none other than "the masking of a primary writing": this is how, for three thousand years, the West "heard itself speak" using phonic materiality. Still, what stands out all the more for me is the broad function of human vocality, for which speech certainly constitutes the principal manifestation—but not the only one and perhaps not even the most important. What I understand, what I hear, is the exercise of its physiological force, its faculty for producing phonation, the activity of organizing this substance. The *phôné* does not immediately depend on meaning, it prepares the milieu where meaning will be expressed; as such, contrary to Aristotle's opinion in *De interpretatione*, the *phôné* does not produce symbols. From this perspective, where orality signifies vocality, logocentrism is extenuated.

Our orality, then, no longer has the same agenda as it did for our ancestors. For them, living as they did in the grand millenary silence where their voice resonated as if on solid ground, the visible world around them repeated the echo of their voice. We are submerged by intangible noises where our voice strives to overcome its acoustical space; yet all we really need are moderately priced mechanical devices to record our voices and carry them around in cassettes.

Nonetheless, it is still a voice. But how and to what extent is it changed by the *mediat* (I use a gallicized term rather than "mass media" in order to limit it to those media using audiovisual modalities to the exclusion of any form of the press). This new orality, a *mediatized* one, differs from the former orality only in certain modalities. After the centuries of the book, the invention of machines for recording and reproducing voices—a development dreamed of for hundreds of years until its realization in 1850—has restored to voice an authority almost entirely lost as well as rights that had fallen into disuse (Chopin, pp. 13–31; Ong 1967, pp. 87–110; Burgelin, pp. 265–70; Charles, pp. 63–75). It is obvious that this detour through industrial metallurgy has modified the conditions for using voice and the extent of its rights and liabilities. Its authority has grown commensurately. Although compromised by the apparatus itself, voice benefits from technology's powerful status. Ong's optimistic thesis on this point still stands. As they transmit messages the *mediats* give language its full and impressive function. Discourse can thereby segregate interlocutors, command or forbid them, throw its full weight against their intentions or their very circumstances—all in order to get them react.

Mediat designates specific mechanisms with specific results. On the one hand they may operate solely on the space of voice or on its dual spatiotemporal dimension; on the other hand they may involve hearing alone or the audiovisual senses. I do not treat the first set (e.g., the microphone), although I do study its sonorous effects in chapter 13. With respect to those that permit manipulation of time—and by that very fact—they resemble books. Then again, the grooves of a record and the imprint on tape have not the least trace of that which defines writing, either perceptibly or semiotically. By fixing vocal sound, they permit its indefinite reiteration to the exclusion of any and all variation. Whence comes a considerable secondary effect: voice is freed from spatial limitations. The natural conditions of its exercise are therefore discombobulated. At the other end of the spectrum, during a performance, the situation of communication becomes quite lopsided in another way.

The features common to these two mediatized voices is that no one can respond to them. Their reiterability depersonalizes them at the same time as it confers on them a communal vocation. By all rights, mediatized orality belongs, therefore, to mass culture. Yet only a learned written and elitist tradition makes it scientifically possible, only industry ensures its materialization, and only big business allows its marketing and distribution. So many dependencies limit—if not eliminate—the spontaneity of voice. The sociality that in day-to-day existence enriches "live" voice is changed into a hypersociality circulating in the networks of telecommunications, constitutive of a new collective bond: a sociality of synthesis, operating on the disjointed and fragmented elements of traditional, structured groups.

The spatiotemporal mobility of the message increases the distance between its production and its consumption. The physical presence of the speaker is eliminated; what remains is the fixed echo of a voice and, for television and film, a photographic image. The listener while listening is completely present; but during recording sessions, he or she is only an abstract figure, a statistic. The sophistication of instruments and the weight of the requisite financial investment add to this distancing (Cazeneuve, pp. 142–51). The message, an object in this respect, is fabricated, expedited, bought, and sold, and everywhere it is identical. Nevertheless, it is not an object that one touches: the buyer's fingers touch only the transmitting tool—record or tape. The senses alone are a concern, in service to a distant perception: sound and, for film and television, sight. Thus a lag time, a displacement of the communicative oral act, is produced.

In a world of primary orality, the strength of speech is limited only by its impermanence and inexactitude. Where secondary orality reigns, writing hides these weaknesses, however imperfectly. Mediatized orality ensures exactness and permanence at the price of quantity and engineering calculations. For the moment, that is where we are today. Already telematic machines erasing distances, but playing with space (without flattening it) and concretizing the object — video recorders and video players, for example — provide optimists the means to foresee new processes of perception, selection, inscription, and integration at the end of which may be found the weight of an undifferentiated presence and the immediate fullness of voice.

Is it not the same optimism (as confused and deceptive as it may be) that today throughout the world leads semi-illiterate peoples wrenched from their primary orality (now devoid of content), and misled by literate powers, to buy transistor radios rather than to subscribe to a newspaper? Is it not the same that leads the down-and-out plugged into their headphones to walk alone among their voices? Is it not the same that has led the Inuit of the great Canadian North to intoxicate themselves with radio programs that are assuming the role traditionally filled in their community by mythic tales (reported by Charron, personal communication, November 1978)?

For many in the Third World, the scarcity of radio and television sets confers on them a truth-value that they have never had for us. It puts the listener-spectator in a more active state of receptivity, invites more engagement of imagination and desires, fascinates or shocks. In the village or in the neighborhood, groups gather around the set, the property of some privileged person, as once they gathered around the local "reader" in order to listen to a book being read.

Likewise, far from breaking the collectivity apart (as sometimes it is accused of doing), the *mediat*, at least at the onset, cements it together. In the French countryside, in the suburbs of French cities until recently, people would ritually watch TV together at some bar; today, everyone has one at home and that community has been lost.

Nevertheless, contrary to common opinion, the *mediat*'s public does not constitute an undifferentiated mass. It exercises its freedom of choice, more so than is generally admitted. It easily accepts what is offered it; it accustoms itself with little resistance. But everything can fall apart suddenly. The *mediats* while pushing toward conventionality at the global level are thereby, paradoxically, generating a traditionalism that used to exist in archaic societies. The man addressed by the media is not fundamentally different from his distant ancestors even if he is pigeonholed by all the forces of mediocrity, blandness, meanness of mind and spirit of contemporary society in conjunction with the immense challenges that inhere in those very forces.

That is why a veritable integration of the *mediats* is unthinkable until a critical effort based largely on traditional culture, transmitted by writing and maintained in an urban setting by privileged means, is produced. In times of crisis or malaise, the solution to one and the silencing of the other lie not in a return to some former, pristine state of affairs but rather in recognizing and surpassing that which up until now has fashioned us. The most present voices that will resonate tomorrow will have cut across the entire breadth and depth of writing.

In concrete terms, there is no orality in itself; rather there are multiple structures of simultaneous manifestations, structures that, each in its proper order, have arrived at very unequal degrees of development. Their common substratum remains, nevertheless, always perceptible (Vico was the first intuitively to recognize this commonality). It results from the linguistic specificity of all vocal communication. For at least two subjects (speaker and listener) this communication carries with it, insofar as it is vocal, the same but not identical investment of psychic energy, of mythic values, of sociality, and of language. As radically social as it is individual, voice marks the manner by which we situate ourselves in the world and with respect to others. Speaking, in effect, implies listening (even if some circumstance hinders it), which is a double movement whereby interlocutors as a group ratify presuppositions based on an understanding. And that understanding, generally tacit, is always active (within a self-same cultural milieu) (Heidegger 1971a, pp. 209–10, and 1971b, pp. 75–76; Lyotard 1984, p. 17; Grice, pp. 44–49, 57–58; Bernard 1980, p. 62; Vasse 1980, p. 63).

A double desire provides both the topic and the locus for speech. It is a desire to speak and a place to where the content of the spoken words returns. The intention of the speaker who speaks to me is, in fact, not only to communicate some information to me but also to achieve this while bringing me to realize his intent and to submit me to the illocutionary force of his voice. My presence and his in the same space put us in a position of dialogue, whether real or virtual, of a verbal exchange where language games are easily released from institutional rules; where slipping between registers, jumping between discourses (from assertion to prayer, from story to interrogation), lends a certain flexibility to the utterance. Is there a rupture in the argumentation, a lacuna in a series of facts, a disconnection in the relationships between your account and the immediate context? A question arises, provokes you, leads the discussion off ironically in another direction (Flahault 1979; Recanati 1979b, pp. 95–96; Kerbrat-Orecchioni, pp. 18–33). There are lateral movements of language, ambiguities that participate in the progressive construction of discourse, impossibilities of maintaining a literal field, a constant opening up to analogical resonances. Only oral language with minimal written contamination engenders the marvelous, preposterous monsters we call calembours and "popular etymologies": *herbe sainte* (holy grass) in French for abysinthe, *lampoule* for a light bulb (*ampoule de la lampe*): this rugged poetry.

A sort of moral effect is produced: the listener has the impression of a more tangible loyalty than that in written or deferred communications, of a veracity that is more probable and persuasive. This may explain why court testimony, absolution, and sentencing are all pronounced aloud, face to face. More than any other form of contact, speech brings to the fore the subjecthood of those individuals that it confronts; it manifests their "place" in the way that Flahault uses the term, resulting both in determinations of the system from which it derives and in a desire-driven commitment (Ong 1967, pp. 217–18; Flahault 1978, pp. 138–51).

Every oral communication is fashioned by voice. A word is proffered by means of voice by those who withhold the right to use it or have given themselves the right. Due to this, every oral communication posits an act of authority: a unique act, one never identically reiterable. It confers a Name, insofar as what is said names the act done by speaking it. The emergence of meaning accompanies a play of forces acting on the interlocutor's state of mind and aptitudes (Hall; Searle; Austin, pp. 67–120; Certeau, pp. 62–63; Lindenveld; Warning 1975; Berthet, pp. 142–46; Guiraut, pp. 92–108; Kerbrat-Orecchioni, pp. 185–89; 1979 special issues of *Langue française*, nos. 42 and 22, and no. 39 of *Poetique*). Since 1945, lengthy series of studies have focused on these points in America, and were taken up twenty years later in Europe: analyses of "speech acts," or of nonlinguistic elements of expression, "kinesics/proxemics." French linguistics deals with discourse or literary texts, the German with "aesthetics of reception."

Therefore, throughout this book, I will articulate my reflections on the idea of *performance*: it is a key term, a touchstone, to which I will have constant recourse. Performance is the complex action by which a poetic message is simultaneously transmitted and perceived in the here and now. Speaker, receiver(s) of the message, circumstances (which the text with the help of linguistic means represents or does not represent) are concretely confronted, are indisputable (Saraiva, pp. 3–4; Fedry 1977b, p. 587). In a performance, the two axes of social communication blend: that which joins the speaker to the author and that through which situation and tradition are united. At this level the function of language that Malinowski called "phatic" is fully played out: it is a play of call and response, of provoking the Other, of request, one that in itself is indifferent to the production of meaning.

Performance constitutes the crucial moment in a series of operations logically, although not always factually, distinct. I count five of them that are phases, so to speak, of the existence of a poem:

(1) Production
(2) Transmission
(3) Reception
(4) Storage
(5) Repetition (in general).

Performance embraces phases 2 and 3 and in cases of improvisation, 1, 2, and 3.

In any society that has writing, each of these five operations is realized either by the sensory, *oral-aural* path (Ong's expression for voice and hearing in a single grouping) or by the intermediary of an inscription destined for visual perception. Theoretically, the combination of these factors allows for ten possibilities. Operations 1, 2, 3, and 5: are they oral-aural (and therefore 4 is purely memorial)? Perfect orality would be its consequence, and 5 is located most probably in a rather stable tradition. Do the same operations contain inscription (with 4, therefore, a library or an archive)? Such would be a perfect process of writing.

By this process a poetics of orality can be constructed. Nine other possibilities remain! In what follows I will consider to be oral any poetic communication where transmission and reception at least are carried by voice and hearing. Variations in the other operations modulate this fundamental orality.

This more or less relative simplification of the facts of the problem finds its methodological justification in one of its consequences: it allows for the differentiation—encouraged as it may be by the history of facts—of oral *transmission* of poetry (including operations 2 and 3) and oral *tradition* (of operations 1, 4, and 5).

Vocal communication fulfills an exteriorizing function within the social group. It assures that a society's discourse about itself, be it serious or futile, is heard for the sake of its own perpetuation. Oral poetry is only one of its modes. Being diffuse and collective, orality reveals that which Maranda calls a ''popular infradiscourse'' (Maranda 1978, pp. 293–94). As one of the activities whose deployment constitutes us as a social body, our voices resonate over near or distant sound waves, like background noise. They are the perpetual sonorous stimulation without which we would be paralyzed by fear.

Hence the double aspect of vocalization that Jousse noted, and that Dournes later reaffirmed, between the *spoken*—every utterance (*énonciation*) emanating from the mouth—and the *oral*—an utterance formalized in a specific manner (Dournes 1976, pp. 272–80). In a societal context, then, voice produces two oralities: one is based on the immediate experience of each person, the other on a knowledge at least partially mediated by tradition. This double polarization also cuts across oral poetry.

In the social arena, an idea of eternal return seems to be attached to speech: an affirmation and a union. I like to talk and I want this pleasure to come again—a tendency repressed in vain in contemporary societies. The knowledge to which I give form by speaking and that becomes yours as it passes through the ear canal is inscribed in a model to which it refers: it is recognition. It tends to rationalize commonsensically: it embroiders on a framework of beliefs and interiorized mental habits that make up whatever group mythology there may be.

Such a configuration of the discourse of communication is the opposite of the scientific discourse described by Lyotard (Lyotard 1984 pp. 25–27; Rosolato 1969, pp. 288–89). Strongly connotative, linked to all the language games that combine social fabric and form, its validity and its persuasive force derive less from what inheres in it than from its status as testimony, in such a way that the criterion of truth bows to another, more fluid one: communication is memory, supple, malleable, nomadic, and globalizing (thanks to the presence of the body).

In the 1920s experts in ethnolinguistics (at the time a new discipline), ethnology, even exegesis (intrigued as it was by the text of the Psalms or the constitution of the Gospels) under the impetus of Marcel Jousse, defined for the first time several anthropological particularities of "oral literary genres": the primacy of rhythm, subordination of the oratory to the respiratory, of representation to action, of concept to attitude, of movement of the idea to that of the body. The work done by Hellenists, including Havelock and Vernant, while enriching these observations, also launched theorization. Their research and that of Parry and Lord are remarkable for having given meaning to the hitherto meaningless expression "oral literature"; their research also showed that the terms of voice and of writing are not at all homologous and that the differences between them have varying degrees of pertinence. Orality can no more be defined by removing certain characteristics of the written than the written can be reduced to a transposition of the oral.

I will not engage in a discussion of the theories erected in the wake of McLuhan's fractious and hasty book published in 1962, *The Gutenberg Galaxy*, having already done so recently (Zumthor 1982b). Ong elsewhere has taken up the major concerns of McLuhan's work in a series of his own works that while acknowledging the far-reaching implications of McLuhan's thesis have managed to add nuances to it (see especially *The Presence of the Word*).

The initial principle is familiar: a message does not reduce to its obvious content, but carries with it a latent content constituted by the *medium* that transmits it. The introduction of writing into a society corresponds, then, to a deep-seated mutation of a mental, economic, and institutional order. A second rupture occurs, albeit less markedly, when manuscriptural writing passes to printing; and a third occurs as mass media begins its dissemination.

From orality to writing in the McLuhan perspective, then, two types of civilizations are opposed. In a universe of orality, human beings — directly embroiled in natural cycles — interiorize their experience of history without conceptualizing it; they conceive of time in circular patterns. Space (despite its deep roots) is conceived of as the dimension of nomadism; collective norms reign imperially over behavior. The use of writing, on the other hand, implies a disjunction between thought and action, a deep-seated nominalism, related to a weakening of language *qua* language, the predominance of a linear conception of time and a cumulative notion of space, individualism, rationalism, bureaucracy.

My book is situated within this perspective, but not without suggesting a number of attenuations to the propositions advanced by the authors who have defined it. In fact, in spite of the apparent validity of the premises and the general verisimilitude of the doctrine, many questions remain unanswered. The answers given over the last years have maintained the oral/written dichotomy only at a very high level of generality. At a strictly factual level or in a historical perspective, these terms appear to be extremes in a continuous series (Cazeneuve, p. 50, 57–62, 89, 138; Finnegan 1977, pp. 254–59, 272; Lohisse, pp. 89–90; Goody 1979, pp. 85–88). Some of the features that put them into opposition are certainly incompatible, if not contrary (such as recourse to the visual in one case, to hearing in another); but the majority are only differences of degree, of one more or one less (so it is, for example, where spatiotemporal limits of the message are concerned).

Still, these oppositions, however attenuated in practice, are more categorical than historical: in every age there coexist and collaborate people of orality and people of writing. Certain societies are ignorant of all forms of writing, or so we would like to tell ourselves. But what exactly is "writing"? Megaliths, property markers, African masks, tattoos, everything that comes under the heading of symbols and social emblems — does all that fall under the rubric?

It is, therefore, only at the level of an abstract typology — appropriate, it seems to me, to clarify certain medial or equivocal facts — that I propose to reduce the extreme diversity of possible situations to four ideal categories: (1) a primary and immediate or pure orality, having no contact with "writing" and designating by this latter word every visual system of symbolization coded in an exact fashion and translatable into language; (2) an orality coexisting with writing and which, depending on the mode of coexistence, can function in two ways: either as a mixed orality where the influence of the written remains external to it, as well as partial and retarded (thus, in today's world, in the illiterate masses of the Third World); (3) or as a secondary orality, one that is (re)composed based on writing and that is central to a milieu where writing determines the values of voice both in usage and in the imaginary sphere. By inverting this point of view, one would posit that mixed orality derives from the existence of a written culture (in the sense of "possessing a writing"); secondary orality, from a literate culture (where every expression is marked by the presence of the written); and (4) a mechanically mediatized orality, one thereby deferred in time and/or space.

From chapter to chapter in this book, I will consider facts borrowed from a variety of contexts: poetry functioning in primary orality, in mixed or secondary orality, or in mediatized orality. The particularities of the latter with respect to the others may appear deceptive, but their definition presents no problem. The first three, on the other hand, tend to get confused in the eyes of the observer, not in theory, but historically and in practice. Classes distinguished in such a way are not in fact ever wholly homogeneous. Pure orality is extensive only in ancient communities that have long since disappeared; the fossilized remains that ethnologists note here and there have little value save as partial testimonials and problematics. Mixed orality and secondary orality divide into as many nuances as there are degrees within the use and spread of writing: an infinity. As for mediatized orality, in the current and provisional state of things, it coexists with the third, the second, even with the first in some outlying areas.

Ideally, pure orality defines a civilization of "live" voice, where it grounds a dynamism, at once both guardian of the values of speech and creator of the forms of discourse needed to maintain social cohesion and group morality. It is a transhistoric function in that it independently brings about changes in general social behavior and in emotional feelings coming from sociopolitical structures: involved in a ceaseless process, albeit sometimes slow, of inculturation, of acculturation, of reinculturation. Poetic forms produced in the successive phases of this history are distinguished on the whole from written poetry in that they offer neither to future critics nor to historians—and no more so than to their public—documents that can be manipulated, ones unascribable to a chronology, in our understanding of it in that they rebuff attempts to be fixed in nomenclatures and in synoptic tables, which, as we know so well, make up the first use of writing.

Even when writing is created and spreads, "pure" orality subsists and can continue to evolve in the very midst of a transformed universe, among the elements of what has been labeled an *archaeocivilization*, filling up the voids of the other. Linguistic problems interfere sometimes to complicate these relationships even more. In a community where written national languages exist alongside local languages that have either remained or have once again become oral, multiple tensions are drawn between a national written literature, an oral poetry in patois, and the efforts, linked to some regionalist movement, to create a literary version of the local idiom. In France, the example of Occitan testifies to the gravity involved in choosing between the values of "live" voice and those of writing for "literate" persons involved in a process that has gone on now for more than a century. Even more dramatically today, this situation has become generalized throughout vast regions of the Third World (Zumthor 1982a).

Writing down stories or poems that up to that point have been in a pure, oral tradition does not necessarily put an end to oral tradition. A doubling is produced: thereafter a reference text is owned, one apt to engender a literature; and, sometimes without contact with the literature, oral versions continue to move along in time. When in 1835, Elias Lonnrot published a selection of epic Finnish songs in the cyclic form of the *Kalevala*, the oral tradition carried on so well that fifteen years later, a new *Kalevala* was published that was twice the original size! One can also cite the Russian *bylines*, the nineteenth-century ballads of northern England, the Spanish *Romancero* dating from the sixteenth century.

Contemporary Africa provides the remarkable example of the Shaka cycle. This warrior, who lived at the turn of the nineteenth century and was the founder of the Zulu Empire, became the hero of lyric and epic songs whose oral tradition runs from his own lifetime to today. In 1925, Thomas Mofolo, an unlettered

Basuto, drew on these songs for the material of a novel, the first literary text written in his language. A tradition grew out of it, in Sotho, in Zulu, in English. This tradition is ceaselessly enlivened by contact with oral poetry, such that after independence, the figure of Shaka—a literary myth loaded with all the pathos of African destiny—reached distant territories: from Zambia to the Congo, to Guinea, to Senegal, to Mali. And the majority of works, in English or in French, which since 1956 have been dedicated to him, have taken on a dramatic form, which is to say the form closest to pure orality (Burness).

Eventually oral poets come under the influence of certain linguistic procedures, certain themes found in written works: intertextuality plays back and forth. At any rate and without exception, oral poetry today is practiced in direct contact with the universe of writing. It does not necessarily imply contact with written poetry, although over the long run that contact necessarily takes place. In this situation of coexistence, facts will be classified all the more according as the point of impact of writing on oral poetic communication is located in the production and storage or repetition of the poem.

From this come the multiple aspects that obscure these interferences, ones capable of sidetracking the critic. Each time, in fact, a part of a poetic communication passes from one register to another, a radical but rarely perceptible mutation is produced at the linguistic level. A poem composed in writing but "performed" orally is thereby changed both in nature and in function to the same extent that an oral poem collected and disseminated by writing changes in the exact opposite fashion (Finnegan 1977, pp. 160–62, and 1978, p. 359; Tedlock 1977, p. 507). It so happens that the mutation remains virtual, buried in the text like hidden riches all the more marvelous for being undiscovered: the feeling that while reading them with one's own eyes, there is an intensity that urges them to be enunciated, that there is a full-bodied voice vibrating somewhere at the origins of their inscription.

Now we arrive at a fundamental question: does the notion of "literarity" apply to oral poetry? The terminology matters little; what I mean is the idea that there exists a marked social discourse, one immediately recognizable for what it is. Despite current trends I disregard quality as a criterion because it is too imprecise. Both poetry and literature are that which the public—readers or listeners—accepts as such, perceiving in them an intention that is not exclusively pragmatic: the poem (or more broadly, the literary text) is indeed felt to be a particular manifestation, in a given time and place, of an all-encompassing discourse that constitutes a trope of discourses ordinarily kept within the bounds of the social group. Signposts stake it out or accompany it, revealing its figural nature—hence the melody vis-à-vis the text of the song.

Yet the mode of reception and the text's insertion into society are not the only ones under discussion. We can reject purely and simply the idea of a doubtlessly functional opposition (and at any rate a heuristic one) between discourses that refer to codes and those that produce phantasms; or, to take up once again (without attaching any more importance that they deserve) the terms to which I had recourse in several of my preceding works, that of "document" (an unmarked discourse) and "monument" (one marked, textualized). It behooves us, certainly, to relativize it, to submit it constantly to redefinition: simply put, it fixes the extreme terms between which a vast gamut of "impure" examples is laid out (Lotman and Piatigorsky, pp. 206–7; Voigt 1969; Milner 1982, pp. 283–84). As such, it cuts across both orality and writing at the same time and produces the same effects. I can outline them as follows:

(1) *Base*: (a) "natural" primary structures (vocal organs, hands, written supports); (b) "cultural" primary structures (language such as it is); whence the base discursive manifestation: *document*.
(2) *Poetic* level, defined by a *secondary structuring*—one that is intentional and results from work—from elements already organized in primary structures, as in: (a) *textual* structuration, bearing on language, and (necessarily), (b) *modal* structuration: *graphic* (akin to drawing) where it concerns writing; *vocal* (akin to song) when it concerns orality; whence the discursive "poetic" manifestation: *monument*.

The corresponding parts of the *textual* and *modal* structures of the monument differ appreciably from written to oral poetry. The textual element dominates the written; the modal is dominated by the arts of voice. In the end, an oral monument would be conceivable—one entirely *modalized* but not at all *textualized*. I doubt I will ever run across an example of it.

The oral poetic text, insofar as it engages a body through the voice that carries it, rejects any analysis that would dissociate it from its social function and from its socially accorded place—more than a written text would. Likewise it rejects dissociation from the tradition that it can explicitly or implicitly claim as its own, from those circumstances in which it makes itself heard. More so than the written text relies on manual or mechanical techniques of the graphic sign, the oral text relies on linguistic conditions and features that determine every oral communication.

Vocal activity is located in time, by which I mean that time does not figure (unless in particular oratorical cases) as a pertinent factor in communication. With regard to the poetic message, in order to be integrated into the cultural conscience of the group, it must refer to the collective memory; it does so by virtue of its orality, in an immediacy: that is why societies without writing are strictly "traditional."

In principle, if not always in fact, the oral message is offered up to public consumption: writing, in contrast, isolates. This notwithstanding, orality functions only in the midst of a limited sociocultural group: the need to communicate that sustains it does not spontaneously look toward universality, whereas writing, split between so many individual readers, buttressed on abstraction, moves freely only at the broad, social level, if not at the universal.

Thus orality interiorizes memory, the same as it spatializes it: voice is deployed in a space whose dimensions are measured at its acoustic range, whether expanded or not by mechanical means, but that it never exceeds. Writing, certainly, is spatial as well, but in another way. Its space is the surface of a text: geometry without depth, pure dimension (if not in the typographic games of certain poets), while the indefinite repetitiveness of the message, in its intangible identity, assures it a triumph over time. The text as a result is completely pliable: I read it, reread it, cut it apart, put it back together, put it down or take it up as I will. It presents itself, in stone or on paper, as a whole and is perceptible as such. Whatever may be the failures, the red herrings (literarily, a play of masks) inherent in the message, a complete grasp of it becomes possible, tending toward the synthetic and therefore abstract.

As it progressively and undauntingly unfurls, the message transmitted by mouth is understood (Gossman, pp. 765–67; Kerbrat-Orecchioni, pp. 171–72; Chasca, pp. 59-63). Only in extreme brevity is it grasped in toto. The listener traverses discourses addressed to him and only that which his memory records is revealed to him as a unity that remains problematical if not problematic when the speaker neglects to pepper the discourse being uttered with markers.

Let us not assume neat contrasts drawn from this comparison. A dichotomy never explains. In like mind with Goody expect no "great division"; moreover, the exercise of binary oppositions all too often unleashes derisible idealist reductions. The idea of discontinuity has value only within a dialectical movement. Everything is historical, therefore, in movement, projected in groups, in spectrums, the extremes of which, albeit definitional, are never more than rationalizations (Goody 1979, pp. 35–36, 246–50). The distance that necessarily separates and distinguishes the observer from the object observed is enough to distort the observation once this distance is posited as essential: me—that.

Ethnology, which confronts *us* with *them* in a unidirectional relationship, is tainted—more than other disciplines—from its very beginnings. "Ethnology," "ethnohistory," "ethnosociology," and "ethnolinguistics" are the same as ethnocentrism, intellectual myopia, an instrument of a knowledge tending to refuse the other, and one that warps almost all our "human sciences" inasmuch as they will not have assumed and surpassed the limitations imposed by our "Western" civilization. We nonetheless are confronted with a problem, for even a general study of oral poetry crosses through several fields of research bearing the same marks (Geertz, pp. 3–30; Derive, p. 15; Maranda 1980, pp. 183–84). African cultures, cultures of the voice par excellence, are today, in their complexity and their richness, almost exclusively the domain of ethnological discourse: a secondary discourse whose object is more a discourse on tradition, on the work of the voice than the tradition and the voice carrying it.

Several ethnologists, for several years now, have been conscious of that which is illusory in the coherence of their discourse; what is fictional in an unavowed alterity (Jason 1969; Smith 1974, pp. 294–95; Fedry 1977b, pp. 593–96; Tedlock 1977, pp. 508–10; Goody 1979, pp. 14–15; Ricard 1980, pp. 18–23; Bourdieu). No discourse is neutral and the latter even less so than others. It tends—often disguised as a tone of colorless chastity that would give the appearance of depth to the least of platitudes—to formulate laws of a social behavior, today called strategies. Perhaps in there the game of a shameful nostalgia, of a mythical return in time, no less than an appetite for power gets played.

Listening ethnologically to oral "texts" ends up "folklorizing" them unless it joins in and participates (disinterested to the point of irrationality) in the very presuppositions of the discourse that the texts embody. Such listening occurs at the deep level of pre-or translogical apprehension where art communicates.

Whence the necessary subordination of analysis to a general, preliminary perception; the subordination of argumentation to the experience of its object. The latter *qua* object belongs to the order of the describable: the theorizable is located at some middle level of inductive abstraction; a deductive approach would imply the a priori recognition of a universal, an ultimate reference, an empty and absurd form.

A frequent approach used by folklorists consists in reducing multiple versions of a song or story to a common form: an archetype by which one is later able to define by cold reflection both the structure and the meaning. This hypothesis implying a universal reader, transcending spatiotemporal limits, is certainly fecund at a given moment of the study; it could not instigate it: it serves as a resonator for a private hearing, a unique foundation outside of which no voice has existence (Geertz, pp. 38–43).

The "structures" are less important than the adjacent processes that support them. Once the facts are proved, described, classified, a typology can be discerned or a supposedly initial and generative schema can be constructed. But the idea of function—which grounds such an approach—if it is not extended to latencies and virtualities of the processes in question, degenerates easily into equivocity or into truism. In some way, every "model" constructed is inadequate; it requires an undisciplined usage that reintroduces the life and creativity of fantasy and error. It also eliminates the simplistic principle of noncontradiction in reasoning (Cazeneuve, pp. 9–10, 66–70; Zumthor 1980a, pp. 73–95; Strauss, pp. 23–24; Coquet, pp. 92–93). What classical science used to designate in the name of truth is nothing more than a discontinuous quality, one that is fragmentary, constantly new to one's eyes, an aleatory guest at the wedding of Philology and Mercury, according to the pertinent allegory of Martianus Capella. The successive rationalities to which our methods refer, and of which in former times they were proud, are only historical variants of an unimaginable unity and that today we are resigned to leaving outside consideration in this necessary empiricism.

Between lived reality and concepts an uncertain territory spreads out. It is strewn with refuse, impotencies, not true/not falses; it is an intellectual bric-a-brac that escapes any attempt at totalization, open only to Saturday morning do-it-yourselfers. Conversely, to bring about the concept means abolishing devouring presences, these monsters by whom it will die. In the midst of these aporias, it is up to you to play and to enjoy: the gain of game and joy are worth the *pain*.

There is nothing "scientific" about the textual analyses of the last twenty years. Between the concept, the inventiveness of the person wielding it, and the interpretation that it is supposed to allow, a complex and unstable triangular relationship is established. The concept programs the action of the analyst at a level too general to be applied effectively to a concrete reality unless poorly considered factors — aptitude, a glance, emotional involvement — come into play. Besides, one arrives at regionalized quasi generalizations: these can (but who will say so?) have some exemplary value and contribute to the enrichment of immediate experiences. No more than that. Whence, at the level of the researcher, an inevitable — a desirable — personalization of intellectual equipment: an *ideolectalization* (if I may dare) of critical language.

Where it concerns a cultural act of vast scope, such as oral poetry, this language is less an instrument of analysis than of translation. It tends to transfer the act into another context (that of my own writing), to integrate it into the plane of intellectuation of a Western university type at the end of the twentieth century. The general, the generalizable, will emerge from a singular perception as such, that is to say in its subversiveness. Hearing the singular only responds to a need for pleasure; within this need, it plays itself out. Interpretation, which comes from desire, chases, interrogates, threatens, tortures this singularity in order to wrest from it a secret of perhaps universal importance that its phantasms will always keep it from definitive understanding (Tedlock 1977, p. 515).

And yet, the number of possibilities is finite. The corpus of Gilbert Durand or Edgar Morin, after Jung, Eliade, and Lévi-Strauss, testifies to the existence of fundamental mythic and psychic configurations, configurations defining the thingness of culture. Linguistics and semiotics contribute to the same restriction of the speculative horizon. With luck we might replace ancient fictions of unity with the idea of probable concordances. (Several points in this chapter are fleshed out in Zumthor 1982a and b.)

Chapter 3
The Arena of the Debate

Are we working at cross-purposes by restricting the scope of this book to a study of oral *poetry* when the more extensive notion of *oral literature* is beginning to infiltrate the ranks of the scholarly.

Several reasons encourage such a restriction. Current research and theoretical elaborations of data differ in quantity, in quality, and in method depending on the type of "literature." Two or three genres have been privileged for over half a century: the short story, the proverb, and the epic. Only the presuppositions of certain researchers pretend to justify these choices. Whatever opinion one formulates, nevertheless, their works serve as a point of departure (in fact, if not always in principle) for everything that is said today about oral literature in general. Whence stem inevitable distortions and, all too often, misleading conclusions. Insofar as I am concerned, therefore numerous studies of the fifties, sixties, and seventies, dedicated to the "living epic," *must* be included in my discussion (chapter 6 is devoted to them); the immense bibliography for folktales, by contrast, will be of little use to me, even though the boundary between story and song blur in certain areas, as in black Africa, where song is often part of story.

Since 1881 when Sébillot coined the expression "oral literature," it has designated in turn, first (and mainly for ethnologists), a class of discourses having a sapiential or ethical finality. In a broader usage, one current with the rare literary historian interested in such problems, it encompasses every type of metaphoric or fictional utterance that has consequences beyond those of an everyday dialogue: folktales, nursery rhymes, jokes, and other traditional discourses, as well as the

32

recitations of ancient warriors, erotic braggadocios, and so many other strongly typed narrations, ones woven into our daily speech (Eliade; Du Berger 1971, sections 01/1 to 01/8 and 10; Mouralis, p. 37).

At the center of a rather vast although highly inconsistent collection, "oral poetry" (in accordance with the definition I will elaborate) is distinguished by the intensity of its features: it is rigorously formalized, replete with markings of a very evident structuration. Every culture possesses its own impassioned system by which the basic configurations in each text produced are perceived by disparate, albeit specific, semantic marks. The oral poetic text appears to harbor the densest of these marks. Whence the impression that oral poetry adheres more closely than folktales to the repetitiveness of a deep-seated collective experience; whence also a particular redundancy and less thematic variations (Lomax and Halifax, p. 236; Scheub 1977, p. 337; Finnegan 1976, pp. 77–78).

Even limited in this way, the field remains immense. My intention is less to cultivate it (forgive the pun) than to move on to the spade work; to gather together rather than to unearth; to regroup in a unified perspective rather than engage in an ambitious synthesis. Beyond even the treasures accumulated by ethnographers in their fieldwork in the midst of traditional civilization, the material to be entertained is virtually infinite. One must proceed probingly taking samples, as prospectors do, of the "plug" and only in those areas that promise a return. Certain lacunae—desirable more often than not—result in my documentation. My research, mostly finished by January 1981, includes a small number of observations and personal experiences from 1975 on, in an unsystematic way in North America, South America, in Western Europe, and in the Balkans, in central Asia, in Japan, and in black Africa. To this is added a considerable bibliography and approximately ten recordings. I have nonetheless avoided a discussion of oral poetry in the European Middle Ages, although I do plan to write on the subject in the future. In this rich and diverse collection I have only cursorily referred here and there to the Spanish *Romancero* and English ballads, the chronologies of which largely exceed the modern period.

The numerous examples found herein make no pretense at being exhaustive. I conceived of them as simple illustrations, if not marginal vignettes.

And finally, the last restriction: as far (however uncertain) as possible, I circumscribe, within "oral poetry," a subgroup—"sung poetry"—focus on it in particular. In so doing, I make my task easier. If nothing else I am persuaded (and I hope to prove) that this artifice leads to of a central point that clarifies the whole scene, right to the outer edge of "oral literature"—if not of all literature.

It would be false, nevertheless, to maintain the idea of hierarchized spheres of decreasing arenas of influence: oral literature, oral poetry, sung poetry. None of these terms reflects a reality clear-cut enough to permit definition. It is a question less of static forms than of converging and diverging dynamisms at the heart of a singular complex movement.

The first stages of analysis warrant positing hypothetically—albeit provisionally—the existence of classes and interdependent groups of classes. Even if it means revising the notion later, one could situate oral poetry relative to various "genres" that it encompasses or to which it is opposed—genres presumably dormant in most ordinary speech acts.

Certainly, the term "genre" poses its own dangers. Its content is being challenged from all sides today and, burdened by conventional values belonging to "classical" Western culture, it lends itself poorly to universalization. Nonetheless, one would have a hard time dismissing entirely a notion that allows the comprehension—whatever may be the cultural environment—of certain varieties of discourses:

(1) those spontaneously identified as such;
(2) those referring to a social knowledge with respect to actions held to be significant;
(3) those responding to a specific expectation for both speaker and addressee and comparable to the imminence of passing into activity.

It is in this extremely broad sense that I will use the word "genre" in this book for want of anything better. I will use it to designate series between units for which there are either functional similarities or similarities that result from configurations of lexical, grammatical, and sometimes semantic features. Still, these similarities must be sufficiently numerous and organized to appear to be programmatic, at least an outline of a common model such that each "work" has its place at the same time as it partially escapes it (Todorov 1978, pp. 44–54, and 1981, pp. 125–29; Genette 1979, pp. 58–59).

For oral literature, the "genres," such as they are, present a particular conventionality necessary to the functioning of communication: the marks reside in the situation as much as or more than in the text (I will return to this point in chapter 8). Yet the situations frequently entail a certain fluidity, as is the case with the easily recognizable and highly mobile "genres" like the riddle, the humorous short story, the proverb, or the ribald ditty, no less than the various prayers of churchgoers. For most ethnic groups of Upper Volta, the folktale, proverb, and riddle are arranged in subclasses according to the age, sex, and social function of the speaker, and sometimes according to the time of day that it is heard.

I will devote part of chapter 5 to examining the "genres" that make up oral *poetry*. But there are others—"nonpoetic oral genres" if you will—with respect to which I have been led to circumscribe my object.

Most ethnologists adopt a system of classification with rather loose criteria, never asking themselves any theoretical questions: myths, folktales, legends on the one hand; proverbs, riddles, ritual formulas on the other; epic; songs; and in

Africa, genealogies, mottos, and occasional discourses. This terminological hodge-podge lacks critical value and is rarely used without vagueness. The past fifteen years have seen various attempts at systematization. These attempts operate by thematic groupings or are based on structural analysis, archetypal interpretation, sociological function—unless they are based on the idea of "cultural modeling" as found in Ben-Amos's work (Agblemagnon, pp. 175–89; Vansina 1971, p. 445; Eno Belinga 1978, pp. 68–101; Köngäs-Maranda; Sherzer, pp. 193–95; Voigt 1973; Scheub 1977, pp. 338–40).

Scholars have arrived at definitions for whole classes of utterances (*paroles*) that users felt had a specific nature in given circumstances. This was accomplished without recourse to "literary" a prioris. Such classification can include even formulaic greetings or insults, traditional wordplays and playing with sounds, tall tales, and popular sermons. The only criteria remain a relative morphological stability and a concrete mode of operation. In this light I have situated the definitional elements that I will propose for various forms of oral poetry (Abrahams 1969; Ben-Amos 1974 and 1976; Houis, pp. 4–7 and 13–23; Burke).

Elsewhere I have had recourse to the vocabulary of the language (*langue*) of the "genres" to be defined: it would be virtually impossible to distinguish between acts that the living language does not record separately (Ben-Amos 1974, pp. 283–86; Bouquiaux-Thomas, I, p. 108; Dournes 1976, pp. 186–89) The French expression for "fairytale" (*conte de fées*) acts as an indicator, perhaps even the proof, of the existence of a "genre" regarded as such in the francophone tradition; the same is true for the word "romance," whereby the Spanish *romance* (in the masculine gender) refers to a completely different genre. Genres, in the final analysis, have no identity other than within their cultural context; features uncovered by analysis become pertinent only through that context: it is a dialectical relationship most often evinced by the vocabulary of contemporary usage in the milieu under consideration, whether it be an ethnic group (in the broadest sense), a social class, or a closed circle of initiates.

And finally, taking historical parameters into consideration complicates the analytic schemata to the point of dysfunctionality; every hierarchy becomes mobile; and, under an apparently immobile surface, systematic relationships are interchanged or come around full circle, new invariables appear, contents transmutate: thus, a number of traditional songs of the Hunde of the Congo reduce to short proverbs, and function as such (Okpewho, p. 247).

As for Jolles's "simple forms," I cannot help but cut to the very quick of his formulation of such an idea. The notion was often criticized, sometimes rudely so, throughout the 1960s. It was completely overturned by Bausinger in 1968 under the guise of approbation. A mentalist theory, it derives from idealistic presuppositions that Jauss barely attenuates and for which he is unable to expand a fragile philological base (Bausinger, pp. 212–13; Utley, pp. 91–93; Pop 1970, pp. 120–21; Ben-Amos 1974, pp. 272–73; Jauss 1977, pp. 34–47; Segre 1979,

p. 577). As a primary linguistic formulation of archetypal attitudes of the human spirit, these ten "simple forms" are meant to provide models for every type of "expression": they are models that eventually, in the course of their actualization, become increasingly "literary." Nothing in this discourse refers specifically to oral poetry. It therefore remains foreign to the poetic horizon.

Although I do not follow this line of questioning right now, I will raise a question that is implicit in Jolles and that impinges immediately on my project: all discourse, is or is it not, a tale (*récit*)? The "simple forms" are, in fact, narratives either directly or in a quasi-oblique fashion depending on the description given them.

By giving Greimas's positions a broad interpretation, one might agree that a generalized and virtual narrativity inhabits every form of organized discourse. Linguistic manifestations restrict it and make it specific by linking it to figurative forms (Ricoeur; Greimas 1970, p. 159; Greimas and Courtès, pp. 248–49). Pierre Janet has already said that that which created humanity is narration. There is no doubt that the ability to tell stories is a definitional characteristic of the anthropological status; that, conversely, memory, dream, myth, legend, tale, and the others, as a group, provide the way for individuals and groups to try to situate themselves in the world. It would not be absurd to posit hypothetically that every artistic production, poetry as well as painting and the plastic technical arts including architecture, is a tale (*récit*) at least in some latent way. And music? Perhaps. Surely it is in a secondary way and by repetition.

What is properly called "the tale" emerges somewhere in a continuous series of cultural facts—but where? Is the label of "tale" applicable to those metaphoric or metonymic names given traditionally in Africa, or among Native Americans, to individuals everywhere, or as happens often in the country, to domestic pets? We have arrived at a limit: a minimal form and an allusive maximum. Whence the existence in Africa of mottos—the detailed explanation of one's name—that scholars have never hesitated to classify as a poetic genre (Awouma and Noah, pp. 3–10; Poueigh, p. 93, 190–201).

For that matter, are speech and writing regulated by the same tendencies? Could we not suspect a Murder of the Tale as it passes from one to the other? Gestural accompaniment, fundamental to every form of oral literature (see chapter 11), can it not be interpreted as a narrative value on which and with respect to which discursive polyphony is disseminated?

These very reasons lead me to remove narrativity as a generic criterion except in those extreme cases whereupon I will explain my reasons. Terms such as "folktale," "myth," and "fable" artificially draw lines within the unlimited field of narrative discourses that are simultaneously self-defining and yet ceaselessly moving. Modal distinctions between prose and verse (themselves very fragile as I demonstrate in chapter 10), between the spoken and the sung, lead nowhere. In several regions of the world folktales are sung, and worldwide there are narrative songs varying in type and length. What principle will we use to decide between this and that? And here again, history contributes to a blurring of distinctions: there is no lack of examples of songs that, once no longer popular, survive as folktales for some time (Davenson, pp. 169, 199).

Sheltered by conventionalized terms like folktale and myth, anthropologists, folklorists, and narratologists have developed their thoughts on oral literature in preindustrial settings; and however sectarian the advances may be, however skewed by linguistics, they cannot be ignored.

For close to a century, the "folktale" (for which at least sixty definitions have been counted) has fascinated scholars and critics (Calame-Griaule 1980a; Segre 1980, pp. 693–94; no. 43 [1978] of *Le Français d'aujourd'hui*, and no. 45 [1982] of *Littérature*). This fascination first arose thanks to the spectacle that this genre manifests on the surface (and perhaps illusorily), both in space and in time. Forms of the imaginary, appearing to be constant, yet all the while slipping and mutating, traverse this genre. This thematic phase in the research has been accompanied by extensive projects to collect and publish folktales from around the world. It continues today. In France, Cuisenier is providing the impetus. Since the 1930s, anthropology has laid hold of this rich material; around 1960, it triumphantly converged with structuralism in the wake of Propp's work. A narrative semiology was born from this union. Exemplary in its scientific pretentions, it has eventually led to principles for a renewed language pedagogy.

At a time when the importance, if not the legitimacy, of literary studies is being challenged, the folktale provides a refuge: within the confines of the domains of writing and of voice, it seems to attest to their continuity and homogeneity. Nevertheless, formalist methods paired with the study of written monuments artificially imprint the mark of writing on their new prey. What occurs is a veritable mutation that is imposed on the object whereas the latter, for all practical purposes, owes nothing to the former. Semiotics, with good reason, has, over the past five or six years, been moving away from studying texts so as to get away from a proliferating, closed world where it would likely have suffocated. It is moving toward the analysis of types of discourse (Pop 1970; Maranda and Maranda-Köngäs 1971, pp. 21–36; Voigt 1977, pp. 226–27).

Similar caveats could be formulated for the many and various classifications of folktales, be they thematic or functional. The sheer size of the material most certainly calls for the use of clear criteria and those chosen thusly cannot be purely and simply rejected. They do, however, leave open the principal question concerning the use of voice. In real situations, the pigeonholes for each classification become permeable, and the manifestations of meaning become more or less hybrid (Paulme; Savard 1976, pp. 58–59) A concrete discourse, far from referring back to typological coordinates, works to destroy the very activity of coordination.

By means of their original tendencies, analyses in a structuralist vein reduce the idea of function to that which is internal to the text. They rest on an opposition between action and composition (or by whatever name they designate them) analogous to that posited some time ago by Saussure between *langue* and *parole*. The poetician — for whom studies on the folktale provide an indispensable forum for comparison — prefers pragmatism, like that of Fabre and Lacroix and Alvarez-Pereyre, to the previously mentioned immanentist conception. This pragmatism would stem from the social functioning and the incessant individual reinterpretation of discourses.

Around 1930, a Canadian Eskimo (or rather an Inuit) confided in his memoirs that telling tales is the stuff of life. Contests between children were even organized. The grandfather would take his tambourine and begin to sing about the Arctic: the hunts, the dances, his wives, the healers of yore. For all its banality, that is what counts first and foremost: each of his stories, more by the warmth of presence than by any pretext, would fill a void in the world; the same one was never told twice because the days change. And the nature of this void in the feelings of the storyteller and his audience would constitute the strongest determination to which the others (thematic, structural, linguistic, whatever one wants) would serve as material and instrument. Even the distinctions between human affairs and the gods' affairs, ones that had no emotional investment for the tribe, became blurred.

What type of knowledge does the folktale convey and what sociological role does this knowledge fulfill, what finality is attached to it? Is it a matter of pure diversion, of an initiatory story, or of something else (Agblemagnon, pp. 150–51, 189; Copans and Couty, p. 12, 16–17)? Let me elaborate on the implications for oral poetry in what follows. Still, one cannot ignore the individual variations that storyteller and audience, by virtue of their particuliar needs and the quality of their mutual relationships, bring to bear on these rules. The folktale for the person who tells it (as the song is for the person who sings it) is the symbolic realization of a desire; the virtual identity that within the experience of speech is established for an instant between the reciter, the hero, and the listener, engenders a liberating phantasmagoria governed by dream logic (A. Wilson). Whence the pleasure of storytelling, a pleasure of domination, associated with the feeling of trapping the listener, someone captured in a narcissistic fashion within the space of an apparently objectified word. Whatever seduction the song may perform operates at another level, although the effect stems from the same order.

In archaic societies, the folktale offers the community an experimental field where it tries out all possible and imaginable confrontations in the voice of the storyteller. Its function as social stabilizer comes from that experimentation. The stabilization survives for a long time in the forms of "primitive" life and explains the persistence of oral narrative traditions, ones maintained despite cultural upheavals: society needs the voice of its storytellers to be independent of concrete everyday life. Moreover, in the incessant discourse that society maintains about itself, it needs message-carrying voices to be wrenched free of erosive utility—for song no less than stories. This is a deep-seated need; its most revealing manifestation is undoubtedly the universality and cyclicity of what we ambiguously call theater.

Several features make it possible to discern the basic unity of an eminent and highly developed form of oral art despite the extreme diversity of its manifestations. The device that structures discourse in this instance is mimetic: it encompasses an entire situation, to such an extent that the effect of language—as one element among others in this situation—is reduced to almost nothing in the most extreme cases and sometimes even wipes itself out completely. The actor leaves the task of verbalization to the spectators. Such is the case with ancient pantomime, our military parades, or the experimental theater of the 1960s by Robert Wilson, Richard Foreman, or Meredith Monk.

A situation of primary oral communication (where the actor speaks to me) engenders a secondary situation (he speaks to another actor) that is posited as primary; the power of the game on my conscience almost erases the sense of fiction: I identify myself with the one who has received these words, with the carrier of the voice that answers. It seems that a human community in order to subsist needs to experience such a split from time to time. At the margins of canonical forms of theater, "popular dramatic" traditions, however literary they may be, have persisted stubbornly since the fourteenth century until today by means of a European social and cultural instinct. Few survive. These are the folkloric continuations of the medieval *mistère* or the remnants of even older rites, from the Italian *maggi* to certain Romanian Christmas songs, to processions with canticles and "missions" that were still alive around 1940 in country parishes (Stewart; Bausinger, pp. 24–27; Abrahams 1972, pp. 352–59; Bronzini, pp. 8–38; Alexandrescu; Finnegan 1976, pp. 502–9).

Theatrical poeticization makes the description of circumstances superfluous: a stageset, if there is one, symbolizes them. Yet, with respect to what the listener-spectator perceives immediately, it does so redundantly. The redundancy weighs heavily on the dramatic message, and periodically one can even see the resurgence of types of "action" theater that try to reduce the gap between the two situations of communication and in so doing to economize on stage sets. The "spoken choruses" that before the Second World War staked out the history of European youth movements required no other symbolization than the presence itself of the human mass to which they were giving free voice.

At play here is a specific quality of voice. In its primary function, before the influences of writing, voice does not describe, it acts. It leaves to gesture the responsibility of designating the circumstances. Tales from oral traditions—it has often been stated—do not have descriptions, unless they be marvellous ones. That is to say they are used to reject the present circumstances, reality. In theater, gesture has a broader scope: the entire stage is organized around it. In the *commedia dell'arte*—one of the limits reached by the theatrical tradition in the West—gesturality was subordinated to language: the guidelines given at the end of the seventeenth century by the Neapolitan, Andrea Perucci, in his *Arte* are an attempt to regulate this subordination by making it irreversible (Bragaglia, pp. 159–271; Couty and Rey, pp. 10–15). Yet in this manner, gesture, far from being stifled by language, valorizes it. This explains the signification of gesture. A tension is created between them, from which the theatrical force extends, put to the service of commemoration, ludic invention, or conjuring up destiny—depending on the time and the culture.

In fourteenth-century Bali, the ritual theater celebrated for all the people inside the royal palace of Gelgel signified the State itself and exposed its substance to the extent that the ultimate finality of this substance seemed to be to produce this Act, and the Speech that it engendered. The relationship of medieval Christian churches to their liturgy (another form of theater) hardly differs from that in Bali (Geertz, pp. 334–35).

In the Japanese theatrical tradition, ritual takes a backseat to play. An art is constituted and diversifies itself in, by, and for a pure action that stylizes and codifies gesture and language with so much exactness that the most personal quality of the actor is exalted by it. His voice, the deployment of his tonalities, his phonic richness are shown off. It is so not only in the No and the Kabuki, both very complex genres, but as well in the more simple forms of the Kodan and the Rakugo (Sieffert 1978b; Zumthor 1981a).

In ancient China, it seems that all collective activities converged on what became a theater and brought forth multiple forms—dance, juggling, peasant feasts, sports, shamanic or royal rites, all grouped around a resurgent voice. The opposite also obtained: an institutionalized voice allied itself with symbolic gesturing. Buddhist preaching played a great part in the formation of many dramatic models in Asia.

The human voice, connected by the work of art to the totality of represented action, unifies all the elements. Cause and effect pretend to reside in these unified elements and thereby justify them. A circularity is established that zealous moralists denounce as diabolical. Puppet theater (it, too, by universal extension) stands as the counterpart to it and acts like an exorcism because the interplay of dolls gathers its meaning by means of a voice that does not belong to it.

All the same, what ties theater to ritual and dance is not so much a commonality of playfulness as a common rhizome. Such common roots are none other than what is conflictual, subjacent to every culture. I will come back to this point in chapters 5 and 15. "A polyphony of information" (to use Roland Barthes's words), theater appears to be a writing of the body in a complex but always preponderant way. It integrates voice as the carrier of language to a graphism traced by the presence of a human being in the evanescence of what makes theater what it is. It thereby constitutes the absolute model of all oral poetry.

I shall no longer refer to theater except briefly in the remainder of this book. The problems it poses have already been amply studied in critical literature. I will admit as a postulate, nevertheless, that all the poetic facts I treat here participate in some way with that which is the essence of theater, that everything said about it in one way or another also applies to them.

Text transmitted by voice is necessarily fragmentary. Certainly analysts of literary data, for their part, sometimes apply the same qualifier to the written word, by virtue of the incompleteness of a Writing that traverses the text without stopping there, by virtue of the tension that sets in between this infinite movement and the limits of discourse. These features are found in the oral text and cannot— inasmuch as they are *text*, an organized linguistic sequence—differ fundamentally from the written word. But the linguistic element is only one of the planes of realization for the "work"; it is from the combination of these diverse planes that fragmentariness devolves. In fact, the tension from which this "work" arises is drawn between speech and voice, and proceeds from a contradiction that was never resolved, a contradiction at the heart of their inevitable collaboration; between the finiteness of discursive norms and the infinity of memory; between the abstraction of language and the spatiality of the body. For this reason, the oral text is never saturated, never completely fills its semantic space.

Moreover, at the heart of the tradition to which it must be referred, oral poetic performance is contrasted as a discontinuity within the realm of the continuous: a "historic" fragmentation of a memorial collection, one coherent in the collective conscious. I will return to this point in chapter 14. The effect of the fragmentation appears all the more evident as the tradition lengthens, becomes more explicit, and embraces more diversity. Thus, each of the native American folktales of the Montagnais studied by Savard is set off in a vast narrative material with indissociable parts and assuming the totality of a knowledge—a treasure on which the narrator draws for each performance according to his desire. In more general terms, all cultures possess "cycles" of legends, epics, songs, virtual superunits whose property is never to be wholly actualized.

The forms of orality that are less strictly traditional, such as contemporary song, blur the effect of "historic" fragmentation. However, such song is often, in fact, perceived and received as a fragment of the group constituted by a given mode, by the production of a given singer or from a given recording company, if not a given variety show. What arouses public demand is totality; what resonds is the fragment.

This economy of the oral text has so profoundly marked our ways that it seems to have imposed itself everywhere, even on the modalities of writing. When widely read newspapers first rolled off the presses in nineteenth-century Europe, was it not (on one hand) a habit inherited from popular orality that urged so many novelists to serialize their works? And the weariness that we feel in the face of organized and consistent discourse today, the pleasure that Roland Barthes extolled in his later work, to write only short, discontinuous pieces—all that is a symptom of nostalgia, is it not?

Chapter 4
Inventory

We may doubt that there has ever existed a culture totally void of oral poetry: the definition I put forth in chapter 1 is broad enough to encompass an almost unlimited number of realizations. The question, then, is how to classify them in such a way that they can analyzed for genre and type, at an equal distance from nontheorizable particularities and a tautological universal.

Performance is present. You can speak to me only in this very moment, and I can hear nothing from the past (leaving aside recorded speech). And yet I know that others have spoken and heard or are doing so right now in a place other than ours. In the same way, there is oral poetry that is addressed to me, here and now; there is that which, uttered long ago, is nothing more than an object of historical research; and there is that which, in my presence now, may be heard beyond me. It is true that I have at my disposal, in principle at least, the freedom to change location in such a way that today, June 8, 1981, as I write these lines in Paris, I am potentially a member of the audience of such and such a griot whom I know in Bobo-Dioulasso. We can narrow the scope to temporal parameters and, for the sake of a preliminary effort, consider oral poetry belonging to the past (where it escapes immediate perception and is verifiable only through archives, yet, by this very principle, indefinitely deployed in time) as separate from poetry *in presentiae*, perceived by the ear in a concrete space but (with exceptions) without a pertinent temporal dimension.

I take an edition of the *Chanson de Roland* down from my bookshelves. I know (or presume) that this song was sung during the twelfth century, although I do not know its melody. I read it. What lies before my eyes, printed or in manuscript form, is no more than a piece of the past, fixed in space, reduced to a page or to a book. This contradiction poses an epistemological problem that praxis alone can clarify empirically if not resolve. By amassing information on the attitudes and manners of this distant epoch, we may try to suggest what happened. There arises an imaginary representation of the *Chanson* as formerly enacted, and we are urged to meld it with the pleasure that is felt (I should hope) in reading it. And in the end we try to account for it, within its historicity.

The ambiguity of the situation is not significantly lessened if the ancient poetic text has been transmitted to us with musical notations. They do, indeed, stand as a mostly incontrovertible proof of orality. They authorize a partial reconstitution of the performance: such is the case with those recordings made by various medieval musicologists including Le Vot. These often excellent recordings make it possible for us to hear the songs of troubadours contemporaneous with the *Roland*. The effects of temporal distance and sensory deprivation are greatly attenuated, although not totally eradicated. The proof lies in scholarly quarrels over the interpretation of ancient melodies.

As a generalization, I would like to propose a classification of oral poetry from the past according to the nature of the markers of orality that afford identification. Again it is necessary to distinguish two situations: either we have a written text at our disposal (reproduction or summary, imitation or literary exploitation of a text uttered at the moment of its performance); or we have nothing but a hollow space, or better yet some recognizable debris, but no text—a proof of absence.

The first case presents complex problems of interpretation; the second, of reconstitution. But these problems are elaborated through different perspectives: interpretation operates based on the particular instance; reconstitution is based on universal tendencies and generic schemata.

And yet, whether there is a text or not, historians and ethnologists, given the slightest hint of orality however distant and unfounded, will allow their Romantic presuppositions (and ultimately their positivism!) of an elemental orality to hold forth: in the beginning there was the Oral. Albeit a chronological verisimilitude, this presupposition is hardly defensible if one turns to a distant past, and yet it cannot simply be taken for granted. I will not, therefore, consider it as such.

For a text preserved in written form, an orality can be established that probably has four types of markers.

In the first instance there are the anecdotal signs: a text composed for written dissemination contains, by means of quotation, another text purportedly borrowed from oral tradition. Such are the poems found inserted into the Japanese chronicals of the eighth or the ninth century or the French *Chanson du roi Chlotaire* (Brower and Milner, p. 42; Zumthor 1963, pp. 51–53). Interpretation often proves difficult: given that it concerns a quotation, how does one measure deviation of the quotation from the performance? The probing nature of this sign remains strong.

Second, there are formal indications—ones resulting from stylistic procedures that are supposedly linked to the use of voice. In consideration of this fact, most biblical exegetes admit the existence of an oral tradition for the Psalms prior to their being fixed by writing. Sinologists have noticed in the *Che-King* poetry (second century B.C.E.) that there are several archaic popular songs linked to peasant feasts. Traces of an ancient custom of improvised poetic tournaments are uncovered in Japanese *haikai*. These joustings were revived in the seventeenth century by Basho, who made them into a literary form by integrating them into the exercise of other genres (Lapointe, p. 131; Dieny, pp. 6–9, 64–65; *Dictionnaire historique du Japon*, II, pp. 24–25 [1970]). The expression by which the text is designated can provide a minimal lexical indicator; hence the expression of a *chanson de geste* (an epic *song*) that figures in several of these poems.

Other equally problematic signs are sometimes sought in supposed allusions to various events that refer us to circumstances implying oral transmission. This type of argumentation has been used in discussing Mozarabic poems of the eleventh and twelfth centuries discovered in the 1950s.

And finally, it is possible to determine inductively, for better or for worse, the ancient orality of a poetic genre, or even of a particular text, by means of contemporary practices. Thus, it still seems possible today to prove the extreme antiquity of the oral tradition of the Southeast Asian epic, the *Râmâyana*, by the continued existence of its public readings. (Its written versions date back two centuries from the beginning of our era.) The same is true for chanted Vedic hymns that are still heard today in India.

In the absence of a text, ambiguities increase and the only acceptable response is to be found at a prudent level of generality.

A written tradition may be related in its entirety to a contemporary or former oral tradition by virtue of verisimilitudes that are drawn from literary history and as such are hypothetical. By such means scholars endeavor to work on Sumerian hymns of the second millennium, Japanese poetry of the High Middle Ages, or Chinese literature from the Sung dynasty (tenth to thirteenth centuries) (Brower and Milner, pp. 39–41; Alleton, p. 220; Finnegan 1978, pp. 493–94).

One can just as well rely on documents that indicate the existence of oral poetry in a given time and place without there being a direct citation of texts or an explicit reference. Hence we find the myopic condemnations both in Buddhist China and the Christian West levied against peasant songs of love or satire, laments, and dance refrains throughout the Middle Ages. The existence of corresponding traditions can be deduced.

Where orality from the past is no longer visible, its signs, however pertinent, can be measured or used only tentatively and in light of current orality. The knowledge to which they allow access is a secondary one that is inevitably problematical.

As noted in the preceding chapter, manifestations of orality are currently defined by their mode of transmission, either direct or mediated. Mediation, in general, implies inscription in audio archives. The text is thereby freed from the immediate constraints of time: at the moment of performance, the song or poem exists both in the present and in a future limited only by the durability of the record or the tape. Once the performance is over, the past is added to this dimension, again with the same limitations.

I would like to suggest some criteria for categorization that are independent of the type of performance, whether it be direct or mediated. I base these criteria on the mode of cultural integration of the poetic messages transmitted by reference to my own present (it being the only one I can understand). Certain ones, emitted by cultures foreign to my own—where I am a Western city-dweller of the twentieth century—have come to me from a "somewhere else" that I identify as such: whether it is a matter of a hunting song heard in the Volta bush or a French folk record. On the reverse side, there are other messages, ones coming from my own cultural milieu, in the heat of its here and now; these I can perceive directly in their function and their necessity—even if some personal reason motivates my rejecting them.

Our technological civilization, with its myths that still tend toward domination by the written model (in Europe, at least), leans toward an occulting of the values of voice. In other parts of the world, this same civilization—being spread over terrain less suited to its rapid implantation—lets us perceive a reality that it condemns in the long run but with which it now colludes. African societies offer the perfect example of this.

Contrary to current prejudice, these other societies have been familiar with the use of writing for centuries. The cultures they have elaborated over the course of their history have made the human voice one of the strongholds of a universal dynamism and the generatrix of cosmogonic symbolisms, but also of all pleasure. (By "culture," in accordance with a rather general opinion, I mean a complex and more or less heterogeneous group linked to a certain material civilization of representations, behaviors, and discourses common to the human group, in a given time and space. With regard to its usage, a culture appears as the faculty to produce signs for all the members of the groups and to identify and interpret signs in the same way; it thereby constitutes the factor for the unification of social and individual activities, the possible locus for an interested party to take the collective destiny into his or her own hands.) African cultures, cultures of the word, having oral traditions of an incomparable richness, are repulsed by that which breaks the rhythm of the living voice; in vast regions (in East Africa and in the center of the continent) no art other than poetry and song is practiced. The Word, a vital force, a corporeal vapor, a spiritual and carnal liquidity, spreads forth into the world to which it gives life, within which all activity rests. In speech originates the power of the chieftain and of politics, of the peasant and of planting. The artisan who fashions an object pronounces (and often sings) the words that make his act fecund. A luminous verticality spurts up from inner shadows, but it remains deeply etched. The word proffered by Voice creates what it says. It is precisely that that we call poetry (Calame-Griaule 1965, pp. 22–26, 174–80; Camara, pp. 237–49; Jahn 1961, pp. 135–76). Yet it is also living memory, both for the individual (to whom naming gives form) and for the group, whose language constitutes the organizing energy. In precolonial societies, praise of the chief helped maintain the identity of his people; its enactment was left to a special group. Its forms were used to define the recognized poetic genres.

All the same, every word is not the Word. There is the time of the ordinary, banal, or superficially demonstrative word game, and the time of the word force. But the latter can be destructive: it is equivocal like fire, one of its images. Whence derives a series of ambiguities, if not contradictions, in its enactment. Popular speech with its inconsistencies and versatility can be placed in opposition to a more regimented speech, one that in certain ethnic groups is enriched by its own foundations, an auditory archive whose workings are restricted to "men of the word." Such men are defined as such, for example, the "griots" of West Africa. Yet, at the same time, speech is female, a "co-naturalness" connects woman to it; a ring set in the lip assures its innocuousness. At the heart of this phantasmagoric world the voice of African poetry arises: it is less a work than an energy, "the work of being in its eternal repetition" (Heidegger 1971b, p. 117).

The opposition thus marked is sometimes clear; often it appears moving or fluid. The blues historically belongs to a black folklore of the American South, dating from the middle of the nineteenth century. Yet the very role it played in the rapid sequence of events and innovations that rocked the musical techniques and the art of singing in the twentieth ensures its having living roots in our cultural consciousness. The proposed distinction remains no less operative, but it has the advantage of taking the play of historical forces into consideration.

The function of oral poetry with respect to the "horizon of expection" of the listeners is obvious: within every rational judgment the text responds to a question I ask of myself. Sometimes it gets explained through mythification or distance, or it may ironize vis-à-vis itself. This connection always remains in our ideologies or in the minutest of our daily memories, even in our love of games or our penchant for the complacencies of fashion. It anchors our deepest emotions and phantasms. From within comes the persuasive force found in the songs of Brassens as well as those of Jacques Brel (albeit of a different style and bent) for Frenchpeople of my generation. But why do I name only those two? Certain songs enjoyed, over a period of many years, such an evocative power that in the common French existence they could be heard daily, hummed by any and everyone; rare was the person who could name the authors; few were they who knew the words of these songs: "Sombre dimanche" during the thirties, or "Les Feuilles mortes" a quarter of a century later.

Great collective passions have accelerated this movement of identification to the point of provoking choral participation by the listeners when the circumstances are dramatized; such were the many soldiers' songs intoned during the wars to calm fears or compensate for losses, like the "Chant du départ" or the "Madelon" of long ago. So many feelings are invested in a poem collectivized in that manner that its explicit theme eventually becomes indifferent and the meaning is absorbed into the context: that is the case of "Le Temps des cerises," which passes as a song of the Communards only by virtue of the identity of its author (Brecy, pp. 77–78). So, too, is it for the nearly mythic "Lily Marlene," a love song that fell into the hands of the armies and was sung from 1943 to 1944 on both sides of the Western Front, each in its own tongue. Likewise for the revolutionary songs, national hymns, all this poetry of often mediocre quality, but which is so engrained in our living oral tradition that despite printed texts they are sung from memory—often only one of its ten lines, with *lalalala*'s to fill in the rest.

When, on the other hand, it comes from another cultural milieu, oral poetry is seen by the listener to be exotic, minority, marginal (by various degrees, depending on the circumstances and the individuals)—as different in that it lacks an immediate respondent. The pleasure it yields is not the question here, and can even be the result of that difference.

What makes something exotic or marginal in one milieu can make it functional in another; and what one senses as different today will perhaps be assimilated or reassimilated tomorrow: jazz, for example, when it was first played in our cities, broadcast outside the black ghettos. But in a chronological cross-section, for every instant of enactment, these contrasts outline the range of the poetic act. From that derives the necessity to grab onto the latter with respect to the cultural ecosystem in which it manifests itself—to perceive it as a conflictual object, at the intersection of the lines of force that, in the majority of our societies, engender such vacillations.

Today, in fact, every form of oral poetry is set against a highly dramatized background. A culture of European origins—tied to technological civilization and in the process of rapid and brutal expansion—dominates the field of the imaginary for most people. It also imposes its stereotypes and increasingly determines its possible futures. At the heart of the European space, two or three centuries have sufficed to corrode, folklorize, and annihilate at least in part the old local cultures, thanks to the irresistible instruments of interior colonization that are perpetrated by means of massive literacy drives and a pervasive press.

From there, too, come the savage defensive reactions included under the name of "counterculture": a collection of protest and fringe movements, at the extremities of political action, most often indifferent to it, and closely allied to certain forms of oral poetry. I will come back to this in chapters 13 and 15.

In the meantime, in the wake of displaced colonialisms a new imperialism has been cast over the African territories and the archipelagoes of Oceania, shattering venerable cultures that had been wise and fragile, but which are now disarmed in the face of this aggression. In spite of the many fragments that have remained, the trauma brought on by rapid degradation does not set up the most favorable conditions for the emergence of new and original forms of life, of sensibility, and of art, among people thus despoiled of their intimate surroundings.

In much of Asia, and especially in the Far East where European expansion encountered very different and highly structured civilizations, an equivocal situation emerged: the majority of ancient, original traditions were marginalized, all the more irreversibly as economic regimes imported from the West were thoroughly implanted in these countries. The marginalization was independent of the numerical relationship betweeen the groups involved: in the minds of the powerful, it is the international technological culture that serves as a point of reference. From the moment national traditions become the object of conservationist measures, they figure only as minor cultural fragments of a historical dynamism.

The effects of two colonizations, the internal and the external, are combined in accordance with the modalities that depend on the rhythm of events and to the geopolitical particulars of the Americas. The natural traditions and mental habits of the autochthonous peoples, of the imported blacks, but also of the majority of penniless immigrants, both European and Asiatic, were crushed or distorted in a single stroke under the steamroller of technological culture.

Fortunately, technological culture does not coalesce into a solid block. Every culture most certainly tends to fold back upon itself and be redundant. But it is never truly closed. It has a fundamental heterogeneity, albeit more or less camouflaged, that is relatively open: through the gaps exchanges are set up. These exchanges carry along with them a given political custom, a linguistic feature, an art, oral poetry, all in accord with certain opportunities rather than necessities and based on an economic model. Thus forms once repressed can surface and take root. What was already committed to the path of folklorization is revived, buoyed by a lively intention, used as a point of departure for a new expression, an expression that is at one and the same time enriched by a tradition and operates as a vehicle for still viable values. It is an expression marked by a sensitivity that I feel to be mine historically, one that invests a creative experience. Meaning is thereby transformed and surpassed.

If the gap is too great between dominating and dominated cultures, such an effort can scarcely do anything short of aborting with full museological honors: since 1925 literacy and industrialization have managed to reduce the traditions of the Mongolians of Siberia to the status of tourist curiosities in spite of a cultural policy that was, in principle, quite open (Taksami).

On the other hand, when solicited by another, I acknowledge the distance that separates us; I discover the immutability of my traditional values in my fear that enrichment means contamination. From that very moment superficial emotion is attached to the exteriorized forms. A meaning is wiped out, and folklorization becomes irreversible. The participant becomes a spectator; social necessity is mythic reference. Under the pretense of ecology, literature can feign to quench its thirst at this dried-up wellspring: this mode harks back to Rousseau and to the *Devin du Village*.

The reigning ideology can seize on these relics as happened in Quebec around 1935–40—the days of Mother Bolduc—when the Church did it to traditional peasant songs; it was so well done that the Quebecois song of today has had to constitute itself mainly in opposition to this folklore. Whence derive misunderstandings when an isolated person attempts the other adventure: the great poet Gilles Vigneault is almost inevitably cast as a regional singer for a non-Quebecois public (Millières, chapters 1 and 3).

Leaving the historical perspective aside for the moment, I can reduce cultures other than my own, ones in remission in today's world, to two types. Some are threatened either by assimilation or by extinction, but they still possess a certain internal cohesion that is nonetheless insufficient to ensure the full functional value that they once had for their traditions. Such is the case in the majority of African ethnic groups or with the Inuit of Canada. Other cultures, disintegrated ones, are on the verge of final dissolution and sometimes take refuge in the sole memory of a tribe, a family, an individual—for example, the old peasant who is the last native informant for a dialectologist or folklorist seeking a lost alpine tradition. With respect to the first case, I will talk about cultural *survivals*; in the second, of *relics*. I am applying this distinction to examples of oral poetry.

Are there any examples of "surviving" oral poetry? With so many from which to choose, I shall cite only those Romanian ballads collected by the Folklore Institute of Bucarest and of which Amzulescu published a collection of 350 titles in 1964. With all the recorded variants there were close to seven thousand texts. These comprise short stories structured in a linear fashion. They amount to no more than a few hundred verses such as is common in small rural communities where amateur peasant singers or singers of the professional class performed the epic *lauteri*. Such epic songs dates back to the sixteenth century throughout what is today modern Romania. There are no less than nine hundred versions of the best known of these songs, the beautiful "Mioritsa." They were published for the first time in literary circles in 1848, but have always been maintained in popular culture as well. Although quite vital until the end of the nineteenth century, this poetry has not withstood urbanization and indeed is maintained by governmental protection alone (Renzi 1969; Knorringa 1978, and 1980, p. 15).

As an example of the "relics," I would point to the Piedmontese songs that Terracini noted in 1908 and which he published in 1959. A seventy-nine-year old woman, the last repository of the village poetic treasury, had sung for him nine short lyrico-epic ballads, each of some thirty verses, that fell into two distinct linguistic groups (one was in dialect, the other in Italian) and which probably represented two separate traditions. The informant, moreover, found these texts interesting less for themselves than for their ability to spark the memory of someone long gone or her own lost youth.

These are very loose distinctions: between functional poetry and survival poetry, the difference derives more, at least in marginal cases, from the point of view of the observer. Thus, the funeral dirges of the Limba in Sierra Leone, an essential element of the funeral rites, remain functional for the villagers who belong to a given ethnic group, but are survivals on the national level. Conversely, Nigerian political parties use songs with alternating invective common to the Yoruba tradition in their propaganda. This has led to refunctionalizing a poetry that would have been nothing but "survival" otherwise. The *haka*, a traditional song of the Maoris of New Zealand, has been used again in protocol ceremonies and adapted to these situations since the Second World War. In 1941, John and Alan Lomax discovered the existence of worksongs among the black inmates in Texas prisons. These songs can be traced back to slave songs but have been adapted to suit the work imposed upon prisoners. Jackson published them in 1972 (Finnegan 1977, pp. 154–55, 220–24, and 1978, p. 292; Vassal 1977, pp. 33–34).

Between survival and relic, there are intersections. Ravier presents the songs that he collected in 1959 in the Pyrenees in much the same way as I have defined "survival"; but his description of the sociological context would lead me to speak of "relics." A dozen villages and hamlets in Lavedan have kept alive the memory of a tradition of poems sung in the Gascony patois in dramatic, satirical, or pastoral tones, and inspired by some past event of local import: the misadventures of a deserter, a memorable hunt, a love story, or a quarrel among shepherds. Some of these can be dated precisely, the oldest one going back to 1830–40 and the most recent to 1943 (Ravier and Séguy). The event was set forth in a narrative according to a compound mode of composition that obeys rules that are not explicit, ones flexible enough to allow for a ceaseless *mouvance* of the text, from performance to performance. They were composed on the occasion of a feast, a collective emotion, a commemoration, and repeated in the coffeehouses, in the town square, at the end of Sunday Mass. They were espoused by the community and succumbed to a sort of anonymity. In 1959 while the research was being conducted, a certain number of informants were able to sing some and recall the story, but the ability to compose had long since passed.

Another principle for classification must intervene and support the first: the rhythms of the traditions in the culture under scrutiny. One distinguishes thereby the long-term effects, those ordinarily designated as *traditional*; the effects of acceleration, whether regional or universal, in the midst of a network of traditions; and finally, the effects of interruption.

Most of our European "folkloric" poetry belongs to the first category. To the second, I assign those poetries that quickly adapted to the novelties of the American continent in the sixteenth and seventeenth centuries; they developed here in a rather singular fashion, to the extent that they constituted huge collections from the eighteenth century on, having typical features and remaining nevertheless within the European cultural continuity and seen as a simple extension of that culture. Thousands of peasant songs from Quebec—whose models came from France and even Scotland—come to mind (see the findings of the Barbeau and Lacourcière research teams). Even more striking are the laments, riddles, lullabies, and scouting songs from Canadian Acadia and the Louisiana Cajuns imbued with British influences. Better known are the drinking songs or courting songs of the *shanties*, the British and Irish ballads in the United States: the body of this old tradition feeds a series of vigorous offshoots—hillbilly, bluegrass, and songs of the Old West—prevalent at the beginning of the twentieth century (Dupont; Rens and Leblanc; Vassal 1977, pp. 52–72, 78–83).

The same phenomena occurred in Latin America in even its most remote regions. Central Chile developed its own popular poetry with typical genres like the *tonada*, grafted on a purely Castillian or Andalusian stem, and removed from the Indian influences of the north and the south of the country. The same persists in Mexico, where the two-volume publication of *Cancionero folclorico* has provided close to ten thousand love songs stemming from Spanish traditions (Clouzet 1975, p. 18; Alatorre 1975).

Between 1850 and 1900, signs of the survival of the Iberian *Romancero* were found first in Nicaragua, then in Venezuela, Uruguay, Argentina, and finally in the Andes. Close to the First World War, they could be found in the West Indies; toward 1940 they were in the southern United States and in Brazil (Menendez Pidal 1968, II, pp. 343–53; Mendoza; Zumthor 1980b, pp. 231, 236–37). Almost everywhere a thematic and musical adaptation had taken place. In Brazil, the vein of the *Romancero* was still quite recently feeding *cordel* literature; in Mexico it gave rise to an even more productive genre, the *corrido*.

It sometimes happens that the impact of an event that has shaken imaginations and consciences will cause an acceleration. In France the Napoleonic epic gave rise to a poetry of "popular" songs using adaptions of old ditties. Béranger made good use of its vigor (Nisard, pp. 495–96). Between 1936 and 1939, during the Spanish Civil War, a host of beautiful war songs sprang up behind Republican lines. Many were based on Basque, Andalusian, or Catalan folkloric melodies or on patriotic songs that had come into the tradition more than a century before (recording of *Le chant du monde* LDX-5-4279).

Other types of poetry, to the contrary, draw their energy from breaking with a tradition felt to be too restrictive. The refusal of time-honored traditions and modeling rules breaks the rhythm of habitual repetitions: a cry is raised, but no clamor. Little does it matter in what terms it is put, ones that may even derive from the depths of a collective memory. What counts is the intention to free the moment of its cares and concerns, be they painful or joyful. The cry is reiterated: we go back in time, but it will be the time of a mode, a self-destructive time, a time that may last a decade or just a season.

In our present situation, all mediated oral poetry, with only rare exceptions, enters into this class, which is naturally open to commercialization. But this story predates the invention of mass media: it has been written throughout the West since the eighteenth century.

The rupture occurs at the moment when changing conditions of existence reach a critical point and come into contact with those very values deemed essential: so it was for the generations who lived through industrialization, urbanization, and in the United States, the conquest of the West. Pioneer songs, prospector songs, and hobo songs are examples in which one can find elements stemming from European traditions but melted within this raging potpourri of nations and poetries into an affirmation of an original self. After 1960 in urban milieus and in the wake of folk revivals, the same explosion took place among the militant civil rights groups.

Personal action can be a determining factor here. The great Alsatian vernacular poet, Nathan Katz, who had been nurtured on the traditions of his Germanic lands, both used and rejected those traditions at the same time, and thereby universalized the discourse on the lips of all those who recite or sing his verses. One should probably mention in this context the Soviet singer and songwriter Vladimir Vissotsky, for his audiences of workers and young people; or the Georgian Ikoudjava, Moscow's Brassens; or the songs of the Pole Chyla, whose forms seem to approximate folklore but are corrupted by a parodic irony and an entirely new musicality (Hell; recordings of *Le chant du monde* LDX-7-4358 and 4581).

Traditional oral poetry with long-standing rhythms will remain functional in its society, a survival in another, and elsewhere a relic. Since travelers, ethnographers, and folklorists have systematized their observations of the moment, a worldwide movement has tended toward a defunctionalization of traditional poetries as they have become the objects of scientific inquiry or of curiosity. In this light, the history of the past 150 years takes on the appearance of an irreversible decline: the end has not yet been fully reached, and who knows which survivals will perhaps tomorrow regain their functionality through some ecological fervor?

The people inhabiting the south-central areas of Soviet Asia—Turkomans, Ouigours, Kazaks—around 1850 still had a major epic wherein their national consciousness crystallized in direct contact with Russian thought. At the end of the century, the colonization of the Pacific islands was such that strong poetic traditions could survive on the Hawaiian Islands for a while longer. Throughout the 1930s, at the very end of their existence as functional songs, the beautiful and mystical chants of the Gond in India—a people considered to be the poorest in all the land—were collected; so too, the epic *yukar* of the Ainus in western Japan; and toward 1940, the last songs of praise of the tribal leaders of the Zulu and the Sotho of South Africa and the Akan of Ghana, that ancient and widespread genre, also got recorded. Ethnologists in the 1950s and 1960s sought out the last remaining poetic traditions bearing a somewhat integrated social functionality throughout the Third World just as urbanization and the transistor radio were on the verge of destroying those traditions: love songs from the Gilbert Islands; circumstantial poems from the Tonga; Somalian war and battle songs; and the mass of mythological poems that the aborigines of the Land of Arnhem in Australia used to sing (Finnegan 1977, pp. 12–13, 29, 82, 100, 113–14, 120, 172, 204, and 1978, pp. 13–36, 98–109, 319–55; Chadwick and Zhirmunsky, pp. 7–19).

We can do nothing more than haphazardly set up this smorgasbord of a heritage. Not long ago, the Mandigo cycle of the Sundiata was effective in maintaining the memory of a past and a gauge for the future of the Mandigo people and the surrounding ethnic groups. In 1975–76, in the slums of Lagos, storytellers and singers would still bring to mind gods and heroes not yet put to rest. What about today?

In 1980, women of Upper Volta, were still singing the ancient words that integrated the rite of their beer production to cosmic mysteries. Did they continue to do so in 1981?

The precipitation of historical periods—common to a technological culture—works against these forms of poetry whose force and meaning derive from their continuity and antiquity. Africa today, due to late acculturation, remains closer to the relics of its past. In contrast, the large mass of material made up of traditional poetries of North American Native Americans constitutes a network of very diverse survivals based on hundreds of different languages and dialects. The "personal songs" in which an individual projects his dreams into a phantasmagoric and liberating discourse have undoubtedly preserved something of their original function for those populations who still compose them. But the songs about intertribal meetings, if and when they still exist, have been taken over by show business: they have become adulterated relics (Vassal 1977, pp. 18–19) Once-sacred ceremonial chants, being a collective tribal property, have survived better: recordings taken half a century apart bear witness to a remarkable solidarity despite (or perhaps as a result of?) their folklorization.

There are, for example, the magic chants of the Algonquins of northern Quebec, despite the disappearance of the long hunting expeditions that gave rise to them; the songs of the pueblo feasts, cosmic invocations that used to coincide with harvesting rites; the medicine songs of the Apache. A glimmering of the richness of this orality is caught in accounts by travelers bringing the first shockwaves of white colonization (Savard 1974, p. 8; Finnegan 1977, p. 83, 100–104,

204, and 1978, pp. 204–33). It may be that since then, the autochthonous populations of North America have managed to readjust their culture in the poetic arena as they were able to do when adapting to the use of horses, firearms, military arts, and agricultural practices: a refashioning of their system of social existence, a reorienting of the treasury of their living traditions in such a way that what has survived genocide represents in part the debris of a relatively recent, heroic cultural work.

The same may be said essentially, albeit less dramatically, about what has transpired in French folklore: the hundreds of songs like those edited by Davenson not long ago or those by Charpentreau. Perhaps some lullabies and nursery songs continue to fill some shadow of a function within more traditional French families. Yet, put all together, the whole set is only a sum of virtualities that no one individual or group can possibly attain. Of the 252 children's songs gathered by Charpentreau, I personally know 82 of them, one-third. I am taking my own experience as representative because in my family we used to sing a lot and I have always liked to sing. Still, of the 82 songs in question, I know no more than 38 of them in full, both text and melody; and more often than not, I have several variations of either a textual or melodic sort for the published form of the song. Of the remaining 44, I know only part of the song, the first verses or the refrain; for 3 of them, I know only the refrain. I am including 15 songs that I learned as an adult (between the ages of twenty-five and thirty-five) and which were part of my wife's family repertoire; one of them, its version given in French by Charpentreau, I only know in Savoyard patois. How many of these texts will my children want or be able to sing to their children? I asked two of my daughters. One who is twenty-eight, university educated, and a mother, provided me with the following information: 48 songs known in full, 8 in part. The other daughter, twenty-five-years old, single, and an artist, said that she knew 23 in full, 26 in part. My son-in-law, who has avowed that his familiarity with this body of knowledge stems mainly from his wife, knows 29 songs in their entirety and 20 in partial forms. Through my daughter, I was able to broaden the scope of this line of inquiry past my immediate family: a Parisian mother, fifty years old, knows 43 completely, 12 in part; of two single people, twenty to twenty-five years old, the man knew 56 whole songs, 10 partially, the woman around 70 entirely, 12 partially. Two hierarchized factors come into play: the "family culture" and age group.

Nothing, however, is terminally lost. A function may appear any day, without warning, for any one of these surviving texts. An artist, having incorporated it, will confer on it a new existence, one integrated to the living culture of his or her times, as, for example, Catarina Bueno had done for Italian folk songs. Or as has happened with more or less politicized regionalist movements that expectantly revive traditional songs to convey their message, and eventually to become songs of action, calling the region's peoples to regroup, to rediscover their ethnic self: such has been the case in Brittany from the Goadec sisters all the way to the *festou-noz* of the 1960s. (Vassal 1980; cf. a series of broadcasts by France-Culture called "La renaissance des musiques traditionnelles," January 1981).

A poetic tradition can once again become functional where an event has acted as an accelerator. Nevertheless, this mechanism sometimes fails to work: the recent forms of the *Romancero*, remnants of which were collected between 1920 and 1950 by Galmes de Fuentes and Catalan, have remained no more than survivals; as relics, we find the two Italian poems of the twenties, dramatic recital ballads about Musolino, the Calabrian brigand (*Drammatica*, pp. 445–64). Contemporary Africa has, in contrast, succeeded in functionally adapting some customary poetic forms. I have already pointed out the Nigerian political songs; they have their equivalent in Zambia. At the time of Bokassa in the Central African Republic, various groups of musicians spread their songs of praise for the Master, who made sure to record them. The imperial coronation especially inspired these poets (Finnegan 1977, p. 230; a dossier distributed by J.-D. Penel in Bangui in December 1980). More subtly, in Kenya, during the Mau Mau wars, the partisans of the Mau Mau sang with impunity, in Kikuyu, their call for revolt using the melody of "God Save the King."

The same diversity in outcomes is to be found in new creations, ones issuing from the disruption of the traditional fabric; initially functional, they easily fall back into a state of survival, if not relic. Such is the case with the majority of the works of the peasant or working-class songsters at the end of the nineteenth century, as well as with the poignant songs of the Beauceron, Gaston Coute, despite the devotion and talent with which Meulien and Pierron have worked to keep them alive. Coute, a contemporary of Bruant, the collaborator on *Libertaire* and *La guerre sociale* (where he published "the song of the week" using his patois like Rictus did his argot), died at thirty-one years of age in 1911, the eve of the day when the world to which he directed his voice was going to disappear (Ringeas and Coutant; recording, *Alvaris* 819).

Part II
The Forms

Chapter 5
Forms and Genres

A form is stable and fixed only under certain conditions; most often it maintains a certain mobility that stems from its own brand of energy: ultimately and paradoxically, *form* equals *force*. The great and mystical Ismailian poet, Nasir Udin Hunzai, honored me in February 1980 by coming to my seminar to sing several of his compositions. When questioned about the "form" of these works, he gave us varying answers that nonetheless testified to his notion of poetic consciousness where "form" is not a schema, saying that it "obeys" no specific rule because it *is* the rule, one constantly re-created, a "pure" rhythm (in both senses of "pure"), that exists only through and within the excitement of the moment, of the encounter, and of the quality of the light.

The production of a work of art is the delimitation of matter: matter that is shaped, provided with a beginning and an end, and that is brought to life by intentionality, even if only latent. In a sociohistorical perspective, form is thus, as Roubaud puts it, a "memory of changes in meaning."

Where it concerns a work of poetry, it is easy to maintain the current distinction between "semantic" elements (those relating to the emergence of meaning), the "syntactic" ones (the relationships between parts), the "pragmatic" ones (the use made of this or that work) and the "verbal" elements (those touching on the materiality of the signs). This distinction will nonetheless disallow all rigidity. In fact, from the moment that a study embraces two or more works, it lends itself to comparison and bases itself on an examination of its discernible variables and invariants. The task of the poetician is to put the invariants in order. Yet the latter come from several levels of expression where the rules of variability (quantity, quality, duration, combination of variables) can differ greatly: such is the anthropological level of archetypes, myths, symbols; the ideological level of the representative schemata, formulas, and commonplace ideas; the literal level of textual features.

There is still no definable "aesthetic level": the problem of the mutual alterity of work and scholar is evinced (Jauss 1977, pp. 11–26, 411–20; Zumthor 1980a, pp. 35–41; Finnegan 1977, pp. 25–26). No doubt the aesthetic value of a work does not depend on its "function" (in an indirect manner), in the sense that I have used this term in the preceding chapter. But judgment based on this relationship comes from the social competence of a given cultural milieu (I noted it in chapter 2) from a *consensus* that presides over both production and reception of what is deemed poetry: all unstable factors within space and time.

The difference between sensorial registers that are problematized by oral poetry on the one hand and written poetry on the other implies that their respective forms cannot be identical. Neither can the levels where they are constituted nor the procedures that produce them a priori be compared.

In slow-rhythm cultures, the functioning of collective memory determines the mode of poetic structuration. The poem seems to be a "rereading" rather than a "creation": its ontological time frame is the very tradition that sustains it. The performance, as the sole manifestation of the work, equals what would for us be an isolated and unique reading, one necessarily unmoored and incomplete. The work is "monumentalized" by what are often extremely subtle marks of its integration into the tradition. In more rapidly paced cultures the time span of the work is displaced or shrinks in accordance with efforts at adaptation or rupture: sometimes it is maintained within the narrow chronological limits of what is fashionable (Kellogg, pp. 532–33; Zumthor 1972, pp. 71–82). Nevertheless, every oral poem, in every situation, makes reference to a concrete poetic field, one that is extrinsic, one other than that which the listener perceives here and now. Written poetry most certainly also refers back to external models, although it does so with less urgency and precision.

Thus the poetic structuration of orality depends less on grammatical processes (as happens almost exclusively in written poetry) than on a dramatization of the discourse. The norm is defined in sociological terms more than in linguistic ones. Yet, for this very reason, oral poetry generally has more rules, and more complex ones, than the written form: in predominantly oral societies, oral poetry often is a much more elaborate art than are the majority of our written productions. To underscore these nuances, I will distinguish as consistently as possible, between the *work*, the *poem*, and the *text*. The work is what is communicated poetically here and now. It is text, sonorities, rhythms, visual elements; the term "work" encompasses all performative factors. The poem is the text and in the final analysis it is the melody of the work, without taking into consideration any other factors. And finally, the text is that linguistic sequence, perceived auditorily, for which the total meaning of its sequence is not reducible to the sum of the particular effects produced by its successively perceived component parts.

The resulting coexistence of these three entities makes it difficult to grasp the specific elements of textual forms of oral poetry. Ethnologists and folklorists tried to get at it in various ways during the 1960s and the 1970s (Pop 1968; Lomax 1968; Buchan, pp. 53–55). Their studies show only a dim awareness of the fact that such forms arose in societies with long-standing traditions and primary orality. That fact alone precludes generalizations and conclusions. The theses of Parry and Lord and the "formulaic" theory (discussed in chapter 6) have long influenced anthropological research on preliterate civilizations. Stylistic features that display some (supposed) analogy with such and such a typical social or mental characteristic become the privileged models: standardized expressions and themes; epithets, slogans, or other qualifiers to distinguish between genres, classifications, and individuals; the importance of ceremonial apparatus; integration of the present historicized moment and erasure of the markings of duration; verbal abundance; and so forth.

Sometimes, however, a monograph, by virtue of the exigencies of its objectives, changes the perspective a little and frees itself of preconceived ideas; such is the case with Dournes's book on the Jorai of Indochina or the short work by Coffin on traditional ballads in North America. Linguistic forms, as such, including deep or surface narrative structures, constitute for both Coffin and Dournes inert elements and from the perspective of the audience they are aesthetically neutral (Coffin, pp. 164–73; Sherzer, pp. 193–95; Dournes 1976, pp. 125–57; Zumthor 1981c; Kerbrat-Orecchioni, p. 170). This *text* becomes art in an emotional setting; it appears in performance and in the totality of the striving and embodying energies of the living work. In this way performance — which in oral communication *is* the poetic object — confers on it a social identity by virtue of which it is perceived and declared to be so.

Performance is, then, an important element of form and is at the same time constitutive of it. With respect to the text alone (such as one *reads* a song once it is fixed by writing), performance acts as sound effects; moreover, it is often felt to be such, and not without a modicum of irritation, by those who have attached themselves exclusively to the values of writing. The text reacts to these sound effects, adapts itself, and modifies itself with an eye to overcoming the inhibition that it carries forth within itself.

This is why — given the need to adopt an analytic approach — I will consider separately first the linguistic forms, then the others by insisting from the outset that this separation is something artificial and that both series are open, in that the one does not come into existence except through the other.

Insofar as linguistic forms are concerned, I have adopted two distinct perspectives to be formulated thus: (1) in this chapter at the level of whole texts and whole groups of texts: the perspective of *macroforms*, on the order of models and "genres"; and (2) in chapter 7, within the texture of a poem: the perspective is that of *microforms*, definable within lexico-syntactical arrangements ("style") and within the effects of meaning ("themes"), especially those in the production of which a social convention intervenes.

I address "themes" only incidentally because they are hardly specific to orality and hence cross horizontally all classes of discourse. Their study, then, rather than stemming from the poetic, stems from history, from sociology, or from an anthropology of the imaginary.

The *macroforms* more or less exceed the linguistic schema. In fact, they encompass the modalities of language of the oral texts that the latter determine; but these same modalities can hardly be dissociated from the nonlinguistic expressive elements, which depend on circumstances themselves linked to the social function fulfilled by performance: a chain of implications that one could, in theory, analyze from any one of its rings.

With respect to the nonlinguistic forms, I group them under the label of the "sociocorporeal," by which I mean the collection of formal characters or the formalizing tendencies resulting, in their origin or their finality, from the existence of the social group on the one hand; on the other hand it is from the presence and the sensorial nature of the body. The body is both the physically individualized body of each one of the persons engaged in the performance and the harder to discern, but ever so real, body of the collectivity such as is made manifest in emotional reactions and common movements (Scheub 1977, p. 363).

For the sake of terminological simplification I speak here of *forms* in the plural. These are none other than the various components of a unique *Form* in each poem (of which the Form is *the* only "form"). Form is equally unique in that it never reproduces itself, thereby escaping the time factor, at the same time as its components, to the contrary, have a tendency to reproduce indefinitely.

By nature or by circumstance, different formal components of the poem are evenly codified: certain ones are rigorously done; others incompletely or in a very loose way; and some escape all codification. The latter cannot be described except with respect to a single performance. I have rather summarily classified the others into two groups according to whether they are a matter of "strict" or "loose" codes: the distinction between these, at once both free-floating and adaptable, is based on the proportion of *signs* (arbitrary), *signals* (metonymic), and *symbols* (metaphoric) that make up its enactment.

In the discussion in chapter 3 of "genres" of oral literature we managed to circumscribe the concept to which I am applying the term "macroform." It is altogether and at once a collection of formal virtualities, a zone wherein individual competencies are brought to bear, a working draft of an abstract model, a grouping of energies and the modality of a tradition. And as such, the macroform — in opposition to raw materials and far removed from poetic discourse—sets up the material that is closest at hand and already partially formulated and that the letter will formalize in a definitive manner while actualizing it. As a program and a desire to exist, the macroform has two elements—*force* and *ordering*, which are respectively the root of this desire and an aspect of a programming.

The presence of this double factor is probably the only wholly universal characteristic of poetic macroforms. The manner by which they are organized and function (i.e., the nature and the rules of the "genres" they engender) differ greatly according to the cultural contexts. Thus, all cultures have produced a love poetry, one of conjuring or of combat, but to say so does little to move us ahead; and the more one seeks to render this information more precise, the more one runs the risk of getting lost in burgeoning regional or particularized manifestations.

The number and the rigidity of the macroforms seem inversely proportional to the degree of technological complexity of the culture under consideration. They grow more and (contrary to common opinion) the inventive force of the poets increases in tandem with the ability of language to create an imaginary universe and socially to impose its pertinence. One of the most learned poetries of the world was that of the Inuit almost a century ago, in a language where a single word would signify both "to breathe" and "to compose a song" (Finnegan 1977, pp. 178–83, and 1978, pp. 225–27). In Europe today, in contrast, the total disfunctionalization of what has become our "folk song" lends a heteroclite aspect to this poetry (taken in its entirety) and denies generalizations. The one-time success of "'caf' conc' "" (café songs), patriotic songs of the nineteenth century, ribald parodies, political satires divorced from their context, relief from the gallant pastorals of the classical period, medieval relics, ritornellos to accompany forgotten dance songs: all these, in a random way, fill our anthologies of "old French songs" where from time to time one of our poets or songwriters finds an inspiration, an image, a rhythm, an emotional theme, without, however, evoking any tradition per se.

The *mediats* bring us to this apparently archaic situation: they demand genres with fixed rules: cop shows, westerns, advertisements. Therein lies the penchant for every "popular" art destined for a quantitatively limitless public (Burgelin, pp. 102–7). The absence of all differentiation is only more remarkable in the unique and exclusively oral art conveyed by these *mediats*: the song. Its musical style by itself is sometimes used to mark it in some specific way, and even more often it is the name of a "hit singer" that serves that function: there is nothing there that works toward the definition of a classification that can be construed as normative.

The entire evolution of European song, from the very beginnings of the technological and industrial era, has tended toward the dissolution of differences, to the erasure of the very vocabulary that used to contribute to their maintenance.

Ballad or *rondeau*, in French, has no usage other than archaeological; *vaudeville* (whoever may have been the mysterious Olivier Basselin, of the Vaux de Vire [popular etymological source of vaudeville—Trans.]) by the eighteenth century had come to designate a type of song in couplets, the couplets sung at the end of a comedy, or a parody, even a potpourri, before becoming in 1792 the name of a Parisian theater. Little by little stripped of their meaning, the *complaint* and the *romance* survive only in those rare, picturesque titles such as the "Romance of Paris" by Charles Trenet and the "Complaint of the Infidels" that Mouloudji sang. Today we simple say *song* (Vernillat and Charpentreau, pp. 68–69, 218–21, 248).

For this reason, I spare myself the trouble of reviewing the numerous and rather incoherent suggestions that, since the middle of the nineteenth century, have been proffered for the purposes of cataloguing and classifying oral poems. From the Ampère report in 1852 to the works by Coirault in the 1950s and to the voluminous Brednich Manual of 1973, they have, willy-nilly or one by one, with more or less subtlety, called on historical, social, stylistic, spatiotemporal, rhythmic, or musical factors (Laforte 1976, pp. 4–8; Brednich): whence derive lists of genres or types, numbering from twelve to around thirty, depending on the principle being used and the scope of the information.

A given number of them are of a great ethnological interest: Bausinger's for its generalities; those compiling the Mexican *Cancionero folclorico*, Laforte's Quebecois songs; in their own right several by Africanists. None, at any rate, is totally satisfying: the more the object of a research project leans toward universality, the more untenable is the hierarchy of elements isolated in the analysis. Besides, the dispersion and the usury of traditional terminologies have made accounting for generic designations specific to each language a delicate matter. Yet one cannot dismiss them entirely, for often they alone provide the means to break the iron grip of ethnocentric classifications. It does matter, then, that the Yoruba have eleven specialized expressions to designate the types of sung poetry; it also matters that the Manobo of the Philippines, according to Maquiso, have a universal term for every type of song or recitation, another special one for the song in its strictest terms, but there are four other ones that designate: the love song; an ensemble of the war song, the planting song, and the harvest song; and two funeral dirges (Bausinger, pp. 66–90, 247–65; Alatorre 1975, p. xlv; Laforte 1976, pp. 8, 26, 46–50, 117–20; Du Berger 1971, sections 11/3 to 11/8; Finnegan 1976, p. 79; Agblemagnon, pp. 119–33; Maquiso, p. 24).

From these speculations arise two universals: the *force* of the macroform is defined in terms of functions; the *ordering* is defined according to the nature of that for which it contains the programming.

The definitional functions of *force* are organized around one of three axes. The first is none other than instrumental causality; in fact, it is the quality of the human intermediary during performance. On this axis we find forms set aside for the use of a particular group classed by age, sex, profession, or a given task.

The governing principle of these groupings seems to be inscribed in language itself insofar as it is a social structure. The observable facts today reveal only approximate similarities, nevertheless ones constant enough to afford suppositions of a profound homology. In those very societies where a long tradition of writing has stripped voice of its originary authority, the orality of the communication remains (at least ouside writing) tied to certain discursive situations: the anecdotal tale, "gossip," secrets told to the person who acts as the repository of secrets for the group, the corner grocery, or the bistro; humorous stories with political dimensions during oppressive regimes where such stories occupy the last margin of freedom; conversation, which is throughout the world the object of rules and censorship and which several cultures have ritualized (Certeau, pp. 66, 150–55; Giard and Mayol, pp. 95–105; no. 30 [1979] of *Communication*); the ludic and agonistic exercise of merchandising; and so forth.

Oral poetry is one of these situations—an eminent one certainly but one in which one hears more or less confusedly the echo of the others. It is, in particular, the echo of those that prolong among us customs as ancient as the human voice undoubtedly is, to each cultural mutation readapted to the circumstances. Medical consultations, by the fact that they contain dialogue (and by the roles thereby institutionalized), assume a situation and a discourse whose first model has grown out of ancestral witchcraft: this model animates psychoanalytic cures today. The utterance once again becomes therapeutic: the voicing of emotions, pure sonorous associations, the rhythm of language and the very position of the listener. In the same position, although not face to face, the analyst practices hearings that make his or her own body echo the voice of the other, less meaning than the sonority, overdetermined by symbolic values in the scene that is played between the two of them.

Teaching, for better or for worse up until today, derives for a large part from the same model: less *what* the voice communicates in the classroom than the transfer established by the teaching relationship. It matters little how differences from one type of culture to another modify the instructional content: here science, there wisdom; for us various subject matters, in other societies, a way of life sometimes stressing individual success, sometimes collective growth. The fundamental feature remains unchanged.

Mediat diffusion made short shrift of traditional scholarly practices: chanted, rhythmic, sometimes versified mnemotechnical formulas—a mediocre and lively poetry that the entire class intoned along with the schoolmaster, the *Barbara celarent* of the Scholastics or listing all the departments of France from my childhood (like memorizing all states of the United States); and so many texts read aloud and regurgitated from memory, like the hundreds of verses of Virgil or Homer that still reside within me today but that nowadays only the sound of my own voice lets me unearth (Barthes; Fédry 1977b, pp. 584–85; Greimas 1979, pp. 3–4; Fabbri, pp. 10–11). Although the old ways have all but disappeared from the curriculum, we are now frantically multiplying seminars, round tables, colloquia, and congresses, these new strategies indispensable for the progress of knowledge; in addition, however, beyond voicing written language at intellectual gatherings, there is a long, universal quest for a restoration of voice.

Elsewhere voice has lost practically nothing of its primitive functions within religious traditions, at the heart of which many forms of oral poetry are composed and maintained. In the dramatic relationship that confronts the *homo religiosus* with the sacred element, a radicalized voice intervenes as both power and truth. As power it is the voice in the breath of which magic formulas are carried out and which in trances the initiate chases out of himself, falling prey to his god: the voodoo of the Antilles, Brazilian *macumba*, but also the rites of the Shakers in nineteenth-century America, the Chlustes in czarist Russia, and less drastically, our own charismatic movements (Rouget, pp. 85–86, 127–28, 205–11, 231–32, 398; Collier, p. 21; Compagnon). That voice is exalted in glossolalia. Beyond a language where everything has been said it posits the word of an absolutely other other; it is a vocal fiction, void of narrativity; it returns to the childhood sources of all voice.

As truth, it is not only the means of transmission of a doctrine but is also in its lived quality the founding of faith. Preaching in organized churches offers a hazy example. A clearer example can be found to itinerant preachers like those of the Yoruba in Nigeria or the American revivalists. Rosenberg has done a study of black preachers whose oratory style he equates with that of singers of epics.

Oral poetry is prone to assume analogous functions. The majority of cultures have or have had an oral poetry (usually songs) meant to sustain some type of work as an accompaniment, especially if it is group work. In Africa, every manual task normally has some kind of song to go along with it. In traditional societies, this poetry has a ritual value; the work becomes a dance, a game, it engenders passion; the song gets involved in the energy of the word, the very strength of voice. Although sometimes very elaborate and sometimes reduced to short repetitive forms, this poetry exerts a double function: it eases the labor by giving it rhythm, but it also disalienates of the worker, who by singing reconciles him- or herself to the work and can thereby appropriate it. In a fictional way the apparent relationships are reversed: the work seems to be nothing more than the auxiliary of the song, in the collective chain gangs of black peasants, *dopkwe* of Benin, Yoruba *egbe*, Haitian *coumbite*, the *troca dia* of Brazil; in the choral groups of parrot hunters in the Congo that Gide described with such admiration in 1926. Throughout Africa there are many other such examples (Finnegan 1976, pp. 230–40; Jahn 1961, p. 260; Roy 1954, pp. 239–48; Gide, pp. 21, 289–92; Collier, pp. 19–20).

In the West ever since industrialization imposed artificial rhythms on working and thereby reduced the creative part to nothing, these forms of poetry have rapidly disappeared. Lloyd and McCormick published the last examples of it in 1967 and 1969. They had gathered them from Welsh miners and weavers in western Scotland. Perhaps there are still memories of hawkers' songs, a secular traditional poetry sung in the Paris and Geneva of my childhood. Collier could still hear them around 1950 in a black neighborhood of New York (Finnegan 1977, pp. 218–19; Neuburg, pp. 247, 296; Collier, p. 23).

Sometimes the poem constitutes one of the aspects of the work itself as in sowing, harvesting, and wine-making songs; sometimes its usage represents the privilege of a closed professional group. If the cultural context highly values this group, its professional poetry may become a major art form; such is the case with cattle praise songs of the Tutsi of Rwanda or the Peuls of Mali — both pastoral and warrior peoples for whom the possession of herds indicates the nobility of the man (Finnegan 1976, p. 206; Smith 1974, p. 300–02; Seydou; Burke, pp. 35–46, 50; Poueigh, pp. 153–56; Vassal 1977, pp. 67–69). More often, it is contrary to the relative marginalization of the group in question that its work songs seem to draw their strength: thus, for example, in Europe between the sixteenth and nineteenth centuries, there were soldiers' songs, sailors' songs, and shepherds' songs; in North America, those of the cowboys.

In the same way, there seems to be a general tendency in natural languages to push toward the specification of certain forms by virtue of age or gender. This tendency influences the status of several sung poetic forms, depending on the group or culture at hand. I will come back to this point in chapters 5 and 12. For us, a once hearty and long-lived tendency is today attenuated. It still defines infant orality quite well. This orality is rooted in the first vocal experiences of the newborn, semanticized by them, and constitutes at the very center of our technological universe the dialect of the last tribe having pure speech. The adolescent moves away from it very slowly, with regret, and often in full revolt. The threshold that he crosses thereby introduces him to this "youth culture" that was so much discussed that it was generalized in the 1950s: based on a rejection of adult commonplaces and the world of writing, it furiously calls forth the savage voice and is comforted by some common adherence to symbols, imaginary themes, and practices, the most universal of which (and largely co-opted by industry) is none other than listening to "pop hits" produced by idols. (Burgelin, pp. 158–70). Surrounding the song and by means of it, new rites of participation become institutions, purveyors of new heroes.

Yet, in the first days of the life of a child, even before a spoken dialogue is set up with her child, the mother enters into the child's game, spontaneously readapting her speech: timbre, level, rhythm, all modified to sing a lullaby, to utter a few words in baby talk. Could this be the foundation (or the indicator) of a specifically feminine orality, the principal factor in safeguarding the central traditions of a group (according to ethnologists and dialectologists)? Among certain peoples, the language of women differs from that of men (in medieval Japan even their writing was different); sometimes it is distinguished by the posturing of the voice. In our own languages we pretend to perceive in passing some stereotyped "women's talk" or a "womanly tone of voice" that amuses us. Both are registers that every human voice possesses physiologically and engenders in each of us individually, in each of our cultures collectively, a tension analogous to that which stems from the separation of the sexes and is not foreign to it (Rondeleux, pp. 49–50, 53; Husson, p. 80; Calame-Griaule 1965, p. 54).

These are games of intonation, ellipses, free falls, rebounds, eroticized wanderings that harmonize chatter—speech with neither memory nor subject, the locus of unpunished pleasure, less the expression of some autonomous reality than a grasp of the body, a vacant desire, acceding thus to communicability, beyond all design (Pessel, pp. 18–20; Cixous and Clément, p. 92; Lamy, pp. 63–70). Or perhaps the litany, that enchanting talk-talk-talk, a ritualized reiteration, the unavowable and eternal recourse to the almighty of the other at the same time as the extenuation of language and its lies. In the depths, the plunge, the flight, then the ripping away that signifies for woman the passage from silence to speech: that flight of the body, let it all go, and here it is that she exposes herself, is present entirely in her voice. The echo of a terribly ancient song resonates herein, one prior to the prohibitions of the law, prior perhaps to language itself—this is why she sings so spontaneously.

On the male side of things, we could conversely put forward the "sweet talk" of the lover's approach, using beguilingly vocal nuances and lexical ambiguities. Men's language, women's language: these distinctions remain virtual, although very general, and many cultures have exploited them for their own purposes.

It is true that the classification of certain poetic genres according to gender derives from professional custom: in Africa or with the Pueblo Indians, songs rhythming millet winnowing are women's songs both in fact and by law. This coincidence does not explain everything. In African villages, the female population forms a very stable living and working community that has its own treasury of songs: work songs, but also lamenting-wife songs, songs meant to accompany men's dances, female ritual songs, teasing songs, ones improvised and used within the group, like jibes exchanged between spouses.

In several societies there are diverse interdictions, infractions notwithstanding, to maintain this division of poetic tasks. By virtue of religious beliefs, ones perhaps connected with fertility rites, the ancient Incan *harawi* was given over to women alone, and the singing of the *lamento* for the deceased, too, is solely their domain. In certain ethnic groups of western Africa and in Rwanda, the right to sing songs about the powerful—genealogies, panegyrics, warrior songs—is disallowed women for political and imperious reasons. Elsewhere it is a social custom, one that has become problematic. Thus, the oral poetry of the gauchos assumes an exclusively masculine role in Brazil, Uruguay, and in Argentina, although not in Chile. During the nineteenth century as the Spanish *romance* was introduced in Brazil, it was considered to be an original creation, men's work; women remained the mistresses of the traditional *cantiga* in the corpus of the *cantoria*. Yet it most probably is more a matter of psychosociological tendencies in this instance than it is of any poetical organization. On the contrary, however, "love songs," even if the discourse is sexually marked, escape from such servility. Some Alexandrine examples, and consequently some medieval ones, have raised the question of the existence of a long tradition of erotic Western "women's songs"—for example, the Germanic *winileodos* and the Portuguese *cantigas de amigo*. In Polish Galicia and in Serbia, the collection of amorous oral poetry was called "women's songs" in the nineteenth century whereas the term "men's songs" was reserved for heroic ballads (Finnegan 1978, p. 206; Valderama, p. 308; Camara, pp. 120, 231, 252; Smith 1974, p. 299; Anido, p. 144; Fonseca 1981, I, pp. 45–46; Lord 1971, p. 14; Bec, pp. 57–62; Elicegui; Burke, p. 51).

Lullabies, as a poetic category with universal implications, fulfill a more differentiated function: sung by the mother or a surrogate, the lullaby is meant to be heard by the infant. Any other usage is merely an imitation of the latter, except apparently in Zulu circles in which each child has his own lullaby, composed for him and which remains his for life, like a name or a epitaph. But, more generally, "children's songs" are supplanting lullabies: the mode of their performance is that of a woman's song. The form, nonetheless, is determined by the image that is drawn of the listener. It shares a given number of formal traits, both linguistic and musical, with what are normally called children's songs (Charpentreau, pp. 9–30; Finnegan 1976, pp. 299–302; Knorringa 1980, p. 19; Roy 1954, pp. 27–71). The same ambiguity characterizes the group of ditties sung by parents to little ones: while bouncing the child on one's knees, encouraging children to take their first steps, to get them to sleep, or to count fingers on a hand (examples of this are found in all the Romance and Germanic languages).

Despite huge cultural differences that affect the assimilation of children into the human circle, there is no society without songs dedicated to this age group—sometimes in a historical fashion, for the distant origins of the text may be literary. Seventy of 250 "children's songs" published by Charpentreau attest to this fact. This poetry nonetheless represents one of the principal manifestations of a specifically child-oriented orality: modulations of language, given the rhythms of the body's breathing, coordinated with sleeping and waking and phantasmagoric shifts in dreams and in words themselves.

Being of a more conservative poetic tradition, the child's song seems to include several universal elements: a tendency to slip away from adult language, or at least to discourse on the outer fringes and with total indifference to denotative meaning; a predominance of rhythm over reference and half-tone; puns, jingles, and jokes; playful or hyperbolic uses of numbers; repetition, openness to foreign linguistic influences. In Canada's Acadia, children's songs are more anglicized than other songs; in the so-called francophone parts of Africa, they are more rife with French words; I would imagine that it is the same for a number of ancient conjuring formulas that have been included in this treasury (Parisot, Introduction; Jaquetti; Dupont, pp. 65–66, 173–83, 306; Finnegan 1976, pp. 305–10). With respect to children's songs, chapter 10 will address a problem: what is meant by *song*? Perhaps a physiological element (the undeveloped vocal cords) comes into play here, reducing the melody to a simple scansion.

Song tends to be a part of children's games: it can operate as a sort of introductory rite, like counting rhymes, used to designate the player(s) and the role(s); as a dramatic component in theatrical games, as are frequent in Africa, like those of the young Rwandese boys who mimic fighting animals, or the girls' moonlight dances in Malinka villages; or sometimes as an illustration or gloss such as a child uses when imitating an adult at work; and finally as a rhythmic backdrop to circle dances—like the *gbagba* of the schoolboys of Bangui in central Africa that Penel collected in 1979–80, gathering some 107 improvised songs (Penel, pp. 27–63).

The connection to play gets looser in little songs to capture animals (for the French, the snail [for Americans, the ladybug—Trans.]); in the singsongs for the days of the week or the letters of the alphabet; in school's out songs to be found in some European countries. Another value, one that is social and oppositive, is at play in children's chase songs for they derive from the folklore of certain feasts (Charpentreau, pp. 31–48; Du Berger, section 11/10; Georges, pp. 178–81; Boucharlat, pp. 34–35; Camara, p. 125).

What figure of childhood is projected in the popularity of song with today's youth—in the rejection of adult values for the mass "youth culture"? And not just any song. Two elements seem to be necessary—although they shift with the rapidly changing fashions—for a "hit song" (Burgelin, pp. 169–74): a particular thematic and lexical similarity to ordinary adolescent discourse (friends, lovers, wanderlust, marginality) and the mediation of a star, a hero, a paternal figure that is set against the world without supposedly having been subjected to the sobering effects of societal conditioning, an Elvis Presley, a Bob Dylan, a John Lennon.

The star, a professional singer, is only conceivable and admirable for being such. Another criterion: many cultures in fact (I will come back to this point in chapter 12) distinguish between professional song and amateur song in their different functions. Besides, a rather stringent opposition is drawn between individual song and group song. Certain songs have meaning only when sung by a group: dancers, drinkers, soldiers; according to Laforte, in the French Canadian tradition, the form that he calls the "song in laisses" was specifically meant for choral singing, such as the "runners in the woods" (Clastres, pp. 123–24, 129; Laya, p. 179; Laforte 1981, p. 264; Sargent and Kittredge, p. xix–xx). We are probably seeing the re-emergence of very old sociopoetic archetypes in adolescent circles in our technological society.

There is a second axis along which the constitutive *force* of an oral genre can be established: its immediate and explicit finality, when it identifies with the social group's will to survive. For our young people today, this is the principle behind hit songs. And yet so many poetic forms become dynamic in the same way — as evident within traditional societies, whereas it is often camouflaged in our world by aesthetic concerns. Hence most African ethnic groups practice mottoes, those short poems added to someone's name or title, to that of an animal, a divinity, even an object, and which by explicating its meaning, integrates it into a history, so efficaciously that the motto of certain spirits sets off a trance in those who hear it (Finnegan 1976, pp. 111–12, 128; Rouger, p. 118, 144–52; Camara, p. 198). The move from motto to song of praise is easy. Upon the naming of a newborn Malinke, the father improvises an epic tirade about the ancestor from whom the name comes — and this while the women dance.

If praise is addressed to the chief, it exalts Power. Panegyric is one of the most widespread poetic genres in state societies, in Africa, in Oceania; this was also true in pre-Columbian America where Inca propaganda dictated its themes. Rich in stereotypes and most often closely tied to quasi-ritual rules, this type of poem assumes forms that for the traditional society refer to the past of the group, ones that are more or less akin to epic forms: songs of self-praise (like those in many ancient societies) by a warrior vaunting his own great deeds whether real, presumed, or fictitious. African genealogies, ones amplified in Rwanda in dynastic poems transmitted so precisely that Kagame, around 1950, could retrace the history of this people back to the sixteenth century just by hearing them; Bantu *izibongo*, in all their complexity and specialization, the accumulation of hyperbolic metaphors and heroic allusions, often juxtaposed without narrative syntax (Finnegan 1976, pp. 206–20; Vansina 1965, p. 148; Smith 1974, p. 302; Bowra 1978, pp. 9–22).

This goldmine is not yet tapped out: some years ago, the griot Kaba sang the genealogy of President Sekou Toure in Guinea. Was it a political maneuver? No, no more so than the Swahili union songs collected by Whiteley around 1960. Rather, it is a merging with tradition that in technological societies assumes the function of cohesion by means of patriotic songs, protest or partisan songs; modern Japan, with its economic miracles, has engendered company songs like that of Matsushita Electric (Camara, p. 299; Finnegan 1976, p. 90, and 1977, p. 217).

The same function operates aggressively in warrior songs. Three more or less universal types can be distinguished: incitement to battle, praise of former combatants, and the song meant to sustain action during battle. The first two types once played an important cultural role in certain traditional societies. Such was the case for the Bantus: in Rwanda, learning military songs was part of the education of young men; in the Zulu kingdom, these songs were a crystallizing element in the national will starting from the time of Shaka's rule and were cultivated, organized, and systematically exploited by the ruling powers. Even today, preserved in memory, there are several old war songs that have been adapted to political and social struggles (Finnegan 1976, pp. 140, 208–20). In our industrial societies as well, warrior poetry continues in its fragmented forms, couched in oratorical motifs of patriotic or revolutionary songs.

Hunting songs are closely related for African, American Indian, and Asiatic peoples. They exalt moral values, the seductive lure of danger, the unforeseeable power of one's adversary and of nature itself: the scansion of the preparation for or the conclusion of massive group expeditions, ones accompanied by dancing, even mimes, and that transform meetings of cynegetic societies or funeral rites of an illustrious hunter into big shows (Finnegan 1976, pp. 101, 207, 221–30; *Recueil*, p. 74).

The instinct for social preservation is no less operative, even though it may be at work only implicitly, in the rarer forms of narrative oral poetry that recount some past event that was important for the community, even if perhaps it is today of little consequence; or in gnomic forms that are frequently found in traditional societies where they contribute to the transmission of common knowledge: in rural areas today we can still find a good number of rhymes and ditties about the weather (Roy 1954, pp. 141–69).

The dynamics that subtend these collective defensive and affirmational strategies are nuanced or inflected in oral religious poetry. This grouping includes all varieties of ritual song: in the West, Christian and Jewish liturgies are performed orally and sustained by age-old written transmission, as is chanting; elsewhere, there are the Hindu and Buddhist hymns; in African cults, songs and dances pay homage to great divinities or accompany initiations, circumcisions, excisions; Melanesian incantations are like those of Mongol or American Indian shamans; chants in their repetitious brevity induce a trance or are brought on by one (see Rouget's recent book on trances; also Dieterlen; *Recueil*, pp. 54–65; Camara, pp. 184–86; Finnegan 1978, p. 146; Foy 1954, pp. 311–51). The introduction in the 1960s of Catholic liturgies in the vernacular has prompted the creation of a new genre, one that is rapidly gaining favor in the Third World: the Mass in vernacular based on local popular rhythms. I heard or rather had them pointed out to me in the Congo, in Zaire, in Chile, in Argentina, and in Brazil—some were astonishingly beautiful. In Ghana, the Methodist church has brought forth new, lively forms of an improvised ecclesiatical song (Recordings: Philips 625.141 QL [*Missa Luba*], 6349.191 Phonogram [*Missa do vaqueiro*], and 14806 [*Chants de lumière*] [*Missa criolla*]; Pathe EMI, PAM 68026 [*Missa a la chilena*]; Barclay 40055 [Voyages collection] [*Missa por un continente*]).

The second type consists of chanted prayers, canticals, poetry of adoration or consolation, for public or private use and not specifically ceremonial. Hence long homiletic poems from Islamic countries have in some instances made it all the way to the heart of Africa, like the well-known Hausa song of Bagauda; there also is the Ethiopian Coptic *gene* in its allusive brevity, the fruit of a sophisticated art that requires a long and studious initiation. All the Christian churches have their stock of hymns of a literary or folkloric origin, ones most often spread by written form but whose usage is entirely oral. In Africa since the independence movements, a noteworthy effort of adaptation of the indigenous practices has allowed the missions to create a high-quality musical poetry that is even choreographed. Everyone knows the role song plays in charismatic movements and in the religious movements for social change, most recently that of the Congo's prophet Matswa; we are all familiar with what that role was during the nineteenth century for the black Christian communities in America in forms that have maintained the in-depth life of traditions brought from lost homelands (Finnegan 1976, p. 91, 167–86, 282; Collier, p. 68).

Several times in European history during religious conflicts, the hymn was at stake. In France, according to Davenson, this form of poetry, stemming from religious wars, was thus created by the Huguenots at the liturgical margins, then by Catholics in response. In eighteenth-and nineteenth-century Ireland, resistance to English occupation gave rise to a series of popular hymns praising the Virgin Mary or the Eucharist (Davenson, pp. 54–57; Finnegan 1978, pp. 169–70, 358–59; Vernillat and Charpentreau, pp. 187–88). Hymns, in their lay dressings, pastoral songs intended for a lukewarm or nonbelieving public, are the stuff of such enormously successful songs as those by Father Duval beginning in 1956; the six hundred thousand records sold in a few short years disseminated some of the most original songs we heard in the early sixties, songs that remind us of the blues and older jazz forms.

The last type we will look at are those songs that illustrate a periodical religious feast. Hence, throughout Europe, Christmas songs, whose traditions are traceable to the fifteenth century but may be even older, convey literary, liturgical, popular memories using melodies borrowed from profane songs and later on even operatic arias (Davenson, pp. 52–53; Poueigh, pp. 249–55; Dupont, p. 283). In different regions of the Christian world, even in Quebec and Acadia, until recently people would go from house to house singing Epiphany and Candlemas songs: these are undoubtedly "Christianizing" customs drawn from ancient pagan traditions, much like Carnival and masquerade songs are tied to Lent.

The third axis of dynamic organization: a more confused finality, one modeled on circumstances, whether it is a question of magnifying them, deploring them, or fearing them. Therein lies, for our society, the sole criterion for a relatively clear-cut distinction within the body of oral poetry.

It evokes in a more or less stylized fashion circumstances of personal existence: drinking songs, songs that exalt emotions induced by a landscape; calling for love or conjuring up death: twin themes that are often connected to deeply uniform realizations of their extreme diversity. Sexuality and indeed death, insofar as they are both lived, are cultural facts; in a physiological foundation, sex and death are no less products of history. Lamenting death, whether sung or rhymed, whether dramatized by sobbing or shouting, is integrated by most preindustrial societies into funeral rituals; sometimes it precedes them or follows them. It has been supposed, and not without some truth, that it is one of the primordial forms of poetic discourse. It is integrated, insofar as it is a dramatic motif, into universal epic art, but it has engendered autonomous—often complex— traditions in most premodern cultures. The fullness that just a while ago the *lamentos* had in rural Mediterranean regions bears witness to an extreme restraint in comparison to African songs like the *imbey* of Cameroon, including an epic elegy of the deceased person and his ancestors (Finnegan 1976, pp. 242–43, 247–52; Haas, p. 23; Dugast, pp. 36–37). Funeral songs as they have been transmitted to us over so many centuries by liturgical song or by an undifferentiated profane music, are still today for most African ethnic groups an element of theatricalization, conceived of as such, to the extent that the same word designates for the Dagaa of Ghana both the text sung and the dance that accompanies it (Finnegan 1976, pp. 147–55; Gide, p. 155; Wilson, p. 72). As late as 1955, for the Iroquois in the United States and Canada, this form of song cloaked political values, and the periodic meetings of the Council of the Confederation of Five Nations would begin with the *lamento* of the deceased heads.

With respect to love poetry where a discourse has been made personal by an I or a You, or has been disguised by impersonal narrative, a very small number of typical motifs have formalized it in songs that generally are quite short—primary motifs based on the experience of desire and universals of the eroticized imaginary, from looking to hoping, from there to pleasure and bitterness. Still, the institution of matrimony, valorized by the collectivity and engaged in the complexity of economic relations figures as a natural element—this as much for the cycles of the body and of emotions that matrimony subjugates or stymies. This may be why all the folklores in the world are rich in nuptial songs. Western culture, since the Middle Ages, has integrated them into the tradition of love songs: marriage becomes the desirable term in this topos—or the obstacle, as in the *malmariées*, stylizing in a single discourse erotic overtures and the sadness of imprisonment (Finnegan, pp. 253–58; Dupont, pp. 245–46; Roy 1954, pp. 74–139). In some regions (e.g., medieval France or modern Acadia), song arises not on the occasion of a marriage but on that which was its moral and social counterpart, a young girl's entrance into the convent.

These are collective circumstances that include everything that—because it is the "reality" of a social group—realizes those virtualities that it knows to be its own: that is what feeds the *topical song* of America. Such are those events that affect the unity of a community, a natural catastrophe, war; more often it is an incident that is less resounding but still laden with meaning that poetry renders immediately perceptible. Or perhaps it is a reaction to a destiny conceived by the powerful, for example, recruiting in czarist Russia and the concomitant cycle of songs.

Today this genre refers to political life, especially in Third World states with a centralized regime. Finnegan cites Mongol songs relating to the Chinese control of that country in 1919 or to a cultural campaign: oral poetry in this instance functions as involved journalism, sometimes manipulating events, in addition to its purported functions. This is also the case frequently today in Africa. Right after the Second World War and as independence movements matured, an oral poetry of political realities (based on local panegyric or invective traditions) went hand in hand with the progress of emancipation movements, and later electoral compaigns: in Tanzania, in Zambia, in Guinea, in Senegal, in Nigeria; in Kenya, during the Mau Mau insurrection; in the Republic of South Africa, refrains in the vernacular satirize police harassment (Finnegan 1976, pp. 235, 272–98, and 1978, pp. 56–58, 67–68; Camara, pp. 270–72). Sometimes an event concerns only a small segment of the population, an individual even, but it arouses in that person or persons a poetic discourse that tends in some obscure manner to dignify it by universalizing it: such are the laments, however maladroit, collected by Dupont in Acadia, and composed during the First World War, by a would-be lover rejected by his beloved or by her father (Dupont, pp. 210–11, 222–23).

Europe in the eighteenth and at the start of the nineteenth centuries, enjoyed a variety of songs defined by the topographical circumstances of their performance: especially meant for an urban public in public places in the city, where the city is set off as such at the heart of a literature of colportage — English street ballads, French *chansons de la rue* (Neuburg, pp. 123–24, 142–43). It seems that such a difference is not evident today; the *mediats* have destroyed it.

All the types enumerated in this way, rather loosely, give way with or without formal modifications, to *irony* and *parody*. The hackneyed terms "satire" or "satirical" designate one of the effects.

Given the magnitude of possibilities, I shall take an example from children's songs. Many of these songs, in France, preserve traces that today may be hardly discernible of what was long ago a caustic allusion to some public personality who was either loved or hated: Henry IV, William II, Bismarck — or King Dagobert, the nickname for Napoleon! After so many years the effects of the irony are no longer felt. We can only presume to know its original impact. In December 1980, while I was traveling in Bangui, Jouve gave me some texts of a series of dance songs that he had gathered a few months earlier from some schoolgirls at a primary school in the city (Jouve and Tomenti). In a traditional form and based on a traditional thematic framework, they had fashioned rather acerbic allusions to the ex-emperor Bokassa and his female entourage that sometimes bordered on the obscene. These children had taken elements from family conversations and spontaneously recreated an epico-legendary cycle, then immediately fixed it into this open and functional poetic form: the ogre, the ogress, and their hated tribe; anthropology and sexual magic culminating in the liberating hero.

The programming mode for a macroform interferes with the nature of its constitutive force in the delimitation of a genre. It varies according to the character of the anticipated textual organization, with respect to the type, the volume, and the context of the discourse.

I am expressing the breadth of the diverse variations in the discursive program in terms of opposition. What I mean empirically by "opposition" are the gradated contrasts rather than absolute ones. There are essentially two kinds of those that affect this type of discourse:

1. "Sacred" versus "profane": on the one hand, the carrier or the creator of myths; on the other hand, ludic or educational with respect to simple everyday knowledge. The difference between these discourses may waiver when it is considered in abstract terms: it gets its reality from performance at the level of reception. The production of a given contemporary singer in a given festival will be received as a mythical or ideological message by one part of the audience and as a game by others.

2. "Lyric" versus "narrative," useful terms in practice (despite the uncertainty expressed in chapter 3) only if the definition is limited to obvious elements, such as Bec does in regard to the French Middle Ages, and tacitly as Finnegan does when she presents the weakness and the relative rarity of narrative elements in African poetry as a pertinent general characteristic of that poetry (hers is a hotly contested opinion, however) (Bec, pp. 21–23; Finnegan 1976, pp. 211–12, and 1977, p. 13; Alatorre, pp. xvi–xvii; Genette 1979, pp. 15–17, 33–41). Whereas "narrative" implies a linear concatenation of interdependent unities, the "lyric" carries with it a circular or unordered addition of unities that are more or less autonomous. These criteria require that the "dramatic" be categorized with the "narrative" and that the "gnomic" find its place next to the "lyric." As a result of these particularities, the "lyric" or "gnomic" poem is generally short, and the very long poems are almost by necessity "narrative" or "dramatic."

We are beginnning here to touch on another field of variables: those that are concerned with the "volume" of the discourse. I am giving two definitions to this term in accordance with its reference to the duration of the performance (long vs. short) or to the distribution of the interlocutors (monologue vs. dialogue or polylogue). In several cultures, length or brevity belongs to the characteristics of a genre and are recognized as such: in Romania, a Christmas carol never has more than one hundred verses; an epic ballad has around eight hundred. Today, in spite of its imprecision, the word "song" implies in everybody's mind something whose length is measured by disk jockeys in minutes and seconds.

Plurilogical forms (dialogue or polylogue) are set in two classes both equally opposable to the monologue: depending on whether the voices alternate regularly, either in a fixed periodicity ("alternating song") or in conformity with external thematic exigencies ("dramatic song").

Dramatic song, accompanied by dance and a minimum of figuration, is distinct from theater only insofar as the general feelings at the very core of a single culture dissociate them. The Chilean *cantata* is just such a case where it was created during the popular Union; hence the very beautiful cantata "Santa Maria de Iquique" by Luis Advis, which was inspired by the memory of massacred miners. The songs alternate between a chorus and a soloist with intermediary instrumentals and recitations. In contrast, there is what amounts to a form of popular theater that is indicated in the Togolese *kantata* with its biblical themes that came out of Christian choral groups in the late 1940s (Clouzet 1975, pp. 90–96, 135–49; Agblemagnon, p. 132).

The alternating song is exchanged between two singers or two choirs, most often between a soloist and a choir. In the latter case, the text is usually cut up in couplets and refrains; but the refrain does not always remain the same throughout the song (as it does in modern Western productions). Historically one can rest assured that the use of the refrain was constitutive of a specific feature of orality: written poetical forms that adopted it borrowed it from some oral genre. The proof is found in the European Middle Ages. The choral refrain manifests in a most explicit manner the need for collective participation that forms the social base for oral poetry. I will return to these concerns in chapters 11 and 13.

The time frame of the alternating song in all its various forms spans the horizon of known histories and cultures. In the West, it is a constant in poetic discourse from Greek antiquity to the Romanesque period to our folklores, all the way to a ballad by Woody Guthrie, one like "Dusty Old Dust," and beyond. Certain peoples, by regrouping form using convention, have made of it a very elaborate genre, albeit one sometimes improvised and having an extremely skillful execution: to the point that the execution may sometimes seem to allegorize the struggle of the individual in the grasp of the complexities of social games. Thus we have the *ajty* of the Kazakhs who, in the nineteenth century, used to celebrate sporting victories; also some latter-day Malaysian *pantuns*, with their quatrains analogous in style to Japanese haiku and improvised by alternating the participants in a poetry contest, or by two lovers, by a dancer and his partner, by the two families in a marriage ceremony. Around 1930, on the Indonesian island of Buru, men and women of the village, in opposing groups, would alternate improvisations of short reciprocal mocking songs; this genre was so well grounded in the way of life that the local language could distinguish five varieties of it. Similar stories have been recorded in Africa and in Spain in recent years

(Winner, pp. 29–34; Finnegan 1976, pp. 103, 232–24, and 1978, p. 73; Huizinga, pp. 122–23; Gide, p. 67; Laya, p. 178; Fernandez, p. 466).

When the song alternates between two isolated singers, it often assumes the form called *défi, altercatio, tenzone*, and other such terms with close meanings and according to the various eras and languages: a stylized disputation purportedly improvised but highly regulated and meant to display the virtuosity of the poets. Arising from a custom in Europe at the end of the Middle Ages, the challenge is preserved in some Aragonese villages and especially in Latin America: Brazilian *desafios* (for which the *Dictionary of Improvisors* was able to list twelve formal types in 1978) or the Chilean *paya*, which the Parra tried twenty some years ago to turn into a political weapon (Burke, p. 111; Fernandez, pp. 464–65; *Dicionario*, pp. 14–44; Clouzet, pp. 89–90).

I plan to group three types of variations under the rubric of "contextuals." The first two are defined relative to a context that is explicitly provided by a tradition or by writing: (1) the linguistic context to which one refers when speaking of "prose" or of "verse"; or the melodic context relative to which one speaks of "the spoken" or "the sung"; and (2) the gestural context that designates especially dance.

Neither of these terms possesses the precision that would at first glance seem to characterize it. They belong, nonetheless, to the central area of the conceptual field where, it seems to me, it is worthwhile to situate a poetics of orality. For this reason, I will treat it in more detail in chapters 10 and 11.

The third type of variation is defined with respect to an implicit context, one arising from discourse itself, according to which it is or is not improvised. I return to this question in chapter 12.

Chapter 6
The Epic

The oral poetic genre that has been most studied up to this moment—other than ethnographic lists and piecemeal historical comparisons—is the epic. Our poetics thus bear witness to the permanence of the Homeric model in our midst in a cultural mythology laden with classicism.

As the ultimate reference for all poetry, the archetypal image of the Poet, Homer in the Germany of the 1780s instigated a new dialectical idea of time, of history, and of philology. Wolf was the first to formulate the question of the initial orality of the *Iliad* and the *Odyssey*. He did it, however, in the narrow and singular perspective of the unity of their composition and the authenticity of their parts. Throughout the nineteenth century, discussions that arose over the "Homeric question" failed to break out of these confines; nevertheless, central to the general movement that pushed European Romanticism to the discovery of "popular poetries," these discussions led some researchers to investigate "heroic poems." Beginning in the 1820s, Karadžić compiled an impressive corpus in Serbia; in 1860, in the far reaches of northwest Russia, Rybnikov noted the vitality of epic ballads, the *bylines*, despite the consensus at that time that they had long since disappeared.

Toward 1900, few regions of Eurasia had escaped this canvassing. The material was accumulating—a vast oral narrative poetry, a polymorphous one, one not really comparable to the diverse forms of folklore. And yet it had not yet aroused any "poetic" inquiries. During the 1930s, English-speaking researchers delineated its scope: in 1930, Entwistle's book on European ballads appeared; then, in 1932, the first attempt at synthesis by Chadwick and Chadwick, *The Growth of*

Literature, compiled all available information regarding "primitive poetry." Then Miles Parry technically formulated the question of the functioning of these texts. Following a concerted effort in Yugoslavia in 1934 and 1935, Harvard became the repository for Parry's thirty-five hundred recordings of epic singers and thousands of his notecards. He had scarcely begun to integrate these experiences in a book, one later entitled *The Singer of Tales*, when he died unexpectedly. His disciple Lord resurrected the title in 1960 for his own synthesis of the work; it sparked heated debate. The influence of his work spread to studies on the Middle Ages and not without arousing violent polemics. The works of Parry and Lord particularly reinforced those of Menendez Pidal on the *Romancero* and the *Chanson de Roland* (Lord 1971, pp. 8–12; Menendez Pidal 1959, pp. 413–63).

Parry had inspired Bowra, who in the wake of the Chadwicks published *Heroic Poetry* in 1952, a work that remains the sole integrative work we have on the epic. Bowra viewed the epic in its historical entirety: from *Gilgamesh* to the present. Marred by a servile acceptance of Romantic presuppositions, his work was further weakened by genetic theories that limited its perspective and by a rigid conceptualization of the "heroic": by eliminating those poems that were not obviously part of a warrior genre or were too short, by ignoring panegyrics and lament, his book—as indispensable as it has become as a resource—is riddled with contradictions that limit its import.

Since then, and in part due to Lord's persistence and Harvard's collections, a large number of monographs and sectarian studies have been dedicated to the "living" epic, so many in fact that Haymes was able to publish a bibliography of it from 1973 to 1975 (today quite out-of-date) including an introduction to Lord's doctrines (Haymes 1973 and 1975; Lord 1975).

Although I lay aside Lord's doctrines for the moment, no poetics of orality can ignore their import even where they merit criticism. Lord was little concerned with theorizing, but he nonetheless provided us for the first time with a framework adequate to the task of describing the epic. As a pioneer in this area, he disallowed any regression to the former confusion of traditional literary history by insisting on the specificity of the oral and its mechanisms of production (Foerster; Marin, pp. 25–43). The classical conception of the "epic poem"— such as Aristotle's commentators bequeathed us and inspired as they are by an ideology of writing—must from here on out be dissociated from, if not impugned, in any conceptualization of the epic.

Defining the epic is no less difficult. Does the term refer to an aesthetic, to a mode of perception, or to the structures of the tale? Some scholars would have it include every type of narrative oral poetry, especially any historical argument, without taking into consideration either solemnity or length. For Tedlock, what is to be called the epic genre, characterized by rules of versification, exists only in semiliterate cultures; in primarily oral societies, the functional equivalent would be the folktale. This thesis appears to be confirmed by information found in

North America in Indian and Inuit groups (such as the Kivioq cycle in Canada), but is disproved by other research. In the end, one might posit, as Bynum has done, that the *epic* is nothing more than a metaphorical designation for oral poetry, based on the Greek *epos* and which for Homer refers simply to words conveyed by voice (Lord 1971, p. 6; Tedlock 1977, p. 507; Charron 1977, II, pp. 273–505; Bynum, pp. 245, 248; Bowra 1978, chapter 1).

It is probably worthwhile to distinguish, as Staiger does, between the *epic poem* as a culturally conditioned poetic form—hence variable—and *epic discourse* as a class of narrative discourse that is relatively stable and definable by its temporal structure, the position of the subject, and a general aptitude for assuming a mythical charge that makes it autonomous in relation to the event. From this point of view, it is more toward the novel rather than the folktale that one would find the bridges that invite comparatists' acrobatics (Marin, pp. 45–47; Oinas 1968). Nevertheless, it is in these terms or in similar ones that one can grasp what makes up the fragile but real unity, inter-and supracultural, of the epic throughout its numerous manifestations.

As an action story, concentrating its effects of meaning in the action and sparing ancillary ornamentation, the epic poem stages virile aggressivity for the sake of some grand venture. Basically, it narrates a combat and selects from its host of protagonists one uncommon character who commands our admiration, although he may not always come out the victor in every test. This prudent definition nonetheless allows many questions to arise. Which archetypes do our most ancient forms of the epic recall? In the Indo-European domain, have they not projected into discourse the myth of the three orders distinguished by Dumézil, those regulators of cosmic movement? Does epic combat include an erotic dimension? Is it necessarily warlike? Does it have philosophical or religious components? Each cultural zone brings to these questions its own answers. Bowra's long list of epic themes is a hodgepodge. Researchers in the Bucharest Folklore Institute have established two hundred thematic rubrics for the seven thousand Romanian ballads collected (Bowra 1978, chapters 2 and 3; Elliott, pp. 235–39; Duby, pp. 16–17; Knorringa 1978, pp. 8–9).

It remains to be said that epic discourses exceed epic poems and that uncertain cases of it are not rare. Hence, in Rwanda—a region where neither the slave trade, the missions, nor colonization have held sway—there are nearly 180 dynastic poems that retrace the history of the country since its earliest days: are these "epic poems"? Is the *izibongo* of the Bantus, with its mixture of panegyric and warrior evocations, one? A twenty-verse-long Baluch battle song—is it an "epic" in the same way that the long Uzbek epic songs are? The short heroic ballads of the Iranians in the same way as the lengthy Turkish compositions? The Arab *qasida* in the same way as the old *hamasa* of Turkey? In contrast, the Kazakhs do not have a special term to designate what we might consider their epic poems (Finnegan 1976, p. 109, and 1978, pp. 121–22; Burness, pp. 129–58;

Chadwick and Zhirmunsky, pp. 106–7, 190–93; Bynum, pp. 242–43; Marin, pp. 14–15, 59–62; Zwettler, pp. 29–30; Winner, p. 68).

Using the terminology suggested in the preceding chapter, we can at least attempt to separate the place and the "moment" whence the constitutive *force* of the epic derives and the terms whereby its *ordering* is programmed.

It seems to me that one could not seriously contest the existence of an underlying model common to all forms of epic song. But if one judges it by its manifestations in space and time, one of the traits of its ordering determines the others just as certain aspects of its force do: the volume of the discourse. Indeed, depending on whether the song is short or long, it is differently marked on several levels.

Being relative notions, shortness and length are in fact very distinct and recognizable within cultures and regions where the two types coexist: as, for example, in central Asia, the heroic songs of the Altai and Sayan mountain peoples on the one hand, and on the other those of the high valley of the Ienissei; or, in our Middle Ages, the French *chanson de geste* and the Spanish *romance*. On the one hand there are thousands of verses, and only tens or hundreds on the other: a Homeric-like epic on the one hand, what I call *ballad* on the other (here the meaning is narrower than that of the Anglo-Saxon ballad as it designates every type of narrative song). It is a question here of two different realizations of the epic macroform without any proven relationship of mutual subordination: the only sure examples of long epic poems coming from a combination of ballads are the literary compilations such as the Finnish *Kalevala* and the Estonian *Kalevipioeg* of Kreutzwald in 1857. Similar attempts were made in our century but failed in Yugoslavia and in Soviet Armenia. The reverse hypothesis (for example, that of Bowra), one that has the ballad formulated after the Homeric type, does not appear to be any more tenable (Bowra 1978, pp. 356–57, 550–53, 561; Chadwick and Zhirmunsky, p. 26).

The ballads collected by Lönnrot in the *Kalevala* have from fifty to four hundred verses. The Russian *bylines* have from a hundred to a thousand, although today, Marfa Kryukova has composed more than two thousand. Anglo-Saxon and Romanian ballads—the two most studied of the short epic poems—rarely exceed five hundred verses. Comparable in number, all the while culturally divergent, the ballads supposedly correspond to an identical deep structure. Edson Richmond has drawn up a definition that is both thematic and narratological, based on a collection of European poems. Buchan's studies and remarks by Bowra and others confirm it: construction of a story with a single episode, in dramatic gradations, or a hyperbolic accumulation of brief juxtaposed episodes—a single character, sometimes collective (three brothers representing a family or a clan), fighting a stronger adversary, often a social group, as a bandit, an outlaw, a rejected prophet, or a solitary wreaker of vengeance; this hero can be

feminine but thoroughly endowed with male virtues; the locale in which it happens highlights the contrasts (Bowra 1978, pp. 330–36; Oinas 1972, p. 106;
Chadwick 1936, pp. 27–76; Conroy; Edson Richmond, pp. 86–89; Buchan,
pp. 76–80).

In opposition to the Homeric-type epic — more diverse, less linear, less exclusively centered on the warrior theme — the special features of the ballad appear all
the more clearly as its rhythmic and melodic structure includes regular recurrences: strophes or couplets in the Anglo-Saxon, Germanic, and Scandinavian
models. When the verses are linked without periodic breaks, as in the *romancero*
or the epic songs of the Balkans, the differences in tone with the long epic tend
to be attenuated. Yet the cultures in which one notices this blurring often seem to
have neutralized the oppositions of length: Serbian and Bosniac poems range
from three hundred to three thousand, and even to thirteen thousand verses;
Greek and Albanian ballads from a few hundred to several thousand (Bowra
1978, pp. 39, 330, 354–55).

Our oldest medieval epics, from what we can determine, had on the average
from two to four thousand verses. Such a length seems common enough for the
long epic. Epic songs of central Asia collected in the nineteenth century show
much the same length for the Uzbeks, the Kazakhs, and the Kalmyks; in contrast,
Radlov heard versions of a single Karakirghiz poem varying from six to forty
thousand verses. The upward limit of the size of the genre is in fact high: only the
social conditions of the performance (place, epoch, periodicity) more or less determine it. Dournes has indicated to me that on the Indochinese plateaus, the recitation of certain epics lasts five to six hours; the Camaroonian Beti epics can take
up to twelve hours to recite (Ngal, p. 336; Alexandre 1976, p. 73).

The *Ulahingan* studied by Maquiso in the Philippines has a large number of
episodes, each of which can constitute an individual performance: up to now, the
shortest one recorded lasts three and a half hours; the longest is eighteen hours,
performed in three sittings. Ms. Maquiso calculates the number of existing episodes to be a hundred; but, for centuries, new ones have been continuously created by means of variation, addition, reduction. One singer, in 1965, claimed to
know 1,355, a figure we must take as symbolic, although no less significant
(Maquiso, pp. 25–37). It is probably in this way that during its oral period, the
immense Hindu *Mahabharata* were formed from the kernel of a tenth-century
B.C.E. royal epic song. Once fixed in writing, they were found to include some
120,000 verses.

Of the three elements of what I have called the generic *force*, the first, the
human *mediat*, seems regulated by a curiously unanimous custom: the long epic
is uttered by a man. To the best of my knowledge, this rule has no exceptions.
The short epic can, in certain cultures, occasionally be performed by a woman.
The ability to sing or recite short forms comes from individual memory and from
the vocal quality; it does not require any particular training. The long forms re-

quire mastery of precise techniques: the performer is a specialist, often a professional. In some cultures, he belongs to a specific caste or, as in the Cameroons, to a society of initiates to whom there is accorded great prestige.

In the traditions of a people, the epic often forms a vast narrative collection that is rather rigorously formalized, but of which each performer on each occasion never recites more than one episode. No one individual in certain African ethnic groups has recited or heard all of the national epic, although he has heard of it and knows its content in a nebulous way. No teller of the *Ulahingan* knows it in its entirety; no Tibetan singers consulted thus far can recite all the segments of the *Ge-Sar*: they allude to one of their brothers, in the East, who is supposed to be able to.

The deliberate finality of the epic, relative to the vital role it fulfills for a given human collectivity, might be expressed in spatial terms: it is less a geographic space for defining a zone of expansion, a "fatherland," than it is the moral scope, cultivated and cared for by generations, lived like a dynamic relation between the natural milieu and the modalities of life. From this relationship, the epic declares its conquest. Like all oral poetry, it is practiced in the center of this space, but it feigns to spread over a much larger area. For its intended audience (which it intends for itself), it is autobiography, its very own collective existence that it recounts within the confines of sleep and neurosis. In this sense, whether incited by the memory of the nearest and least uncertain event, it erects its fiction; and this fiction also constructs a collective benefit, a plane of reference and a justification of behavior. There is no "heroic age," and the "time of myths" is not that of the epic: there is nothing but the incessant fluidness of lived experience, a natural integration of past and present. The information transmitted by the poem can, therefore, be modified according to circumstances throughout the course of its tradition. For a long time, the epic of the Ghanian Gonja intoned the seven mythical ancestors in all their connections to the seven current chiefs. Sixty years after the first recordings, the number of heroes was reduced to five: political changes had abolished two of the ancient chieftains (Okpewho, p. 75; Marin, pp. 42–43; Goody and Watt, pp. 307–10). The epic is no museum piece. There is no history so to speak, but rather a perpetually re-created song of truth.

Being so tightly implicated in that which creates the stability and the continuity of a group, the epic is no less a joy of storytelling and of listening. If it manages to instruct and comfort, it does so through this joy. The epic denies the tragic. Catastrophes are nothing but an opportunity for honor. Although the hero is crushed and the people caught in his misfortune, epic discourses transcend both individual and collective death. It posits a model for action, designates the origins and the final days of an ethnic group, gives to Order the form of rhythms. Both times that Maquiso and her groups recorded the *Ulahingan* of the Manobo, the youth of the region were so moved by hearing this poem on the tape recorder that several of them wanted to learn to sing it. Once revealed to itself, a whole moribund culture seemed to want to live again. This may be the reason for which the epic song narrates combat against the Other, the hostile stranger, the enemy outside the group—whether the latter be a nation, a social class, or a family (Bowra 1978, pp. 29–30, 70–79; Havelock, pp. 93–95; Elliott, p. 243; Maquiso, p. 7; Sieffert 1978a, pp. 21–22). Perhaps the *Heike* of the Japanese alone, far from using this brutal process, suggests the unanimity of a people in the narration of civil strife: whence derives a distrust of heroism; whence the nuance, the impression of threatening transience, the absence of glory without some remorse.

The epic tends toward the "heroic," only where "heroic" means the exaltation of a sort of community superego. It has been noted that it finds its most fertile grounds in border regions where there exists a prolonged hostility between two races, two cultures—neither of which obviously dominates the other. The epic song crystallizes this hostility and compensates for the uncertainty of competition; it foretells that all will end well, proclaims at least that we have righteousness on our side. In so doing, it forcefully arouses action. During the conquest of Algeria, around 1840, the French officers would prepare the Beni-Amer recruits for battle by having them sing the epic ballads of their poet, Si Mest'fa. I have heard that two or three years ago Somalian radio invited singers of epics to the station to support soldiers engaged in the campaign against the Ogaden.

If such is the all-encompassing finality of the epic genre, its pretext, a factor of *ordering* and a generator of tales, seems to be able to be linked to one of two types: those that Bowra called "shamanic" and "heroic," where he finds the first to predate the second. Nothing is less certain, and the distinction necessitates a great deal of nuance. I prefer to oppose "historic" to "mythic," similar terms in a double polarization acting within the same discursive field. The opposition between profane and sacred, pertinent as it is to the majority of other oral genres, is more or less neutralized by the epic. There are supposedly human forces being put into play on the one hand; and, on the other hand, there are supposedly superhuman forces, phantasmagoric figural forms that engender the representation of a universe felt and wished to be forever different. But between one and the other of these ideal types, the borderline is poorly controlled. The ontological status of the characters (human-divine) is distinguished in very few cultures; and for those very ones that do not confuse the conqueror and his tutelary god, time and tradition are meant to muddle the distribution.

Among the predominantly "historical" epics, we could name the Mandingo *Sundiata*, the Japanese *Heike*, or the French *Chanson de Roland*, all of which have a more or less large number of narrative sequences that contain some reflection, direct or indirect, of military or political events from the national past. A good dose of "historicity" escapes all overarching generalizations: the poetry of the *Sundiata* seems to convey enough verifiable information about medieval Mali to constitute in the eyes of historians a valid source (Niane, 1975a, pp. 7–11, 21–22, and 1979, pp. 9–10, 152–53). On the contrary a strong archaeological dimension is called for in order to read the story of Hellenic migrations of the first millennium that lay just below the surface of the *Odyssey*. Distance in time no doubt blurs the image—but that is not the question. The story provides the epic poet with a malleable narrative framework, one less important for the information it contains than for the emotions will arouse. The same action, from one poem to another, from one version to another, can be traced to a different hero—and vice versa: characters from different epics can be brought together under the same roof.

Certain cycles in their entirety carry with them throughout the centuries the indelible marks of a foundational event beneath the mask of successive and uncertain transpositions. The permanence of that event is exactly what constitutes the cycle. The Tartar invasions of the thirteenth century are still found in the background of Russian *bylines* for which the real historical context according to scholars ought rather be the border squabbles between the Great Russians and the Petchenegues: everything gets reinterpreted here with respect to an important memory, one occulted but active in the collective unconscious. One by one the figures of Ivan the Terrible, Peter the Great, and Catherine II engendered other cycles or were integrated into preceding ones. The Serbian epic, with its very diverse subjects borrowed from guerrilla attacks on the Turks starting in the sixteenth century, preserves the original details of the battle of Kosovo; Albanian ballads, those of the Scanderbeg victory (Bowra 1978, pp. 22–26, 86, 388, 511–12, 523; Oinas 1972, pp. 100).

In accord with these incessant remakings, a circuit tends to get established that leads from the historic to the mythic, and sometimes vice versa. The cultural context shows itself to be more or less favorable. In societies without writing, these exchanges are intense. In the Cameroons, the *mvet* stages imaginary tribes situated in a utopia space—at least, the poet and the audience experience them as such—but it has been proved that they were the real fatherland and ethnic group up until the eighteenth century for the people who later migrated into the forest. As for the principal narrative theme of the *mvet*, it exalts the struggle of man against natural powers, be they visible or invisible, and man's accession to immortality. The tradition of the Tibetan *Ge-Sar*, a six-hour-long fragment of which was collected in Nepal by Helffer and published in 1979, has been around since the tenth century; various written versions of it circulated, known then as edifying books, in lamaseries before the Chinese invasion. Centered on the doubtless historical figure of a conqueror aspiring to universal royalty, the *Ge-Sar* forms a cultural and religious summa so dense and complex that certain bards could sing parts of it only by reading from a manuscript (Ndong Ndoutoume; Helffer, pp. 1–8).

The lengthy *Ulahingan* provides the typical example of an epic with a strongly "mythical" predominance. Through its nine versions and many divergent points, in recordings that span from 1963 to 1975, the same deep narrative schema survives: initial patriarchy, imposed tyranny, flight to freedom, the messenger bearing salvation, visions, miraculous signs announcing a complete restoration, discovery of the *sarimbar*, the divine carriage that rises to heaven under the guidance of Agyu, the divine father-hero, and finally the general attainment of joy in paradise (Maquiso, pp. 56–57). Is this a schema of biblical origins crossbred with local traditions? It is not impossible that this is the case, but we know that the autochthonous populations of the Mindanao were subjugated long ago by Muslims from Indonesia: does this historical memory preserve its traces in this myth? In the 1920s and 1930s, three successive messiahs came to the Manobo, speaking in, they assured the people, the language of the gods and promising to lead the faithful to the paradise of their ancestor Agyu. One of these ventures resulted in bloodshed with the Muslims of the region. In the sect that survives today, some poor devils still await the *sarimbar*.

No epic is totally devoid of historical ingredients regardless of the mythic opacity of its discourse. In Western eyes the ancient *Romancero* and even (despite the character) the English ballads of Robin Hood are more "historical" than the Voltaic tales about Princess Yennenga, ravished by a rampaging horse, and who, lost in the forest, is mysteriously impregnated and becomes the progenitor of the Mossi dynasty. By what criteria? The universal feature of the epic, even more than its warrior element, is this interpenetration of elements, and although contrary to modern attitudes, it is still indissociable for traditional civilizations. The birth of the African epic hero is always extraordinary: in the Fang story, Akoma Mba spends 150 years inside his mother (Okpewho, p. 93). The character is perhaps "historical," but the epic moves forward in a collage of emotional indicators and allusive metaphors, dependent on a foundation that they dissimulate.

Moreover, the "marvelous" is only the anecdotal ornament of the "myth," and the myth stems from the general programming of discourse. But in its own turn, it depends perhaps on history by virtue of very distant implications: Penel, in an unpublished essay on central Africa, indicates that the majority of societies without a state ignore the creation of world myths (linked to the existence of a strong power), but that their mythology concerns, rather, land division among men. Perhaps such a distinction would account for the diversity of epic models where it gets integrated into history. In the same way one would oppose those myths that confirm an order and those that seem to oscillate between order and disorder, between affirmation and dissent. Which forgotten conflicts between dominators and the dominated would be resolved at the level of the imaginary? Paradoxically and not without irony, one might argue that the function traditionally fulfilled by this epic interpenetration of myth and history has been taken over—at the very time when our technological universe was being institutionalized—by systematic philosophies. Hegel, Marx, August Comte—these were our last epic poets.

Epic discourse contains features that are virtually universal; other discourses, differing within their cultural milieus, remain stable within themselves. Its structures and functioning have been elaborated on everywhere at great length for some time now: it is a traditional discourse, in the strongest sense of this term, one relatively closed and sometimes archaic, but mostly it is laden with internal references, with allusions to itself, and it aggrandizes its own significance. A general tonality presides within (Bowra 1978, p. 493). Although one may find here and there epic parodies, and although humor, if not the grotesque, may contribute to heroic figuration, the epic is basically serious. Aristotle defined Homer's poetry as "pathetic." In several regions of the world, epic singers when interrogated, describe their song as sad and unhappy, and they sometimes link its recitation to long and perilous nights (Finnegan 1977, pp. 110–12; Bynum, pp. 251–53).

Although epic discourse often integrates monologues and dialogues, it is "impersonal." Ainu poems are the only exceptions I know to this rule: their heroes tell of themselves. The message uses conventional structures that are definitional of the genre and specialized in their exercise of a function: introduction (of the whole or of an episode), conclusion, emblematic descriptions, modalized by the immediate context, embroidering into the basic framework of the typical picayune "true details" of the tale, "real" effects that make the epic a mimetic genre: those that lend their seal to the ballads about Anglo-Saxon outlaws, whether it concerns the Scottish border or the Far West: to the stories of the *matamoros* of the Hispanic *Romancero fronterizo*; those that populate the Mongolian epics about unbeatable horse-racing princes, ravished princesses, and talking horses, or that show the king on the telephone in a Serbian epic sung around 1930 (Bäuml and Spielmann, p. 70; Havelock, p. 87; Bowra 1978, pp. 163, 178–79, 189–97, 475).

The short forms seem more rigorous in their adherence to predetermined patterns and get their expressive power from conforming so closely to their inherited procedures. Buchan has provided, in this vein, a remarkable analysis of English ballads and demonstrates therein the persistence and efficacy of simple but easily diversifiable compositional modes, either binary or ternary, as well as indefinitely reproducible narrative turns of phrase despite their reworking the same themes: a perfectly coherent evolution of the system has been clearly drawn since the sixteenth century (Buchan, pp. 87–144).

Conversely, the long forms, in relation to a traditional scene, are constituted both by contraction and expansion without being marked by necessary progression: the art of the poet consists not only of pulling on the thread of the tale without breaking it but also in adapting its matter and nuances to the fleeting, unstable, and forever absentminded demands of the audience; to keep their interest all the while watching out for the physical effort the performance exacts from the participants. Whence come the accumulations, the digressions, the associative slippages, the moves into the gnomic, to the lyrical, a sometimes refined and sometimes crude fugue. The performer, at each and every moment of the performance, concentrates on the episode in progress, and more or less loses sight of the whole; whence his indifference to chronology and, in general, the difficulty he experiences in ending. In light of that problem, the Aristotelian idea of unity, applicable to the short epic, does not lend itself at all to the long epic, whose ultimate value, rather, seems to be *plenitude* (Okpewho, pp. 179–93).

The epic is composed in verse; where it is evident in Western traditions, this characteristic has been disputed elsewhere. Prose might alternate with verse in the works of the people of central Asia as well as those of some African ethnic groups. Therein lies a technical question that I will discuss in chapter 9. Regardless of its verse structure, it is rarely grouped into strophes or couplets in the long epic (Chadwick and Zhirmunsky, p. 336; Helffer, p. 461; Bowra 1978, pp. 36–39).

The epic is "sung." This term should be taken in its broadest meaning, such as I will define it in chapter 10. Certain epics, even very long ones like the *Ulahingan*, are sung entirely in the recitative mode. Short poems are generally melodic. In some cultures, the singer alternates the two registers, one flatter, the other sharper. Often, as in central Asia, playing instruments accompanies epic declamation to the extent that the singer is designated, as happens with the Yugoslav *guslar*, by the name of his instrument rather than the name of his poem. Elsewhere, as in the African *mvet*, the intervention sung by a chorus can cut into the tale.

No specialist today can doubt that epic discourse is the product of a refined art. Still, its universal aspects have been much less questioned than its microforms over the past thirty years. On that score, rightly or wrongly, we have tried to answer the question (and this without recourse to classical terms haunted by Homer and Virgil) whether there is an "epic style" that is identifiable as such. We can assume that the epic where it is meant to be transmitted by voice shares the general linguistic characteristics of all oral poetry: I will examine this in chapter 7. But it seems to present some specific features that, once discovered by Parry and Lord, have been recently overemphasized by commentators (Lord 1959; Bowra 1978, pp. 221–53; Burke, pp. 122–28). Whatever criticism one can level at these speculations, they nonetheless result in the definition of a mode of rather complex expression, what the French call "formulaic styles."

Rather than as a type of organization, the formulaic style can be described as a discursive and intertextual strategy: it inserts and integrates into the unfolding discourse rhythmic and linguistic fragments borrowed from other preexisting messages that in principle belong to the same genre, sending the listener back to a familiar semantic universe by making the fragments functional within their exposition. These fragments, these *formulas*, appear in the epic song in varying numbers depending on the age, the poets, the circumstances. The textual fabric of the Slavic and Asiatic epics presents, it would seem, a high degree of formulaic density. Attempts have been made to measure this density in the epics of the Middle Ages in Europe: the norm would have been from thirty to forty formulaic verses out of one hundred for the oldest French *chansons de geste*. Moreover, Fochi's research on Romanian ballads suggests that the formulaic style, far from being archaic in the heart of an epic tradition, would be the relatively late product of an evolutionary chain (Lord 1971, pp. 17–22, 131; Duggan 1975, pp. 81–82; Fochi, chapter 5; Winner, pp. 69–71; Bowra 1978, pp. 222–23). The structure of verse and the constraints it engenders most probably play a role here, no less than the talent of the singers and their acquired habits.

Each poem constitutes an original verbal unit (*unité de parole*) governed by laws that belong to it alone; formulas are inserted as unmarked terms that in and through this insertion acquire their function and their meaning. It has been widely observed, particularly in Asia, that formulas travel from one genre to another, from proverb to epic to folktale, a mass of polyvalent handiwork in the service of discourses that are, themselves, quite marked; that is what Dournes calls "formulism," in its concomitant state of spirit and mode of expression (Dournes 1976, pp. 133–78).

Several definitions for the formula end up partially contradicting themselves. Everyone agrees on the banal fact that it deals with a textual schema that is indefinitely reusable: the interpretation of this fact varies according to the breadth of the theoretical objective. For Bausinger, every cultural practice can become formulaic: the formula constitutes a *Kulturgestalt*, a formalizing dynamism, a collective property of the human collective. Two types can be distinguished, each with a given number of varieties: "functional" formulas that exercise a constraint on discourse, and "ludic" formulas in which, with respect to this constraint, the tension of the game is manifested dialectically. On the contrary, in a linguistic perspective, Zavarin and Coote take into consideration every stereotype, a more or less stable linguistic habit determining lexical and syntactic choices in a given situation (Bausinger, pp. 66–90; Zavarin and Coote).

For Parry, who built his theory on "Homeric epithets," the formula was a group of words with a fixed metrical structure that expressed a certain idea or nuclear image. The epic poem engages a system of formulas that are connected by rather complex, either semantic or functional, relationships of equivalency, complementarity, or opposition. The manner by which an epic poet dominates and exploits this system constitutes (in his eyes as well as those of his audience) one of the criteria by which his art will be judged. With Lord, his students, and his detractors, the definition is relaxed and for given points made more specific. Today the lexical sequence is not considered more important than the structuring factors such as prosody, syntax, and the distribution of key terms (Goody 1979, pp. 199–200; Lord 1975, pp. 9–17; Chasca, pp. 22–43). Alongside formulas in the strictest sense, we can identify formulaic expressions: both show latent structures on the surface of epic discourse. The latent structures, more so than the verbal form the essence of the epic. Certainly any Johnny-come-lately rhymester is capable of imitating or adapting a group of oral epic formulas to a written work: if their artificialness strikes us, it is because writing has lopped off their roots and reduced them to a stylistic trick that has meaning only in relation to a profound and implicit conception of the world.

Nagler has systematized this conception of the oral epic style by proposing a *generative* definition of formulas. This term for him goes back to a group of phonetic, syntactic, lexical, rhythmic, and semantic correspondences that constitute the model that underlies all formulaic occurrences in the mind of the oral poet. Each formula functions as an allomorph, not of any one particular formula, but rather of the model. The group of formulas, in a never-ending series, weaves into the text a resistant and supple network between whose parts meaning circulates.

The model, in fact, comes into play at each level (of sounds, words, syntagmatic and prosodic configurations) by means of a double engagement: internal, on the formulaic sentence; external, on the entire text. As a result, every formula is, in principle, situated at the crossroads of eight relational perspectives. In effect, often one or the other of these is clouded over or may even be completely erased. Thus, Zavarin and Coote distinguish "analytic" formulas (those having a concrete signification for which no context allows a broader interpretation) and "synthetic" formulas (ones that direct every object or analogous situation to its first referent). Others emphasize a given level of realization of the system: especially the semantic level or that of the rhythm. Some privilege two or three indissociable levels: rhythm and lexicon, as Dournes does; rhythm and grammar, done by Renzi with respect to Romanian ballads; rhythm, syntax, and lexicon, as I have proposed for the French medieval epic. Various works on the short epic, like those of Knorrigna, in more detail than those by Renzi or Anders on the Anglo-Saxon ballads, have shown that the functioning of its formulaic style is comparable to that in the long epic (Zavarin and Coote, p. 2; Dournes 1976, pp. 134–42; Renzi 1969, pp. 17–70; Zumthor 1972, p. 333; Knorringa 1978; Anders).

Formulas exist *within* a tradition and cannot be dissociated from it. Collective tradition—a given culture as historical permanence—keeps a more or less considerable quantity of formulas, available at any time for any poet schooled in his art. It happens that certain formulas, in the same way as dialectical features, have only a limited area of diffusion within the territory in question: that does not change at all the output of the system. Other formulas, the property of a particular poet, who sometimes gets them from a master, come from a personal competence that is at once durable, stable, and repetitive. The study of medieval texts has suggested a distinction between "internal" formulas (which appear only in a single poem) and "external" ones (which are common to several).

A number of various classifications have been proposed: formulas of introduction, of dialogue, of action, of adjectival or adverbial qualification such as Webber gives for the *Romancero*; empty, full, matrixed, gnomic, adjectival formulas of dialogue, of calls to the public, such as Okpewho gives for Africa. Although few serious studies (comparable to those of Duggan on the *Chanson de Roland* and that of Helffer on the *Ge-Sar*) have been dedicated to this question, it seems that there exist a certain number of epic universals, ones relative to the values and the exploitation of the formulaic expression (Webber, pp. 181–203; Okpewho, pp. 138–43; Duggan 1973; Helffer, pp. 381–99, 408–22, 430–37).

Dournes has noted that from one state of equilibrium to another a harmonico-melodic theme is composed. The network of associations and correspondences is more and more broadly used as the discourse is played out, whereas, in that same way, polysemia is reduced and the personal mark of the singer gains ground: replays, variations on an *obligatory* theme (obligatory due to the audience's familiarity with it); diversity at the heart of similarity, the basis for a technique whose means, although diverse, differ only a little (Dournes 1976, pp. 180–81; Havelock, pp. 89–93). Formulas stabilize and maintain. Tending toward hyperbole, they bear witness to the poet's acceptance of the society for which he sings; but he accepts this society less from personal choice than by virtue of the role given to him by the collectivity—that of guardian and herald.

Epic recognition operates on the thread of the poem in and through formulas, analogous perhaps to the effect produced in the most archaic cultures by lists of names or catalogues that they construct and preserve with care and from which formulaic expressions may initially derive. Both sign and symbol, paradigm and syntagm, the formula neutralizes the opposition between the continuity of language and the discontinuity of discourse.

Thanks to Lord and his students, the study of formulaic style has managed to develop into a quasi-autonomous discipline to the detriment of other poetic elements of the epic. Often, in fact, it is reduced to rather derisory formula hunting. Lord, however, has always taken care to distinguish between "formula" and what he calls "theme" (in the way that others use "motif"). This distinction seems to refer to the two constitutive levels of the poem, that of the plot (*récit*, i.e., the deep narrative structures) and that of the story (*histoire*, i.e., the manifested semantic units). The distinction has never really been explained or elaborated satisfactorily; whence derive the misunderstandings, omissions, and hasty generalizations from which this "theory" largely—and it must be said rightly at times—has suffered.

What is called the Middle East—from Iraq to the Aegean Sea—has bequeathed us, through later transcriptions, the most ancient epic monuments: the Akkadian

Gilgamesh, the Sumerian *Su-nir*, Homer. In our eyes these examples seem isolated in time: such isolation is doubtful. Over the course of the twenty centuries of the Christian era, it would be hard to find a long period when documents did not indicate to us, here or there in the world, the existence of some living epic. We can rest assured that, during the small number of millennia that make up "history" for us, epic usage was continuous, albeit not general in the region.

It is possible that some regions or types of cultures have never known the epic: we can point to ancient Egypt, to China, or to the collectivity of Native American civilizations. Once again we need to come to some agreement over definitions. Finnegan considers the *Ballad of the Hidden Dragon* to be a fragment of an oral Chinese epic from the eleventh century (Finnegan 1978, pp. 493–510). Several authors, until recently, have questioned the existence of African epics. Perhaps traditional black societies do not differentiate its notion: for the Fang, the Boulous, and the Beti of Cameroon, the word *mvet* designates the musical instrument, the person who plays it, the heroic story he sings while accompanying himself, and the knowledge to which he thereby bears witness — more or less everything that we encapsulate under the heading of *culture*.

Most scholars today admit nevertheless that numerous ethnic groups, mostly in west and central Africa, have had a large corpus of epic poetry that is now dying out (Jahn 1961, pp. 170; Kesteloot 1971b; Eno Belinga 1978, pp. 25–28; Okpewho). There are, for example, the Peul epic of *Silâmaka*, collected by Seydou; the Wolof *Madior*, the Tukolor *Kambili*, whose hero is King Samory, the adversary of the French at the end of the nineteenth century; or the epic collection, comparable in some respects to our classic model, of the versions and diverse parts of the *Sundiata*, as it exalts the memory of the founding conqueror of the empire of Mali. The Ghanian *Bagre*, studied by Goody in 1972, based on a version of some twelve thousand verses, presents a different, ritually dramatized aspect: its oration is interspersed with mythic recitations that the audience echoes. In Cameroon, Alexandre has taken an inventory of fifty epic songs that last from four to ten hours; in 1971 Clark collected the Nigerian *Ozidi*, which extends over seven consecutive nights; in Zaire, the existence of an epic genre still alive for the Luba was slowly revealed in the 1970s. More toward the south, to find this type of poetry one must go all the way to the Zulu territories where there is the cycle of narrative and panegyric songs about Shaka.

The question must be posed then: Is there or is there not a connection between the type of society and the epic? Does the epic arise only in determined sociological conditions? Does the first emergence of an epic happen in groups dominated by a warrior or a priestly caste? Kesteloot told me in 1980 to see in the epic and courtly erotic poetry inseparable products characteristic of feudal or clannish societies. My colleague M. Voltz, from the University of Ouagadougou, who is an expert on ethnic groups in the region, has assured me that the Paleo-Sudanese populations of Upper Volta, living in segmentary societies (clan or village types), without any state organization, have no form of heroic poetry, but that the social and mythic functions fulfilled elsewhere by such poetry, for them, are performed through masks: abstract designs, with the value of writing, commemorate indefinitely a myth of origins (Voltz). The Mossi conquerors, masters of the country since the sixteenth century, imported the state and the epic, but today remain excluded from mask ceremonies.

I do not doubt the correctness of this theory, built on solid semiological considerations as it is. But can we generalize on the basis of it? It seems that one could apply it easily to central Asia and less so to eastern Asia. The Mongolian epic was constructed in the wake of Genghis Khan: a sort of strange and distant parentage unites it in the thirteenth and fourteenth centuries, across the immense spaces of Eurasia, with the last epic songs of feudal Europe, no less than to the Armenian cycle of *David de Sassoun* or to the Byzantine *Digenis Akritas* of Anatolia. These traditions, products of the great political upheavals throughout the interior of Asia at the time of our High Middle Ages, remained viable until the beginning if not the middle of this century. They proliferated at the heart of the politically best insulated populations: Turkomans, Kirghiz, Kazakhs, and their allies, for whom diverse forms of the oral epic maintained the memories of a heroic past with an astonishing rigor; hence, the songs based on the fight between Yermak Timofeyevich, the Russian conqueror of Siberia, were acceptable to the majority of the Turkish peoples. Events from the seventeenth century are easily identified in the Yakut epic. The circulation of legends and poems must have been intense, despite the language barrier: the Turkoman bandit-hero Korogh was commemorated in song by the Kazakhs, in the same way as the Georgian *Visraminiani* recast the Persian *Vis-er-Ramin*; the Mongol *Gesserkhan* was related to the Tibetan *Ge-Sar*, in a name that the Greek *Kaisar* or the Roman *Caesar* seems to recall.

Despite the rapid disaggregation of old Siberian cultures since the 1930s, the far eastern territories of the Soviet Union still have a considerable number of epic survivals, the collecting of which has not yet finished. In the People's Republic of Mongolia, Bawden heard several epic songs sung in 1967 by a shepherd from a collective farm. A man of many years, he was able to give explicit information about his art and the changes that had affected it for over thirty years (Finnegan 1978, pp. 463–92).

For all these peoples a connection indubitably exists between the epic and some form of the state (and this goes for the Tamil of Sri Lanka, in Indonesia, or here and there in Polynesia). So it is elsewhere. The Ainu of western Japan, who today are somewhat assimilated but until recently were considered to be some of the world's most backward people, have several mythic epics: the *Kutune Shirka*, recorded in the 1920s, has no fewer than six thousand verses; the *Ainu yukar* has versions ranging from three thousand to ten thousand verses long; the *Oina yukar* is still sung today. The small tribe of Manobo has maintained its immense *Ula-*

hingan all the while subsisting with difficulty for centuries now on the margins of societies that have successively ruled the Philippines (Kindaiti, pp. 56–61; Maquiso, pp. 1–8).

As it disentangled itself from the logical criteria of Aristotelianism, Romantic criticism tended to see the epic as the manifestation par excellence of "primitive" societies. We know now that this is not valid, even if by "primitive" one means "chronologically first." The Turkish epic tales attributed to the singer Dede Korkut, contemporaneous with medieval migrations, might trace their origins to former court poetry (Finnegan 1978, pp. 413–14). In Japan, where poetic influences from the continent were limited to an educated lyricism for many centuries, the epic appears suddenly, two hundred years after the *Genji* novel—like a *Chanson de Roland* that would follow Proust's *A la recherche du temps perdu.* The trilogy of *Hogen, Heiji,* and *Heike,* brought about by the military and political events that shook the empire between 1150 and 1180, remained part of the oral tradition until very recently; and even today, one can find about ten professional reciters of *Heike* in the country. Written versions have proliferated throughout the centuries—more than 150. No one doubts the role played by the *Heike,* one of the most fascinating epics of humanity, in coming to national consciousness and in fixing the language (Sieffert 1978a, pp. 7–25).

Our technological civilization feels repugnance for the epic. Perhaps our mass communication has made mediation by specialized poetic forms useless, and it has recuperated the fundamental epic function: the exaltation of the hero and of the exemplary exception to the rule. It can be supported, whether in film representations like the western or, in more generally by the system of star making that reigns in the marketplace of songs, literature, and the arts (Cazeneuve, pp. 91–94; Burgelin, pp. 114–22; Gili). Elvis Presley, the defeated vanquishing hero, and so on.

These substitutions are sufficiently discernible only in the forefront of our contemporary culture, where it is quite aggressively manifested. In everyday attitudes and practices, the actual exclusion of the epic is less evident. Repressed in its traditional autonomous forms, it becomes a parasite on others. Many French revolutionary songs about the capture of the Bastille up to the Commune and beyond have an "epic vein" that is quite hard to define: a mythification of lived history through narrative redundancy and a universalization of meaning. Many of the Pyrenean songs that Ravier collected can be considered to be heroic ballads, much like Woody Guthrie's "Tom Joad" or Jean Cuttat's "Noël d'ajoie."

In those societies where oral traditions have retained something of their former vitality, multiple testimonies attest to the extreme resilience of the inherited epic forms, their resistance to the hostility of the lettered milieu, their ability to absorb new motifs, to apply themselves to lived experiences without being altered profoundly—like the very heroes of whom they sing—not to die without long battles. The Malaysian poet Dokarim was still singing at the end of the nineteenth century about the wars led by the Dutch in Sumatra; a singer of the *Dambili*, Seydou Camara, in 1973, introduced the "Man of Paris"—De Gaulle—into his verses; a version of the *Sundiata* replaces arrows with bullets and shows the hero mixing his powder with gold, silver, and centaury, a magic mixture used by archers. One Cameroonian epic puts the German major, Dominik, on stage; others have episodes from the Second World War, even Zorro! The same happens in the Fiji Islands. In Yugoslavia during the partisan wars, epic stories about Tito were circulating. In Soviet Russia, the revolution made life hard for the *bylines* for many long years, it being officially declared proletarian art. Marfa Kryukova, born in 1976 to a family of singers known for four generations to folklorists, had her day of glory in the 1930s: she sang about the heroic Chapaev and the expedition to the Artic; she composed and peddled a long poem retracing the life of Lenin, from his adolescence to his funeral. Concerning the great man in the image of the *bogatyr*, a traditional epic warrior, Krupskaya, Voroshilov, Stalin, and Trotsky the Traitor are profiled in the general recent history. The Mexican genre of the *corrido*, recognized since the middle of the nineteenth century but formally stemming from the *Romancero*, twenty years ago was still resisting the pressures of television, as is demonstrated by the beautiful poem about Gregorio Cortez collected by Paredes from the Chicanos of the Rio Grande. (Bowra 1978, p. 116–17, 339–40, 469–71, 562–63; Okpewho, pp. 75, 176; Finnegan 1978, p. 474; Paredes 1958).

Chapter 7
At the Level of the Text

In 1936 the idea of a linguistic specificity of oral poetry was first suggested by J. Meier in his work on the Germanic *Kudrun*. This idea had already found its way into the thinking of certain biblical exegetes like Jousse. As evident as it had become by 1950, it remained rather abstract. The spread of the Parry and Lord theory after 1960 led to refinements, of the idea, albeit of a grossly overgeneralized version. Many researchers, mostly from English-speaking countries, in fact, wasted no time in setting forth the equation: oral style = formulaic style. From 1966 on, dissenting views began to accumulate. Today a tendency toward skepticism and a refusal to see a verifiable mark of orality in formulas prevails (Stolz and Shannon; Fochi; Finnegan 1976, p. 207, and 1977, p. 69–72; Benson, pp. 334–41; Fowler, pp. 1–28; Gossman, pp. 765–66; Chasca, p. 40–42).

The formulaic theory *qua* theory is clearly insufficient. It does not take the internal necessity of the poetic *text* into account. From the linguistic point of view, a text—be it oral or written—remains a text, springing from critical methods (whatever they may be) of which it is, as a text, by definition, the object. It necessarily carries the marks of this status: what a Navaho storyteller called his "pretty language" and what African poets identify in various ways. A poetics of orality should focus less on these marks than on the unstable relations from which stems the particular economy of the *spoken* text at the level of the concatenations of elements and their effects of meaning. This *spoken* text is what (in a terminology that today is outdated) Menendez Pidal has called the Spanish "traditional style": its intensity, its tendency to reduce the expression to its essentials (where essentiality is equated neither with simplicity nor with brevity); an absence of emotion-dampening tricks; the predominance of speech acts over descriptions; the plays of echo and repetition; the immediacy of narrations that accumulate into complex forms; the impersonality, the intemporality (Iser, pp. 110–17; Barre-Toelken, pp. 223–25; Finnegan 1976, pp. 265–66; Menendez Pidal 1968, I, pp. 58–62).

These more or less clear-cut features demonstrate the poetic opposition that distinguishes voice from writing by means of their functions. The written text, since it endures, can fully assume its future abilities: the misunderstood Romantic author is persuaded that he will be understood by the next century. The oral poet is not allowed such a thought: he is too closely subject to the present exigencies of his public; on the other hand, he enjoys the freedom of constantly reworking his text, as demonstrated in multiple renditions of songs.

Besides a few premature and disputable syntheses such as Greenway's, studies in this domain have rarely produced anything more than a few monographs over the past twenty years (Greenway 1964, pp. 106–48). They often manage to escape generalization: what the "oralist" seeks to separate within the continuity of the real are discourses rather than texts, messages-in-situation and not completed statements, drives rather than stasis or, to put it in Humboldt's words, *energeia* rather than *ergon*. This object has to be trapped; but first the trap has to be invented and we have not yet even taken the first step. One thing is sure: it is only in perceiving—and in analyzing—the oral work in its *discursive* existence that we can entertain its textual existence and, after that, its syntactic reality. By giving a broad meaning to these terms, one would posit that herein there is no grammar without rhetoric, nor the reverse; nor is there between them any hierarchical relationship: there is a simple, directed fluidity. Oral poetry is constituted therefore in what Likhatchev calls an "etiquette," a type of formalization that makes the poet a master of ceremonies (Likhatchev; Chadwick and Zhirmunsky, p. 22; Okpewho, p. 202).

Performance proposes a text that, as long as it exists, can carry with it neither erasures nor regrets: a long written work may be drafted in fits and starts whereas the oral one has no rough drafts. Poetic art consists in the poet assuming this instantaneousness, integrating it into the form of his discourse. Whence comes the necessity of a specific eloquence, of an ease in diction and phrasing, of a power of suggestion: an overarching predominance of rhythms. The listener follows the thread; no going back is possible: whatever the desired effect, the message has to make itself heard from the start. Within the framework of such constraints—more than within the freedom of writing and the intention guiding its use—language tends toward immediacy and a transparency that is less one of meaning than of its linguistic beingness, outside of all "writable" ordering.

Oral African poetry illustrates the fecundity of this alliance between an unshakable rule and an indefatigable spontaneity. In assuming the responsibility of the word, universal energy, this poetry calls on being: it describes nothing; rather it connects the images projected on the screen of a future to which they have given rise. It does not create pleasure (although it may give pleasure), but forces the present to make sense, so as to buy back time, so that reason dries up and gives way to fascination. Language (*le langage*) exhausts all its efforts on this plan that both subtends and fulfills its desire for form. The encounter, in performance, of a voice and a listening requires an almost perfect coincidence of denotations, of principal connotations, of associative nuances, between what is uttered and what is heard. The coincidence is fictive; but this fiction constitutes the essence of oral poetic art: it renders the exchange possible by dissimulating the residual incomprehensibility.

The form in its own turn will mimic the work, will stylize the creative flow without breaking it, whence the gaps, the false starts, the repetitions, the illogical parts. The Peuls shepherd songs described by Seydou are modeled on the wanderings of the flock, a verbal and temporal flux outside narration. This flow unceasingly connects sequences of a luxuriant vocabulary. There sonority gives rise to structure. Other ethnicities blend onomatopeia, empty sounds, and cries with articulated language, however imperfectly it may adapt itself to the rhythm (Finnegan 1976, pp. 232–34, 241, 263; *Recueil*, pp. 108–9; Jahn 1961, pp. 169–70).

From this comes the observer's impression that the verbal aspect of the oral work is less refined than its prosodic or musical ones: such is the point of view of a culture of writing. Poets in a predominantly oral culture who have been questioned about their art describe it in terms that evoke a mastery of discursive outbursts that produce significations inconceivable outside the very forms they invoke. "Meaning" takes on the French equivocity of *sens*: direction, vector, more than end product. The great Orpingalik, a Netsilik Inuit, used to say to Rasmussen: "My being is song"; Lord's Yugoslav *guslar* were unable to distinguish between the notions of "word" (*mot*), "message" (*énoncé*), and "verse" (*vers*), confusing them all within the idea of sound and voice. In the same way, the Navaho storyteller studied by Barre-Toelken spoke of his own tales only in terms of language (*langue*), and not of narration. Hugo Ball used to situate himself in a similar perspective starting in 1916; William Burroughs does so today (Finnegan 1977, pp. 178–80; Lord 1971, pp. 25; Barre-Toelken, p. 223; Chopin, pp. 9–42).

For this reason, a poetics of orality, whose object is the functioning of a discourse, cannot base its theory on aesthetic criteria, except with respect to its choice of examples, reflecting the personal tastes of poeticians, integrating their analyses with the joy that such examples give them and without which their words would have no meaning! Beauty is judged only in performance (whatever meaning one may ascribe to the word "beauty"): how does one generalize? The "axiological" horizon of an oral work and the values the work poses and proposes borrow as much from textual mediation as from the mediation of voice and gesture (Okpewho, p. 52; Todorov 1984, pp. 45–46). What remains, when the abstract categories (stemming from writing) are thus emptied out, is the statement of a fleeting agreement, of a momentary reconciliation between an expectation and what suddenly responds to it: this brief encounter.

Jacques Brel stated one day to Clouzet that song is not an "art." Developing this assertion into a series of paradoxes, he had meant to accentuate the "artisanal" aspect, but managed only to show just to what extent he was a prisoner of the literary conceptualization of poetry (Clouzet 1964, pp. 6, 46–47). Yet no one will deny, I think, that Brel was a great poet, but *we* feel it to be so, in his *song*. The term "song" refers back to a mode of aesthetic existence that is not of the same kind as that which we currently call "poetry"; *we* refer back to our (historically and spatially determined) culture.

One example: the majority of recently published Acadian laments can, in all fairness, be qualified from a "literary" perspective as flat, clumsy, bookishly clichéd, lacking any overt attraction. Yet Dupont's research in 1973 testifies to the breadth of this "folklore," which just yesterday was quite alive and for which up until 1965 new creations were still being collected (Dupont; Rens and Leblanc). Rooted in daily experience and in the historical consciousness of isolated populations of the Canadian Finistère, it has had the important function for at least two centuries of accompanying the collective existence of these people in a discursive counterpoint: that of the poetic function par excellence, the mythification of lived experience.

Davenson remarked that textual variants, following one on the other throughout the course of a tradition, almost inevitably produce, at one moment or at another, *the* perfect version. Let us agree that a given song, in the course of its existence (however long it may be), had its moment (moments?) of beauty: like a face, like a body, in the eyes of those who loved it, according to the desires it aroused. Today, when a song shows commitment and exhorts action, it may be scarcely more than a chanted slogan. But, through the slogan, there may pass a "poetic current," as Henri Bremond used to say long ago. Speaking of the Chilean songs of Popular Union days, Clouzet tried to sort out the many factors at play in their dual levels of operation: that of the initial design and that of long-term reception. (Davenson, pp. 132–35; Clouzet 1975, pp. 80–82). The song that after such a long time is able to produce enjoyment for whoever sings it or hears it must possess a quality that others do not. But the capacity for enjoyment is itself culturally conditioned. This may be the reason that members of a community embellish their traditional poetry with a special beauty (but one that for others is often questionable).

In the end, what is important is the harmony of an agreement between the formalizing intention of the poem and another intention, one not as clear, diffused in the social existence of the audience. Thus, in African cultures, the art of words is never proposed as a goal in itself. As magic appeal, poetry informs the collective request that human beings address to things: that they come forth in their totality; that they let themselves be engendered by the word (*le verbe*); that they be created present! The poetic sentence is pronounced in the imperative, the poet orders time, speaks from the past about the future; its place is the cradle of its people (Jahn 1961, pp. 151–53; Thomas, p. 415). What eventually will be analyzed by the poetician will be those words in their ontological depth: rhythm that is the architecture of being, symbolic articulation, image, mirror, denomination, participation in what animates the universe—and all these at exactly the same time.

It is more or less true for all oral poetry. In the field of anthropological structures, voice precedes the graphic: vocal art, by means of one of its roots, is anterior to everything; in one of its essential features, it remains "primitive." We know today the degree of complexity (contrary to previous opinion) that this adjective generally designates. For half a century, ethnography has been adding to a list of "literatures" or highly elaborate oral genres found among so-called unevolved peoples. This elaboration uses the number of hierachized rules at play to determine value. It appears all the more subtle where the poetry in question has shown itself to be more resistant to external and literary influences. Since the 1920s, this characteristic has been noticed in the Malay *pantuns*; in the thirties, in the Gond love poetry of central India; in the forties, with the Tatars of Ienissei; around 1950, for the Somalians, in the Zulu, Sotho, and Hausa panegyrics; after 1960, for the Arnhem Land of Australian aborigines; and for some time we have known of the extreme, formal finesse of the pre-Islamic Bedouin poetry of Arabia (Finnegan 1976, pp. 58–67, 71–72, 83, 88–89, and 1978, p. 5, 14, 73, 99, 319, 445; Chadwick and Zhirmunsky, p. 221; Hamori, pp. 3–30).

It does not seem that these are the givens of civilization. Their number and distribution lead us beyond ethnography to ask a broad question: oral poetic language, such as it is and in every circumstance—does it not carry with it a fundamental tendency to complicate structures of discourse? It thereby, or so we would think, imprints in the fleeting *spoken* (*dit*) the trace that transmutes it into a "monument" and removes it from the circumstance of common words. Written poetry, for which graphism of any sort assures its triumph over time, has more freedom in the choice of media, however transparent they may be. A vital instinct pushes oral poetry to explore, to exploit to the maximum the resources inherent in vocal communication, to attempt to exhaust them in a gigantic "primitive" feast.

This tendency, subject as it is to every distortion, appears to whoever is considering it to be qualitatively indifferent: everything is good that seems directed toward the goal. There is no doubt that this weakness in oral poetry makes it very susceptible to literary influences, sometimes (from our point of view as literate people) the least fortuitous ones. However, for as long as the cultural tradition that produces it remains sure enough of itself, it can, by absorbing and mastering a written model, pointedly attain some rather remarkable successes. In slow-rhythm cultures, these successes enter into the tradition and contribute to fixing it in place. In "style" cultures, such as ours, they trace, discontinuously, in pointillistic fashion, the axis of a field of forces.

The fleeting nature of oral time, interfering with the desire to produce a durable effect, determines a set of rules, procedures, and compositional tricks used to put the text in order. Being almost universal in their implementation, they vary according to several parameters:

(1) The type of natural language where they are first put to work. Thus, numerous languages have no infinitive: all verbs are personal; several Native American languages do not use indirect discourse: all discourse is direct, and this can cause considerable consequences for the composition. African languages have a particular class of words, called "ideophones," or "sound ideas," which are expressive terms used adverbially to individualize action. One dialect has up to thirty ideophones for the single idea of walking; yet the density of the ideophonic network is one of the characteristics of African poetic language;

(2) Particular customs and "styles" that, in certain cultures, distinguish classes of age: hence, in Africa, old people often do not tell stories or sing in the same manner as the young;

(3) "Period styles" characteristic of Western art: melodramatic or "realistic" songs from the turn of the century (even today with Edith Piaf) used to follow rather rigorously coded rules, ones easily recognized by listeners;

(4) Local styles, at the very heart of a specific cultural arena: for half a century, there was in Paris a Montmartren style, after 1945 a Left Bank style; in American folklore, one can find particularities attributable to the mountain folk of Appalachia (Barre-Toelken, p. 225; Finnegan 1976, pp. 64–66, 71–72; Dugast, p. 31–32; Vernillat and Charpentreau, pp. 170–71, 212–13, 215–16; Edson Richmond, pp. 145–55).

General tendencies are no less marked. Thus oral poetries, no matter where they come from, display a common ineptness at verbalizing descriptions, be they of beings or of objects, other than by a listing of qualities that lacks perspective. And here, too, it often occurs that an integral signal marks the beginning and end of the poem, as if to isolate it by a double strike from the flow of ordinary discourse. Several cultures demonstrate this propensity, especially in folktales; hence, for Turkish storytellers there corresponds to our "Once upon a time" a succession of absurdities meant to get the audience in tow. A special intonation or an instrumental prologue (sometimes a whistle according to Seydou's account of the Peuls) fulfills the same function for songs. But it happens that the effect is textually emphasized: the first verse of the epic songs recited by the Fijian Velema, around 1930, was always pronounced by an ancestor albeit conveyed by the poet's lips and was easily identified as such upon hearing it. Elsewhere, an easily recognizable, stylized introduction—nonetheless spoken—immediately precedes the song: so it is for the Manobo studied by Maquiso, or in certain Louisiana hunting songs (Coyaud, p. 329; Hymes 1973, pp. 33–34; Finnegan 1978, p. 474; Dupont, p. 294).

In the absence of the signal, perhaps we hesitate: what surges forth suddenly from the flow of our discourses—is it a poem? Or is is only a new emergence of the interminable poem, be it latent or emotive, that coexists in all that the human voice utters? Where it concerns texts with a high degree of semantic cohesion and filled with stable linguistic forms, the question has little meaning. But those are exceptions in the multitude of oral poetries (Finnegan 1977, p. 107).

Yet, this lack of external limitation of the poem, the flux in its textual borders, comes from within: from the absence of *unity*, in all the senses that a rhetoric of writing could give to this term. The oral text, for the most part, is multiple, cumulative, many-colored, sometimes diverse to the point of being contradictory. In ancient Japan, as elsewhere, one tries to correct this feature by introducing other signals, ones meant to make abridged elements stand out in the body of the text, to make them more perceptible to the ear. The team of researchers who compiled the Mexican *Cancionero*, while examining songs collected from all over the country, could publish only some isolated couplets: the migrations of these couplets, the exchanges—a sort of generalized *mouvance* of these cells of discourses—kept anything but provisional aggregates from being seen in the majority of songs where they were grouped together (Brouwer and Milner, p. 62; Alatorre 1975, pp. xvi–xvii). This situation (common for many folklorists) has led Mexicans to distinguish two types of oral poetry: one with a necessary and traditionalized ordering of the parts, which remains stable from performance to performance; as well as one whose autonomy of the parts allows each performance to propose a new order, to add them up, to transfer them, to suppress them without destroying the impact of the song.

This distinction appears to be valid well beyond the borders of Mexico. But it will be necessary to introduce a third term into the classification, one found in most cultures: the very short poem, whose dimensions allow for an almost simultaneous perception of its entirety within the auditory memory of those listening to it. But where are the limits of brevity? Of the one hundred songs collected by Görög-Karady, nineteen have fewer than five verses, fifty-three have from six to twenty. Where is the cutoff? It would be worthwhile to take the length of the verse into account, the rhythm of the language, the role of the music. A very

brief African poem becomes long through repetition. In a rather arbitrary fashion, I will say that a very brief poem, an almost instantaneous one, does not go
beyond five to six lines, in one or two simple sentences, like the Spanish *jota*.
Among the Malinke griots' songs that Camara published, certain ones do not exceed this number; this is comparable to condensing the eulogy of the liberation of
Paris into five verses (Görög-Karady 1976, pp. 25–31; Camara, pp. 270, 303;
Fribourg 1980a, pp. 114–22).

Historically, certain poems of this type, established through a long tradition,
can be the leftover debris of longer compositions, ones fallen out of common
usage; but their fragmentary character has been forgotten. French folklore provides many examples. In contrast, several cultures (in Hawaii, Ireland, and the
Arctic) have conventionalized brevity into a genre. Aong the Santals, in eastern
India, men and women improvise very short poems—rarely more than six
verses—at the end of ritual singing. In Somalia there appeared around 1945 a
form of song that squeezed its erotic or political theme into two verses. The
balwo, as it was called, soon became popular among city youth. Not long after
another genre was invented; it was made up of a long series of these distichs put
together end to end (Laforte 1976, p. 87; *Languages*, pp. 216–17; Finnegan
1977, pp. 107–9; Kesteloot 1980, p. 39; Wardropper, pp. 179–80).

Brevity presupposes discursive concentration, governed or not by explicit
rules. The Malay *pantun* weaves a constellation of sonorous and lexical relationships into a tight quatrain. The Senegalese Sereres practice a genre that con-
denses into three verses a whole poem of such complexity that, according to
Kesteloot, it takes the ethnologist an entire page of dense commentary to understand it. The space of the discourse, compacted yet overloaded with allusive values, leaves room only for the nuclear elements of the sentence, upon which elip-
sis and suspension confer ambiguity, if not an apparent semantic vacancy that
deliciously limits the listener's interpretation. At least one of these principal
terms of the utterance is thrown into a unnamed circumstantial context: the subject or the object, often the verb, the answer to the question asked or the question
that the text seems to answer, the designation of the thing itself whose description
it sketches. Meaning emerges from a nonplace, from an unsaid, within the mind
of the listener, here and now, and can be modified at each performance.

The most often cited examples of the very short genres belong to ancient and
stable traditions. Still, technological society is familiar with a poetic happening,
which if not identical, is at least analogous: the infamous three-minute rule imposed on our singers by disk jockeys and record producers. This rule has been
fastidiously followed since the invention of the LP record and has limited the
maximum length of commercial songs. Whence stylistic and thematic constraints, the necessity of a certain laconism, and the play of suggestion.

The songs of Bob Dylan and then of the protester Phil Ochs were, in 1966–67,
the first to overstep the bounds—at the risk of being refused by radio stations—

and still be successful recording texts lasting up to eight or nine minutes, even thirteen. Yet, in the same period, songs for both authors and public came to be envisaged as works of art and thereafter counted as both music and poetry. Are these two facts connected? It has not prevented a strong tendency toward brevity from continuing to predominate in this art (Clouzet 1964, p. 7; Vassal 1977, pp. 191, 224). I have examined two hundred songs by fifteen French and American singers from the years 1960–70: the listening time of 42 percent of these texts lasts from two to three minutes; 31 percent, from three to four; 15.5 percent, from one to two; 7.5 percent, from four to five; the rest are negligible (1.5 percent, less than one minute; 1 percent, from five to six; 0.5 percent, from seven to eight). The only time spans used by all the artists and which constitute a "normal" range run from two to four minutes.

The extreme brevity of a poem neutralizes the effects of its duration. The discourse rests within the limits of the distinctions proposed in chapter 5 — those between "narrative" and "lyric," "dramatic" or "gnomic." Beyond a certain threshold, conversely, time intervenes in the operation of the text, and the poem is inscribed into one or the other of these registers. Each one of these possesses its own semantic direction: the "narrative" tends to exhaust the signified within the signifier, the "lyric" rejects it (Chasca, pp. 45–46). Whence from one end to the other, in a given culture and at a given period of time, there are some specific formal tendencies. However, no poem realizes either exclusively or fully the latter; there always subsists an uncertain fringe, heterogeneous bands, reflections: "lyric" in narration, or the reverse. The oral text seems to fight against its model, to hinder the extreme consequences of the principle to which it adheres.

Thus, in practice, narrative dramatic poetry uses every type of procedure at its disposal to integrate the redundant indicators of its "phatic" function within the structure of the discourse: prospective, retrospective, justifying, digressions, ornamental stases, apostrophes, exclamations, rhetorical questions, passages from "he" or "they" to "I," to "you," the use of introductions such as "see here" or "listen," descriptive schematizations, enumerations. From there comes a general artificial tension that allows language to change direction with the exigencies of the linearity of events (Knorringa 1978, pp. 113–38; Ong 1972, p. 2; Jauss 1980, p. 127).

Crossing registers betrays an effort meant to produce a semantic surplus in performance and to set up an amazing diversification within the heart of poetic *meaning*. For this reason most probably, "lyric" and "gnomic" traditions, for their part, have devised various mixed forms that allow them to impose a conventional order on discourse. The most widespread of these are the ones I call "pseudonarratives," the most typical example being the medieval songs of *fine amor* in Europe. What constitutes the utterance for them is the indefinitely reiterated exposition both of a desire prey to its phantasms and at the same time of an intellect that denies their reality. The textual surface, although sometimes chaotic, is summarily organized according to a latent narrative schema: vision, meeting, request and waiting, abandonment or rejection, each of these terms serving as a memorial reference outside the text for one of the given propositions. The system was still operative not long ago in our sentimental melodies.

Another mixed form is that of European popular poetries and their American extensions that have been catalogued as "enumerative" or "recapitulative." Laforte has counted no less than twenty-two varieties among "traditional French songs" alone. The principle is to link successive couplets by inserting into each one of them a lexical item borrowed from an ordered group: number, name of the month or day of the week, letter of the alphabet, a piece of clothing, a part of the body, a social class. The order is more or less associative. In the "linking" songs there is in an associative series, marked by refrain, at the beginning of each group, the last element of the preceding group. Such techniques are to be found today only in children's songs. They are still at the disposal of the "artistic" song. Examples can be found in Brassens (for example, "Au bois de mon coeur"). Moreover, they do not belong to our tradition alone. They can be found elsewhere throughout the world: Finnegan has noted a genre in Hawaii in which the utterance is cut into four couplets, referring to the four dimensions of the Polynesian space: above, below, on earth, and on the sea (Laforte 1976, pp. 69–85; Finnegan 1978, p. 289).

Therefore, it is less a border for separating the registers of oral poetry than a large area open to smuggling contraband. Buchan, in his study of Anglo-Saxon ballads, uses the label "tonal structure" for the interferences in register found in the poem. In certain cultures, where the opposition is more clearly maintained, the "lyric" or "gnomic" song intervenes, in its purity of register, as an ornament of a narrative discourse: it is so in Hawaii and in Africa, where the genre labeled "chantefable" by Eno Belinga systematizes this technique of montage (Buchan, pp. 133–43; Finnegan 1978, p. 256; Eno Belinga 1970).

Oral poetry and written poetry use an identical language: the same grammatical structures, the same syntactic rules, the same base vocabulary. Yet neither the distribution of usages nor the strategies for expression are the same. In this respect orality carries with it its very own tendencies, presumably universal ones. The lack of preliminary studies in sufficient numbers precludes any closer study. I restrict my brief comments, therefore, to a few points that to me seem tenable.

First, the relationship between the duration of the discourse and the number of phrases in the "lyric" register: this fact was noted by M. and R. Harcourt for some 1,000 couplets of Quebecois folk songs, of which 956 have only one melodic phrase (to which a linguistic phrase corresponds), the remaining, atypical, 44 songs are grouped into three classes (Harcourt and Harcourt, pp. 50–53). The couplets with one phrase can be grouped into four classes according to whether this phrase is articulated in one (2 percent), two (37.7 percent), three

(44.7 percent), or more (15.6 percent) units. A rule for the genre can thus be imputed (recent African examples are found in Zadi 1978, pp. 174–76; Camara, pp. 269–71, 302–4).

I too have analyzed several hundred central African songs collected (but not published) by Penel. They are rarely divided into couplets, but their average length does not exceed fifteen to twenty-five verses. Approximately half (46 percent) have from one to six phrases; 52 percent have from six to eight. These proportions come close to those established by the Harcourts. Another coincidence is that songs with refrains rank high among those in which the couplets have the most phrases.

Second, syntactic structures: the frequency of parataxis characterizes all oral genres, including the epic. The narrative register tends to juxtapose elements without subordinating them and does so in a two-dimensional space. The lyric register does so by cutting the discourse into short affirmations, exclamations, imperatives, and series of discontinuous accumulations; in the extreme, verbs disappear: there are no more phrases but rather a parade of liberated nominal elements. In contrast, the gnomic register (or its parody) regroups articulations by collapsing their arrangement and tends to make the phrase an accumulation of simple equations. The discourse, whatever may be the metaphoric charge, is made into a series of actions stripped of their circumstances.

Third, figures: just as they adhere to the same grammar, writing and orality come under the jurisdiction of the same rhetoric. The differences appear between them when the elementary figurative factors (displacement, substitution, transference), acting within the depths of the text, are manifested on the surface in specific, culturally conditioned forms. Tibetan oral poetry, strongly influenced by Lamaistic writing, and for which traditional procedures are exactly coded, has no fewer than ninety-three types of figures of which a certain number, congruent with the nature of the language (various plays on particles), have no equivalent for us (Finnegan 1977, pp. 112–16; Helffer, pp. 385–94).

In Africa, the strong imagery of the oral poem does not seem to have a different nature than our own poetry (even taking its extreme density into account). What differs here is neither the "style" nor its deep source, but the functional linking from one to the other: the African word generates the image; the motor of the poetic discourse is the word itself: pronouncing the word is what erects it into a symbol of the world. The image is idea, but it abolishes the autonomy of the latter: discourse acts like riddles do for us (Jahn 1961, pp. 171–73; Kesteloot 1971a, pp. 3–5; Thomas, p. 418).

Whence stems the eminent function of the proper name, a revelation of cosmic energies for which the vehicle is the location; whence the considerable space allotted it in traditional African poetry, which endlessly returns to this poetry to stimulate texts. This feature, moreover, is found in most cultures, although motivated differently. There are incantational or simply evocative continuations of names of places, people, divinities, peppering and orienting the discourse or, sometimes, confirming an irony.

Finally, the vocabulary (if not the grammatical forms) used in poetry is generally demarcated from that of everyday usage. It so happens that it gets far removed enough to obscure (intentionally or not) the meaning. Certain Native American populations specify their diverse varieties of song with the help of the same number of ceremonial languages, defined at the same time by the choice of words and their pronunciation. Köngäs-Maranda told me that in the Solomon Islands the women sing lament in pidgin, a language ordinarily for men only and one that the women never use in other circumstances. Throughout the world there are abundant fixed idioms with rules transmitted like recipes for trade, and received socially as "poetic," "learned," ones sacred and always venerable. Their preservation through time can be attributed to external constraints such as versification; in general, they survive by themselves.

The influence of written literary language, even if foreign, plays a role here: the style of the Tibetan singers associates forms imitated from Sanskrit with dialectical terms from eastern Tibet. In Europe and in America for several centuries, oral poetic styles have been saturated with elements that come from literature, sometimes reduced to the status of clichés, but apt to produce by contrast some intense emotional effects (Finnegan 1977, pp. 109–10; Cirese, p. 45; Davenson, p. 16; Roy, p. 281; Sherzer, pp. 184–92; Helffer, p. 381). One of the features of our folk songs is the casualness with which they play with these elements among others, sprinkling the text here and there with bits of a Louis XVI style and of *il tombit, je le cherchis* [literary preterite forms rarely used in French today—Trans.], lost testimonials to a popular language contemporary with Rabelais: an apparent verbal arbitrariness, deeply motivated by the need to distinguish and exalt the voice of the poet.

Whatever their historical origins, the vocabulary and the grammar of oral poetry are often perceived as archaic, unless quite simply they mimic archaism! This is what has been noted in both Asia and Africa regarding the epic. But the tendency is more general, and the art of our contemporary singers is scarcely free of it. In societies with long traditions, the old forms that convey the song thus are often no more than the vestiges of an antique, sacral language. So it is for the Dogon and the Manobo, for whom the language of the *Ulahingan* alone allows them to communicate with the gods. The ritualized archaism of the panegyrics of some African ethnic groups makes them so opaque that they require an interpreter. For the Ainu, the exact opposite takes place: the *yukar* are sung in an ancient ritual idiom that is today still accessible to the whole group, whereas the local dialects have evolved to such an extent as to preclude mutual comprehension—the last refuge for historical unity! Analogous evolutions, or perhaps, a blind effort to return to this source are observed elsewhere in our midst. A given nursery rhyme whose origin is no mystery is so altered that it resembles some magic formula: *Eins, zwei, drei* in German become the French *Amstramgram* (but is this really the etymology?), the voiding of meaning, aspiring to primitive glossolalia, as were the onomatopoeia and the engine noises that shook the songs of the first rockers: the *scat* (Bowra 1978, p. 389; Finnegan 1976, pp. 117, 131; Coupez-Kamanzi 1970, pp. 8–9; Eno Belinga 1978, p. 105; Maquiso, p. 40; Hilger, p. ix; Hoffmann and Leduc, p. 23).

Most probably it is the same need that leads traditional poets and singers to privilege a given grammatical form, multiplying the uses of a certain affix, tense, or nominal class, within the authorized limits of the structure of natural language, but outside the norm. They constitute, therefore, an obvious mark of the type of discourse that they propose for an audience (a Fijian example is given in Finnegan 1978, p. 473).

At any rate, the form of the poem thereby manifests that the message transmitted comes from a universe that is at the same time alien and warmly welcoming, solemn or exalting, perhaps a little dangerous and (as with childhood memories or Father's words) not at all on the same level of reality as day-to-day existence.

Secret poetic languages, used in several cultures, particularly in Africa, tend to have the same effect. Conventional "Javanese" or argots connect singers and storytellers together within some brotherhood: they are less peculiar vocabularies than rules for altering existing vocables. Thus, on the lips of Manobo singers, the *r* becomes *l* or *y*: I doubt that this deformation comes solely from a musical constraint as Maquiso proposes. The lexical deformation can be used as an ironic procedure, as in the political songs of the Spaniard Pi de la Serra (Eno Belinga 1978, p. 105; Maquiso, p. 40; Wurm, p. 44).

When a situation of diglossia reigns as a result of circumstantial pressures and individual initiative, one of the languages present can assume a particular poetic function, for example, the *joual* of the Quebecois singers around 1970 in a context of national pretensions, rather than the tearful patois of the *P'tit quinquin* of the populist Desrousseaux in Lille in 1853; likewise, the songs partially or entirely in Breton by Mikel Laboa or Manex Pagola. Sometimes during a performance, discourse, begun in one language, is set in motion on another, for a more or less long period of time, for the purpose of setting off a reaction in the audience: hence Brel in the bilingual song "Marieke," or Carlos Andreou evoking in alternating stanzas of Spanish and Portuguese the destiny of the Iberian Peninsula. This technique is used frequently around the world. Examples are to be found in rural Ireland as well as in the United States (Millières, pp. 90–108; Brecy, pp. 70–72; Vassal 1980, pp. 85, 168–72; Wurm, pp. 159–62, 172–74; Clouzet 1964, pp. 98–99; Finnegan 1978, p. 173; Hymes 1977, p. 437).

Thanks to some material given to me by Penel, I have been able to study this phenomenon more closely in the Central African Republic, the songs I examined had recently come from an urban source and were expressed in Sango, the local language. But numerous foreign words appear that are not current in everyday speech and thus were chosen with semantic or stylistic intentions: words of Lingala, the language of Zaire, popularized in Bangui by radio, put on the air by Zairian singers are enjoyed throughout central Africa; French words seem to follow certain rules of use (Penel, pp. 70–72). I have counted four hundred of them in several thousand occurrences in some eight hundred songs. If one eliminates the helping or lackluster words attributable to the accompanying of diglossia, there remain series with strong cultural valorizations, names of numbers (indicative of education), days of the week (international calendar), and some others; emotive terms make up 50 percent of the total and have the highest frequency. The expressive effect is only too obvious; however, it is not certain that the singers have a clear and conscious idea of it; they have automated its use.

Most of these procedures contain some phonic rule for their initial staging: the manipulation of the linguistic datum contributes to the use or reinforcement of rhyme, alliteration, all sorts of sonorous echos, or, more generally, it accentuates the scansion of the rhythms. I will devote chapter 11 entirely to this question. When they attain a certain density, these games influence the formation of meaning. Finally the sentence, the words themselves, are erased in concatenations stripped of coded signification, pure sonorous suggestions. I have found in Banguissi songs published by Jouve and Tomenti and Penel some examples illustrating the successive degrees of this rise of a phonic joy and the transformation it provokes in the linguistic datum:

Absurd "text," made up of juxtaposed syntagms, without any grammatical or semantic relation;
A phrase borrowed from a foreign language, not understood and greatly altered;
A litany-like accumulation of isolated words without context;
A succession of proper nouns in apostrophe, outside the sentence;
The use of ambiguous monosyllables, interpretable as signifying words or as interjections, onomatopoeia, outcries;
Refrains of the *tralala* type, evoking or not a word in the language;
A phonic series having lost any relationship to the code;
The litany-like repetition of such a series (Jouve and Tomenti, texts 3, 6, 8, 9; Penel, texts 7, 11, 13, 23, 31).

One has every reason to presume that any group of texts, no matter how widespread, sampled in whichever oral literature, would furnish similar examples. The final two or three degrees of this scale are not distinguishable from vocality, which we have already assumed is connected to dance.

In the most widely held opinion of ethnologists (and the rare poeticians familiar with their works), the constant and perhaps universally definitive feature of oral poetry is the recurrence of diverse textual elements: "formulas" as Parry and Lord use the term, and more generally, every type of repetition or parallelism. None of these techniques, certainly, is the exclusive property of oral poetry: Jakobson saw in them the basis of all poetic language; in a limiting fashion, Schwab sees them as characteristics of nonEuropean poetries. All this does not preclude that a close tie, and one that is undoubtedly functional, attaches them to vocalization (Gossman, p. 765; Finnegan 1977, pp. 130–33; Goody 1979, pp. 205–6; Schwab in Eliade, pp. 128–62).

This connection is evident in dance songs where the rhythmical exigencies confer on the text a necessary iterative aspect. But at the deep level where the properties of the living word (as opposed to writing) are constituted, it is narration — every narration — that is spontaneously repetitive: made up of repetitions that embellish the first as they interpret it in such a way that the new element of the tale leads back to the gloss itself. The narration begins a dialogue with its own "subject," as Greek tragedy once did. This fundamental tendency more or less polarizes all the genres of oral poetry.

The rhythm resulting from the recurrence is marked at all levels of language: orality does not favor single sonorous echoes. Repetitions of stanzas, phrases or entire verses, prosodic or syntagmatic groups, turns of phrase, grammatical forms, words, phonemes, as well as effects of meaning — discourse capitalizes on everything. The repetition is submitted to the regularity of parallelism, opposing the members two by two; it can also be freed from this numerical rule. It is localized in privileged sites, or it invades the text. It takes up its theme identically once again, or effectuates a partial variation; it is constructed in a rigorous sequencing or according to diverse modalities of alternation.

Nothing in the usage of these figures allows for the reduction of the verbal techniques of oral poetry, nor even for imagining that they are indispensable. Empirically, one notes nevertheless the considerable role they play, if not in all the texts, at least in all times and places, independent of cultural conditions. They are found, more or less set forth, but identical to themselves, in texts as diverse as English ballads, Malinke women's songs, a song by the Soviet Okoudjava, or most of Woody Guthrie's Dust Bowl ballads; the blues, in its old forms, depends on the play of recurrences (Sargent and Kittredge, pp. xx–xxii; Buchan, pp. 150–55; Burke, pp. 122–23; Camara, pp. 275–78, 307–11; Collier, p. 42; Oster, pp. 263–67; recordings of *Le chant du monde* LDX 7-43-58 [no.7] and Folkways Records FH5212).

These recurrences weave associative threads into the discourse. The threads, multiplied, crisscrossing, engender yet another discourse, one operating with the elements of the first as does a dream with fragments of waking experience, for the benefit of the phantasms to which the dream gives a face. As the song plays itself out, equivalences or contrasts with subtle nuances (for the context is modified, even if imperceptibly) are established. Each one of them, received as new information, lends to the familiarity to which this voice invites us. The *Mamita mia* that arises in the second verse of a famous Spanish war song—a parody of the popular romance, *Los Cuatro Mulatieros*—with no relation to the rest of the sentence, then repeated two times per couplet, appears at first to be gratuitous, but little by little it makes sense allusively (the mother, the distant beloved). It ends up being the most important element of the poem, constituting by itself a whole plane of signification (Scheub 1977, p. 347; Gossman, p. 766; recording *Le chant du monde* LDX-S-4279 [no. 2]).

For this reason, beyond stylistic combinations, the recurrence becomes the principle of various modes of composition:

(1) The *litany*: An indefinite repetition of a single structure, be it syntactic or partially lexical, some words being modified on each repetition, in such a way as to mark a progression by slippage and gaps;

(2) *Overlapping*: the same slipping repetitions, not of phrases and sentences, but rather of parts of the text (stanza, couplet, section). The similar *laisses* of the French epics of the Middle Ages provide a refined example but one which is the property of that culture alone (a good African example can be found in *Recueil*, pp. 162–81).

(3) The regularized *echoes*: the text is dotted with repetitions at fixed intervals, sometimes crossing each other, and which, framing and supporting the discourse, confer on it a particular force. Thus, a given element (sound, word, syntactic form, seme) will figure at the beginning and at the end of uneven verses; another element, even verses; the one and the other can reappear in medial configurations. The system lends itself to variations of an infinite number. It has been applied to all epochs, in all cultures; even written poetry often uses it, in its aspiration to rediscover the harmonies of voice.

We could cite as well some techniques more clearly tied to the melodic structure of the poem: verses sung twice, a third time; plays of reiteration that make a couplet the dilation of a verse, if not of a unique term; and, even more general, the practice of the refrain, constant or variable, distributed in regular intervals or not, glossing the couplet or contrasting with it, sometimes reduced to an evocative name, suspended in the extrasyntactic void, or with pure vocalities.

Whatever its form, discursive recurrence constitutes the most efficacious means to verbalize a spatiotemporal experience, to make the listener participate in it. Time runs on in the fictive intemporality of the song, starting at the moment of the inaugural word. Then, in the space that the sound engenders, the sensorially felt image is objectified; from within the rhythm a knowledge is born and is legitimated. Some disrupted cultures based their notion of the world on repetition and parallelism so that their stories and their oral poetry "were inscribed" in the fleeting nature of the voice: for example, the Hopi and the Zuni Indians in the southwestern United States; the Polynesians of Hawaii. Fuegians or Toungoui used to evoke the same forms of discourse to excite a shamanic trance, opening up access to the Powers; we can discern the far distant echo of these magics in the liturgies of the pop festival (Finnegan 1978, pp. 206, 257; Rouget, pp. 178, 190–91, 432; Lyotard, pp. 21–22). Should we also mention again the incantatory repetitions of certain songs by Brel?

All the features mentioned here are found in the texts of our singers—the only "oral poets" produced by our industrial civilization, at least until further notice. The technical constraints of using *mediats* do not seem to have upset the foundations of a poetics immanent in the diversity of cultures and adhering to the ontology of the living voice.

Certainly, in the midst of the "Gutenberg galaxy," one does not sing, without necessarily submitting to the influence of literary models or relying on various techniques of writing. It is a fact of intertextuality. In that intertextuality there are manifest all the moving, diverse, contrastive, and attentive (to common discourses more than to the research of the personal avowal) features of oral poetry—as it is turned toward the already known rather than toward the unheard of. Borrowings, reuses, remakes of every dimension: this very gesture that in cultures having a long rhythm, constitutes "oral tradition" and that, in the short, staccato rhythm, forms our mutations, embraces other, more numerous areas, but does not change in nature. Today and for some time now, it holds true: the song writes itself. No matter: the goal of discourse remains nonetheless the corporality of voice alone.

Part III
The Performance

Chapter 8
A Circumstantial Discourse

Only the use of the text accords reality to the rhetoric on which it is founded; only its vocal actualization justifies the rhetoric. Whence the necessity for us to define "situations of communication": Houis in considering African proverbs distinguishes between the distinctive features of performance based on the listener's role—either simply listening or an active exchange with the speaker where this exchange may be either *necessary* or *useful* (Houis, pp. 6–10). For oral poetic communication, however, there generally corresponds a situation of *listening*: it is worth our while to analyze this more closely.

In questioning the nature of the oral poetic form in chapter 5, I had suggested that *performance* can be considered as both an element of it and its principal constitutive element. Performance fully realizes and determines all the other formal elements that have no more than a virtual relationship to the performance. African lamentation singers (all women) are able to reproduce their poems only at real funerals (Finnegan 1976, p. 164, and 1977, pp. 28–29, 89, 241–42; Gossmann, p. 778; Jason, 1977). By incurring a singular type of knowledge, poetic performance is comprehensible and analyzable only from the point of view of a phenomenology of reception.

Inside or outside the text the conventions, rules, and norms regulating oral poetry encompass its occasion, its public, the appearance of the one transmitting it, its short-term goal. To a certain degree the same may be said about written poetry; but, in dealing with orality, the collection of these terms refers to a totalizing function that cannot be broken down into diverse, concurrent, or successive finalities. In the vernacular of northeastern Brazil, the word *cantoria* refers to poetic activity in general, the rules it imposes on itself, and the performance.

This latter term, first adopted by American folklorists such as Abrahams, Dundes, and Lomax, refers to a creative social event, one irreducible to its components alone and during which particular properties are effectuated. The importance of this event and of the properties it manifests are measured, according to Hymes, by the distribution of three characteristics, one or two of which are necessarily contained in the performance but never all three at once: interpretability, describability, iterability (Hymes 1973). This broad criterion makes it possible in principle to classify every form of orality, poetic or not. Hymes adds another: absence or presence of taking responsibility; whence a distinction between *behavior*, *conduct*, and *performance*.

Several cultures, conscious of the power behind effects produced in this way, carefully codify the choice of performative components—time, place, and participants. Thus, in many cases in Africa, the use and control of the social imaginary by the privileged means of poetry have for traditional societies as much or more importance than those of economic surplus value do for us. Whence imperative prescriptions or taboos. Vocalization of poetry postulates a collective accord (and its counterpart, censorship), without which the performance could never completely be concretized (Calame-Griaule 1965, pp. 470–73; Bouquiaux and Thomas, I, pp. 106–7; Brower and Milner, p. 57). Then again, one can distinguish between the linguistically immutable song, one tied to precise circumstances, often uttered by specialists, and the one that is more or less improvised in conjunction with a personal or local event (as is the case in Penel's account of the Azande of the Central African Republic). The language of ancient Japan had different terms to designage these two types of orality.

The freely performed text, one without the overture of written poetry, one interpretable ad infinitum, varies constantly at the connotative level to such an extent that is is never the same twice: its surface is comparable to that of a lake on a windy day. The text of a fixed performance tends to immobilize its superficial reflections, to harden them into a thick shell surrounding an ancient storehouse, a precious deposit that warrants enclosure: we stand at attention for the national anthem; we go to church on Christmas Eve if we want to hear the midnight service. In the end, the poem remains incomprehensible outside the situation. To change the circumstances is to modify the meaning and social function of the received text: a revolutionary song becomes a marching song, a love song becomes a political chant, and so on.

Performance implies *competence*. Beyond knowing what to do and what to say, performance displays a knowing-how-to-be in both space and time. Whatever the spoken or sung text evokes through linguistic means, performance imposes on it an all-encompassing referent at the corporeal level. It is through the body that we are time and space: voice proclaims it, an emanation from us. Writing, it is true, also carries with it the measure of space and time, but its ultimate goal is to free itself from them. Voice happily accepts its servitude, and, starting with this primordial yes, everything is colored in language: nothing here is neutral any longer; words babble; they are loaded with intentions, odors, they smell of human beings and earth (or of that which human beings substitute for them). Poetry no longer comes from the categories of doing, but rather from those of process: the object to be fabricated is no longer sufficient; it is a matter of reviving another subject, one external, observing and judging the one who acts here and now. For this reason performance is also the instance of symbolization: the integration of our corporeal relativity within the cosmic harmony signified by voice; the integration of the multiplicity of semantic changes within the unity of a presence.

As an action (a double one at that: emission-reception), performance makes *actors* (sender, receiver, one or many) present and enacts the *means* (voice, gesture, media). With respect to the *circumstances* that inform its context, I relate them to the parameters of space and time: the subject matter of this chapter (the means are considered in chapters 9 to 11, the actors in chapters 12 and 13).

Performance is doubly temporalized—by its own length, and by virtue of the moment of the social duration into which it is inserted.

I have already mentioned certain extreme terms: recitation time for a long epic or for a short song on the radio. From a few minutes to several days—it is less important in and of itself than it is for what causes it. Certain causes depend on the text itself: its length and the mode of recitation or of singing as dictated by custom. These two factors sometimes tend to neutralize one another: the long Zulu panegyrics are uttered in a fast voice, in an uninterrupted stream. The *pantun* of Malay and the Somalian *balso*, in contrast, are performed using a slow rhythm with a repetitive melody that considerably lenghtens the performance of their two or four verses. Other factors regulating length come from the particularities of the given situation of communication. In evaluating the real length of the Nigerian *Ozidi*, Okpewho has observed that it is measured less in terms of time (seven evenings) than by equal spacing of the episodes, that is, by virtue of a narrative economy imposed by the physical and social conditions of the performance.

The emotional relationship that is established between the performer and the public can be no less a determining factor, provoking every type of dramatization or display of the song: intervention of the poet in his own play demands a great deal of elasticity but engenders great freedom. Neither author nor listeners can predict the time frame of an unmediated performance. Its length is made to adhere to a culturally motivated rule of probability (Burke, p. 139; Finnegan 1977, pp. 122–24; Okpewho, p. 267 n. 8; Lord 1971, pp. 128, 132; Calame-Griaule 1965, p. 485).

The event of the performance, extracted from sociohistorical time, is never indifferent, even if it disengages itself from the latter and more or less transcends it. Thus, every performance—such as it is, as a fragment, fictitiously isolated from real time—carries with it some inherent values that may change, be inverted, the next time the same song is sung: it matters little; there will always be values, even if negative ones. From this point of view I distinguish four performative situations, according to which the moment of the song is inserted into a "conventional," "natural," "historical," or "free" time.

In the first group there is every type of *cyclical time* whose rhythm is fixed by custom: the time of rites; the time of ritualized human events; normalized social time.

In most religions the performance of liturgical poetry is articulated in ritual time. In Christian countries, innumerable hymns are found in that time; their usage constitutes for us one of the last almost pure oral poetic traditions. In the world of Islam, one of the disciples of Nasir Udin told me that the poems composed and sung by his master, meant to be recited immediately before or after communal prayer, are actually glosses of the prayer itself. The ritual connection is sometimes relaxed, but connotes, in the manner of an originary mark, banalized performances. Ages ago, one of my peasant neighbors, a dyed-in-the-wool nonbeliever, would bawl out church songs while sawing wood, thoroughly scandalizing the women of the neighborhood. The *Kutune Shirka*, a sacred poem of the Ainus, was still sung around 1930 both for shamanic ceremonies and for winter evening leisure (Finnegan 1978, p. 463).

Performance can correspond to the celebration of a particular and periodic feast that it characterizes: across Europe, Christmas carols, whether in dialogue form or not, are today disappearing; in Spain, the *jotas*, are improvised and danced for the feast of the Pilar Madonna, and the initiatory songs of the Dogon of Mali are reserved for the feast of Sigui, celebrated every sixty years (Roy 1951, pp. 171–225; Fribourg 1980a, pp. 114–22; Eno Belinga 1978, pp. 78–81).

Various public and private circumstances influence the common destiny in some way and measure recurring events whose frequency is hard to predict: birth, marriage, death, combat, victory. For many societies, every event entering into these series arouses a prescribed performance. I have indicated in chapter 5 the poetic genres defined by such periodicity.

The series of steps in a collective chronology resulting in a public convocation is what I call normalized social time: announcements, posters, letters of invitation, all for which the penny readings of nineteenth-century England provided one of the first widespread examples. In the industrialized world, without exception, singers' performances are articulated within that time: a commercialized time of *show biz*. In an analogous though culturally different custom, the Muslim singers of Bosnia around 1930 used to intone their epics throughout the evenings of Ramadan in village cafés where the men would gather after the day's fast (Neuburg, pp. 243–47; Lord 1971, p. 15).

Natural time—the seasons, days, hours—provides an abundant poetry, one that for us now is folkloric, its moorings in experiential time: by virtue of a direct connection to cosmic cycles, like serenades or our ancient dawn songs, or those of medieval "May Days," those brought forth on St. John's Day in mid-August; or in an indirect way, the worksong in total subservience to these cycles—in Asia, rice planting and in France the sowing and sometimes even the harvesting of grapes. The night, warm with mysteries, is a forceful time that most civilizations deem susceptible to human voice. Either they prohibit its use at night, or else they make the night its privileged, if not exclusive, time for specific performances: in Africa, that of the tale; for the Jorai, that of myths; for the Siberian Tatars that Radlov visited, the epic. Sometimes the entire night is ritualized, like that of Holy Saturday for the ancient Christian liturgies. For the Malinke, the night that precedes circumcision ceremonies is filled with discordant songs and cries, accompanied by pounding drums, a purifying verbal orgy (Gaborieau, p. 326; Finnegan 1978, pp. 445–46; Dournes 1980; Rey-Hulman 1977; Camara, pp. 185–86).

"Historical" time is that which an unforeseeable and noncyclically recurrent event marks and measures as it touches an individual or a group. Among the Maori of the nineteenth century, the victim of a reprimand or an insult would compose a song to attenuate its maleficent import. Among the Gond of India, young people court each other by means of improvised songs. In several regions of the world, the return from a fruitful hunt engenders occasional poetry that unites the voices of the hunters much as the voices of drinkers join at the end of a peasant banquet. This type of performance includes almost all the political and protest songs, ones that today form a considerable part of living oral poetry. An effect of distance is produced rather quickly between the text and the event that it illustrates or commemorates. An ambiguity can thus arise, the message becoming transformed as it draws away from its event. But strong poetic effects sometimes result in these slippages: Osvaldo Rodriguez's "Laura" bears witness to this in Chile's recent troubled times (Finnegan 1978, pp. 15, 292–93; Clouzet 1975, pp. 72, 207).

The connection of performance to lived experience is readily overextended. What remains alive is the marvel of the song. The joy or the sadness that the event or the mood provokes can, in turn, arouse the pure desire to sing rather than the taste for a particular song: the text matters little; what counts is the melody. The "historical" relationship is broken; time is unleashed.

Time connotes *every* performance. This rule abides by the nature of oral communication and can have no exception. In ritual performance, the connotation is so strong that it can by itself constitute the meaning of the poem. In *free-time* performances, ones problematically situated along a chronological chain, the effect tends to get diluted; it is never completely effaced. That I am suddenly taken by the desire to sing or to recite verses, with no apparent reason, at nine o'clock in the morning, at noon or at sunset, while on vacation or while going to work, cannot be indifferent, and modulates in some fashion the meaning of the poetic word that crosses my lips.

Yet, the spatial modalities of performance interfere with those of temporality. The place, like the moment, can be aleatory, imposed by circumstances foreign to poetic intention: a given recital by the Basque singer Lertxundi, supposed to take place in the village square, happens in the church as a result of a sudden storm (Wurm, p. 84). We remark a tension between the spatial and temporal connotations: in the farmyard, my woodcutter with his hymns, recuperable tensions, ones mimetically exploitable though also dominated and operative, tending to produce poetic effects. But most probably, serendipity does not really rule. An attraction, often subtle, issuing from the phantasms of the performer, seems to provoke in a given place, in a given type of place rather than any other, a particular performance. This spatial configuration appears stronger and more constant than the temporal ones. I do not doubt that this difference depends on the ontology of the voice.

Human societies have somewhat rigorously exploited these virtualities by institutionally privileging certain locations. When a ritual norm intervenes, it ties a knot of identification between sacred time and space, thereby mimicking some utopic eternity: the liturgical chant in the temple; the cosmogonic poem in the midst of the assembly of Nepalese orants; or the Mandingo epic that is recited at the historical dwelling of Kamabolon (Garborieau, p. 320; Niane 1975b, p. 160). All cultures possess or have possessed their sacred spots, umbilical cords, rooting human beings in the earth and bearing witness that they came from that ground; and I cannot remember ever reading that to any one of these places there did not correspond some incantatory or poetic practice. There remains, in differentiated societies, more than the traces of this former state. Religious practices contribute to its maintenance. But at the very end of secularizations of every type, sacredness is interiorized and is camouflaged by simple specialization: hence, throughout the world, the spaces readied for dance and the vocal performance that generally accompanies it.

Ancient motivations, beyond outward changes end up institutionalizing custom. For this reason, since the sixteenth century, theaters have been progressively isolated in our cities. For Native Americans of the lower Saint Lawrence region who are not as far removed as we are from magical resources, there are on tribal lands places more appropriate for gathering, for binding the totality of the spiritual and corporeal faculties into an unbending whole. These places are known, they are named. It is there that song is performed, myth is recited, memories of the old hunters are recounted (Bouchard, pp. 9–10).

For centuries now in our cities, the streets have been the favorite place for reciters of poetry, for singers, for satirists. It has become so again, furtively, intermittently in revivals in London in 1976, at the debut of the group Jam. The street: not fortuitously, not always for lack of finding a roof, but by virtue of a plan integrated into a form of art. Con-Square slave recitals in eighteenth-century French New Orleans up until the Civil War may have, in the long run, engendered our jazz. When the latter took shape around 1900, its first recitals took place in the streets and in parks. Several European cities, those blessed with a temperate climate, still had at the beginning of our century areas where oral poets, hither and yon, in the company of charlatans and jugglers, could always meet and perform and where everyone knew they could go to hear them: the Plaza Mayor in Madrid, the Piazza Navona in Rome, San Martino in Florence. Paris had, at least until Napoleonic times, its Pont-Neuf. Can the Beaubourg Plateau today be traced to this tradition (Burke, pp. 107–9)? Those were wide open spaces. More recently, upset by the invasion of the automobile and the progressive disappearance of street life (before the palliative invention of pedestrian zones), the concentration was reformed in the network of shelters (cafés, cellars, ateliers) often embracing an entire neighborhood like Saint-Germain-des-Prés or Greenwich Village. Clubs for songs opened and operated, much like town bistros where communal singing neutralized external conflicts.

The evolution of urban behavior joins in Western Europe with a tradition that goes all the way back to the end of the Middle Ages. For such reasons, the majority of more or less important cities promoted closed spaces for the performance of oral poetry to the status of an institution: declamation, improvisation, versified dialogues and song. Thus, the *puys* and "rhetorical chambers" of the fifteenth, sixteenth, and seventeenth centuries; but above all, starting in the seventeenth century, the "cabarets" and singing clubs, after 1850 the French "cafés-concerts," the London music hall, an uninterrupted chain that leads all the way to our dinner theaters. In Paris, the long and tumultuous history of the successive *Caveaux*, between 1729 and 1806, opened the modern era of song, where song had become in this milieu a literary genre, whereas the *goguettes* (several hundred in 1845) gathered together its popular clientele, attracted solely by the pleasure of song. Around 1880, Emile Goudeau, first in the Hydropathes and then in the Chat Noir, created a formula for alternating recitation and singing that made Montmartre's fortune in the Gay Nineties.

The existence of these places, the social function they assumed, must necessarily have marked the art of the singers or the men and women of letters seduced by this mode of diffusion. The image of the real space where the performance took place was integrated into the poetic project. This is why one saw, oddly enough, during the French Revolution, several patriotic clubs transformed into singing societies. Then, over the course of the nineteenth century, libertarian and social circles gave ample room to song in their meetings. During the Commune, the Bordas had the people applauding *La Canaille* during concerts held in the Tuileries Palace or at the Hotel de Ville. The South American *penas*, first literary clubs then later singing clubs in Argentina and in student milieus, appear in this new form in Santiago, Chile, in the 1960s. What the Parras started up in 1965 was the spot in Latin America where for eight years singers and political poets met and exchanged works. It was one of the places where the great though short springtime of the song got ready for the triumph of the Popular Front (Vernillat and Charpentreau, p. 8; Brecy, pp. 67, 290; Duveau, pp. 480–86; Clouzet 1975, pp. 35–38).

The nature of the place, appropriate for bringing together a mix of people for a predetermined length of time, for professional leisure time; its commercialization, even partial (one pays for its consumption); the technical necessities of programming — so many factors dramatize the poetic word and push declamation and song toward some form of theater. I will not go into the extreme example of the African group Okro de Lome, which for some years now has been in the process of creating, under the title of "concert," a new oral genre, one polyglot (French, English, local languages), reaching simultaneously into *commedia dell'arte*, song recitals, and instrumental concerts for its roots (Ricard 1977).

Located in a particular place with its relationship of order that is both genetic and mimetic, performance projects the poetic work into a *setting*. Nothing, in what constitutes the specificity of oral poetry, is conceivable if not as a sonorous part of a signifying group where colors, odors, mobile and immobile forms, ones animated and inert, all play together, in a complementary fashion, as the auditory part of a sensorial group where sight, smell, and touch all take part equally. This group stands out from the continuum of social existence, without (despite certain tricks) dissociating itself from it: the place of the performance is taken from the "territory" of the group, it depends on it in every way and is thus received.

Inevitably, albeit to a small degree, performance is rampant with parasitic noise: acoustical sounds or fragments of useless discourses, ones stemming from the nature of all oral communication and skewing the semantic perspective; but other noises are also specific: a poor physical layout, overwhelming decor, indiscrete instrumental accompaniment or, at another level, the effects of censorship, whether authoritarian or spontaneous; and finally, for the outside observer, stranger to the active group of participants — ethnologists recording a "primitive" feast or medievalists studying the epic of the twelfth century — intercultural distance. Whatever it may be, the "noise" tends to disorganize the performance by upsetting the system of information that it has as its function to pass along. The art of the performer tries to recuperate, as much as can be done, this heterogeneous element, to transform it in its own turn into information, correlated to the intentional message even if it means distorting it to the point of perverting the message. Only the purely temporal sound effects, the chronological distancing, exclude such plays. Historians of poetry know this only too well (Lotman 1973, pp. 124–27).

Recuperation of noise? The interpellation of an intruder, integrated by rhythm and mimicry, is blended into the poem that it enriches by this episode: I have found several examples in Romania as well as in Africa; or the improvisations suggested by a disturbed audience reaction; or the dissimulations, the desired ambiguity of a poetry on which weighs a moral or political censorship but that makes that very censorship work for its own designs, for good or for ill. Or as well, sought, integrated, mastered by voice, noise dramatizes it, intensifies it, extends it beyond conventional meanings (as in the songs recorded by Joan Baez in Hanoi in 1970, with the backdrop of American bombings). The reason for the noise counts from now on among the presuppositions of poetic discourse; the cause is itself discourse, absent but real: the poem refers back to the cause, whose terms in the end function with respect to itself like the elements of a universal anaphors. But these terms simultaneously refer to the moment of utterance—the performance, drama, and psychodrama—as much as to an external referent, one more and more blurred as the pathos or irony of the voice is intensified. The communicative function makes it prevail over meaning, texts, rhythms, time, and space concentrated in an implosion of meaning rather than dispersed in a discursive chain of signifiers.

The interaction of space and time thus opens in every way sensorial and intellectual perspectives and offers everyone a chance. The message is *published*, in the strongest sense that one can confer on this term, the current usage of which, relative to printed writing, makes a wretched metaphor. Performance is *publicity*. It is the denial of this (de)privation of language that gives way to neurosis.

Chapter 9
The Vocal Work I

Every poetic word (whether mediated by writing or not) rises out of an uncertain interior space, one named by metaphors: source, foundation, ego, life, and so on. Strictly speaking it designates nothing. An event is produced in a somewhat aleatory fashion (the rite itself is no more than the inveigling of fate), in the soul, on the lips, in a hand. An ordered system disintegrates, another unveils, a system is opened, and universal entropy is suspended (Gaspar, pp. 9–13, 86–92). It concerns a place and time where, in an excess of existence, an individual encounters history and in a dissimulated, fragmentary, progressive fashion, modifies the rules of his own language.

A voice speaks, not just an epiphany of language: energy without figure, intermediary resonance, fleeting space wherein the unstable word is anchored in the stability of the body. All around this poem-in-the-making there swirls a nebulus that has just spun out of the chaos. Suddenly a rhythm surges forth, dressed in wordful tatters. They are vertiginous and vertical, a streaming jet of light: therein everything is revealed and formed. Everything at once: the one who speaks, that about which one speaks and to whom one addresses oneself. Jakobson long ago indicated (by a game) this circularity by referring to the "incantatory function" of language (Valéry, pp. 1322–23; Bastet, pp. 42–45; Chopin, p. 77; Dragonetti, pp. 157–68; Genette 1976, pp. 119–33; Jakobson 1963, p. 21). The appropriate characteristics of every oral communication are interiorized in this secondary state of language. Signs, it has recently been said, become things; the transparent becomes opaque. But as well, the opaque becomes translucent. The poem questions signs (the question is also torture), tries to turn them

126

around, so that the things themselves *assume* meaning. In the ray of this word a very small sector of the real suddenly lights up and lives, alone at the center of omnipresent death.

For this reason the discourse of the poem cannot be in itself its own end. The *closure* of the text (its barrier, its wall) is dismanteled: in the breach the seed of an antidiscourse is introduced, transgressing (in a specific, marked manner that differs for each place) common discursive schemata. (Stierle, pp. 430–35). Within the vibration of voice, the thread that connects so many signals or experientially determined markers to the text is stretched to the breaking point. Whatever referential strength remains in the poem stems from its focusing on the contact between subjects bodily present in performance: somebody whose voice carries and somebody who receives it. The closeness of this contact is enough to make sense, just as happens in love.

Triumph of the *phatic*. Listening as much as vocalizing overflows speech. These are the primary functions of the libidinal body (its language [*le langage*] it is a secondary function), through which metonymy and metaphor move toward each other. Writing, if by chance it intervenes, neutralizes these ambiguities. In oral poetry an undeniable state of affairs is defined in clear terms—the *Sitz-im-Leben* of Bultmann-inspired German critics: within the Orphic dimension of the meaning, according to C. L. Bruns's definition of the "Dionysiac" impulse, where Nietzsche situated the origin of "music" (Rosolato 1969, p. 298; Berthet, pp. 127–31; Bruns, pp. 232–62; Nietzsche, pp. 48–52).

The desire for live voice dwells in all poetry, but it is in exile in writing. The poet is voice, *kléos andrôn*, according to a Greek formula whose tradition can be traced all the way back to primitive Indo-Europeans; language comes from elsewhere: from the Muses, according to Homer. Whence the idea of *epos*, the inaugural word of being and world: not rational *logos*, but rather that which the *phôné* presents, active voice, full presence, the revelation of the gods. The first of the poems consisted of "making" the *epos* like an object and depositing it in our midst: *epo-peia*. "The Nature of Language" (Heidegger's *Das Wesen der Sprache*, the French title in translation being *Le Déploiement de la parole*) from within divulged words, hidden in ambush at the site of the poem, in man's own stead, "the relationship of all relationships" (Lord 1975, pp. 9–10; *Iliade* II, vv. 484–92; Derrida 1973, pp. 15–16; Heidegger, pp. 57–108). All poetry aspires to being *made* voice, to *making itself* heard one day: to seizing what is individually incommunicable, where the message gets identified with the situation that engenders it, in such a way that it plays a stimulating role, a sort of call to action.

Therefore several cultures in the world work the voice of the poet as if it were material, imposing on it a highly valorized, conventional "mannerism" (often nasalized or high-pitched): so it is for the Zulu *imbongi* as well as for the Malian griots (whose code contains eight vocal modes), the Appalachian hillbilly singers or the *cantadores* of the Brazilian *sertão*. According to Dournes, modes of vocalizations are used by the Jorai to distinguish between poetic genres. In Tibet the *Ge-Sar* is sung in an ordinary register in the voice of a man as opposed to the falsetto of monastic ritual (Finnegan 1976, p. 137; Calame-Griaule 1965, pp. 485–87; Devereux; Rycroft; Dournes 1980; Vassal 1977, p. 61). These are manifestations of a universal tendency from which our own contemporary culture is not exempt.

From its initial outburst poetry aspires, like an ideal term, to purify itself from semantic constraints, to get outside language, ahead of a fullness where everything that is not simple presence would be abolished. Writing occults or represses this aspiration. Oral poetry, in contrast, welcomes its phantasms and tries to give them form; whence the universal processes that disrupt discourse: absurd phrases, repetitions accumulated to the point that meaning is exhausted, nonlexical phonic sequences, pure vocalisms. The cultural motivation varies; the effect remains. In Tibet, the epic song loses its force, so says a singer, if one does not intone the formula *ala-tha-la*, stripped of sense, three times repeated: is this an effect of the magic power of voice? The Fuegians salute the arrival of a guest with joyous vocalizations, abandoning themselves to this pure pleasure, like French teenagers I used to hear singing a popular American song without understanding a single word of English.

An effort at disalienating voice, the end result of which might be the field hollor of the black farmers of Louisiana, or the yodel that resembles it, a shepherd's song totally free of language, reduced to three notes and gleaning its effects merely from the contrast between the vocal registers; Swiss and Tyrolean folklore has spread it throughout Europe along with lederhosen and feathered hats. But the yodel does not reduce to this picturesque image. Physiologically conditioned by the natural milieu (solitude, the purity of the air), it has been heard from the Rockies to the Himalayas, in every massive high mountain region. Is this not like the emblematic realization of a total poem, one outside language? The same goes, perhaps, for the Inuit musical game *katadjak* (which means "threshold," "passage") found throughout the great Canadian North: a fragment of a sentence from a tale or a myth, a group of words posed as a riddle and repeated simultaneously by two women or two children, face to face, face touching face, until out of breath, progressively dwindling, eventually recognized only as an infinitely iterative syllable, a phoneme, and is finally reduced to the breathfulness of a breath, breaking out finally into laughter (Helffer, p. 431; Bowra 1962, pp. 64-66; Collier, pp. 21–23; Beaudry; Charron 1978b).

A worldwide speech, with no distinct signification but one that the body of the other fills with an allusive meaning while hearing it. The purified sound is identified with the "point of cessation," with the place and the instant of the lack where (close to all surface realizations) language cannot not "take the Fifth," like a witness might do. Dante long ago had an inkling of it, and the idea of poetry set forth in his *Convivio* and in his *De vulgari eloquentia* is based on the memory of an empty space where the pure sonority of speaking, one prior to all articulation, erupted on the first day, then during materialization, in a first sentence, in the form of a vocalic concert *a-u-i-e-o*—what in Latin takes on the appearance of the first person of a Verb (Rosolato 1968, p. 292; Milner 1978, pp. 38–39; Pézard, pp. 449–50, 591; Dragonetti, pp. 53–54; Vasse 1979, p. 134; Tomatis 1978, p. 17; Meschonnic 1975, pp. 60–68, and 1978, pp. 160–79). A fluidity between two unsaids (the absence of speech and interior speech), the locus of voice is the crux of the matrix, in the confines of absolute silence and the noise of the world, where it articulates itself on the contingency of our lives.

For this reason the poetic voice takes charge and stages a continuous knowledge, without breaks, homogeneous with the desire that sublates it. More than the tale (which Lévi-Strauss and Gehlen focused on), oral poetry constitutes, for cultural groups, a field of experimentation of self, making mastery of the world possible. The value judgments this speech arouses are founded on the qualities of voice, the vocal technique of the one reciting or of the singer, as much as or more than on the content of the message, a confirmation of what one knows.

For this reason again, voice, more so than writing now, assumes in poetry an explicit, erotic discourse. The only poetic form that in all cultural contexts creates itself in such an overwhelming fashion immediately accessible to the collectivity is the love song. In the diversity of its rhetorics it is fixed but always reinvented: speech outside time, outside space, indefinitely salted with reassuring formulas whose paradigm is the unspeakable call of desire; but also, constantly, a rupture and a new surging upward, a wish to tell of the new renewed (Gans, p. 131; Berthet, p. 130; Bellemin-Noël, p. 132; Durand, pp. 387-88). Raised up toward an unknown, unforeseeable subject, an empty listening, song, in its very enactment, reaches the real receiver, the desired one, the virtual future of the singer, his Other.

Still, through the course of their history, the cultures that human beings invented have inconsistently integrated the poetic values of voice. Africa remains—but for how long?—its triumphant soil. Yet, on the world scale, other factors seem to enter into play: societies deprived of visual arts, and those that live in a poor and austere natural milieu (generally the same), provide a privileged terrain for every type of oral poetry: in Africa itself, the Somalis of the desert, the peoples of the forest; in the Near East, the Bedouins; in central Asia, the Kazakhs; in India, the Gond; in Indochina, the Jorai; in the Arctic, the Inuit; and the Australian aborigines—as if the ecological misery, while suffocating other artistic activity, concentrated the energy of a civilization in the work of the voice (Finnegan 1978, pp. 13, 98–100, 224, 319; Winner, p. 29).

Whence, perhaps, the vital function song has assumed for our youth over the past twenty or thirty years, inside the intellectual, aesthetic, and moral poverty of the world that we have made for them. But at the same time, for reasons intrinsic to their art, for a growing number of newly arriving poets, so it seems, in the pale of writing, a quest is being mounted, though ever so slightly anarchic, for the lost values of the living voice. The custom, already an ancient one, of public readings and recitals used to consist in proffering a writing. The invention of the phonograph, which unfettered the materiality of voice, led Apollinaire and some of the first Cubists to use this instrument in a creative way, engraving thereupon those scandalous "vocal texts." For Ungaretti, voice alone could fix the text, the authority of which would emerge from recording rather than writing. Readings by the poets themselves were published on recordings: Ungaretti, certainly, Claudel, and before them, Céline, Joyce, Audiberti.

A movement—whose scope and long-term implications are still not yet fully comprehended—was taking shape, one that wasted no time reaching all the industrialized countries of the world: Henri Chopin has written an entire book on it. Already at the turn of this century, at the two extremes of Europe, Italian and Russian futurists confronted the masses in poetry tournaments. Around 1960–70, immense halls listened to Yevtushenko recite his verses, while readings in the Café le Métro in New York brought together some one hundred people twice a week to hear Jerome Rothenberg, Jackson McLow and friends. Other meeting places opened up thereafter, like Saint Mark's Church, a renaissance today commercialized on—the same research in Hungary, in Romania, as in New Zealand, in Canada, in Latin America. Each year an international competition is held in Amsterdam; "Nuits de la poésie" in Montreal have brought together surging masses. Nowadays poets write with an eye to performance, and this intention informs their language. Certain ones reject written mediation and improvise, modeling their discourse on the resources appropriate to the mouth, speech and silence, glottal stops, breathing, those of the body itself, pressing the microphone to their hearts so that the audience can hear their heart beat.

Yet, from Pierre Albert-Birot to Kurt Schwitters, Michel Seuphor or Paul de Vree—the precursors—to Henri Chopin, Novak, or Burroughs, "sonorous poetry" has taken on the proper form and situated its voice, integrating the *mediats* with the production of voice. Starting around 1950, in fits and starts, voice came to reflect critically on itself. In France the magazine-record *OU* would soon start publication; in Germany, Niklaus Einhorn was founding the *S-Press Tonband*, publishing reel-to-reel tapes and cassettes of poets such as Cage, Heidsieck, and McLow (Chopin, pp. 11, 43–52, 135–39, 259). In São Paolo, the Afro-Brazilian singer Caetano Veloso created a vocal drama in a marginally articulate language from a "concrete" text by Augusto de Campos. In France and in Germany, since the 1950s, the old need to make language burst apart has been at work both on graphics and sounds of a poetry called *spatial*. In the United States in the 1970s, *Talkings* by Rothenberg and poems in the anthology *Open Poetry* reorealized the discourse of writing, situating the "text" in the domain of coagulating vocal speech, where it is reclaimed by a radical *dialogism* (in the Bakhtinian sense of the word): that of an emergent language, in the energy of the event and the process that produced it there (Bologna 1981, section 2.6; Henry and Malleret, pp. 69–70; Garnier, pp. 15, 22, 41–80; Quasha, pp. 486–89).

Submersion at the bottom of voice: the twelve hours of recording for Belgian radio by Philippe Sollers, whose writing for many years now has had no other theme than voice, and whose *Paradis* without doubt has realized, as perfectly as is possible today, the polyphonic reconciliation of space and time, of living speech and the written word. Influenced more or less by the aesthetic of Max Bense, others choose to examine their relationship to language, the sensory import and polyvalence of that relationship. The writing-happening posits the utterance as a visual equivalent of the oral message.

The linguistic work of the voice is defined and evaluated by virtue of two parameters: modal and prosodic. I will return to this in chapter 10 when I discuss mode. With respect to prosody, I use this term in the most general sense to include all that that comes out of the rhythm of poetic speech.

The prosody of an oral poem refers to the prehistory of the spoken or sung text, to its prearticulatory genesis, the echo of which it interiorizes. For this reason most performances, whatever the cultural context, begin with a nonvocal prelude, the beating of an object, not with dance, the preliminary musical measure: the frame is thereby exposed, where voice is going to be deployed. Fundamentally, oral poetry has only prosodic *rules*. Okpewho, with respect to African genres, goes so far as to support the idea that this poetry does not have transmission of intelligible content as a function, rather only sounds and rhythms (Lord 1971, pp. 21–22; Kellogg, p. 531; Finnegan 1976, p. 239; Okpewho, p. 60; Meschonnic 1970, pp. 65–97, and 1981, pp. 31–39). A paradox, but not at all a countertruth. Rhythm *is* meaning, otherwise untranslatable into language.

At a high level of generalization, the notion of rhythm is applied equally to neurophysiology, to music, to poetry, and to history—all in one. One would, along with Lusson, call on a universal rhythmic human activity, an activity distinguished by ritual, pragmatics, techniques, aesthetics: with regard to poetry the *measure* is no longer included as a single quantity, but rather as a bundle of qualities. In this perspective, mathematics and music provide the only apparently effective language of analysis. I am thinking here of the research done by the Parisian group of the *Cahiers de poétique comparée*, and I place my work low in their hierarchy of concepts (Lusson 1973 and 1975).

Based as they are in the physical and, universally recognizable as such, rhythms are no less diversely perceived, exploited, and connoted from culture to culture. Cultural conditioning can atrophy certain perceptions and exaggerate others. In so doing, rhythm ceases to be primary: its absolute predominance in human activities would be established only at the end of a long historical trail, along which impasses would have been avoided. Perhaps African civilizations, enduring for millennia, have avoided them. It remains that, throughout the world, in the well-known words of Mayakovski, rhythm constitutes the magnetic force of the poem. By returning, voice systematizes an obsession; by syncope, it makes signs explode into a virtually hysterical symbolization: thus a knowledge freed of temporality, identified with life itself, the immemorial beating of life, is transmitted (Nettl, pp. 62–76; Lyotard, pp. 21–22).

Whence, at the very heart of a cultural tradition, the extraordinary resistance that rhythmic formulas offer to the usury of time—better than any other element of poetic art (rhetoric, themes, the social role itself), apt to maintain itself, unchanged or almost, beyond even the disintegration of a language, the overturning of the ideological context, the withering of an aesthetic, the geocultural displacements. The system of versification that the Romance languages used, from the High Middle Ages to the nineteenth century, and without any appreciable break during this millennium, prolonged the Latin system of the Low Empire, itself (taking into account the changes intervening in the nature of the accent) differing little from the classical system. The first Occitan troubadours around the year 1100 brought back from their travels among the Muslims of Spain the form of the *ghazal* that they adapted to their language, although by all appearances they knew no Arabic.

The very complex rhythmic impression that performance creates comes from the confluence of two series of factors: corporeal, therefore visual and tactile (I will treat this subject in chapter 11); and the vocal ones, therefore auditory. However, these last ones operate on two levels: first, that of the recurrences and the parallelisms (about which I wrote in chapter 7), producer of rhythmic effects at the level of the constructed phrases, of the motifs, of the words or the meaning, necessitating the mediation of linguistic knowledge and of a practiced auditory memory in order to be perceived; and second, that of the sonorous manipulations, even as immediately perceptible, in principle, in the ignorance of the language used: thus informed only by my experiences as a medievalist, one day while hearing a Pakistani poet in Lahore, I was able to identify with little difficulty a *ghazal* performed in Urdu, a language of which I do not know a single word.

The play of these diverse factors is projected into the proper space for the performance, engendering poetry there that is never the same. The game, however, is not without rules, imposed more or less *de rigueur* by a tradition, a style, a pattern, the artist faithful to himself and his inertia. Thus, the art of Zuni reciters recorded in 1966 in New Mexico by Tedlock consists of vocal modulations using silences, emphasis, tempo, volume, pitch, duration—all in a refined way. Tedlock, in publishing these texts, had recourse (in the manner of our written poets since Mallarmé) to typographic contrasts in the size, disposition, and spacing of characters, however insufficient to render this vocal gesturing. Each performance thus creates its own rhythmic system, even if the units used to make it are always the same. It may happen that some such games are superimposed on a system of regular versification: from there perhaps the nonlinguistic final *e*'s ("le cheval-*e* du roi"), some *s*'s or *t*'s that harmonize liaisons and that performance introduces, as variation, into many French folk songs as well as the Spanish *Romancero* and popular Italian poetry. Peul shepherds proffer their praise of their herds in a tone that requires the poet's full individual respiratory capacities: this open-air discourse, carried out within the moving herd, reels off four hundred syllables a minute (seventy between two breaths) in a loud voice, for a quarter of an hour without slowing down, without difficulty, in phonic clarity (Meschonnic 1970, pp. 65–69; Tedlock 1972; Menendez Pidal 1968, I, pp. 108–21; Seydou).

Most cultures, conversely, resort to conventional rhythmic systems, the norms of which are based in either musical or linguistic customs; in our contemporary music, these two criteria coexist and interfere.

The conventions founded on language-based features are pertinent only to the units felt to be the simplest: periodicity of accents, words, grammatical forms, figures, or sounds. In fact, the physical complexity of the latter offers several possibilities depending on whether the convention or usage privileges the oppositions of height, length, or intensity, valorizes the high or low pitched, the clear or the murky, the diffuse or the compact (Kibedi-Varga, pp. 110, 148, 149; Croquet, pp. 99–109; Lomax 1964).

The structure of natural language orients conventions. Between the third and fifth centuries, those who reigned over eloquence and poetry during the Roman Empire were overthrown by the evolution that made the oppositions of intensity prevail over those of duration in Latin phonology. Peoples speaking tonal languages (like the majority of Africans and many of the Far East) in the course of their history have focused on systems dependent either partially or entirely on the regularity of the *tones*—therefore on the oppositions of height about which it is impossible to furnish a legible written image by phoneticians. J.-D. Penel has recently sketched out an analysis of such a system in a hundred central African songs. Some cultures like those of the Luba in the Congo, the Burmans, and the Thais have made these oppositions enter into a set of complex rules, where they are combined with other linguistic features in unstable and highly significant contrivances (Fédry 1977b, p. 595; Penel, pp. 66–70; Finnegan 1976, p. 265, and 1977, pp. 96–98). An element intervenes here, one of such practical importance to the African scene that it has led some ethnologists to propose the classification of poetic rhythms into two groups according to which the movement of the voice is or is not coordinated with that of the body. The oral poetry of the Yoruba, one of the liveliest in Africa, has recourse, depending on little-studied schematizations, to tonal differences alone, to the extent that a Nigerian intellectual defined poetry as the art of tones.

At the communal origins of vital rhythms, of language and of poetry, the African imaginary has situated what the summary language of Westerners confuses under the label of "tom-tom" or "drum." One of the original characteristics of sub-Saharan civilizations is the importance of percussion in social functioning and linguistic comportment. Most certainly other peoples, like the Inuit, have attached a quasi-magical value to the "drums"; the gong for Buddhists, the church bell for Christians, belong to the same symbolic field. But the *dundun, cyondo, mudimba, lunkumwu, snambi,* and other "drums," with or without skins, in all shapes and sizes, utter true speech, exhale the breath of ancestors. A tribe deprived of its drums loses confidence in itself and breaks down (Charron 1978; Faik-Nzuji, pp. 19–22; Zadi 1977, pp. 451–52; Mutwa, p. 54; Jahn 1961, pp. 187, 214–15).

As source and mythical pattern for human discourses, the beating of drums accompanies in counterpoint the voice pronouncing phrases on which existence depends. It marks the base rhythm, sustains the movement that it animates with its syncopes and its downbeats, provoking and regulating handclapping, dance steps, gestures, arousing recurrent figures of language: by these, it is a constitutive part of the oral poetic "monument." In listening, percussion, able subtly to mark tonal differences, acts on the key event of language. The messages it transmits are not translated into an alphabet similar to our Morse code. Immediately intelligible, they are "spoken" by the drum in a register that is a language having a unique articulation, holding within itself diverse linguistic levels, the singular tonal level. To compensate for the ambiguities brought on by the disappearance of the other sonorous features (vocalic timbres, consonantal oppositions), a system of periphrastic formulas enables the substitution of a rather long figure for the "word" so as to facilitate its decoding by expanding the number of tonal combinations (Yondo, pp. 112–15; Ong 1977b; Alexandre 1969).

Used in this way, percussion constitutes, structurally, a poetic language. Handled expressively, as is the rule, the drummed sound is enriched by effects of intensity and melodic connotation that sometimes allow it—as, for example, with the Yoruba and the Akan—to relay the song in the course of its performance. It thereby assures the memorial conservation of discourse. It constitutes a specific and privileged oral tradition at the heart of Tradition: it conquers distance, for it carries for five to twenty kilometers; above all, it abolishes time, protects from its attacks. Slave owners in the New World understood this and prohibited the use of drums on their plantations. Its use, however, is transmitted and is maintained today in Haitian voodoo, Cuban *santeria,* and Brazilian *macumba.* Several ethnic groups possess veritable drummed poetic genres, like those of the *tumpani* of the Ewe of Togo: it was a *tumpani* that on April 27, 1960, proclaimed independence to the bush. They include very formalized announcements of public or private events; emblems or "drum names"; poems made from linked proverbs; invocations of divinities; and panegyrics. In 1923, R. S. Rattray published the transcription in both the local language and in English of a very long drummed poem that traced the history of an Ashanti group. He had recorded it just prior to publication in southern Ghana. Faik-Nzuji recently transcribed a dozen beautiful ritual Luba poems, one of which, beaten at funerals, contained more than a hundred rhythmic units, each from four to twenty-eight syllables long (Rouget, p. 120; Agblemagnon, pp. 128–31; Collier, p. 17; Okpewho, p. 62; Finnegan 1976, pp. 481–99; Faik-Nzuji, pp. 23–28).

The preceding considerations open up the singular perspective in which to ask the question: prose or verse? All cultures have created, while manipulating the acoustical elements of natural language, a secondary auditory level of language, some artifices of which put the rhythmical markings in order (Havelock, pp. 93–95; Milner 1982, pp. 285, 300). That is perhaps the principal aspect, the one that determines the others, of the "monumentalization" by means of which poetic discourse is constituted: domesticated, the rhythms of speech inscribe the mark of a human order in the universe.

Is this secondary level of rhythm identifiable with verse? The example of modern European languages inclines one to answer in the negative: the rhythmical richness of their literary styles is indifferent to conventional versification. But where can the line be drawn? If one slips in time (what was it in the Middle Ages?), in the cultural space (in China), or in the register (of the written to the oral), the picture is completely blurred. Does one get song to intervene—the question almost completely loses its meaning: a text composed without its own rhythmic structuration, if it is sung, assumes the rhythm of the melody in performance; thus, a passage from "Comment peut-on être breton?" by Morvan Lebesque, sung (and recorded) by the group Tri Yann in 1976 (Ben-Amos 1974, p. 281; Vassal 1980, p. 132).

In the Western tradition, the existence of distinct concepts of poetry and prose is part of our Greco-Roman heritage and depends more on antiquity's idea of *metrum* than on some natural fact. This notional group, once it is taken out of its limited sphere of application, threatens to lead to absurdities: have we not heard it said that oral "literature" is in verse in order to facilitate its memorization? The reverse evidence is found in the facts: the opposition verse/prose cannot be universalized (Marin, pp. 19–20; Finnegan 1977, pp. 26–27). The Hunga poet Nasir Udin, who used to sing for me in his native language (Burushaski), barely understood (although he was a good performer of Arabic and Persian poetry) my questions about meter: his answers indicated that he was playing, in a very personal way, the natural rhythms of his language, adapting them to the melody.

From 1925 on, Marcel Jousse rejected the distinction between prose and verse: such a distinction, according to him, had no meaning outside writing. Jousse restricted his definition to a "rhythmic oral style." This idea, a bit too short, can truly be applied only to pure oral facts, in societies with a long tradition: for example, in Polynesia, according to the analyses of N. Chadwick, or in a very general way, in black Africa. Various modalities of poetic language are distinguished there by the intensity of the effects of rhythm that they carry with them: effects realized in performance and thus tied to circumstance more than to a predetermined structure (Jakobson 1973, p. 69; Meschonnic 1981, p. 35; Chadwick 1942, p. 28; Jahn 1961, p. 189; Okpewho, pp. 154–55). The text, if by an artifice that isolates it from this context, appears prosodically to be almost formless: the voice of the performer formalizes it according to the concrete and immediate exigencies of a given music, a given dance, given exclamations or movements in the audience.

What is needed then so that at the heart of a "rhythmic oral style" there is what is properly called versification, such as we are familiar with in European languages? The relative constancy of a rather precise model, determining by brief discursive sequences; a rather clear separation of the measures (hence, popular European oral poetry has no enjambment): signals for beginning, end, even intermediary stop, or regulated division of pauses? These criteria are necessarily fluid and debatable. The same Zuni text, in verse for Tedlock, is not so for Hymes (Kidebi-Varga, pp. 43–46; Finnegan 1977, pp. 90–92; Hymes 1977, pp. 438–40, 451–52). Japanese experts hesitate: the *Heike* is prose for most of them but not for others; for an apprentice singer I consulted in Nagoya, however, this is but a war of words.

The uncertainty comes from the diverse levels of language lending themselves rather inconsistently to rhythmical equivalencies, to the "principle of metrical concordance" (according to Guéron), despite supposedly universal algorithms that would regulate its formation, or so they say. To see clearly in this matter, we lack a sufficient number of studies interpreting the genre such as those that Halle and Keyser have dedicated in generative terms to classical Arabic and Old English, or that Guéron has done for nursery rhymes; or on the historical level, Laforte's work on French songs in *laisses*. (Halle and Keyser; Guéron 1974, and 1975, pp. 142–54; Ruwet 1980, p. 22; Laforte 1981).

In the wake of some historical accident, two systems of versification based on different, if not contradictory, principles can coexist in one practice. The example of Latinity in the Low Empire is not an isolated occurrence. Turkish still uses an old syllabic versification for oral tradition alongside quantitative metrics from Arabic and Persian. Common usage and opinion attach an aesthetic or social connotation to concurrent systems: popular versus high, old versus modern, banal versus refined. According to Laforte, a popular French custom of song is opposed (if not at the level of principles, at least at their application) to a literary model (written or oral). Cirese expresses himself in similar terms with regard to Italian when he points out the syntactical formalism of folk verse (Chadwick and Zhirmunsky, p. 336; Cirese, p. 43).

In general, oral enactments of a system of versification are more limited than writing. Whereas individual writing, with the freedom that is its own property, easily evades the system by interiorizing it, voice can only ease it by forcing its rule on some particular point. In this way, in languages with a rigorous syllabic versification, oral poems often have hyper- or hypometrics: Acadian laments; Romanian ballads where the heptasyllable may float between five and eight feet according to the melody; epic verses in Old Spanish, if not, as has been claimed, in all epic verse. The activities of Brazilian improvisation artists as they vye with one another lead them to create—in a rather rigid verse framework inherited from the Middle Ages—numerous new types of verses or couplets, or to make the traditional rules more complicated (Edson Richmond, p. 90; Dupont, pp. 240–41; Knorring 1978, p. 14; Menendez Pidal 1968, I, pp. 89-90; Duggan 1975, p. 76; *Dicionario*, pp. 45–52).

However rich a given versification, the flexibility of its enactment and the harmonies made operative, it is almost always possible to discern its major point of fixation among the elements of the language: for the traditional French system, the number of syllables; for ancient Latin, their length. All the aspects of natural prosody can thus be valorized. Exterior influences, it is true, sometimes contribute to skewing the tendencies. In a part of Muslim Africa, the Arabic model has repressed several of the customs indigenous to local languages such as Hausa or Swahili. On a worldwide scale, the geographic distribution of the principal systems of versification does not always correspond to those of the families of languages (Finnegan 1976, pp. 73–76).

Several types of versification are distinguished, nonetheless, with relative clarity. They are, in fact, based respectively on (1) the syllabic quantity, by virtue of more or less complex alternating short and long schemata; (2) the distribution of tonalities, a distribution generally combined with another element, syllabication or alliteration; (3) the accent, combined or not with a syllabic count: Ainu epic verse has accents that the singer emphasizes by hitting some object; the Serbian epic verse, from eight to fifteen verses (most often, ten), has three accents, rarely four, distributed according to a precise rule; (4) the lexical or syntactic parallelism like that in the Psalms, or in the Zulu *izibonga*, which associate it, during performance, with a vocal modulation that makes the verse both a respiratory unit, a unit of meaning, and the panel of a diptych. This parallelism is combined with syllabication in the *Ulahingan* of the Manobo: a basic syntactic sequence, made up of seven syllables, or by a multiple of seven up to thirty-five, posits an utterance that will be repeated with little or no variation from one to four times; (5) the number of syllables, definitional for the majority of Far Eastern systems, from China to Indonesia. Often associated with some distributive rule touching on accents or tones, the syllabic count sometimes floats a little bit, as in epic Tibetan verse, in principle having seven syllables, in three or four syntactic segments; but, in the published versions of the *Ge-Sar*, a verse of five counts for eight, by means of adding on an initial element: an accident that seems to be thematically motivated. In the final univocal mark, an uncertainty about the limits of the verses: is the octosyllable of the *Romancero* truly one of them, or half of a verse of sixteen (Finnegan 1976, pp. 69–71, 129–30, 163, and 1977, pp. 93–94; Opland 1975, p. 196; Maquiso, p. 40; Guillermaz, pp. 20–25; Heiffer, pp. 427–30; Menendez Pidal 1968, I, pp. 92–99)?

And so certain peoples (and they are probably numerous) have rhythmic customs too vaguely coded for one to be able to speak about a system. Thus, the funeral songs of the Akan of Ghana, the great poetic genre of this ethnic group, display irregular and diffuse phonetic or tonal groupings, based on a rhythm marked by sobs, cries, pauses, and body movements.

Another factor differentiates systems: using (or not) stanzas or couplets to disrupt discourse at regular intervals. The distribution of these techniques does not coincide with the division of genres: the long epic, generally without interruptions is, in French medieval tradition, set off into "laisses," which make up the narrative units of the story; the short epic is generally stanzaic, but not in Romania, where during performance the story, as if by compensation, is punctuated by instrumental interludes. It has been thought possible to discern a geographic distribution based on regions of cultural influence (Fochi, chapter 4; Edson Richmond, pp. 82–83). In this hypothesis, the systems with interruptions would have originated in Northern and Western Europe. There is nothing profound in that. It is otherwise assured that a break, without exception, corresponds to a melodic repetition: in the simple type, like that of traditional European songs, the same melody is repeated for each couplet. The coincidence is neither general nor perfect.

Everywhere where versification is punctuated with breaks, oral poetry uses only a limited number of basic strophic forms, sometimes combined (rather than blended) into larger units. The study of the oldest medieval literatures and of modern folklore enables us to recover, in almost every case, the original distich, tercet, or quatrain: the quatrain itself here and there is less an autonomous rhythmic formula than the result of the consolidation of two distichs; thus, in many of the popular Mexican *coplas*, two verses of stock exposition are followed by two verses of gloss. English ballads, in contrast, are almost all in quatrains, and very few in distichs. The sestet comes from the conjunction of two tercets or of a quatrain and a tercet: the trace of the suture often remains obvious as much in the poetry of the Brazilian *cantadores* as in the folklore of Western Europe. Davenson saw an imitation of written poetry in couplets having more than six verses. All the while preserving a simple structure, these combinations can multiply over the course of time: Laforte catalogued (in a considerable collection of texts: seventy thousand volumes!) twenty-nine types of couplets in French folk songs (Alatorre 1975, p. xxiv; Fonseca 1981, pp. 121–40; Davenson, p. 17; Laforte 1976, pp. 26–29, 43–52).

In many languages, the poetic structuration of rhythm includes, beyond those accentual, quantitative, or tonal elements of natural prosody, the timbre of sounds:

a complex phenomenon, for which it is possible to distinguish at least two aspects, namely, the phonematic suites and their harmonic potential (Nyeki, p. 127; Coquet, p. 100). Written poetry in the West has valorized the effects of this order to such an extent (as if to erase the tarnish of writing!) that it sometimes seems to be completely drained. Oral poetry plays with it with less subtlety, but with more panache.

It has occurred that one uses them as marks of the vocal unity of discourse: hence it is in dialogued genres that, in order to confirm the organic space between the parties, the diverse sonorous recurrences will unite. In the texture of the message, every repetition of a phoneme starts a rhythmical chain: to break it or to prolong it is a decision that comes from the individual art of the poet, one enlightened and oriented by tradition. The African griots demonstrate a mind-boggling virtuosity in this, and certain Brazilian *cantadores* are scarcely less proficient. Tibetan, Nepalese, and Mongol singers obtain analogous results, thanks to a particular morphology in their languages by doubling or tripling the radicals or particles by highly semanticized terms (Heiffer, pp. 381–87; *Dicionario*, p. 17; Finnegan 1978, p. 39). In the multiplicity of possible sonorous echos, the majority of versification systems have valorized and regulated one or two of them: alliteration and rhyme. The first involves the initial consonants of words and is realized in long series; the second involves final syllables and is realized in couples or in short series.

Alliteration constitutes a necessary rhythmic element in the poetic practices of some traditional societies. So it is for the Somalians; for the Mongols it marks the initial syllable of several consecutive verses. The Anglo-Saxons of the High Middle Ages alliterated all the accentuated words of the verse. As for rhyme, it has been argued that in the pure form of identical syllables, repeating at regular intervals in syntactically corresponding positions, it appears in oral poetry only in those societies that have a rather general written output (Finnegan 1977, p. 96). And so one can explain the rhythmic perfection of the Malay *pantun* or of English ballads by means of the cultural context and the coexistence of a literature.

It could be doubted. The fact remains that in versifications with rhyme, the identity of the rhyming syllables is rare in oral poetry: rhyme is reduced to the vowel, or even the closeness of two vowels with a similar articulation (*oi* rhymes with *a* in popular French songs); if the consonants that follow are different, the rhyme is nothing more than *assonance*, the most frequent form in popular European poetry and that can even be found in Fiji, associated with parallelism. Less frequently, *consonance* assures the recurrence of consonants, but not of vowels, and is closer to alliteration.

All these processes join together in most oral poetics; one of them in general has more weight in the mind of its performers and their public, without eliminating the other. It is felt to be constitutive of verse; the others are only "figures." Hence, in Romanian ballads, the rhyme of which is manipulated adroitly by some singers, this rhyme, according to Knorringa, is less important to the system than alliteration and assonance (Finnegan 1978, p. 473; Knorringa 1978, p. 15). In traditions (like that of Homeric poetry) that have not regulated acoustical echoes for being such, these echoes can nevertheless constitute essential figures for the performance, in the same way that the length of phonemes does for French verse.

Localization of rhyme or assonance in the verse also varies: at the beginning, in the alliterative form for the popular Finnish tradition, as for the Romance and Germanic languages; at the caesura, as in certain medieval, Latin, or vulgar styles. The systems based on syntactic parallelism include in agglutinate language a rhyming effect with a grammatical origin: an identical suffix necessarily repeats in the verse at fixed intervals. Certaom Turkish languages of Asia have drawn a rule from this particularity (Chadwick and Zhirmunsky, pp. 337–38). With respect to the distribution of "rhyming places" throughout the poem as a whole, it depends on the local traditions and probably on the abilities of the performers. Introducing rhyme or assonance into a system of oral versification does not imply that it affects all the verses. Far from it: many, if not most, texts rhyme only one verse out of two, three, or more at random intervals — for example, the Acadian laments, a large number of French songs, and English ballads. The intervals seem, on the contrary, to be regular in the Hispanic *Romancero* and in the traditions through which it is maintained in Latin America.

The quality of the sound is in general abandoned to the invention and talent of the poet. Some societies, however, seem to have introduced on this point a norm, if not a rule. I have already discerned traces of it and noted the recurrent effects in the works of the twelfth-century *trouvères*. Buchan was able thereby to extract the dominant tendencies determining the choice of rhymes and assonances in the English ballads. Mongol singers artistically spread out verse by verse their language's two classes of vowels (Zumthor 1972, pp. 220–23; Buchan, pp. 151–55; Finnegan 1978, p. 39).

Chapter 10
The Vocal Work II

In the ordinary use of language, what is *spoken* (*le parlé*, but here less ambiguously, *le dit*) uses only a small part of the resources of voice; neither the amplitude nor the richness of the timbre of voice is linguistically pertinent. The role of the vocal organ is to emit audible sounds conforming to the rules of a given phonematic system that does not come from any physiological exigencies, but rather makes up a pure negativity, a nonsubstance. Voice remains in retirement, on reserve, denying its own freedom. Yet being so removed, voice sometimes breaks forth, shakes off its restraints (even if it entails accepting other, positive, ones): *song* (*le chant*) thus arises, scattering voice's abilities, and (through the priority accorded these abilities) disalienating speech.

Spoken, language makes voice its servant; sung, language exalts the power of voice but, in so doing, speech is magnified—although at the price of some obscured meanings and a certain opacity of discourse: speech is magnified less as language than as affirmation of power. The mythic values of live voice are thereby exalted. The voice of Thoth, the Egyptian god of speech, of magical formulas and of writing, is heard like a song. An equivocal power, it musters its defenses: the physiology of the vocal cords alone did not motivate the Italian tradition of vocally as well as sexually inoffensive castrati. When Giovan Batista Veluti (he being the last of the castrati) died around 1800, something had changed in the profound relationship of Western man to his voice (Bologna 1981, sections 1.8 and 2.1; Schneider, p. 173).

Song arises more from musical art than from grammar; as such, it is classified among the manifestations of a privileged signifying practice, probably the least inept at touching the umbilical space of the subject in us, there where the symbolic order of a culture is articulated upon natural powers (Ruwet 1972, pp. 41–49). In the *spoken* the physical presence of the speaker is more or less attenuated; it tends to blend into the circumstances. In song, it is affirmed, claims for itself the totality of its space. For this reason most poetic performances, in all civilizations, have always been sung; and in today's world, song, despite its debasement in the commercial sector, constitutes the only veritable mass poetry.

Through this relationship of opposition between the *said* and the *sung*, then, I can define the *mode* of performance.

Yet, here once again, arises the question: where is the line drawn? The cultural milieu conditions the feelings each of us has about these differences. What the voice of the African griot proffers is, for his ethnic group, neither speech nor song, but rather an utterance both pleasant and mysterious where forces, perhaps quite formidable ones, circulate. Those of the blues—commonly called *talking* to separate them from the others in the American South—constitute a discourse with a strongly accentuated rhythm, slipping deftly into sung episodes and set apart from ordinary speaking, but somewhat conforming to local customs. What passes here for song would elsewhere be speech with sound effects (Oster, p. 259; Finnegan 1977, pp. 118–19; Bouquiaux and Thomas, III, pp. 902–14; Calame-Griaule 1965, p. 490; Lotman 1970, pp. 70–75; Werner, pp. 102–27). Empirically the existence not of two but of three modalities is accepted: spoken voice (in French, *dit*), measured recitation or psalmody (in English, to *chant*), and melodic song (in English, to *sing*). Medieval liturgists used a similar scale, limiting the extension of the first term, *recitatio* to the *dit* rendered poetic by an artificial rhythm.

The *dit* of oral poetry, marked in this fashion, is found along a continuum with the recitative, and the latter differs from song only in scope. From one to the other, slippages are produced. Every society, every tradition, every style sets up its own safety catch. Ethnography would incline me to presuppose that there is song in every oral poetry and that every oral poetic genre is also a musical genre, even if the users fail to recognize it as such. This affirmation needs modification, based on factual proofs in particular cases. Cultures, over the course of time, have inconsistently and varyingly valorized voice; I noted this in chapter 9. From this stems the diversity of criteria. The Manobo, according to Maquiso, associate song with every sacred discourse, to the extent that one of them, converted to Christianity, would sing his prayers in the mode of the *Ulahingan*, instead of saying them. There is a people in Asia who sing all their activities, private or social; another group speaks them. In Africa, song and poetry are not consciously differentiated and those people who European travelers since the eighteenth century have been calling *griots*, and have rightly been presenting as professional musicians, the Arabs have been designating by a word that means "poets" (Bausinger, p. 247; Maquiso, p. 42; Chadwick and Zhirmunsky, pp. 214, 218; Collier, p. 8; Camara, p. 5).

What is being questioned here is a foundational element of all culture: the nature of the mutation that is operative in the physical link between sound and language, at the very moment when the poetic "monument" emerges. In a perspective opened up by Schopenhauer and Nietzsche a century ago, melody was made out to be the original principle of all poetry: the musical matrix nurturing the desire for the poem to come (Nietzsche, pp. 52–66; Calame-Griaule 1965, p. 528; Vincent, p. 25; Durand, pp. 386, 400–403; Rosolato 1968, p. 297; Rouget, pp. 185–88, 433–34). By necessity, it is instrumental or it is song, that is to say, a modality of language; and this modality constitutes, to use Calame-Griaule's expression, the "maximum of speech": the eminent manifestation of the magic of voice, the archetypical Orpheus, assumed by all our mythologies, even current ones. For the Native Americans of the mountains, song is a sonorous dream: it opens a passage toward the world from where it comes. For us, it gives form to a power about which we know only one thing: that it is going to reconcile oppositions and master time.

Whence, once again, the universality of "love songs": song eroticizes discourse far beyond meaning and desire. Music slips into the gaps of language, works its corpus, sows it with its own mythic projects: in the most inconsequential of our songs there still shines an extremely ancient incantatory fire, the echo of rituals in which the shaman evokes his "trips" (in the sense that drug users make of the word), the interiorized memory of the secret chant intoned on the athanor by the alchemists of the Renaissance.

A culture acts on the individuals forming the social group like a continuous program; it provides them with gestures, words, ideas, according to each situation. But, at the same time, it proposes techniques of disalienation for them, offers them areas of refuge, from where to banish, at least fictively, undesirable drives. Art constitutes its principal technique; but, of all the arts, the only one that is absolutely universal is song.

The idea and the naming of culture thus imply the activity, throughout its duration, of a *song function*, one vital to the society in question. This profound need accounts in part for a major episode in European history: the creation of opera, over which, lest we forget, the Orphic myth presided! In 1600, Peri's *Euridice*, and seven years later Monteverdi's *Orfeo*, fixed a genre in which humanists, preoccupied with restoring the power of music by connecting it indissolubly to poetry, believed they had found the Greek model for this harmony. In fact, they reestablished unbeknownst to themselves the modern equivalent of archaic rituals of trance and possession (Bowra 1962, p. 241; Rouget, pp. 327–37). But this new art, conceived of as the highest form of song, appeared and spread in the era when, throughout the West, writing and the visual were triumphing within a literate culture and for several centuries would put a damper on the values of voice.

Alban Berg in his 1930 preface to *Lulu* listed six "degrees of musicality" that make up a continuous spectrum: what is simply spoken; what is spoken with orchestral accompaniment, without rhythmic constraints; what is spoken with the orchestra and include tempo; somewhat sung speech; half-sung speech; and sung speech. (The terms used here are those used by Orlando, who in answer to a question, discussed this passage with me. I have not been able to examine the German original.) Songs performed spontaneously by young children provide a comparable gamut of modalities. A sort of spoken-rhythmed mode predominates in the youngest, but rather quickly, depending on the abilities of the individual, is transformed into what an adult can recognize as a song.

None of the distinctions thus delineated has any absolute pertinence. They contain meaning only as applied to the description of a concrete performance and relative to that performance. The griot Amadou Jeebaate, renowned today in Gambia, uses two modalities of speech when he executes an episode of the Mandingo *Sundiata*: one with rhythm (and instrumental accompaniment), the other sung; the parts sung are in a different dialect (B); however, certain rhythmic parts, also in dialect B, cut into the story (in dialect A), attributing, as if parenthetically, praise to subsequent characters; all the passages in dialect B recur at more or less equal intervals. The extreme complexity of the textual and vocal relationships engendered by such a system prohibits any simplifying reduction. In the execution of Romanian ballads, "song" alternates with the "recitative" in accordance with local customs. Certain performers sing the entire text; others recite up to 60 percent of the poem. The same fluctuations are found in the performances of the Manobo *Ulahingan*; the same holds for the Jorai of Indochina. From one to the other of these modes, the tempo becomes fluid, ceases to be perceived; rhythm is what abides. Some African epic singers use this difference, depending on the situation, to create expressive effects. Tibetan singers of the *Ge-Sar* use two modes, one of which is clearly melodic, but for which no rule presides over their distribution; and each performer plays their alternation to his own liking (*Recueil,* pp. 108–25; Fochi, pp. 109–15; Maquiso, pp. 4–38; Dournes 1980; Okpewho, pp. 214–15).

Some contemporary singers, Brassens, Montand, and others, have exploited modal contrasts of this type: contrasts free of a possible division of the text into "verse" and "prose." In a stringently versified composition by the Irishman Percy French, the spoken intervenes regularly into the sung, like a modal refrain (Finnegan 1978, pp. 196–97). A number of African ethnic groups have systematized such alternations. The author of the performance combines story and song, according to various procedures and customs: part of the story is sung, the rest spoken; or as well, a refrain, sung by the audience, marks articulations in the story; or then again, a poem of praise or lyrical effusion is intoned at a particular pathetic moment. For the Xhosa, the genre of story called *intsomi* is often built on a song whose theme it makes explicit: whence the mobility of the narrative element (Eno Belinga 1970; Agblemagnon, p. 142; Finnegan 1976, pp. 244–47; Vansina 1971, p. 453).

From the dramatic circumstances of certain collective performances, there emanates an emotionally charged unanimity of design. The affirmation of self, by the voice of the group, is triumphant in choral song—the "Marseillaise" or the "International"—or perhaps it requires rhythmic scansion alone, strongly accentuated by the number of voices in unison, as one used to hear in the "speaking choirs" of the 1930s or around 1970 at the Swiss meetings in the Jura where the people would intone a refrain of a poem by Voisard.

However much "music" and "poetic text" (in the broadest sense of these two terms) perform together, does not one predominate over the other in the listener's mind? The relationship uniting them is neither simple nor constant. An ideal gradation seems to be drawn: at one extreme there would be a discretely rhythmic and slightly melodic diction leaving the text to impose its force and weight, as does the epic; at the other, such as an operatic aria moving by the pure musicality of voice, the words have little to do with it. Having traversed the long space separating these extremes, does one still feel "inside" the realm of poetry, or rather has one crossed over into music? Has one gone over the line that demarcates the separate domains wherein the full sovereignty of each one of these arts is practiced? Where does one put the romantic lied, like those written by Schubert in 1813–14 based on texts by Schiller and Goethe (Massin, pp. 550–59).

Gradation is not really what is at question here. The values attached to human voice prohibit the conception of a degree zero. Even when intervening as a simple expressive support, to emphasize the words, scansion and melody project a new dimension into the space of the poem: "vocal structuration" creates a specific form (see chapter 1). In the epic, across the lied all the way to the operatic aria, what is produced is less a slow passage of pure poetry into pure music than a progressive investment of poetic language by musicality. In the extreme case, the text becomes inaudible, such as on the lips of the Xhosa bards or rock singers; for peoples like the Russian Tcheremisse, the Watusi of Africa, the polar Inuit, it gets diluted into syllables that are scarcely articulated (Oplang 1975, p. 190; Bologna 1981, section 2.1; Hauser).

There are no steps in this movement, no scales to number. Each performance as a rule yields to an evaluation of the expressive powers at play and of the relation that is established between them. But this evaluation is made by virtue of the parameters of which the listener is not always conscious: it depends, in fact, on the extent of the means of execution, on the intention presiding over reception, and on cultural habits.

As for the means, they involve both the melodic richness (on the far end of the scale, the performer is a virtuoso) and the strength of the orchestration (instruments, number of voices engaged in the song). These two qualities can be dissociated; their effects are comparable. (I will have more to say about this.)

As for reception, a certain "horizon of expection" determines it: circumstances, opinion, publicity, and my own desire lead me to participate in a given performance *qua* concert, show, poetry recitation; once this schema is formulated, it becomes difficult not to remain its prisoner. For such an audience Schiller's mediocre poem *An die Freude* taints the "Hymn to Joy" of the Ninth Symphony from which, as a poem, one cannot isolate it. For the music lover it matters little: the platitudes of Maeterlinck, depending on the disposition of the spectator, destroy *Pelléas et Mélisande*, or the music by Debussy, in contrast, can divert attention from their prattle. In the Brazilian *cantorias*, neither the singers nor the public seem to valorize the musical part, although it is definitional for the genre: judgments that at various intervening moments accompany performance weigh on the rhythm of the verses, never on the song: one complains if a syllable is missing, but a wrong note passes unnoticed (Fonseca 1979, p. 192).

Custom, collective prejudice, ideologies all enter, in the final analysis, into the ability of the performers as well as audience members to perceive a separation between the two arts joined together in song, and to think about the relationships they entertain. Traditional African societies do not seem to recognize a difference any greater than that between "verse" and "prose" (Jahn 1961, p. 102; Calame-Griaule 1965, pp. 527–42; Camara, pp. 115–23; Laya, p. 178; Okpewho, pp. 57–58; Lomax 1964). Spoken discourse is for them only a degradation of song. The word is maintained over the course of time by its musical quality (whence so many texts that have become obscure, even incomprehensible), but it is as speech that it remains effective in rites.

Africa, for this reason, is exemplary and brings to its achievement what elsewhere remains a partial tendency or a failed evolution. One could set up the inventory of these universal "Africanisms," memories of the mythical time when language and music were one. In the most diverse regions of the world, ethnologists have remarked the impossibility for many oral poets to recite one of their texts without singing it. Does not the mystical or communal trance that Rouger describes—sought after and provoked by African cults, but observed also in several Islamic and Christian sects—involve the most formidable effort (even unto death) to erase all distinction between speech, music, and dance (Okpewho, pp. 58–60; Rouget, pp. 428–31).

From the bottom of a world broken apart by the corruption of writing there arise in our own day and age calls for this unity. It is not enough to focus on oralizing poetry, as I have indicated in chapter 9, one must *sing* it. The efforts by poets like Luc Berimont have culminated in attenuating the indifference and the deafness of the literary milieu in France. The early death of Brassens (which occurred as I was writing this chapter) is unanimously deplored as that of a great poet: he is placed in the lineage of Villon so as better to pass on the news; in fact, it *does* pass. Many composers since the Renaissance have put texts of poet-writers to music. But this custom, in the 1950s and 1960s, was renewed along the aesthetic and social lines of the cabaret song: Aragon's poems sung by Catherine Sauvage, or Verlaine's *Gaspard Hauser* done by Moustaki. More recently, Angelo Branduardi, a strong peasant "rocker," based his first songs on the texts of Essenine and Neruda, seizing on this poetry as raw material for music, spectacle, incapable of living otherwise.

Poetic speech, voice, melody—text, energy, acoustical form—actively united in performance cooperate in the singularity of a meaning. Too few detailed studies up until now have focused on this semiosis. The remarkable work by Amzulescu and Vicol on the Romanian ballad have merely opened the door. The typology for which they have laid the bases gives value to the intensity of the semantic exchanges between text and melody, to the extent that their dissociation would render the poem absurd (Amzulescu 1970; Vicol; Knorringa 1978, pp. 15–8). Scattered remarks by ethnologists or comments by performers confirm this point of view. It is at the level of meaning that the union is sealed: the meaning is its gauge; the rest flows from it. In societies with vast epic collections, the performance of which never exhausts the telling, it often happens that the characters or the episodes are stamped with a musical mark that is used to identify them. This is true of the Tibetan *Ge-Sar*, the principal witness being Ms. Helffer, who used thirteen characteristic "timbres," assuring us that each hero of the poem had his own, but that no singer could know them all. The singers of the Japanese *Heike* distinguish nine modes of recitative depending on the theme of the passage. The Manobo song of the *Ulahingan* has four tones: two of them (one more melodic, the other heavily scanned) alternate in the tale; the other two are used, within exact guidelines, at precise moments of the performance (Alatorre 1975, p. xix; Helffer, pp. 463–503; Maquiso, p. 41).

The use of refrains interferes with the production of meaning. Technically, the refrain is a recurrent musical phrase (sometimes instrumental), chopping the song into subunits, and the performance into distinct moments; a verbal phrase is generally associated with it. Three types of phrase-refrains coexist and can, in exceptional cases, coalesce: the first uses rhythm, rhyme, or number to wrap up each segment into a unified *and* regularized versification system; the second forms an autonomous unit between what comes before and what after; the third is connected, however autonomous it may appear, to the preceding unit by a melodic or verbal signal (Laforte 1976, pp. 117–20; Roy 1981).

The semantic effect thus produced either reinforces the signification of the preceding or subsequent parts, or it introduces a new, independent, often allusive, ambiguous, even intentionally contrastive element into the ambient scenario. The autonomy and the mobility of the refrain favor intertextual games: text or melody can reproduce or parody earlier song, or some written or oral poem.

Some traditions can be established, such as the one that led court poets in thirteenth-century France to draw a number of their refrains from peasant dance songs. Such examples of are innumerable and are found in all cultures.

I am drawing near to the practice of musical intertextuality, frequently found in European poetry, as well as in Chinese, and not unknown elsewhere: the use of "timbre," a tune taken from a preexisting song and for which the author adapts a new text, even if it entails over time, if the tradition endures, the timbre's being more or less altered. In this way a considerable number of "popular" European songs perpetuate Gregorian melodies, court music, operatic arias. Conversely, in a crisscross of sacred and profane, Christmas carols and canticals have popular melodies taken from pastorals and lover's laments (Laforte 1976, pp. 108–12; Guillermaz, p. 20; Brecy, p. 11). In the eighteenth and nineteenth centuries in France, most widely popular political, satirical, and protest songs were composed on timbre; certain ones were called *vaudevilles*. Beginning in 1717, Ballard published the *Clef des chansonniers* (the *Guide for Songsters*), a repertoire of melodies dedicated to this purpose.

In opposition to timbre, there stands improvisation, to which I shall return in chapter 12, it being an ambiguous term that refers indistinctly to melody and words: one can be improvised and not the other, or vice versa. What are, on the other hand, the limits of what is improvised? I will discuss in chapter 14 the variants for oral poetry: but, in pushing it to the limit, one would have to consider in good faith every variant, even infinitesimal ones, as improvisation. The oral poet, more so than the writer who has at his disposal the time lapse of writing, works in an artisanal frame, a workshop where there is at his reach not only tools but prefabricated materials (musical and verbal) that are not entirely raw. In traditional societies, using these fragments is absolutely required; elsewhere, they are products of a transitory style, launched by a fashion, and do no more than propose themselves for the poet's use.

Here, too, where is the line drawn? The poet Nasir Udin assured me that he re-creates his melody at each performance by means of an internal need. In fact, he has at his disposition a treasury of rhythms and melodic schemata whose bases inhabit the popular music of the Hunza, and from among which at the moment of intoning, he chooses what he needs to form his song. Does he improvise? I was unable to convey what I meant by this word to him. The text of his song had been prepared, and done in a very "literary" way. The melody reinterpreted it, in subsequent and changing circumstances in such a way as to fulfill all expectations. Certain cultures have created analogously improvised oral poetic genres, ones defined by this very character—at least at the beginning, for the vagaries of beginner's luck inevitably brought about written intervention: hence the blues, improvised on a traditional, highly formalized base; hence also the original flamenco (Oster, p. 267; Wurm, pp. 71–74).

When an instrumental accompaniment resonates with song, the two musics are conjoined in the operation of voice. And yet always a tension is drawn: through the acoustical difference there passes a functional demarcation. Whence the ruses instigated by certain customs: the Brazilian *cantadores* alterate voice and instrument during the performance. Then again, they use, as do most epic singers in the world, only a single instrument, a viola or a guitar. But, the greater the number or diversity of the accompanying instruments grows, the greater the tendency to weaken the formal requirements intrinsic to the poem. The eventual result would be a symphonic orchestration with some scarcely audible, banal words, unless the song, once it became choral, assumed a breadth and complexity sufficient to its reimposition—but would not one thereby exceed the definition of "poetry"?

Probably, within this competition, there is a moment of equilibrium in which the instrument confirms the voice: in French as in Italian, within the etymology of the word "accord" (in tune), heart, concord, and the chord of the lyre all coexist. Accord, being "in tune," nonetheless cannot be identical in all cultures. In Africa, the mythic value attached to musical instruments joins them irrevocably to human voice in a common signifying word. In Malinke, the same word means "to speak" and "to beat drums." Warnings and taboos for the use of various instruments include the entire social group in all aspects of its life. Senghor declared around 1960 that he writes his poems in the desire to hear them sung accompanied by African instruments, that is, in the fullness of their meaning (Camara, pp. 51, 106, 115–19; Guibert, pp. 144–50).

It has been noted that the rhythmic and heterometric complexity increases from group to group, as one moves from east to west across the black continent, and reaches its greatest wealth along the western seaboard, from Senegal to Nigeria (Okpewho, p. 62): the very regions from which were uprooted millions of those who, as slaves in the New World, eventually created "Afro-American" music in the Antilles, Brazil, and the southern United States. This music, which for a half century now has spread around the globe, has reintroduced into our minds an almost magical feeling about the sonorous object. It can be doubted that without this influence the guitar (itself a product of Spain) would have assumed the value of a cultural symbol that it enjoys today across three continents, nor that the spectacular use of the electric guitar by Bob Dylan in Newport in 1965 would have provoked such an uproar.

The instrument has been sacralized (but was not the *biwa* of the Japanese *Heike* singers as imbued with divine power?); fetishism has become so profoundly anchored today in mass culture that it functions as well in the opposite direction; the Cuban *salsa* is the "sauce" of the trumpet, the flute and the saxophone amplified and dramatized by congas and maracas for Ruben Blad's songs in the magnificent voice of Celia Cruz. But there is no regional movement in Europe that, folklore or not, does not try to reinstate traditional instruments, for example, the Basque *xalaparta*, the Armorican *biniou-braz*. In Chile, too, during the 1960s, the *tumbadura*, the *bongo*, and the *rabel* of the Andes were sought after. Cabaret musicians that I met in Bangui lay aside imported and expensive instruments like guitars and saxophones in favor of traditional harps, flutes, and tambourines, ones that they could build and repair themselves, financial necessity forcing a return to the basics.

The primitive forms of what Collier circumspectly calls the "popular music of American Blacks" were slowly set apart from the old traditions of African song and influenced by melodies and instrumentation from Europe in nineteenth-century Louisiana. This long process of maturation ended around 1900. During the second decade of the century, black music—both vocal and instrumental—invaded the United States; ten years later, it reached Europe at the same time as "Negro art" was coming up from colonial Africa and was beginning to disturb the once immutable modes of art appreciation, heretofore identified with "nature." A war had just revealed the failure of so-called modern society, the disintegration of which had begun and that henceforth would survive only as a referential myth.

History was offering this revenge to Africa, after slavery and cultural genocide—before the independence movements, that derisorily were devoted to the same myth! The musical revolution unleashed around 1915 by some black bands in New Orleans has spread so far from its homeland and has known such amplifications that its original features are more than a little changed: but not the essentials, strong enough to have modified the musical taste and habits of the masses on three continents in less than two generations and to have overthrown the presuppositions of an aesthetic (Jahn 1968, p. 65; Collier, pp. 16–42, 57–94). The rhythmic innovations of Stravinski in the same period, the implantation of the serial system, came from a perfectly assimilated classical tradition. Jazz was going to Africanize the world.

Strongly outlined are accentuated tones, syncopes, and double-beat rhythms for which the percussion instrument provides the base, upon which the clarinet, trombone, and saxophone are set apart in jazz and toward which voice counterpoint moves. Speech loses the monotony that syntactic regularity engenders; discourse is constructed polymetrically: the periodic return of a moment in which all measures are superimposed assures its coordination and force, and assumes in its unity the adventitious rhythms of alliteration, paronomasia, and anaphora. From primitive jazz to the avatars of rock and reggae, styles, inspirations, and designs have evolved. The verbal elements of such an art almost inevitably escape the formal norms stemming from the practices of writing: undoubtedly they are no longer even perceived as "poetry," but as a component of a total action. Aesthetic distance is crushed, that which would have enabled the identification of the song as an autonomous art. A massive unity is forged in the depths of a consciousness. The function of the text loses all clarity; its paucity and its mediocrity often cancel its impact: only music and dance remain. But therein lies the result less of a system than of the insufficiency of many authors. In the United States, the work of Langston Hughes has been proof for more than twenty years of the possibility of a jazz in which speech, both purposeful and active, preserves its power, its right, its ability to persuade. In France someone like Boris Vian has made up beautiful songs based on a great variety of "modern" rhythms, parodies of rock and roll composed with Henri Salvador in his attempts to create a jazz song or French blues (Jahn 1961, pp. 100–101, 187–088; Collier, pp. 88–122, 139–40; Rouget, pp. 105, 430; Jemie; Clouzet 1966, pp. 82–85).

These musical practices require another, different type of verbalization. Few poets have yet explored these dangerous zones: the experiences to which the poets of writing have for a half century now devoted themselves concerning words and grammar constitute at best, for an oral poetry yet to come, a preliminary clearing off, the sketching out of usable strategies: not that they remain too close to some sort of absolute threshold; but they unfurl themselves in a direction and by means that are not those of voice. They remain, with respect to voice, out of phase.

Yet these are mental tendencies and practices appropriate to traditions of pure orality that confer — in a way provocative in the midst of our world of writing — their original nuance to the music of Afro-American provenance: the frequency of improvisation, the accessory role of the written in the composition, moreover often the work of an instrumentalist; the predominating wish to establish an immediate contact with the listener; a general design of communicating rather than pleasing. Whence the violent coming to consciousness provoked by the musical revolution of the least conventional writers on both sides of the Atlantic. In writing, disquieting memories are revived. In 1939 there appeared in Havana an anthology of Afro-Cuban poetry with rumba rhythms. The American "Beat generation" borrowed its name from what was for a time a style of jazz. Kerouac was said to get his language from Parker and Monk more than from a literary tradition, and he compared the Proustian sentence to that of Miles Davis on the trumpet (Collier, p. 76). In France, where Cocteau had already discovered the blues, an alchemy was perpetrated in the work of Boris Vian, trumpeter and chronicler of jazz: *l'Ecume des Jours* is no less vocal than the songs.

This entire art stays fundamentally (despite various misadventures) connected to speech, to explicit language formed in the throat and on the lips. It maintains the intermittent memory of one of its roots: these revivals in black churches in the South, so saturated with the presence of African music that they evoke voodoo; collective ectasies in which, with respect to the holy place, hands alone continue the percussion: the first spirituals, brought forth the day after the Civil War, and the Gospel; then, their profane equivalent, the blues, a genre, in my opinion, that is the most accomplished of contemporary oral poetry. As a concise and rigorous form, like the sonnet of long ago was in the perfect equilibrium of its twelve measures, three by three, on a quarter-time rhythm, a verbal phrase by a musical phrase, but always shorter than the musical one, and the obligatory recurrences, highlighted by a guitar *cauda*. In "classical" blues the curve of the vocal part lets us hear again the ancient structure of the antiphonal chant of traditional Africa: the continuous phrase in a unique voice has replaced alternating solo and chorus. The instruments have relayed this latter, but hereafter they are subordinated to the dominant function, the song. Contrary to a common notion, it would be impossible to say that the blues are an individual song, as opposed to the collectivity of spirituals. In its deepest motivations, the blues depends on the common destiny of a downtrodden people; by its implicit finality, it returns to this people. Whence its "sadness," produced technically by the "blue notes," between major and minor, equivocal, impossible to play on the piano and perhaps stemming from the "intermediary tone" of West African languages (Jahn 1961, pp. 252–62; Oster, pp. 260–61; Vassal 1977, pp. 42–44; Collier, pp. 38–39).

The diffusion of these types of musical poetry spreading out suddenly with such energy in the region of the Caribbean and tropical America was bound to touch *Africa mater*. It did so with violence, but provoked—a return shock—in urban and Westernized milieus first curiosity, then a new passion for traditional song, the practice of which continued in the bush and forest. Since independence, in several large equatorial cities—Lagos, Douala, Brazzaville, and above all Kinshasa—groups of singers set themselves the task of re-creating a music integrated with contemporary modes based on genres practiced in the villages. The political commitment that these forays generally carry with them, and the necessity of getting an explicit message across, confer such an importance on the words that they find their autonomy in instrumentation. Local stars like Jean Bikoko or Anne-Marie Nzie of Cameroon synthesize Afro-American styles and popular forms like the Beti *assiko* or the *mokassa*: a necessary rupture in the invention, ceaselessly reiterated by adherence to only the universal musical model of today, linking the five continents on a background of jazz and Brazilian, Argentinian, and Cuban dance.

The function of these neo-African composers differs little from that played by singers elsewhere who quest after the living roots of humanity in and among a hodgepodge of folklore: Alan Stivell in Brittany, Maria Del Mar in Catalonia. It brings to mind the role that the great voices of American folk-rock, Bob Dylan and Phil Ochs in the 1960s, had assumed between a rural folk-song—socially implied by its themes and the defrocking of its language, but technically rudimentary—and an urban rock and roll, coming from the blues and already completely commercialized. Thanks to musical regeneration, song redeemed speech (Vassal 1977, pp. 260–61).

Chapter 11
The Presence of the Body

Orality cannot be reduced to vocal action. As an expansion of the body, vocality does not exhaust orality. Indeed, it implies everything in us that is addressed to the other, be it a mute gesture, a look. In chapters 1 and 10 when I spoke of "vocal structuration," I meant to emphasize the specificity of *oral* poetry. Perhaps, however, it would be better to use "corporeal structuration." Gestures and looks, in fact, are of equal concern. In the following pages, I will subsume both under the terms "gesture" and "gesturality."

Body movements are thus integrated into a poetics. Empirically, one notes the astonishing permanence that associates gesture and utterance (both in long-standing traditions and for those with sequential modes): a gestural model is part of the "competence" of the "interpreter" [in the French sense of *interprète*, i.e., actor — Trans.] and is projected into performance. The *actio* of Roman rhetoric had no other objective. Whence for the audience member-spectator, a complementary expectation and, during the action, a progressive transfer of the desire that animates the gesture of the performer, culminating in a collective trance, imposing, as the offbeat of jazz singers, its discontinuities into the midst of an equilibrium, nervous jumps into the stream of time. Most probably this is only an extreme manifestation of the ever-present vitality that connects the speech being formed to the look that is given and to the image it gives us of the body of the other and of his clothing (Calame-Griaule 1980 and 1982). The actor-interpreter, during the performance that exhibits his body and its setting, does not call on visuality alone. He opens himself up to contact. I hear him, see him, virtually touch him: a very close virtuality, one strongly eroticized; a nothing, an offered hand would suffice—an impression that is all the stronger and more repressed should the audience member belong to a culture that prohibits touch in its social relationships. Another, internal, tactility is awakened: I feel my body moving, I am going to dance.

Certain cultures have developed a more spectacular gesturality than others and have better exploited its expressive potential. Whence the interest in ethnology since its inception: in 1881, Mallery published his observations on the "sign language" of Plains Indians, a work that was reprinted ninety years later! Mauss's studies, "Les techniques du corps," and Jousse's *Anthropologie du geste*, however outdated, are nonetheless classics; and the bibliography already contains five hundred entries. Starting in 1909, a medievalist was involved on his own along these lines; K. von Amira analyzed the elements of juridical gesturality in the *Sachsenspiegel* miniatures, a repository of German customs written around 1400. Nothing, however, of any importance followed it until Le Goff's and Schmitt's works at the end of the 1970s (Le Goff, pp. 352–401; Schmitt 1978a and b; Fédry 1978a; Guiraud, pp. 49–59, 72–91; no. 10 [1968] in *Langage*).

The problem, on the contrary, had arisen ten years earlier rather urgently in the Africanist camp. Africa, once again, the universe of gesture as much as of voice, provided a privileged field of observation. The vast and beautiful thesis by Gasarabwe, written in 1973 and published five years later, presents gesture as a rite. Within a meaning-producing space, rite situates and confirms a world of lived experience, but such a world without that space, would begin to lose its reality. In a similar vein, Derive put forth a system of written translation of performance that allows the integration of tonal and gestural movements (Gasarabwe, pp. 69–166; Derive, pp. 62–63, 95–102, 188–241).

The execution and placement of gestures, in a given cultural milieu, cannot be completely aleatory. Are they coded? If so, how and to just what extent? Is gesturality homologous to language? At best, certainly, a gesture can be analyzed by its discrete features; but these features are combined directly into signifying units, without the intermediary articulations inherent in linguistic signs and that assure them a possibility of variations in an unlimited number. Assuming and exceeding ethnographic information, American semiology of the 1960s seized on these questions. The extremely technical nature of most of these works and their research, often exclusive of quantifiable and systematic elements, significantly reduces their usefulness for the poetician. The analysis of gesture in its relationship with voice modulations necessitates methods not yet developed. Material accumulated thus far has at least afforded a beginning synthesis of some general anthropological interest in the work published by V. and F. Bäuml in 1975 (Sebeok, pp. 1–6; Mounin; Cosnier; Bäuml; Berthet, pp. 141–42).

Nevertheless, the relationship between gesture and the other elements of performance does not cause problems at the level of meaning. Even if the performer leaves none of his gestures up to chance, certain ones will signify and others simply attract my attention, my emotions, my goodwill. Certain ones set up a corporeal staging; others simulate speech. And yet no gesture is exact; gesture always has an outline, one that is also temporal duration: Is there not a point in the outline, an instant in the duration, when meaning emerges, when it attains its fullness, when it is laid bare? In passing from convention to "realistic" mime, can gesture be called arbitrary or motivated?

Calame-Griaule, in one of the first essays expressly to formulate the problem, distinguished two types of opposing gestures: "descriptive" (mimetic) and "social" (conventional), each of them containing several subtypes. She thus reoriented Thomas's summary classification of gestures into "formulaic" and "indicative or expletive" gestures (to which were added the "gestures of intonation') in accordance with ethnolinguistic data. Jason in the United States in 1977 arrived at a similar perspective. Insofar as the complex relationship of gesturality to language is concerned, it seems today that it requires three series of definitions, depending on the extent to which the gesture redundantly completes the speech act; that in specifying the speech act, it dissipates any ambiguity about the act; or finally that, in substituting itself for speech, it provides the spectator with information that betrays the unsaid. Scheub, in a remarkable study of Xhosa storytellers, adopted this formula, but completed it with two essential points. He showed, in fact, the existence of gestures having a purely rhythmic function, gestures correlated to the musicality of the performance and not directly to language. He also recalled the semantic depth of certain gestures, ones laden with temporally variable cultural symbols, ones able to be reinvested with new values at each performance (Calame-Griaule 1976, pp. 919–26; Thomas, p. 415; Jason 1977, p. 105; Cosnier; Scheub 1977, pp. 355–59).

I shall adopt here a pragmatic view and distinguish only between gestures based on the size of the space within which they are deployed:

(1) Facial gestures (looks and mime);
(2) Upper body gestures (head and chest);
(3) Gestures using the whole body.

Together they contain meaning in the manner of hieroglyphics. Gesture transcribes nothing, rather it produces figuratively the messages of the body. Gesturality is defined therefore (as is utterance) in terms of its distance, tension, and patterns rather than as a system of signs. It is less governed by a code (if not in an always incomplete and local way) than submitted to a norm.

This norm, in turn, comes from a structuration of behavior, one tied into social existence: gestural *savoir-faire* is an art that no culture (not even anticulture) lacks. Yet, the more an art of the body is elaborated and wants to distance itself from banalities, the more it is wrapped up in a network of rules and regulations rendered explicit by an adequating pedagogy: Bouissac demonstrated this regarding the circus. From appropriate civil behavior to ballet, a continuity is maintained despite several intermediary steps. All the imaginable forms of poetic performance are distributed along the varying degrees of this scale. In the most strictly formalized performances (like those of the Japanese *rakugo*) (Zumthor 1981a), the codification of gesture seems to dominate that of the text. On the contrary, however, in those performances least dependent on circumstances and most approximate with respect to norms, does not every song contain, at least by way of the mouth, its own articulatory dance?

In whatever manner the social group orients it or limits it, the function of gesture in performance exhibits the primary link that attaches poetry to the human body — what Jousse expressed in speaking about verbal-motor art, or the ancient Chinese in denoting lyric by a term associated with the idea of a foot tapping on the ground. In an essay on Andalusian poetry meant to justify his own activities, Lorca insisted on the magical origins of the arts for which the body is the instrument and argued that a late historical development alone has dissociated dance, music, and poetry (Wang, p. 356; Baumgarten, pp. 328–29; Derrida 1967a, pp. 260–62, 284). To this we can attribute the profound inability of these arts (despite all appearances and all the erroneous truisms) to "express" what is individual. More than to written poetry, this paradox is applied to oral poetry, which (in the way that Artaud understood it in theater) requires a totality, challenges the interpretive distance, eliminates allegory and all that, by means of its forcefulness, separates the sign: from speech, breath.

Written poetry, it is true, is created by strategies that allow it to integrate the approximate equivalent of some gesture into its text: always partial, ambiguous, conditional. This is the source of its aspiration to reject these subterfuges, to recast itself as voice and dance. In oral poetry, the text has immediate recourse to such markers: to the body to modalize discourse, to explain its design (Scheub 1977, pp. 351, 354; Thomas, p. 414). Gesture engenders the external form of the poem in space. It grounds the poem's temporal unit, by a scansion of its recurrences. In the monologue of the griot, dance must surge forth from time to time so that the story may progress.

Contemporaneous corporeal expression links gestures of all sorts in a series. A movement of the entire body is generally accompanied by a gesticulation of the arms and head as well as by miming and a particular look. Poetic performance can suspend this chain intentionally and admit as pertinent only the gesture of the face, or that of the arm or some nonexpressive dance. Poetic vocality, I have already shown, sometimes confers a function on silence: likewise, gesturality can integrate "degree zero gestures" in a significant way. The Jorai myth singers make no gestures, according to Dournes. Houis has provided me with African examples where the speaker was perfectly immobile. Photographs obtained for me by one of my students working on the *Ulahingan* show a singer seated at a kitchen table, forearms flat, the upper chest and head stationary, with a distant look. Droplets of sweat, I have been told, bead on the back of his neck. Undoubtedly the feeling of sacredness, the presence of ancestors in the discourse, perhaps the remains of a tradition of initiatory teachings motivate this immobility — unless either a sexual or social taboo intervenes, one that is analogous to the Touareg one that prohibits the reciter from making any gestures while he exercises his art before his father-in-law (Dournes 1980; Calame-Griaule 1980).

Mime by itself or a look by itself (to the exclusion of all other gestures) is rarely encountered in performance when the performer wants to provoke a "zero effect" in the rest of the corporeal space. A contradiction here opposes materiality and meaning: the limitations of the possible movements of the face, despite the eminent symbolic value of the organs it contains. Most cultures have reduced this weakness in two ways: (1) by makeup, which increases the scope and visibility of gesture (hence, for us, that of the actor, of the singer, under the stage lights or in the spotlights and, more significantly, that of the clown); or (2) by masks, which fix the features beyond all gestural possibility. Certainly, in traditional civilizations, the figurations of the mask introduce the wearer and its spectators at once into the mythical universe to which they aspire, for example, masked dances duplicating certain Tibetan rites. But it is at the level of a face that the mystery is accomplished. Yet, from the face the voice wells up, and the mask necessarily muffles it or amplifies it. The Dogon have invented the mute mask; that of the Northwest American Kwakiutl is shaped in such a way as to denature the voice of its wearer. The Western tradition, from Greek tragedy to medieval carnivals and the *commedia dell'arte*, offers a rich variety of examples: always discourse arises from an emblematic and immobilized face (Stein 1978, pp. 246–47; Bologna 1981 section 2.1; Finnegan 1976, pp. 509–15).

Several cultures, certain traditions, and some artists in their individual practices attach an exclusive value in performance to the gestures of the upper members of the body and the head, gestures perhaps associated with mime, perhaps not. It is enough to impose a seated position on the performer to make any movement of the body altogether impossible. In the Japanese *rakugo*, for example, the extreme economy of authorized gestures permits the actor to use only his hand, forearm, and head. And the gestures of Tuareg reciters are inscribed in what Calame-Griaule calls the "storyteller's square," a space whose extreme dimensions go from the belt to the back of the head and from one hand to other of half-open arms (Zumthor 1981a, pp. 28–29; Calame-Griaule 1980). Hence, as well, beyond language, the seated dances of Bali. If the performer holds a musical instrument, like the Cameroonian *mvet* singers do, this additional constraint prevents him from making hand movements.

When the performance requires the figuration of the entire body, the figuration can be accomplished in two ways, although not necessarily combined:

statically, as posture, or dynamically as "dance" — modulating a discourse (this will be mime), or what is properly called dance.

Mime normally shapes and surrounds poetic performance in all cultures. Totally present, the body plays the discourse. The scope of the incorporated movements, the degree of dramatization can differ greatly — it does not matter. In Africa, where tales mimic each other, certain ones (for the Ewe and the Yoruba) are barely distinguishable from what would for us be theater. In the Bobo funeral ceremonies of Upper Volta, dances, songs, and discourses imitate sequences of events in the life of the deceased, his tics, the timbre of his voice, his walk. The few remaining epic tale tellers in Japan today mime their stories like actors. Jelly Roll Morton, the illustrious jazzman of the twenties, prided himself on having invented *stomps*, those pieces of rhythmic provocation meant to get the audience moving (Collier, p. 95.)

From *mime* to *dance*, the opposition arises from the same general order, gradual and uncertain, as that from prose to verse, and from the *said* to the sung. In and of themselves the end terms of the series are not rigorously defined. I would define mimes as those half-dances that make up — their rhythms from artisanal gestures or the emotional outbursts of stylized grieving — the majority of work songs or laments like those that I saw in the Central African Republic. On the other hand, dance will be those collective movements symbolically accompanying the war chants of western Africa (Finnegan 1976, pp. 153, 208–11, 238).

Dance, in fact, inverts the relationship of poetry to body. When dance is accompanied by song, the song prolongs and underscores a movement, illuminates it: discourse glosses gesture, as does the song a Nepalese bard sings while dancing among the workers planting rice. And it is not simply by chance that the first diffusion of jazz in the United States coincided with the "dance boom" that somewhere around 1910 replaced the panting figures of polkas and waltzes with ragtime rhythms and rocking and sliding movements (Gaborieau, p. 236; Collier, pp. 76–77). The institution of dance halls, characteristic of our culture, came about at this time.

It is true that many dances, mute as they are, do not as such concern poetry. However, the absence of speech takes ascendancy sometimes as an index and arouses a meaning complementary to that which the corporeal movement engenders. Such is the case for masked African dances, the silence of which is interpreted ritually as something beyond language. It is also the case perhaps for dances whose movements are linked in a rather easily "readable" narration for the sake of the audience: our pantomime; the Tibetan *cham*, closely tied to Lamaic ritual, and the danced processions of medieval Christianity (Calame-Griaule 1965, pp. 523–26; Stein 1978, pp. 245–46). The purely corporeally moving arabesque of what is disdainfully called a "belly dance" spatializes the interplay of the flute, drum, and the entire orchestra: the entire body of the dancer, made musical, becomes song within its very materiality.

The line that separates such spectacles as Western ballet from the Japanese *ma* of Hideyuki Yano is not clear. All human cultures seem to collaborate in some vast theater of the body, in infinitely varied demonstrations, in techniques as diverse as our everyday gestures. On this "corporal" stage oral poetry where suddenly it appears as one of the actions that plays itself out there. For this reason, during a performance, unless strictly prohibited, the performer passes from immobile mime to dance, from dance to "looks" and draws from these contrasts a harmony that is all the more intense as it is perceived in the midst of a perfect unity. Sometimes, while the entire body is moving and participates, one of its gestures is more laden with meaning than the others: hence Indian dances in which the essential message comes from hand movements, the rest of the body only forming the context (Ikegami, pp. 389–90).

Dance is that pure pleasure, corporeal motion without the pretext that it is, by that very fact, conscious of itself. From solitary dancing to dancing as a couple to dancing collectively, the warm perception of possible unanimity grows. A contract is renewed, signed by the body, sealed in the effigy of its momentarily freed form.

Dance exhausts the qualities common to all human gestures in their plenitude. It exposes what is elsewhere occulted; reveals the repressed; makes latent eroticism burst forth. The traditional dances of Africa—still grafted on the movement of the first word, memory of a cosmogonic libido anterior to the desires with which it is filled—impudently testify to it. While the West experienced the triumph of the model of writing, Europe, by tricking its slaves, became frightfully aware of this art. *Calinda* from Guinea, *yucca*, and the subsequent *rumba* (whose name may have meant "umbilicus" in the Kongo language): a dancer improvises a song to which the spectators take up the rhythmic refrain by clapping hands, men and women together, a potential orgy justifying condemnation by Baptists and repression by masters. Some Incan dances evoking the same mysteries of genesis had already succumbed to the same fate, although surviving even today clandestinely (Jahn 1961, pp. 83–84, Collier, p. 67; Valderama, p. 310).

Being an irreversible time of pure *differance* between successive tensions, beyond figural representations, sensual enjoyment (*jouissance*) rather than pleasure: dance precedes song itself. According to Bowra, it issues forth from the rite whereby the human body imposes its order on the Universe. Ancient Chinese wisdom conferred on it the role of guarding the world in its proper course and confining nature to goodness. Mastering space, dance and gesture come no less from inside (Bowra 1962, p. 241; Huizinga, p. 14; Ong 1967, pp. 157–58). They evolve during the performance, like voice: a figure of lifelike life; but, unlike life, one can stop them with a look, fix them, paint them, make statues of them. For this reason they are affirmation rather than knowledge, and less proof than test.

In several archaic cultures, a danced poetry accompanies the production and manipulation of fire: its rubbing, the sparking flame, the forge, a symbolic mirror where a primordial realization of irreducible likenesses is reflected. In this light song is no more than the verbalized aspect of dance, and dance requires a particular aptitude, one tied to the possession of a power. Hence, Malian griots traditionally hold title to the realm of public speaking and govern certain dances. Female—but never male—amateurs (it is significant) may under exceptional circumstances dance them, but then the style gets modified: when the griot gives a show, the woman succumbs to symbolic action, for her power is other, as is her body. In the Nigerain *Ozidi*, epic speech itself returns to silence from time to time and leaves to dance alone the stylized figuration of collective actions, battles, navigation, the evocation of spirits; the reciter of the *Mwindo* epic interrupts himself to dance the songs that he inserts into his tale (Durand, pp. 385–88; Camara, pp. 108–15; Okpewho, pp. 52–54).

Such is the anthropological background of "danced songs" or the "dance songs" that every known culture possesses, and this undoubtedly represents a primary phenomenon of all poetry. The ritual origins for many of these songs is still palpable in Africa, as it was not long ago in the Hawaiian hula, where poetry, music, and choreography constituted a liturgy for the patronage of the goddess Laka (Finnegan 1978, p. 256); similar rituals were performed in the European countryside, until two or three centuries ago, involving maypoles or Saint John's fires.

In group songs—either of figures, as in the square dances still prevalent in North America, or in circles or chains as in the Provençal *farandole*—gesture and voice, regulating one another, cement the unity of the game and reveal a common plan. But circumstances manage to dramatize it; it is the community of a destiny that is sealed. The cohesive effect of rhythm can increase by using taps, hand-clapping, or other means of a forceful scansion. The part sung, accompanied or not, is generally done by a soloist or a choir, and the dancers take up its echo or answer it with a ritornelle; hence, probably, for most medieval dances, from which the modern technique of songs with refrains seems to have come. Closer at hand we have the eighteenth-century *branle*, which in 1792 may have given its rhythm to the *Carmagnole* (unless the latter was based on the melody of some Marseillaise dance spread by the Federalists), and the Breton *kan ha diskan*, brought back to honor in the 1950s by the Goadec sisters. Conversely, in Africa today, as yesterday for Native Americans, here and there in European folklores, a solo dancer performs in the middle of a circle formed by the singer-spectators to whom the unanimity of their double function ties him (Burke, pp. 114–15; Brécy, p. 16; Vassal 1980, pp. 59–60). The "basket dance" that I saw the Pima Indians of Arizona perform celebrates springtime and evokes the fertility of the earth in movements of a mute choir of women, while immobile singers comment on this mystery.

Couple dances, such as those that we still do today, seem appropriate to modern Western society. More obviously (but superficially) connoted by eroticism than are our group dances, the former symbolize, from one partner to the other, the play of their desire, without integrating it in any explicit manner into collective cycles. The golden age of these dances coincided, throughout the seventeenth, eighteenth, and nineteenth centuries, with that of the triumphant bourgeoisie. For this reason undoubtedly the profession of the dance master is disappearing from our lives. From the already remote days of the charleston, and even more so since the Second World War, dance for us, still in rhythm with the song of the soloist, has once again become a collective festivity, dissociating couples into disalienated individuals, but, at the same time, plunging them in a unanimous unfettering: a return to what the tango was before being borrowed by Europeans, a psychodrama for the proletariat of Buenos Aires.

The text of these dance songs, determined by its function, is related to the gesture it verbalizes. It may be brief, cut short, reduced to a call, an allusive exclamation, a maxim; or larger, extended to broad strophic returns lending themselves to emotional modulations and to mythic evocations. The necessary regular recurrence or rhythmic units—gestural, vocal, instrumental, and consequently, textual—makes, conversely, the composition of explicitly narrative dance songs almost impossible. We can cite some isolated examples: Faeroe islanders used to dance to the singing of heroic ballads; sixteenth- and seventeenth-century Spaniards danced to recitations of the *Romancero* (Menendez Pidal describes a ball of this type that he attended in August 1930).

Once ancient rituals begin to be disarticulated, an unceasing movement is established between dance songs and the other forms of oral poetry. In the French tradition, from the fifteenth century on, dance couplets were composed on the melodic framework of popular songs, or vice versa: the "Court ballet" of the seventeenth century made this practice a common occurrence. In the eighteenth century, parodying songs, ariettas from the Foire theater, and songs from the Caveau all used tunes taken from opera ballets. In the nineteenth century, most dances were accompanied by songs or used "tunes" from other compositions. Records and radio have reinforced this double movement, and the history of song since the twenties would be impossible to recount without that of dance. It happens sometimes that we dance to a hit song (for example, Boris Vian's "Déserteur") that was not written for that purpose: without undergoing any formal modification, the text thereby changes its function but not its nature. We can logically maintain that the dance song no longer exists for us as a genre (Vernillat and Charpentreau, pp. 75–77).

What the contemporary world, in the disruption of traditional values, seems to have effectively rediscovered, in a savage and impassioned way, is the totalizing function of dance—one that excludes generic distinctions. For the Chiripa Indians, the dance leader was designated by a name signifying "song master," and symbolically that was understood to mean the carrier of the sacred message (Clastres, p. 62; Herkovits, p. 276). But is not this circularity—linguistic, aesthetic, mental—common to most purely oral cultures what young people alienated by our centuries of writing seek pathetically to recompose, to close up again, in festivals and discotheques, in the trepidatious mediocrity of hit songs, beyond the sundering of body and language?

The body wears clothes, finery; indissociable from them, however, the relationship that connects them may differ. Apparel in fact can or cannot be codified, amplified or not amplified by accessories. The kimono, the scarf (*foulard*), the fantail of the *rakugo* storyteller are rigorously codified, as are the belt, the knife, the scarf, and its knots for the gaucho singer. There remains a margin of variation: the color of the kimono, the form of the knots. Insofar as accessories are concerned, they are sometimes only one of the musical or vocal instruments of the performance, on which an eminent value is thereby conferred, one as deictic as symbolic: the guitar or the microphone, in the stylized usage our singers make of them (Zumthor 1981a, pp. 29–30; Anido, pp. 163–67).

The clothing of the performer assumes various values. Neutral, deprived of eccentric signals, it blends the reciter or the singer into the audience, from whom he is distinguished only by his role as *porte-voix*, perhaps highlighted by this apparent banality: such is the Romanian ballad singer in a Carpathian village, among the drinkers with their caps and their knit vests, he belongs to them; such is the old North American Quebecois storyteller, in jeans and pullover, seated on the steps of his prefab house; such are French cabaret singers.

In other circumstances, the clothing coincides by its general style or by some notable detail with the ornamentation of human beings themselves, thus presented as outside the common, associated with current stereotypes of beauty or power in the social group where they exhibit their art. Crests of wild animal skins and cowries, fur robes pieced in geometric designs, multicolor blouses of Guinean griots, the heavy jewelry of their women accompanists, the antimony grey eyelids, the lips bleeding with kola, and our silvery harnesses on rock singers, the sailors' peacoats of the Dexys Midnight Runners. Seydou Camara, the epic singer recorded by Bird, wore the same outfit, covered with amulets, as the hero of his poem; Rureke, the *Mwindo* singer, holds the scepter of his hero in his right hand; the *Ozidi* singer, his hero's sword (Camara, p. 112; Ma, pp. 93–94; Okpewho, p. 43). Ritual traditions interfere; or perhaps the ornament is ritualized: a threshold is soon crossed. Beyond that it is no longer the person but the function he or she provisionally incarnates: sacred or profane symbols, emblems by which lived or dreamed experiences of a collectivity are perpetuated, colored finery and hairdos of the traditional Pekinese theater, the leather shirts of Vince Taylor, if not more recently Maurice Chevalier's straw hat. Cosnier's experiences prove the importance of the role played by visual elements in the impression that the words addressed to the audience make on it if not on the very interpretation itself. The performance exploits this feature of nature.

Moreover, the rite inverts itself, erasing the presence of the person for the sake of a fictive, paradoxical, or negating function: the clothing becomes disguise, completed on the spot by a mask. However, taking into account some archaic rituals or occasionally even today satirical songs during Carnival parades, such an occurrence is rare in the practice of oral poetry. Performance seems to repudiate this legerdemain of the personality from which voice emanates.

Beyond the body, the "setting" — all that which falls under the gaze is sometimes controlled in the same way and with as much rigor as clothing: we are reaching here, in interconnected forms, the confines where oral poetry becomes theater, totalization of the space of an act. Ending up with a design integrated into oral poetry from its primal song, theater remains to date at each performance a virtuality completely ready to be realized.

Gesture, clothing, setting, and voice are projected into the space of the performance. But the elements that constitute them one by one — corporeal movements, forms, colors, tonalities, and the words of language — together compose a symbolic code of *space*. Place, space: according to the words of Certeau, are opposed as language is to speech; system to mobility; arrangement to speed; appropriation of what gets juxtaposed and coexists as the show plays on (Certeau, p. 208; Scheub 1977, p. 345). In seventeenth-and eighteenth-century Europe, singers and actors in the marketplace under the international appellation of *saltimbanci, mountebanks, Bankelsängers*, by means of their acrobatics gave birth to the space where their voice was deployed — like Peter Townshend, the rocker of "My Generation," anthem of the 1960s, coming onstage in a fireman's get-up, a glass in his hand, a boxing glove around his neck, breaking microphones and amplifiers with the noise of firecrackers. The repetition or syncopation of gestural units coincides with those of vocal accents and linguistic forms: in harmony or intentional dissonance, it confirms its cohesion, encloses in this space the time frame outside the time of discourse. The "pure" form of the oral poetic work is what remains from the dimension given to its space by gesture within memory after words are silenced. Such is the aesthetic experience of performance.

Yet this space is not identical with the extent of perception alone. Partially qualitative, it grounds symbols, provides an operative zone for the "fantastic function" designated by Gilbert Durand. In the space of geometries, the actions that make up our destinies are inscribed; in the space of performance an action engenders itself from itself, casting a spell over destiny (Sartre, p. 165; Durand, pp. 472–80; Ong 1967, pp. 163–67; Durand 1981). Whence the euphemism of gesture, whatever its visual aspect. For this reason, the idea — however obscured—that gesture is but an ornament of oral poetry is enough to pervert and sterilize all interpretation. What gesture re-creates, longingly, is a sacred space-time. Voice, personalized, resacralizes the profaned itinerary of existence.

Part IV
Roles and Functions

Chapter 12
The Interpreter

In the preceding chapters I have used the word "poet" to indicate the one who, executing a performance, is at what is perceived as the source of the oral poem. It was a provisional simplification. Poet subsumes several roles, depending on whether it is a matter of composing the text or speaking it; and, more often, in more complex cases it is a matter of composing it, composing the music for it, singing it or accompanying it with instruments.

These roles can be filled by the same person or by several people, individually or in a group. The diversity of possible combinations largely accounts for the extreme variety apparent in oral poetry. It engenders misunderstandings by literary historians. Our attitudes, fashioned by practices of writing, push us to join the ideas of text and author; at the same time, our sensitivity, distorted over the past one hundred years, leads us to identify (I already indicated this in chapter 1) oral poetry and folklore, that is to say, anonymity and impersonal traditions.

None of these prejudices accounts for the facts. The distribution of roles, in the production of the oral work depends only minimally on the cultural conditions. Africa offers as many examples of performers who are not composers as the opposite, and the composition of the text does not always coincide with that of a melody. Yet, do the variations in performance of a traditional song make the performer an author? I return to this question in chapter 14. For the French, Boris Vian performed works for which he had composed both text and music, or text alone, music alone or neither one nor the other. Brassens and Brel usually sang their own poems, but wrote texts and musical scores sung by other people. Most rock singers are authors of texts, composers, *and* musician-singers; but this unity dissolves when, the music having crossed the ocean, a French songwriter like Claude Carrere or "Jil and Jan" translates the American original (Finnegan 1976, pp. 105–6, 266; Hoffmann and Leduc, pp. 41–42; Vassal 1975, p. 172). Of one hundred songs selected piecemeal from the 1960s, and not sung by their composers, I count forty-four for which text and music are by the same author; fifty-six are by different authors.

Still, shall we not consider a collaboration, however secondary, and one that constitutes a major part of the work of a writer and musician (like Prevert and Kosma some time ago) to be somehow equal? Would it be worthwhile to take the qualitative disproportion that sometimes exists between roles into account: mediocre songwriter versus talented musician, or both being no more than sources for a popular singer? From this stems a functional hierarchization that impinges on the mode of reception of the work. Finally, would it be correct to classify separately songs that derive from putting to music poems written for other purposes, poems often from long ago and by writers recognized as poets, for example, Aragon's verses put to music by Leo Ferre? We are all the more hesitant given that, in our experience, a song rarely belongs to the exclusive repertory of a singer: one of the roles is then, in fact, mobile. All things considered, the same holds for the oral poetry of traditional societies.

The "free" performance does not differ essentially from the former: an individual, without any particular qualifications, sings or recites — for himself or for others — a preexisting poem or perhaps one that he has composed himself, either by embroidering on another text, another melody, or by producing an original work. The pure pleasure of singing or telling motivates him; or as well, an event that has taken place in the group, provokes joy, irony, or anger.

In every exercise of oral poetry, the role of the performer counts more than that of the composer(s). Not that it eclipses it entirely, but it is apparent in the performance that it contributes all the more to determining auditory, corporeal, emotive reactions of the audience, the nature and the intensity of its pleasure. The action of the composer, preliminary to the performance, depends on a still virtual work. As happens every day, no less than what took place in earlier oral civilizations, a song is spontaneously associated with the name of the one who executes it in such circumstances; a traditional hymn, with the social or vocal quality of a given singer. To refer to the author is the mark of literacy.

From this, perhaps, comes the idea that oral poetry, without exception, is anonymous. The term deceives us if we do not specify the poetic roles on which it depends. Lacourcière assured us, with respect to the folktales and songs of Quebec, that the "author" is not a role in oral literature: the "work" comes to us thanks to a chain of intermediaries of whom we may at best know only the most recent ones (Lacourcière, p. 224). This abrupt judgment reflects a widespread opinion among ethnologists; it stems from the fact that their reference model remains (whether consciously or not) written literature.

Calling on the anonymity of a text or melody indicates not the simple absence of a name but rather an insurmountable lack of knowledge about it. For this reason performance itself is never anonymous. There are in fact two causes for the lack: either the thickness and opacity of the time span or the manifold disparity wherein several persons have one by one adjusted the elements of the work. But there is no absolute anonymity. Certainly the audience, in general, pays little attention to the "author" (Finnegan 1977, pp. 187–88, 201–2; Bowra 1978, pp. 404–7). Such indifference does not imply that the audience denies the author's existence, even if mythical. In more traditional societies, the performer well knows that the question will sooner or later be posed: Where did you get this from? The question will always make sense. The exactness of the answer matters little.

Ravier, in his research into Gascony ballads in 1959, sometimes got contradictory information concerning the identity of rather recent authors, which reveals perhaps, as much forgetfulness as camouflage. The Fijian singer Velema, recorded by Quain in the 1930s, announced which ancestor was expressing himself through Velema's mouth and how that ancestor had communicated the song to Velema in a dream. A given African singer recites the genealogy of those from whom he gets his song; or as well, he names himself at the onset, provides the name of the master who instructed him in his art, and sometimes mentions the price he paid. Nasir Udin, who claims the dignities of an author, names himself at the end of his song as the spokesman of the community. At least, when the singer thus 'declines' his name, the phrase by which he does so is often integrated into the poem, is therefore interiorized, and refers to the very design of the performance. The *folhetistas* of Brazil, still close to their original orality, apparently sign their booklets in acrostics, which does not preclude plagiarism whatsoever, since all that is required is a modification in the acrostic (Ravier and Séguy, p. 72; Finnegan 1977, pp. 178–83, and 1978, p. 7; *Literature*, pp. 20–21).

The general cultural context plays only an ancillary role. Anonymity is not in itself more "primitive" than literary appropriation is a mark of "advanced" civilization. The Inuit Orpingalik proudly asserted to Rasmussen in the 1920s the proprietary nature of his songs. What is at stake are the ideas we still have about the individuality and autonomy of the poetic production, as well as the very notion of the author. In this light, to oppose orality to writing explains nothing. By reflecting on the written, contemporary criticism has managed to dissolve the author into his text, and to deny him the right to put himself in a creative and exterior instance, the exclusive domain of meaning. Western culture since the twelfth century, as it has become increasingly secularized, has transferred to the keepers of writing the ancient theological conception of the divine Interlocutor (Gossman, pp. 770, 773; Certeau, pp. 240–41). Little by little, "literature" as it has come to be known took shape. Language in the future would no longer serve as a simple exposé of a mystery of the world, would no longer be the instrument of a discourse itself beyond question: henceforth, language makes itself; piecemeal discourses no longer get their *authority* only from the individual who utters them.

This ideology today is falling apart, and tomorrow perhaps only the publishing industry will retain the memory of it and its fiction. Many other cultures will never have taken this detour: that they will be condemned to death changes nothing. In this manner Eno Belinga proposes to substitute, where it concerns traditional African cultures, the idea of a "second thought" to that of author (Eno Belinga 1978, p. 67).

Nevertheless, authority, for us, implies juridically consecrated possession. But poetic appropriation is not in itself a new idea nor one particular to Western ways. The majority of societies, even the most archaic, recognize and sanction an exclusive right of use or possession of certain poetic products (certain songs belong to a village, a brotherhood, a family, an individual), and the beneficiary of this right, according to the ethnic groups, will be the composer of the poem, the reciter of the one to whom it is dedicated. Such is the case in several regions of Africa and Polynesia, as well as for the Inuit. The poem is property: it is saved, preserved, willed — in certain cases it is exchanged (Finnegan 1977, pp. 203–5; Copans and Couty, p. 183). What sets us apart is the commercialization of this property, the financial consecration of its exploitation: the author's copyrights. But copyright is linked to the use of writing, in such a way that the songwriter and the composer, to whom no listener may perhaps pay attention, receive revenue from a performance by a third party: a procedure that in the same move excludes the public who is thereby denied all sense of participating in the production of the work.

In what follows in this chapter, I will consider only the roles that are really implicated in performance: these I designate together by the term "interpreter." The interpreter is the individual whose voice and gestures are perceived during performance by sight and sound. He may also be the composer of all or part of what he sings or says. If he is not, the relationship that connects him to previous composer(s) will be questioned. The public adopts the same attitude toward the interpreter as toward an author: memory and title of a particular song get connected to the name of one of the singers who makes it popular so that it appears to be his property. Hence "Lily Marlené" by Marlene Dietrich, to the detriment of Lale Andersen.

No universal rule regulates the way in which an interpreter fits into the society to which he belongs. The inventory Finnegan sets up shows that all the conceivable possibilities are in fact realized somewhere: societies in which all the members have equal mastery of the traditional treasury; others where its use is limited to a small number of professionals (Finnegan 1977, pp. 170–200).

In certain African villages, all the women compose and sing lullabies, nuptial hymns, and funeral dirges; all the men know work songs or initiation songs; the children do nursery rhymes. But this division of poetic tasks carries with it neither exclusive nor veritable specialization. The Somalians, empassioned amateur singers, are unaware of professional aspects, despite the extreme complexity of their poetic techniques and the rigorous standards by which any audience will judge them; the same situation is also found among peoples as different as the Pueblo Indians of New Mexico and the Inuits of Canada. The Xhosa of South Africa, to the contrary, distinguish among three types of interpreters in their midst: every man with the gift for improvising within the rules; individuals who know how to recite and develop poems memorized from their clan's storehouse; and specialists charged with composing panegyrics. In central Asia of the nineteenth century, only specialized male recitants used to recount heroic poems of the Turkomen and the Kirghiz; but, for the Yakuts and the Tungus, the same office was filled by women having no particular schooling. The Mongols, today largely a literate people, not only preserve their oral poetic traditions, but it also seems that a growing number of amateurs are cultivating this art, once reserved for traveling bards or minstrels allied with a princely court or a lamasery (Finnegan 1976, p. 104, and 1978, pp. 29, 41, 99, 123–24, 207; Beaudry, p. 39; Bouquiaux and Thomas, I, p. 108; Kesteloot 1971a, p. 3; Opland 1971 and 1975, p. 186; Chadwick and Zhirmunsky, p. 213; Bowra 1978, p. 41).

The interpreter may be a professional belonging to a stable, institutionalized group, a privileged person connected to power. The archetype of this would be the poet-shaman of societies without a state. Once the state emerges, religious values of performance are connoted politically, and the connotation eventually supersedes the original signification: at the end of this deviation, the poet fulfills the function of official soothsayer, panegyrist, or appointed bard. So it was for the pre-Islamic Arab poets, persons who as rulers of the word, repositories of the collective memory, singers of the ancestors, were as indispensable as the sheik to the life of the tribe (Rouget, pp. 185–96; Finnegan 1976, p. 88, and 1977, pp. 188–89; Abd El-Fattah, p. 163; Stein 1959, pp. 304–7). So it was, too, for the Tibetan singers of the *Ge-Sar* who, by miming their epic, used shamanic techniques to evoke a divinity for incarnate characters.

This secularization of the interpreter may result in making him into a functionary, as used to happen to the *imbongi* of the South African chieftains of long ago: as the people's messengers, moderators of power, historians, comedians, they were chosen by the community for their eloquence, their judgment, their ability to move people. The institution survived Christianization and even the formation of the Republic of South Africa. The last *imbongi*, those of today, cut off from their tribe, forced into literacy and urbanization, having become teachers, policemen, taxi drivers, have been reduced to seeking radio engagements, to performing at funerals and political meetings. Unless they have the chance to scratch out paperwork for some local chief, their only contact with the life of their people takes place through newspapers. Yet, even if they have had recourse to writing, their oral poetry lives on, and still today there are those who take up the calling of the *imbongi* (Opland 1975, pp. 192-94, 199–200).

West African griots (see Camara's 1976 book on the subject) in the precolonial states filled an eminent political function in the hierarchy where the relationships of solidarity cross and where discourses are institutionalized: counselors to kings, preceptors for princes, members of a hereditary caste, possessors of an activity based speech. The immunity they enjoyed—and still do today—unleashes the occulted threat of words. Satirists, buffoons, ready to turn the chief himself into the butt of derision, the chief for whom they are the exclusive messengers, repositories of oratory techniques, of epics, genealogical songs, and instrumental music—they are feared and disdained at the same time. Political parties (for example, in Guinea) use them today for their propaganda; some private societies or families use them to celebrate their feasts. Show business entrepreneurs cash in on them. In 1978 I even managed to hear Mali's Bakourou Dekou Kouyate in concert in Los Angeles. His rather pessimistic comments about practicing his art contrasted strangely with those of a griot from the Ivory Coast, Madou Dibore, who in 1973 while talking to Zadi spoke convincingly of the necessity of his social function (Finnegan 1976, pp. 96–97; Camara, pp. 7–9, 104–5, 156, 180; Zadi 1978, pp. 154–64).

Within their oral poetic traditions, certain societies set apart a special area, one reserved for specialists, whereas the rest stays open to free and common use. In the Cameroons, for example, there is the *mvet*, the masters of which form a professional, initiatory, and very prestigious association. Sometimes the specialization alone does not suffice to feed its man, so that the singer, in order to vary his clientele, is forced to enlarge his repertoire greatly. The audience of a Toucoulor singer requires him to perform pleasant songs, dance songs, ritual songs, and to finish with a fragment of some epic—all in a single evening. Seydou Camara around 1970 sang, in addition to the *Kambili*, more than fifty various poems for Bird (Alexandre 1976, p. 73; Okpewho, pp. 35, 40).

There is another type of interpreter: the "free" professional, independent of any institution, although sometimes joining in more or less marginal brotherhoods like the *skomorokhi* of ancient Russia or medieval minstrels. They live by their art or aspire to do so. But societies show themselves inconsistent in their favoring of such financial autonomy. The Serbian *guslars* interviewed by Lord and Parry used to exercise their epic art professionally at given times, but practiced as well a utilitarian trade—farmer, shepherd, schoolmaster, café keeper. Only a begger could allow himself to be only a singer. The same holds true today in several regions of Africa and Asia (Bowra 1978, p. 431; Finnegan 1976, pp. 92, 97–98;

Lord 1971, pp. 17, 20; Okpewho, p. 37; Burke, p. 104). As regards our patented singers, those aspiring to stardom, how many are not, at least temporarily, guided by the need to eat?

In traditional societies, freedom from institutions almost necessarily implies nomadism. Only a sedentary and monopolizing profession puts a stop to it. But, even there, there resurges a mininomadism during the poetic exercise and within a limited area—albeit symbolically reduced to making the rounds in a neighborhood—a nomadism inseparable from the "freedom" of an art, freedom less by choice than from the usury of an organism once the guarantor of oral poetry: griots without patrons today walk the roads of Africa. Students who around 1960 were carrying protest songs to villages in Chile followed the straight line of a tradition (Niane 1979, pp. 5–6; Clouzet 1975, p. 44).

Until approximately 1850, all of Europe was crisscrossed by poets, singers, nomadic reciters, entertainers using voice and gesture, who were not stopped by linguistic borders: persons sociologically identical from people to people all the way to the far end of Eurasia: akin to the Kirghiz or the *Heike* singers in the monk's yellow robe, the *biwa* in bandoliers all along the green countryside of Japan (Burke, pp. 91–96, 103; Chadwick and Zhirmunsky, p. 218; Sieffert 1978a, p. 21).

Industrial society has not totally eliminated this nomadism, the relics of which it preserves, those traces of a past gradually meeting extinction, if not of a freedom that this same society renounces: America's rambling men like Woody Guthrie, who in 1926 at age fourteen traveled across Texas with his harmonica, going from ball to festival, from café to beauty shop; dropouts like Tom Rush, thirty-five years later, from Harvard to Saint-Tropez and the Latin Quarter; in England, Donovan and his guitar. But, in a more general vein, nomadism as co-opted by the system, for us, takes on the appearance of something left to chance (more so than is the case with these tours without which recording artists would not be able to "break in") and to the *laws* of the marketplace, however ironic this appellation may be (Vassal 1977, pp. 97, 263, 308).

Every professional exercise of poetry presupposes that there has already been an apprenticeship, one consecrated by public opinion. The existence of specialized schools is not confined to graphemic societies. The Maori of New Zealand and several Polynesian groups educated their singers up to the end of the nineteenth century in specifically chosen locales, under the direction of responsible masters and in accordance with programs fixed by custom. The ancient Rwanda and the Ethiopians used to train their court poets in the same fashion; we can also speak of the schools for bards in medieval Ireland. These examples nonetheless remain exceptional: our over educated world itself has, outside the confines of its music and dance schools or its public-speaking courses, no organized teaching of oral poetic arts. The only broad type of apprenticeship is thus the one that, while taking place alongside one or several experienced artists, combines imitation of these models with progressive and critical practice sessions. This is true for most of our singers, as it was for the Yugoslav *guslars*, and as it still is for the griot caste. Sometimes, student and master belong to the same family, and so dynasties of singers evolve, like that of the Ryabinines in the Lake Onega region whose history Russian ethnologists have been able to retrace and whose works they have identified for a period of 150 years (Finnegan 1976, p. 87, 1977, p. 189, and 1978, p. 290; Lord 1971, pp. 21–29; Bowra 1978, pp. 417, 429–30, 454).

The very fluidity of the procedures of apprenticeship erases all clear-cut distinction between the "free" professional at the beginning of his career and the expert amateur, as there are in the Calabrese or Greek villages and the "criers" required to sing the lament. This ambiguity is especially felt by folklorists working in rural European or American settings to gather material. In search of authoritative informants, they are generally limited in their choices to rather old people, survivors from a premodern culture, one that for centuries has been cut off from its collective sources, who procure texts and melodies that they identify with their own past. This was the case for a Quebecoise peasant woman recorded by Brassard. At ninety-four years of age, she could still intone in her quavering voice songs that she had learned some eighty-seven years before; she was quite happy to tell her life story. To speak of amateur status would have no more or no less meaning than it would for all of us who sing "for our own pleasure." It is only the place where this pleasure is rooted that differs from one to the other.

Yet, sometimes, "art"—or what the marketplace so designates—becomes involved: "someone" discovers a popular and talented singer, a tradition that is still vigorous and significant. The exploitation of this discovery, whether by recording or some other technology, erects (at the media level) a secondary professionalism; and the latter, beyond the merchandising of the intermediaries, sometimes engenders a new form of poetry, a source of collective pleasure. Certainly, the "unpolished" singer, recorded without any preparation, may be delivered to album connoisseurs at large, as happened in 1970 to the ballad singer, Granny Riddle, in Arkansas. Hers was a fascinating, though definitively lost, poetic lanaguage recorded by Abrahams. In contrast is the example of Ralph Rinzler, who around 1960 unearthed Doc Watson in North Carolina and got him to record his first two albums accompanied by his family: and so opened the classical era of American folk music. A bit later, in England, the Young Generation Trio discovered the Cooper family; in Chile, Violeta Parra collected the *cantos a lo divino* or *a lo humano* from the local *puetas* in the mountains (Finnegan 1977, pp. 183–87; Vassal 1977, pp. 66, 297; Clouzet 1975, pp. 23–24).

None of the types of interpreter, distinguished as I have done here, is defined by an opaque line. Medial or mixed figures are not lacking, and their number increases in societies with shaky traditions (Finnegan 1977, p. 200). In our industrialized world, the ordinary steps in the career of a singer retrace and encapsulate the complete series of these possibilities: from the spontaneous amateur to professionalism and institutionalization. What were initially widespread social forms are nothing more than a repertory of successive individual situations now, one tending ultimately toward stardom, the motivating force. The anthropological foundations have not, for all that, changed.

And yet nothing in the existence of several categories of interpreters allows us to see a projection of the division of the human group into antagonistic social classes, rich/poor, dominating/dominated, noble/common or enslaved (Finnegan 1977, p. 195). A situation of fact, stripped of every customary sanction, sometimes results from the mode of literacy (as in sixteenth- and seventeenth-century Europe or just yesterday in Latin America): if the dominant class hoards the techniques of writing, all that which belongs to orality becomes virtually the object of repression, and the oral poets become, rightly or wrongly, the spokespersons of the oppressed.

The history of oral poetry across the world reveals a constant of another type, one that in an archaic regime of the collective imaginary has been able to address a strong ritual and social value: the blindness of many singers. The Greeks of the first generations of writing, in the fifth, fourth, and third centuries, interpreted the name "Homer" as meaning "the blind one." Chinese tradition attributes the diffusion of poems collected in the ancient anthology of the *Che-King* in part to blind musicians; Japanese tradition attributes the anthology from the thirteenth century of the Taira epic to their blind singers—and we may suspect that that is no more than a mythical view, for Japan has never been lacking in blind epic storytellers. Professor T. Shimmura was still able to produce one for a congress of medievalists in 1979 (Bowra 1978, pp. 420–21; Guillermaz, p. 8; Sieffert 1978a, p. 21).

Traditional Africa used to surround its blind griots with a mysterious prestige; today, according to what Alexandre told me in 1971, the blind bards, numerous in Cameroon, no less than leprous poets or those afflicted with other infirmities, are said to pay thus, in their flesh, for the quasi-sacral privilege of mastering epic art. In November 1980, I was led to Bamako to find Ba Ousamana, a griot known all the way to Mali for the strength of his voice and his memory; blind since birth, he possesses supernatural gifts, and it is considered an uncalculable privilege to be able to attend one of his performances. One of my students, a Ghanian from the Dagaa group, furnished me with a detailed report on an illustrious blind man from his native region, Zacharia, a musician and singer, repository of a vast repertoire of dance songs and a talented improviser, a poet who organizes millet beer gatherings that still echo with ancestral magic. In 1981 in Brazzaville I met a young illiterate singer-composer, Emile Ndembi, born in a village in the bush and blind since the age of two, who was attempting with great energy and talent to "break into" the city. He was living his blindness as a challenge, interiorizing thereby exactly what ancient myths? Perhaps in the manner of a René de Buxeuil in Paris between the two wars.

Similar stories are reported in traditional societies of the Far East: Javanese or Yakuts of the nineteenth century, Ainus of the twentieth. In societies still ignorant of our notion of handicap, individuals deprived of sight keep themselves integrated in groups by earning their livelihood through speech. But, under socio-economic pressure, other values are on the lookout, however confusingly, even in the West. The legend that surrounded Blind Lemon Jefferson, one of the first recognized blues singer in the South during the 1920s and later, around 1940–50, the stories about Doc Watson, Ray Charles, and Stevie Wonder stem from their blindness at least in part, as in Louis XIV's France the legend of the illustrious Savoyard, "Orpheus of the Pont-Neuf" (Chadwick and Zhirmunsky, p. 228; Finnegan 1978, p. 463; Vassal 1977, p. 65; Collier, p. 40; Vernillat and Charpentreau, pp. 223–24).

All of Europe up until the dawn of the contemporary era (if we are to believe the literary and pictorial clichés) was crawling with blindmen, wandering or sedentary, singers, actors, poets of all hues. Milton himself, having lost his sight, dictated *Paradise Lost* to his daughter: the manner in which he composed it, without the help of writing, made him the greatest genius of this group of people. Popular traditions attribute to blindness a particular vocation, a marvelous aptitude to spread works of the voice, either by word of mouth, or by media, through the sale of the most humble printed materials, unbound sheets, songbooks, mass-produced novels: so it is in most Celtic, Germanic, and Slavic countries. A patented corporation in the seventeenth century gathered together the blind romance singers of Sicily. When in England in 1820, Buchan left in search of old Scottish ballads, it was a blind beggar, James Rankin, who provided the material for his collection published in 1828 (Burke, pp. 97–98; Bowra 1978, p. 440; Sargent and Kittredge, p. xxx).

The Iberian Peninsula and then Latin America have, more than any other parts of the Western world, valorized this mysterious function of the blindman: the term *ciego* since the fourteenth century has come to designate in Spanish every popular singer, and *romances de ciegos*, until the end of the eighteenth century, meant a poetic genre of which the disseminators, if not always the authors, were for the most part blind. Madrid for a long time had a congregation of blind storytellers dedicated to the Virgin and, around 1750, it was so esteemed by the public powers that several tribunals provided it with criminal cases to use in creating successful romances. Until almost 1900, the blind were assured of a monopoly in the sale of the small unbound monographs called *pliegos sueltos*, the medium of an abundant popular literature intended for orality. Toward 1925, automobile traffic had chased most peddlers from the cities. Caro Baroja noted the last of them in Madrid in 1933 (Caro Baroja, pp. 19, 41–70, 180, 310–11).

The same evolution occurred in Portugal. In the Brazilian *sertao*, to the contrary, the time of blind singers is barely past. For two or three centuries the *cegos da feira* had traversed these regions, singers then peddlers of *folhetos*, disdained by the "real" poets and more or less assimilated to the class of beggars, sometimes poets themselves (like the blind Aderaldo Ferreira, dead in 1967 after having, four years earlier, published his memoirs) (*Literatura*, p. 148; *Dictionário*, p. 11; Zumthor 1980b, pp. 230–31).

Societies still close to the archaic forms of the imaginary mainly correlate the image of the blindman to the declamation of the epic, confiding mythically the harboring of the Primary Word to one who is only Voice. Blind and clairvoyant, Tiresias, Oedipus, the one on whom the divinities load their entire awesome power. A second archetypal view relays the common vision (G. Durand, pp. 101–303; Zumthor 1980b, p. 239). Cut off from the symbolic and moral values attached to the eye, the blindman is the old King Lear of the Celtic legend, mad and cruel — or else, somber translucidity, the Seer beyond the body, the man forever free of writing.

The mode of activity of the interpreter during a performance differs according to the number of those assisting him or sharing his role — and the presence or absence of musical instruments.

First case: the interpreter recites or sings alone in the presence of an audience; so it is for the majority of professional singers in all societies.

Second case: two interpreters recite or sing alternatingly, in a sort of contest or debate. All ages and cultures provide us with examples, sometimes rigorously regulated ones, as, for example, with Nordic peoples, from Finland to the Canadian Arctic. During the nineteenth century, the *Kalevala* was sung in Finnish villages by two interpreters seated face to face, holding hands and rivaling the other's excellence. The same coded dramatization in the *desafios* of northeastern Brazil, or those of the gauchos of the south. For the Kirghiz of the nineteenth century, in Spanish Gallaecia some ten years ago, as also for the Inuits of Greenland today, singing duels, sometimes episodic in nature, serve the need of social preservation by providing an outlet for personal or group hostilities (Huizinga, p. 124; Ainido, pp. 152, 167–69; Finnegan 1077, p. 223; Fernandez, pp. 464–65).

Third case: the song or declamation of a soloist is supported by a choir or alternates with one. This type of performance, very frequent in Africa, used to be found in several Afro-American genres during their first dissemination. The action of the soloist generally dominates that of the choir, in length, in strength, in expressivity, or in what follows conventionally as happen with "refrain repetitions" or in the recitation of the *qasida* for the Bedouins of the Sinai, where the audience repeats together the last word of each verse (Finnegan 1976, pp. 228–29, 259–62; Collier, pp. 35–37). But this predominance is fragile. It suffices for the choir members to get more intensely involved in the performance for their part to begin to overshadow the solo.

In an extreme case, the solo is reabsorbed, and there is a pure choral song: this is the fourth case with its strong social function. No one part, in fact, is distinguished from the group. The interpreter is a unanimous group. The number of its members (a minimum of a duo) and the eventual division between them of the tasks matter little. To this mode of execution is owed the renaissance of the European art of song since the beginning of the 1930s. Duet singers, like Pills and Tabet, Gilles and Julien from my adolescence, or the jazzmen, Charles and Johnny; fuller groups like the Comédiens Routiers de Chancerel, before the Frères Jeff, the Frères Jacques, the Trois Ménestrels, the Quatre Barbus or the Compagnons de la Chanson—French examples, but France is not the only one to have them. In a town rather removed from the beaten tracks as is Bangui (in the Central African Republic), there were during the 1970s some twenty more or less ephemeral groups. In America as in Western Europe and the Soviet Union, the rediscovery of the folkloric song and its assimilation by a new vocal music (aspiring confusedly to giving its collective fullness to the poetry of voice) were due mainly to the activities of such groups between 1930 and 1960 (Lohisse, p. 95; Vernillat and Charpentreau, pp. 123–24; Vassal 1977, pp. 66, 152, and 1980, pp. 61, 110, 123–25; Bahat, pp. 330–31; Rytkheou, p. 14).

The four modalities of execution distinguished in this manner in practical application get reduced to some twenty combinations according to the usage they entail of musical instruments.

The absence of all musical accompaniment characterizes, in modern Western tradition, those performances that are spoken, perceived as clearly distinct from song. It is not the same for those in which the oppositions are attenuated. With respect to the sung performance, received as such, it is or is not, in all cultures, accompanied by virtue of ritual or aesthetic choices, sometimes valorizing vocal energy alone, sometimes engaging it in concert with instruments.

First usage: the absence of any instrument is worthwhile interpreting as an demonstration of the strength and harmony inherent in voice.

Second usage: the singer accompanies himself, as does the Senegalese griot on his lute, the Sudanese poet on his harp, or our singers on the guitar. It is physically impossible to have recourse to wind instruments; acoustics make percussion accompaniment scarcely desirable. String instruments, the most abstract of all, are therefore privileged: locus of concentration a symbolic charge; means of reinsertion of human vocality among the universal rhythms it has subjugated (Camara, pp. 108–10; Dampierre, p. 17; Finnegan 1976, p. 117; Anido, pp. 158–59).

Third usage: this complex role doubles itself in that a musician accompanies the singer; whence the possible reintegration of wind or percussion instruments. This is universal practice, the most common perhaps that the history of oral poetry records; in medieval Europe it used to constitute (if we can judge from pictorial representations) its most ordinary means of diffusion. It reigns, still today, in flamenco where between voice and guitar there is established a dialogue of intonations and tones that tends to surpass figuratively the conditions of the language (Wurm, pp. 73-77).

Fourth usage: an orchestra or band accompanies the speaker or singer. I mean here two or more musicians, and instruments of varying types, playing either continuously or sporadically. It is in this way that African oral poetry functions as a general rule. The structure of old, custom-bound societies was projected (as in Togo) into the complex institution of orchestras that would signify their various elements by mythically representing the Word and the energy: village, neighborhood, brotherhood, chieftain's or war leader's orchestra (Abglemagnon, pp. 115–17). By means of the Afro-American detour, that need for a "band" has returned to us, beginning in 1930 with jazz, then with rock and what followed. The singer and "his group": photographed on the album cover, a polycephalic poet whose existence responds certainly to a technical and commercial necessity, but implies distant presuppositions and carries with it great consequences in the long run for this art, returning in this way to some unreflective and violent unanimity.

The fifth "usage," rarer and more complex, results from the combination of several others: auxiliaries help the reciter or singer, one by one or simultaneously instrumentalists, singers, mimes. The performance, totally theatricalized, is diversified into cosmogonic action around the central and exemplary figure of the principal voice: hence the Pahari epic singer in Nepal; the Do dance in the Toussian country of Upper Volta; or, closer to home and in an even more spectacular fashion, between several stars of our time, a Diane Dufresne.

There is no performance without memorial action, and this action, perceptible at one or at several levels of formalization, can be automatized and integrated into the system or, in a given particular case, it can be intentional: whence the opposition that can be made between what in oral poetry is *mnemonic* or *mnemotechnical*.

The relation the interpreter maintains with the poem he transmits is manifested in various ways according to the mode of vocal and gestural dramatization. Public reading is the elementary form of it. We do it generally on a platform, before a microphone, or in the spotlight: a means of accentuating its artificiality. Other cultures distance it less from the body. But the role of memory always remains accessory here. Voice utters a writing and does no more than project a reflection of its own virtues. All the other techniques of performance are founded, to the contrary, in principle, on the operation of *memoria*, in the broad sense that rhetoricians of long ago used to ascribe to this term.

Memory, in fact, for cultures of pure orality, constitutes—in time and partially in space—the unique factor of coherence. As the use of writing expands, its social importance declines, as well as its power over individuals—slowly and not without repentance. Nothing ever eliminates it (Ong 1967, pp. 22–60; Finnegan

1977, pp. 73–87; Yates, pp. 42–113; Bowra 1978, p. 355; Tedlock 1977, p. 507; Fry, p. 45). The question gets asked then, less about its power than about its functioning.

Three characteristics of memory appear to be determining factors: its selectivity, the tensions it spawns, and its universality. The first exerts its influence on the milieu of traditional culture. Each interpreter (unless he exercises ritual functions) possesses his own repertoire, set out from the memorial treasury of the community, and often somewhat unbounded throughout the course of the years. The work of Lacourcière on Quebecoise songs reveals that there never exist two identical repertoires and that, if an informant knows on the average some fifty songs, certain other ones may be able to provide up to five hundred (Lacourcière, p. 227; Bowra 1978, p. 439). None of them, on the other hand, distinguishes between the authentic and the pastiched, the old and the new: all that he knows presents itself at the same level. But selectivity operates at the heart of the performance: text, melody, and gesture are adapted to performance; whence the "variants" I discuss in chapter 14.

The memorial action carries with it constant tensions, energetic currents between an individual pole and the collective desirous of poetry: the appetite for a personal enjoyment, the taste of a beauty—these interfere in the motivations of the performance with social convention, rites, fashion, contracts, the demands of the other. Whence a situation of virtual conflict, enriching for the community: ethnologists have often noted that in preindustrial cultures, all it takes is a singer who is more talented or enterprising than the others to make a once immutable tradition suddenly change. All the more so in our culture where the temporal dimension is blurred.

In the technological milieu, in fact, the transience of traditions reduces memorial tension; but, bringing it back to the proportions of our modalities, it converts the tension into dramatic opposition between the values of the masses and those to which the interpreter adheres intimately. The interpreter, a simple cog in the machinery of production and diffusion of poetical messages, is submitted to strong pressures, due to the high degree of recycling in this industry: whence the necessity of a self-discipline, one more rigorous than in archaic societies that impose themselves on their messengers. The system exercises a pitiless selection, whose sole constant criteria, called "talent," is the difficult simultaneous adequation of its being offered up to public and private demand, to the contingencies of programming and to personal vitality (Burgelin, pp. 57–65).

The "universality" of the memorial functioning in the end constitutes one of the most general traits of oral poetry. What transmits voice, as the words get linked together, exists in the memory of the performer as an entity: a profile with uncertain regions, vibrations, *mouvance*—not a totality, but a totalizing intention, already endowed with the means to manifest itself.

Neither the letter of the text nor the melody, as such, is absolutely important. "Memory lapses," "blanking out" during a performance is less an accident than a creative episode: traditional cultures, by inventing the "formulaic style," had integrated these uncertainties of living memory into their poetic art. But, as well, have not our singers found their own formulaic style in the wake of jazz? These are ways of telling for which the appropriate mode of the interpreter is to make *remembrance* (my coinage) predominate over memorization: where remembrance is in opposition to pure and simple recall of the already known, the re-creation of a knowledge constantly questioned in its very details, and for which each performance instigates a new integrity.

In terms of a Derridean inspiration, Yaounde, apropos to Sheikh Hamidou Kane, used to speak of the simultaneous operation of a double speech: the interior, "pneumatological," and the manifest, "grammatological," that it realizes. Oster, in his research in 1960 on the blues in Louisiana, stated that at the end of the performance, most singers had only the vaguest idea of what they had just played: what stayed in their memory referred to the norms of a genre rather than to a text (Ngal, p. 335–36; Oster, p. 268).

These singers, one would say, were improvising. But what exactly is improvisation? In principle, it is a coincidence between the production and transmission of a text—the text being composed *within* the performance, as opposed to those that were composed *for* the performance. In fact, improvisation is never total: the text, produced on the spot, is so by virtue of cultural norms, even re-established rules. What is, for the improviser, the weight of these norms? What constraints perhaps result from them?

The popular Aragonese songs studied by Fernandez, or the *chansons express* in the fashion of the Parisian cabarets at the beginning of the century, appear to be instantaneous creations. But this "poetry in movement" that they make us grasp, this operation in which they implicate the listener, do they not lead back to the manipulation of voices heard, of a common language, of a tradition? The improviser has the talent to round up and immediately organize raw materials—thematic, stylistic, musical ones—that he blends with memories of other performances, and often, memorized fragments of writing. Or he may, if he belongs to a more formalized tradition, construct, as blues singers do, day to day, using standard elements, texts that are forever new.

But the talent of the performer does not suffice, were it within these limits, to ensure the success of the improvisation. A cultural agreement, an expectation and a predisposition of the public, and a collective attitude toward memory are no less indispensable. These conditions are neither everywhere nor always connected. From this comes the impression among ethnologists that a given population is "more talented" than another in improvisation: the Kirghiz of the nineteenth century or the South African Xhosa, who, around 1970, had already provided a good number of improvisers for radio broadcasts. The cultural agreement or the expectations take specific form when a poetic genre is defined within a community by the fact that one improvises it: one calls to mind the Andalusian flamenco in its original form; the multiple popular models of the Brazilian *versos do momento*, precisely coded and with a sometimes dazzling virtuosity; and the *desafios* with their themes imposed by the audience who watches out for any impropriety or trick (Chadwick and Zhirmunsky, pp. 218, 228; Opland 1975, pp. 187–88; Wurm, pp. 72–74; *Literatura*, p. 16; Fonseca 1981, p. 23; *Dicionário*, pp. 15, 17).

The drummer in an African village transmits news, the exchange of which constitutes the link between individuals and groups. But this obvious function covers up another, more profound and less differentiated one, which is to proclaim history, to claim a consciousness and to arouse its voice. For this reason, during the time that he beats, a taboo protects him, a sacred personage: the missionaries, for their part, persecuted him as a sorcerer. The Tupi of Brazil, if we believe Soares de Sousa at the end of the sixteenth century, forsook eating a captured singer, the carrier of a discourse the motivations and forms of which belonged to another reality, where differences between men are abolished (Jahn 1961, pp. 216–17; Clastres, pp. 49–50). Myths about the presence of the oral poet in our midsts, the models of behavior that such a presence engenders actualize an archetypal situation—certain beings, in the social group, have of themselves received the mission to explain a knowledge, certainly a common one, but one folded back on itself and ineffective. Vocalized, according to customary norms, by the elected mouth, this knowledge operates in three ways: biological or mental, it awakens and whips up an energy; cultural, it imposes a rhythm, in order to submit it to itself and to make it serve the brute world; discursive, it constitutes itself in a story. One could even hold that oral poetry results from an accumulated operation at the first of these levels and at at least one of the other two.

Chapter 13
The Audience

Audience members "take part" in the performance. The roles they play contribute no less than that of the interpreter. Poetry, therefore, is what is *received*; but its *reception* is a unique, fleeting, irreversible act, and an individual one, for it is doubtful that the same performance is experienced in an identical manner (except perhaps in a rigorous ritualization or a collective trance) by any two audience members. Any subsequent recourse to the text (if indeed there is a text) does not re-create the performance. Once the risk is accepted the spectator, like the reader confronting a book, becomes implicated in an interpretation wherein nothing ensures its correctness. But, more than the reader's, the spectator's place is unstable: narrataire? narrator? these functions tend to exchange themselves endlessly at the very core of oral customs (Charles 1977, pp. 15–6; Lyotard, pp. 20–21; Jauss, 1978, pp. 243–62; Paulme).

The gestures and voice of the interpreter incite a response in the spectator, a response of voice and gesture, one that is mimetic and, in line with conventional constraints, delayed if not repressed. Certain oral genres, conversely, have regulated the response by programming it: forms with responses, refrains, all dances, even silent ones, that give rhythm to the song of a soloist or a choir.

The fundamental ingredient in "reception" is, therefore, the action of the spectator, recreating for his own use, and according to his own internal configurations, the signifiying universe that is being transmitted to him. The traces that this re-creation impress on him belong to his intimate life and do not necesssarily and immediately appear outside. But it may happen that they are exteriorized in a new performance: the spectator becomes, in turn, interpreter, and on his lips, in his gesture, the poem is modified perhaps radically. Hence, in part, traditions are enriched and transformed. Arab Sufism may have designated this creative *mouvance* by using the ambiguous word *sama*, which some translate as "listening to mystical songs" and others as "ecstatic dance" (Rouet, pp. 350–53).

We could distinguish, therefore, without paradox, two roles in the person of the spectator: that of receiver and that of coauthor. This doubling comes from the nature of interpersonal communication and whatever may be its modalities over the course of time and across space; its effects vary little. Two rather frequent situations, however, entail exceptions, and these are more apparent than real.

The first is solitary song or recitation. The interpreter has for all appearances no audience other than herself. The genre of oral poetry that occasions such performances matters little: singing while working, while walking, at the steering wheel of a car, singing for one's own pleasure, all naturally adapt to it. And yet, is the listener ever really erased or completely interiorized? The flock of the singing shepherd receives the voice of its master, and perhaps the reaction of the beasts makes them the obscure coauthors of this performance. The *yodel* of the mountain man, at the end of Valais or in Wyoming, calls to the forests, the peaks, a Nature present in the wind and who sings within him in its turn.

The other situation, one less precise, has in common with the latter nothing but the absence of a differentiated audience. But, containing a plurality of interpreters, it disseminates among them the roles of reception. In recitation or song that is integrally choral, where all the copresent individuals in the performing arena take part in its execution (as happens in many societies at present) interpreters and audience are intermixed, yet, at the very heart of the communal action, a variety of instances function distinctly: while singing with them I hear them sing, and the feeling of this community confirms my desire to sing, which increases the entire joy of song for us.

The audience member is not necessarily the designated recipient (*destinataire*): African songs praising the leader are meant for him, but the entire group is the receiver and coauthor. The distinction becomes evident when the hero sings about himself (Finnegan 1976, pp. 116, 139).

This, once again, is an extreme situation. Houis not long ago, in generalizing about African storytellers, delineated a typology of "reception behaviors." It is articulated on the more complex notion of "situations of communication." By identifying "reception" with the "listening situation," he was able to distinguish "refrain listening" from "silent listening." Finnegan, for her part, adopted a functionalist perspective and opposed performances where the audience is "totally" involved to those where it is more or less a tourist (Houis, pp. 9–15; Finnegan 1977, pp. 217–30). I will combine the dissymetric principles of these analyses and join to them a numerical consideration: does the audience account for one or several individuals? One can thereby obtain less a classification of performance genres than a simple list of possible enactments. At most one can observe that certain poetic forms are realized in one manner rather than in another: thus, for example, a revolutionary song generally requires the "total" involvement of numerous listeners, in a "refrain listening."

These descriptions avoid a particular problem: the reciprocity of relationships that are set up between interpreter, text, and audience member during performance and that provoke the interaction of each of these three elements with the other two in a common game.

Whatever he says, the performer, even if he is the author of the text, does not talk about himself. The use of *I* is of little importance: the spectacular function of the performance makes this pronoun ambiguous enough that its referential value is diluted in the consciousness of the audience. For the speaker or singer that very movement unleashes solitude and communication starts. For the audience, the voice of this *character* who addresses it does not completely belong to the mouth from which it emanates; it comes from within. In its harmonies the echo of an elsewhere resonates albeit weakly. Traditional societies distinguish clearly between the operation of the interpreter and that of an authorized language, one impersonally transmitted, to which the interpreter only lends his talent: consequently the audience judges him and definitively accepts or refuses any individual innovations (Burke, p. 112; Charles 1977, p. 38; Finnegan 1977, pp. 205–6). Our style-conscious societies do not function in a radically different way: the listener expects a certain discourse from the interpreter, a language whose rules he knows, a language freed of all proprietary exclusion. What is said or sung for him cannot be autobiographical: the signature that would authenticate it is lacking. Nothing is signed in vive voce.

This impersonalization of speech lets the listener take it more easily into account; to identify what is felt with what has been said. Yet nothing is more misleading (where it concerns even archaic societies) than the idea that the voice of the community speaks through the lips of a storyteller or a singer, that the consciousness of a people is expressed by him. The oral poet as much as the literate engages in power plays that are either adopting or challenging them, but where never pretending neutrality, just as the poet's own tradition or style can never be neutral. If he is speaking for others, the poet's discourse, never completely appropriable (as opposed to writing), stays constantly available to other voices that resonate within his.

In the course of a performance, diverse linguistic indicators, either rhythmic or gestural, indicate these interactions, and sometimes amplify them through their demonstration.

In the dramatic arrangements of performance, certain ones seem to have as their apparent function to maintain contact with and hold the attention of the audience. Thus, in Africa the interpreter can introduce by means of text or gesture a familiar detail, one apt to create complicity; or perhaps he manipulates some symbolic object that brings the spectators closer: these are everyday procedures in traditional societies and ones for which we can find equivalents in our own. Then again, the interpreter addresses this audience, integrating words of encouragement or reproach into the rhythm of the poem (Okpewho, pp. 231–32, 236).

Conversely, the audience intervenes, at the risk of upsetting the flow of the discourse or song. The Manobos encourage the reciter of the *Ulahingan* with their cries or foot stompings. The Mossi of Upper Volta engage in a dialogue and punctuate the narration. "Do you follow me?" the performer asks. "Yes," the audience responds, though less laconically, "Yes, master." The audience of an African epic, conscious of upholding tradition and assuming the role of those responsible for the common cultural good, controls the singer, calls him back to order if he strays or lets his fancy wander too much, requires him to go back if he has passed too quickly over an episode they consider important (Maquiso, p. 42; Okpewho, pp. 194–201; Barre-Toelken, pp. 224–25).

At the very heart of the theatricalized universe to which they, both one and the other, belong for so little time the audience member reacts to the action of the interpreter as an "enlightened amateur," both consumer and judge, often hard to please. Modern societies in which old traditions of orality are kept alive, even isolated, have preserved intact the use of these interferences: from the popular *cantorias* of Brazil to the subtle *rakugo* of Japan. Elsewhere, under the empire of the written word and of our technologies, growing unaccustomed to voice and even the constraint of inherited "good manners" have not entirely repressed the occurrences; and, for our youth in the presence of their stars, passion, voice, and gesture erupt openly.

The peripetiae of a drama with three participants that is thus played out between the interpreter, the listener, and the text can have an influence on the mutual relations of the last two, the text adapting itself in some way to the quality of the listener.

In traditional societies, it sometimes happens as a result of previous programming: a given African song is not pronounced, is not accompanied or danced in the same way among men as among women; among the initiated as among the uninitiated. The myths of the Australian aborigines are the object of songs differentiated by clan. In a less exclusive fashion, the Yugoslav *guslar* used to sing their epics in taverns where the audience was made up entirely of men and hence of connoisseurs.

Today in our midst traces of these ancient practices endure: we see them as answers to an inquiry; they are integrated into an aesthetic design (or, for the media, a commercial) that determines its information. A given style is addressed to one age group or social class rather than to another. When, at the beginning of the 1960s, François Hardy and Sheila began to temper what was originally a brutal rock and roll into bubblegum rock for the benefit of well-heeled youths, rock remained the territory of poor suburban adolescents until its revival in 1973–74.

For nations in the sway of authoritarian regimes, as was Franco's Spain, a tone or a new style of oral poetry first gets implanted in university settings and stays there alone for a long time (Agblemagnon, p. 118; Eno Belinga 1978, p. 87; Derive, p. 70; Finnegan 1977, pp. 233–34, and 1978, p. 320; Lord 1971, p. 14; Hoffmann and Leduc, pp. 42–43; Wurm, pp. 56–57).

A more supple adaptation of the text to audience occurs during performance. The interpreter spontaneously varies tone or gesture, modulates the enactment of the utterance (*énonciation*) according to the expectations he perceives; or he deliberately modifies the work (*énoncé*) itself, despite the prevailing custom. (Finnegan 1977, pp. 54–55, 192; Okpewho, p. 71; Lord 1971, pp. 16–17). Epic singers observed by Radlov around 1860 in central Asia would adapt their stories to the changing moods of their audience: the immediate situation would move them to recompose a whole poem by adding to, cutting, and transforming it with deft mastery. African storytellers do the same. Parry and Lord's Serb or Bosniac *guslar*, when they were singing in mountain villages, molded their text to the noise of continual comings and goings of curious onlookers, cutting parts, repeating some, changing others to suit the needs of time and place.

The rules governing certain oral genres program this mobility of the text: in fact, they anticipate the parts requiring active intervention by audience members. African traditions offer numerous examples of it, among which one can distinguish degrees of inclusion of the public. The recital of the Congolese *Mwindo* is accompanied by the humming of the young people seated around the interpreter, and their drumming defines the rhythm. In alternating performances of the Nigerian Ijos, the entire audience sings a fixed couplet in chorus, responding to the soloist's variations (Okpewho, p. 63; Laya, p. 178).

Most of these techniques are found again elsewhere or in other times. Is it not a variant that is found in the mysterious refrain marked on some of the manuscripts of our oldest medieval *chansons de geste*? In 1969 with my own ears I heard in the Rawalpindi bazaar a group of men scan in short outbursts the song of a blindman whom they encircled and to whom they were avidly listening. *AOI* of the *Chanson de Roland*! For the Yucatan Mayas, the performance of a storyteller contains a role intermediate between those of the performer and the audience: the "respondent," usually the very person who has requested to hear the story and thus constitutes a living link, a privileged one, by whom life circulates between what is said and what one hears (Tedlock 1977, p. 516).

Thus, the listener contributes to the production of the work in performance. The listener is author, scarcely less than the performer is author. Whence the specificity of the phenomena of reception in oral poetry.

Performance *figures* an experience, but at the same time it *is* experience. As long as it plays, performance suspends the activity of judgment. The text that proposes itself, at the point of convergence of the elements of this lived spectacle, does not call for interpretation. The voice that utters it does not project itself there (as speech would do in writing): it is given, in and with the spectacle, all-present; and yet, no more than the performance, the spectacle is not closed. It challenges exegesis, which will intervene only after its inscription in writing — that is, after being put to death. Its meaning is not such that a ''literary'' hermeneutics can serve to explain it, for basically and in the most widely accepted sense of the term, it is political. It proclaims the existence of the social group, reclaims the right of speech, the right to its life. The investment is more than some thematic pretexts: it is an indiscreet desire to compensate for complacency, crying out to the other to create a dependency. Hence, perhaps, the connection will strengthen itself, the menace will be appeased, hidden forces will surge forth.

For this reason the oral poetic text pushes the listener to identify with the purveyor of the words that they experience in common, if not with these very words themselves. Beyond the negativities inherent in every aesthetic use of language, beyond the radical indifference of the poetry *qua* poetry, performance unifies and unites. Such is its permanent function. A Mayan storyteller asked Tedlock impatiently, for Tedlock seemed far too unconcerned; ''When I tell a story, do you *see* it, or do you just write it down?'' I couldn't say it better (Tedlock 1977, p. 515).

Hence, at the level of the listener and of reception, the truly historical dimension of oral poetry shows itself. The existence of the latter, whatever form it may take, constitutes in the long run an indispensable element of human sociality, an essential factor in social cohesion. We know how, despite the frightening cultural aggression of which they were victims, despite the systematic destruction of the old tribal cadres, the blacks of America managed to keep a collective consciousness alive by means of song.

In the cold fragmentation of today's society the same life-sustaining reaction associates song with all the efforts meant to help threatened communities or those who are soul-searchers: in the streets or the bars of the disenfranchised neighborhoods of our urban centers, at Larzac, or with the Markolsheim strikers. Whence the creation forever renewed of (sometimes rather humble) groups, musicians, and singers, going ahead of these anonymous people who wait for them without knowing it: the ''Folk of Lace Street'' of Jean Dentinger in Upper Alsace, and so many others. From this comes the continual composition of songs some of which will end only by emerging on the horizon of universal poetry — but where will people have learned the rudiments of the language of their rediscoveries: the partisans' song of the Second World War; or the ballad of Farabundo Marti for the FMLN militia of El Salvador?

Oral poetry masters the very pulsations of the body and the heartbeats of life that gives birth to its rhythm and bends them to its order. From this internal tension, from this initial quasi contradiction, there comes an energy from which it derives its formidable unifying power. It does not differ at all by nature from any other oral communication, but in terms of capacity, it remains incomparable. In archaic societies, using audience members who receive it and on whom it acts, it targets the dead as its ultimate recipients: founders and guarantors, outside all vicissitudes. We have secularized all that, that is to say, we have lost the sense of analogies. Yet the elementary emphases of the oral poetic work always function at the root of this art, despite historical distortions, cultural mystifications, and the partial sclerosis of surfaces. What has transpired among us for some twenty years proves that in the end nothing is really broken: a continuity inscribed within the network of our languages and the economy of our bodily powers has perhaps allowed us, beyond the circumscribed territory of scribes and pharmacists, to anchor the great spiraling circularity to the vertical balance that we once embodied.

For an audience the use of the *mediats* masks this continuity — less so, however, than would appear to the critical eye. For the masses who are so little concerned with historical models, the *mediats* have restored the omnipresence of continuity to voice; in so doing they have brought common poetic sensitivity back to a state bordering on that of our pre-Gutenberg ancestors.

To the best of my knowledge, it is still the case that no one has yet dreamed of using the telephone for transmitting poetry. I am astonished by this. Reposing in fact on the individual entrenched in his own existence and the voice of another (as both body and speech), the telephone conveys an erotic current, latent or manifest, a source of a linguistic energy comparable, at a distance, to that which elsewhere was subservient to the shaman's incantation, the song of the enchanter or that of the lover. Whence the protests of given individuals ("I don't like to call on the phone"); whence the repugnance that answering machines inspire in others. But perhaps the primary destination of the telephone suffices to render it poetically useless: made for conversation and exchange rather than for communal affirmation, it implies no *audience* in the sense that I use this term, but rather an *interlocutor*, all of which embroils the distribution of the roles.

Like the telephone, in a much smaller measure, the microphone increases the vocal space and reduces auditory distances. Maintaining the view and the physical presence of the body, it makes the performance technically better without modifying any of its essential elements. It is to this that we can attribute the universal success of this instrument that has become (since 1937, when Jean Sablon, a singer with a weak voice, lent it to political orators) the almost obligatory medium for all vocal poetic transmission. Thanks to the microphone, rounded out by the amplifier (if not by microphones attached to instruments), word and music are becoming truly public. By this *publicity*, business as much as artists gains something. The audience and its space continue to expand all the way to far removed acoustical limits, albeit to the detriment of an immediate visibility (in certain circumstances).

This makes it possible to assemble crowds: at once to spread the strength and authority of the interpreter, and to permit listening by a given number of individuals so that any personal relationship between them is suspended; a collective passion is substituted for it, culminating in the admiration of the hero. Since the 1940s, American hootenannies have been improvised, ones that later were to take hold in Paris, at the Raspail Boulevard Center, between 1964 and 1967. The folk songs of a Guthrie or a Seeger triumphed there, before the great wave of rock concerts that Johnny Halliday brought to France in February 1961; the protest song festival in Cuba in 1967: twenty thousand, fifty thousand up to one hundred fifty thousand audience members (Vassal 1977, pp. 105–6, 138, 148; Clouzet 1975, p. 39).

Since Juan-les-Pins, in August 1961, the use of the microphone, for Vince Taylor, has become an art; the instrument itself carries a quasi-sacral function at the very heart of a ritual, exuding repressed violence, crowned by ransacking the stage, a symbolic universal destruction. But these furies had only one moment, a rather brief one, whereas the trend of festivals endures: festivals promoted by the establishment. The Newport Folk Festival (which in its early years was a financial success, but also debuted Joan Baez and Bob Dylan), from 1959 to 1970 was unanimously the best concert. In France, after 1968, rock concerts became, despite the distrust of authorities, scheduled events and took on the appearance of a liturgy whose faithful practitioners little by little lost their faith. Yet the technical and human potential of these concentrations of listeners remains untapped. From time to time, there are vast events where the collective fervor triumphs in an explosion of joy as, for example, happened with Alan Stivell and his Breton group at the Olympia in 1972; as in Larzac in 1974 (Hoffmann and Leduc, pp. 39–41, 174; Rouget, p. 408; Vassal 1977, pp. 148–50, 175–76, and 1980, p. 110).

Records, tape recorders, cassettes and radio, the auditory *mediats* tend to eliminate, along with vision, the collective dimension of reception. Then again, individually, they reach an unlimited number of listeners. The broadcasting of Afro-American music is due principally to their use — and thus, in part, the "cultural revolution" that accompanied it. According to Collier, in 1914 alone (even before the first jazz record was cut), twenty-seven million 78s were sold; in 1921, one hundred million (Collier, pp. 72, 77–78).

A blind and deaf apparatus takes the place of an interpreter. Certainly the listener connects it to a human being who exists somewhere. Exposed to a lone voice, however, the listener receives no other invitation to participate. The listener probably re-creates (in an effort to master this purely sonorous universe) the absent elements of an imagined performance. But the image evoked can be intimately personal only for the solitary listener. The performance is interiorized. Despite what is currently being done in groups (especially in light of dance), these *mediats* are better adapted to solitary listening experiences and eventually to criticism.

Still, it is necessary to distinguish between them. Records, tape recorders, and cassettes leave the listener with a large freedom of choice: the record manufacturer imposes on me his choice of ten or twelve songs that he cuts on the same wax; but I am the only one to decide on listening to that particular record, then another and can even modify my program in the middle of its execution. Tape recorders and cassettes, within the means of everyone and being easy to use, release me from this final servitude: I record at will.

Radio, on the other hand, flows in a continuous discourse, and is entirely programmed by others; the same negative freedom is given me in the supermarket: accept, change stores, or hit the reject button. The relative passivity required of me predisposes me to believe that what I get is exactly what I expect. It is an illusory interiority that, quite probably, some twenty years ago made for the success in France of the program *Salut les copains*, followed for a number of seasons by a unanimous generation of teenagers, brought back into line by the established order by this same show. Listened to on transistor, radio emphasizes its atomizing effects: light, mobile, and inexpensive, the transistor individualizes performance even more without necessarily deepening it, and lends itself to long stretches of solitude without really penetrating them. Even to the very ends of fields in the Third World, it is a familiar sight today to see a peasant bent over his field, transistor in hand, but the voice deafened by the noise of his machinery. With headphones, it is accomplished: all social lines are cut, the intoxicated Walkman zigzags between us, empty-eyed. Total interiorization—in what madness?

Despite the distortions that radio thereby imposes on the functioning of orality, it is already well implanted in the "developing" countries who often do not yet have full access to television. Adapted to the demand of barely literate populations, the radio is in the process of relaying traditional singers, all of whom are aging. Nevertheless, it alters little the external form of the oral poetry that is transmitted to us. Whence inevitably, a folkloric exploitation: the radio of the Solomon Islands dedicates a mere quarter of an hour per week to indigenous songs and tales. The northeastern Brazilian stations leave a place for the *cantorias* singers. Radio Yaoundé broadcasts *mvets*; Radio Dakar, the *Sundiata*; Radio Mogadishu, Somalian bards. Does the relative importance of the movement, in Africa at least, foretell the emergence of new forms of poetry where presence, reduced to its sonorous elements, suspended by mechanical mediation, would reestablish itself at some other level (Finnegan 1977, pp. 155–58)? Already African political parties in countries without a press have discovered the efficacy of a propaganda molded in the forms of hereditary song and transmitted by transistor.

Reconstituting the image of a presence, the audiovisual media threaten their user less with this symbolic confinement. The universe they propose has the appearance of integrity and truth; it provokes a potentially nonalienating exile.

In cinema, the darkness of the room doubly influences the viewing audience. To all appearances, it gives them again their solitude; yet in a confused way they know they are together—enough so that sometimes a common reaction takes place. The projected image, concentrating its light, its colors among our shadows, proclaims itself to be different, coming from somewhere else, shooting forth from some crack opened in the wall of our world. It addresses itself to me. I see and I hear. But the sonorities clear within me an imaginary field that is larger than sight. The play of sounds on and off screen gives rise to an auditory diegesis for which the visual realm plays only a supporting role. By means of the window of the screen, the viewer of objects and actions "bigger than life," my eye perceives only a slice of the reel(real), framed by shadows. But the frame does not enclose what the ear hears. It seems that the situation of direct performance is reconstituted.

We know about this deceitful appearance. Yet from its origins a direct line connects the varying forms of vocal art, especially song, to the soundtrack. Since the days of the silent film, many films have been demonstrably potpourris of current songs, accompanied by piano: from *The Jazz Singer* with Al Jolson, in 1927, the first commercialized "talkie" until *Honeysuckle Rose* by Jerry Schatzberg introduced at Cannes in 1981, the chain is unbroken. A lively circulation passes from one to the other of these registers. The raspy voice of Marlene Dietrich, Lola in *The Blue Angel* in 1930, set up a tradition that is still alive. There are few singers among us who have not composed for cinema or aspired to do so (Cazeneuve, p. 110; Vernillat and Charpentreau, pp. 63–64; Vassal 1977, p. 107). Records, radio, even TV are instruments of broadcasting; film is a *form*. But song often escapes the scenario for which it is destined and by which it is disseminated. It then engages in an autonomous career. Then again, some successful songs in other moments give birth to a cinematographic work of the same title: for example, *Ramona* from 1936 on, *Rio Bravo* by Howard Hawks in 1959 or, an extreme example, *Lily Marlène*, source and theme for at least four films. After seeing *The Grapes of Wrath* in 1940 in New York, the enthralled Woody Guthrie composed one of his most beautiful ballads, "Tom Joad."

Television opens a dialogue without responses: private, intimate, but eliminating a book's would-be distance—illusory conversation. But what good is it to react? The encircling zone of silence shortens it to the point of disappearing. On the backdrop of a continuous discourse, ephemeral communicative effects, ones scarcely realistic, are drawn. Even if by chance the program takes place live and is not prerecorded, voice is assured an earthly space but loses all temporal dimension: fallacious return to a situation of primary orality.

The tele(interpreter) vision, whether hidden away in a cabinet or sitting in the center of the living room, imposes itself, intrusively, with servility or bad conscience. Even turned off, it remains present, signifying symbolically the technicity whose the fruit it is and the type of sociality that has made it possible: it is never reduced to its instrumental function alone. To use it implies the acceptance of its language (if not of the content of this language) and of the typology of the genres of discourses it proposes. But, among the better established of these genres there figures song, whether integrated or not into a variety show. Whence television's essential function in the preservation of oral poetry at the end of our century: more than film, in which the performance tends to dilute itself in a narrative fiction; much more than records, which leave the eye out of the circuit (Berger, pp. 107–15).

What is questioned here is the relationship between reality and consciousness. Has the use of *mediats* modified it? Or is it itself, modified as it is, what has made the *mediats* possible? Within technically unchangeable (so it seems) limits, the modalities of reception can differ greatly depending on the nature of the cultural milieu. The spectator whom the media reach is a singular and historic being; whatever techniques of brainwashing that one uses on him, it is through his history that he perceives and through this history what he reacts (Corbeau, p. 335).

Between him and what he hears there is interposed, it is true, the programmer: a new person on the performance scene, a commercial organizer who knows his clientele only through sociological cross-sections and market studies. The consequences of such a system have often been decried: they operate only to the advantage of the stars (Bertin; R. Cannavo in *Le Matin* April 6, 1981). Yet the passivity for which the viewing public is reproached stems less from the *mediats* than from social causes: absence of appropriate education and the program's profit margin (commercial or ideological). The listener is thereby stripped of all possibility of reacting to the works as they are transmitting to him, to cooperate in their "creation." Several attempts, until recently marginal at best, nevertheless prove the existence of this possibility (Cazeneuve, pp. 60–63, 218–19; Berger, p. 18).

Theatricalized, direct oral poetry engages the spectator's entire being in the performance. Mediated oral poetry leaves something inside untouched. The passage from one mode of reception to the other represents a considerable cultural mutation. I was assured in Upper Volta in 1980 that the radio broadcasts of griots had but a small listenership in the bush. The sensuality of a presence was lacking. Ong had a similar experience in Senegal (Ong 1979, p. 6). A relatively homogeneous society interiorizes this effect of mutation, without losing consciousness of it. Upon returning to Africa, I asked Jean and Brigitte Massin for their opinion as musicologists: how do records and live concert hall performances differ? As for the first, they recognized a technical prefection that today is almost absolute, as well as the advantage of a solitary, more intimate listening experience. But the second, imposing and particularizing its spatial dimension more totally, mobilizes attention and thereby the unity of the performance, emphasizing the elements of personal invention while listening.

The audiovisual media return the eye to its function. But what I have called in chapter 11 *tactility* remains lost, despite the gimmicks invented long ago by Griffith and Abel Gance, huge maps and eyes within eyes. The look I put on the screen cannot be the same as the one with which I caress objects; it is more abstract, devoid of eroticism. Whence, perhaps, the temptation for programmers to exhibit on screen the entirely external signs of an exaltation of the body, an incitement to narcissism in the bathroom.

Thus, in the mediated performance, what is properly called participation—collective identification with the received message, if not with the sender—tends to give way to a solitary identification with the proposed model, all the way (we note among our youth) to the point where these solitudes join together massively. The model is the savoir-faire or the behavior of a Hero. Stardom, in our world, is an indispensable factor in the functioning of the *mediats*, as "heroism" was for the ancient epic. But, and we know it, the hero type of our mass culture is the singer: nothing yet has taken away the magic of voice (Burgelin, pp. 134–47, 152–53; Cazeneuve, pp. 91–96).

Film and TV are exposed to an omnipresent and pitiless eye. Their technology tends to emphasize imperfections that direct performance tones down. We end up by dissociating the recording of the vocal and the gestural: in playback mode the singer or actor opens his mouth before the camera, but it is a record that we hear. Certainly, the perfection of the product is not always attained, as we know all too well. But integrated in the very project of the media, perfection orients technical research and the corresponding financial investments. No doubt this is (obscurely but efficiently) perceived by users. It seems to me that this is one of the causes of the fascination exercised by television over children and of its intrusion in their fantasy world. The baby on her mother's knee turns from the mother to look at the set, even when turned off. I am referring here to Berger's work that speaks of a rebirth, as traumatizing as the first, vis-à-vis an infant's sudden immersion in televiewing.

Seated in an armchair of the movie theater of in front of his TV, the listener-spectator consumes images and sounds. He necessarily makes something out of it. If the world where he exists were to offer him holes in which to stash them, undoubtedly he would make objects out of them, in the same fashion as the old *patenteux* (licensors) of Quebec. But there is no longer any room for objects today. Images and sounds fall, apparently useless, in the microsociological context of each one of us; they flow there in the matrices of the imaginary serving in the piecemeal building of a day-to-day mythology (Certeau, p. 11; Corbeau, pp. 333–34).

All has become spectacle—"live." Reality replaces Primordial Time; the Real, the original. We, no less than our ancestors, need myths to survive, prostrated as we are like Plato's men in the cave. Forms coming from elsewhere are projected on the wall. Certainly, we do not totally confuse the real outside with these shadows; simply, we prefer the shadows. However, it sometimes happens that the image strikes us so strongly that we must rise up and go see. A message is launched, outside there. The Voice of a poet resounds therein (Berger, pp. 52–55, 64; Cazeneuve, pp. 100–103).

Chapter 14
Duration and Memory

The work transmitted in performance and deployed in space, in a certain manner, escapes time. It is not, in fact, insofar as it is oral, ever exactly reiterable: the function of our *mediats* is to palliate this inability. A repeat performance is always possible; in fact, it is the exception that a work is not the object of several performances: it is never, by necessity, the same. From the first to the second or to the third playing of a record, changes remain minimal: one type (various psychic dispositions of the listener, circumstances) would have as much effect on subsequent readings of a book; others are specific, like acoustical conditions. In the series of declamations of an epic, in contrast, the modifications are sometimes so great as to obscure the identity of the work.

At any rate, *false reiterability* constitutes the principal feature of oral poetry. It grounds its mode of existence outside performance. It determines the preservation of oral poetry. This preservation can result from two different practices, ones that today are somewhat contradictory though generally cumulative: either *archiving*, by means of writing or electronic recording, which has the effect of stabilizing all or part of the elements of the work (verbal, acoustical, or visual even if it concerns a film or a video disk); or *memorization*, either direct or indirect through various mediations, such as the one that, as it passes through writing, requires an interiorization of the text.

Archiving stops the currency of orality, stops it at the level of *a* performance. This fixed performance loses that which makes up the movement of life but preserves at least its ability to excite other performances. I can sing, make someone sing, and vary a song that is read in parts or one heard on a record I like. The play of competition will perhaps lead me to make another edition of this work, to record another interpretation of it: a chain that poses delicate problems of methodology for the ethnologist (whose practices are necessarily inscribed in this plan) (Derive, pp. 58–64).

Memorization, a natural method of preserving oral poetry, remained the only viable means for even graphemic societies as long as the use of writing was not widespread: in Europe up to the end of the nineteenth century or to the middle of our century depending on the region, and even today in much of the Third World. Beyond the threshold of technology from which its relative importance rapidly decreases, memorization continues to fulfill its office, in the margins of the archive.

Goody emblematically observed that oral societies possess storytellers and bands but not novels and symphonies. The oral text, from the very fact of its modes of preservation, is less appropriable than the written text; it constitutes a common good within the social group wherein it is produced. It is thus more concrete than the written: the prefabricated discursive fragments it conveys are both more numerous and semantically more stable. Inside a given text during its transmission, and from text to text, we can observe interferences, encores, and what may be allusive repetitions—all facts of exchange that give the impression of a circulation of wandering textual elements, combining themselves with others at each and every moment into provisional compositions. What constitutes the "unity" of the text (if one accepts such an idea) belongs to the logic of movements more than proportions and measures: to perceive this unity, in performance, is less to state a necessary organic whole in the text than to identify the latter among its possible variations (Goody 1979, p. 72; Zumthor 1981b, pp. 15–16).

The complexity of its mode of existence precludes studying oral poetry other than through the perspective of rather long time frames. Still, it is worthwhile to distance any historicizing perspective that pushes research toward an origin where ulterior developments would be contained in their germinal stages. I would rather insist on the equivocity of the temporal status of the work that is at once both unable to be situated in abstract time (i.e., the external measure of becoming) and inconceivable outside a time that is concretely and interiorly lived.

As a direct consequence, its spatial status is no less equivocal. From the space that inheres in each performance and that constitutes its real dimension another space is engendered, an extrinsic one, due to the multiplicity of successive performances. Although this effect is hardly discernible when these performances take place in the same location, the effect of this exteriorization can become considerable when a large-scale geographic displacement results (Finnegan 1977, pp. 134-36, 139–42).

In Europe and in Asia, we have at our disposal numerous reliable documents for dating the tradition of many works. The *Rig-Veda* in its earliest versions, whose transmission in Brahmanic circles has remained (despite being written down) oral up to today, must have been contemporaneous with Homer. It is a unique and extreme case. More modestly, a certain number of French "popular songs" have been recognized since the Middle Ages. Several have gone to Quebec: in a group of 355 *chansons en laisses* (epic songs having what more or less amount to "stanzas"), Laforte has noticed two from the thirteenth century, one from the fourteenth, and eleven from the fifteenth. Of some three hundred English and Scottish ballads taken from the Child collection by Sargent and Kittredge, around ten can be dated back to the thirteenth, fifteenth, and sixteenth centuries; but how many others are as ancient without our knowing it (Finnegan 1977, pp. 135, 150–51; Davenson, pp. 116–18; Laforte 1981, p. 8; Sargent and Kittredge, pp. xiii–xiv)?

In Africa, in Oceania, for Native Americans, the absence of proof does not preclude the presumption of ancientness for some poems or cycles of poems. Thus, several Maori songs exalt the lands they used to inhabit before settling in New Zealand, perhaps in the fourteenth century. The Sundiata of the Mandingo epic poem, a historical person, died in 1255. How long did it take for the poem to be formed, a poem that today griots like Mamadou Kouyate still sing (Finnegan 1978, p. 290; Niane 1975, pp. 24–37).

The geographic dispersion of oral poetry is not always clearly marked. It happens sometimes that very similar forms associated with almost identical themes are found in traditions of peoples living far away from each other and who historically have had no contact. Is this a fortuitous cultural interference due to the adventure of some solitary navigator? Or are they independent creations that manifest the existence of a universal model? These questions concern only a small number of isolated cases. Most facts assured by poetical dispersion have been drawn from the entire range of well-known itineraries: migration routes, trade routes, and pilgrimage trails. Sometimes the history of an individual or of a group provides a plausible explanation and one that in its details is always dubious (Finnegan 1977, pp. 153–54).

There is nothing less mysterious than the movement by which, in the wake of the Spaniards, Portuguese, French, and English of the sixteenth to eighteenth centuries, popular European poetry swarmed (I noted this in chapter 4) over the American continent, as well as to Madeira (where a previously unknown version of the *Cid* was discovered in our century) as happened with the Sephardim exiled to Morocco at the end of the fifteenth century. Ballads collected in England and Scotland in the eighteenth and nineteenth centuries were rediscovered by Sharp in 1930 on the lips of Appalachian mountain folk in the hinterlands of Kentucky, Virginia, and the Carolinas. Some of these songs have been found in Australia

(Menendez Pidal 1968, II, pp. 203–38, 306–65; Sargent and Kittredge, pp. xiv–xv, xxvi; Finnegan 1977, pp. 136–37).

Once imported, these poems can be maintained over a long time in a form that changes little. But the need that allows them to survive in small communities of immigrants works on them from the inside and eventually transforms them: around these relics new traditions are formed, ones that, all the while maintaining certain original features, are developed according to a new rhythm and differing tendencies: hence, the Appalachian hillbilly originating in the English ballad (Vassal 1977, pp. 58–63).

Happy circumstance sometimes allows a somewhat small group of migrants, established in an allophonic milieu, to preserve its cohesiveness, its language, and something of its oral poetry. Such islands, unceasingly threatened by submersion, dot the map of zones of migration across the world. My colleague, E. Seutin, has secured for me recordings of songs in French or in the Walloon dialect still in use among the elderly of some rural families in Wisconsin, in a region that agriculture opened up to Belgian immigrants around 1860. This group, spread out over isolated farms, managed to maintain some social cohesion until around 1940. The majority of its songs were hits in cabarets in Liège around 1830–50. The singers today, although often ignorant of French (but speaking a type of Walloon), have preserved an almost pure form of the original (Lempereur).

From time to time a fortuitous discovery reveals the path of an isolated work, transmitted by some uprooted person and that in other circumstances might have been able to engender an original tradition in the land of exile. Thus, Costa Fontes, doing research among Portuguese immigrant workers in Toronto, got from a seventy-seven-year-old woman from the Azores, a *romance* related to the war in Paraguay (1864–70), from all evidence brought to the Azores by another migrant returning from southern Brazil (Costa Fontes, no. 489).

Where there are no population shifts, an osmosis can be produced between neighboring sectors of a rather homogeneous cultural and geographic locale: versions of the Tibetan *Ge-Sar* are sung in Mongolia and in certain cantons of China; the Chilean "new song," in the 1960s was on its way to covering all of Latin America (Finnegan 1977, p. 135; Clouzet 1975, pp. 60–61). Linguistic borders do not suffice to stop this movement; but the lexical, syntactic, and above all rhythmic affinities of these contiguous languages facilitate it. Hence for many centuries, the circulation of oral poetry was intense between the various Scandinavian linguistic zones and sometimes even reached Scotland (Burke, pp. 54–55).

A comparable movement of a lesser scope (consequent to the power of written traditions in these territories?) unites, in the popular milieu, up until the beginning of the nineteenth century, the Romance languages. The song *Donna Lombarda*, probably composed (according to a very old lengendary theme) in the sixteenth century around Turin in the Piedmontese dialect and using the tune of a Christmas carol, was collected in a half dozen other Italian dialects, in a French version in the Massif Central and in Quebec, in Spanish, and even in Albanian! *Gentils galants de France*, with its very old tradition, is common, with, it is true, notable variants, to both France and Spain. The dramatic *romance* of *Bernal Frances*, whose hero was one of the victors of Grenada in 1492, spread to the entire Hispanic world, to Argentina, and to the Judeo-Spanish communities of Turkey; but we also have Catalan, French, and Piedmontese versions, none of which alter the metrical structure of the original (Foschi; Davenson, pp. 204–6; Menendez Pidal 1968, II, pp. 320–23, 361–62).

The translation from one language to the other can bring about failures that contribute to thematic fluctuation: a Spanish *romance* composed at the end of the nineteenth century (and perhaps inspired by *Bernal Frances*) recounts the tragic death of the spouse of Alphonse XII in 1878. Still, in the Portuguese version found in Brazil, the name of *Alfonso Doce* was taken to be *Le doux Alphonse* ("sweet Alphonse"), which radically alters the equilibrium and the meaning of this sad story. How many European adaptations of American texts sung to rock music have maintained the primary violence of the texts and their allusive power (Moreno and Fonseca; Burgelin, p. 176)?

How, and just how far, does the work remain the same all the while changing by way of double detour? The controversial notion of "tradition" attempts an answer. Ethnologists of the current contextualist school refer the term back to a scientific construction more than to a cultural product, and the discourse used comes from an ideology whose functions are ascribed within our own social field (Ricard 1980, p. 21). In fact, it is easy enough (by observing the mechanisms of imitation by which a society is comforted and perpetuates itself) to circumscribe *some* traditions, much less to define *the* tradition. Here I am considering rather, from afar and above, this depth of social time that, more or less, at every instant of its duration, tends to neutralize contradictions between the present and the past, even between the present and the future.

We may deny these contradictions here and now whereas elsewhere we pride ourselves on them in a purely verbal or behavioral way, deliberately or unconsciously: diverse types of coexistence of temporal depth, possible criteria for a typology of cultures, and of poetries. "Traditions": multiple answers to the challenge that the transience of all that our language designates throws in our faces: a "naturally" primitive perception of our fragility, the equivalent of what is operative within the transformation of the natural milieu. The social group, collectively, refers itself to the universe as its end and its guarantee, and interiorizes this reference by consenting to the norm thus objectified, relative to what it is necessary to know and how.

As long as this effort remains unreflective, thought and language — being close to their archetypes — are continuously readapted, in brute time, with elasticity and not too many constraints. Reflection opens the doors of history and introduces the risks entailed in inheritance. Perhaps today the cultural behavior of a youthful generation left to fend for itself demonstrates its desire to cross back through the doors in the opposite direction—if it can.

Through this network of perceptions, customs, and ideas there develop and persist "oral traditions" (Slattery-Durley, pp. 8–9; Bäuml and Spielmann, p. 64; Lapointe, p. 139). Language (*la langue*), the cement of the collectivity, manages to acknowledge the ancestors' names and deeds as well as give the group its everyday reason for being. And yet speech (*la parole*), the interiorization of the story, does not play itself out in time, as would a sequence of events; rather it follows successively and dialectically upon itself, in a constant reorientation of existential choices, affecting the totality of our being-in-the-world each time it resonates. In order to confirm or protest, the voice I hear throws its fragile sonorous interconnection between two unexpressed voices murmuring in us, too deep to penetrate the marketplace: the past voice that our forebears speak in us, and the other voice, which challenges them (Ong 1967, p. 176; Rosolato, p. 301). It is thus that at one and the same time we get propelled forward yet remain captive.

From this, according to Goody (and refuted by Vansina), comes a "homeostatic" equilibrium between a society and its oral traditions: what, at a given moment in the historical trajectory, no longer corresponds in this discourse to a present need becomes the object of a "structural amnesia," and survives as an empty form or disappears. If an overwhelming cultural trauma follows, the society that undergoes it will require several generations to reconstitute the general economy of the collective speech (Goody 1968, pp. 27–67; Vansina 1971, p. 457; Scheub 1975): thus, old Europe after Gutenberg, colonial Africa, and our "West" in its confrontation with the computer. Instability and functional ambiguity are the major features of the "images," like those Scheub calls complex forms—mental, linguistic, and corporeal—whose performance embodies our traditions.

These traditions exist less by themselves than they are engendered in the memory of those who live them and live from them: the cumulative knowledge that the group, as a group, has of itself, and that it invests in language according to thematic or formulaic rules. These rules and modalities of their usage differ depending on the types of cultures. Archaic societies possess a greater capacity for absorbing individual contributions and for assimilating them into more or less restrictive customs; the expansion of the scope of communications, the diffusion of writing, then the establishment of a regime assuring it preeminence contribute to the weakening of memories and to the acceleration of the rhythms of transmission: contradictions inscribed from now on within language itself, and within the relationship it maintains with the body. From this emerge new social roles: the intellectual, the poet, the "author" (Certeau, pp. 157, 162–65; Havelock, pp. 93–94; Goody 1979, pp. 73–74; McLuhan 1967, pp. 136–39).

Nevertheless, compared to the other elements foundational to the conscience of the community, oral poetry does not come out of what Zonnabend calls "long memory." With the exception of highly ritualized mythical forms, oral poetic discourse is much less durable than we used to think not long ago: its dynamism dissimulates the fragility of its linguistic, vocal, and gestural elements, elements devoted to what in an earlier work focusing on the medieval text, I called *mouvance*, designating thereby the radical instability of the poem (Finnegan 1977, p. 53; Zumthor 1972, pp. 68–74).

But this instability is conceivable and perceptible only in performance, the same as a discourse is only "on location." When for my own pleasure I intone one of the songs drawn from my memory I assimilate it for a moment to my living consciousness; then it falls back into silence. The passionate rock or salsa fan participates in what is felt to be a tradition (or a trend, which amounts to the same thing), but this participation is demonstrated by the intensity of the pleasure associated with a *particular* performance, relative to a *particular*, circumstantial expectation (Hymes 1973, p. 5; Houis, pp. 8–9; Burke, p. 89; Lord 1971, p. 22). Most probably tradition is nothing more than conditioning that has become (for a more or less long or short time) habitual for this expectation. It is an "open" or "closed" conditioning according to the schema proposed by Houis, the conditioning of a "public" or "selective" expectation, to which the "active" or "passive" carriers of a more or less delayed response address themselves, albeit one that I recognize.

What the voice of the poet reveals to me in effect is—doubly so—an identity, one afforded by that presence within a common space, one in which looks are exchanged; one also that results from the convergence of knowledges and from the ancient and universal evidence of *meanings*. Woody Guthrie used to declare that he wanted to be "the man who tells you what you already know." Lotman showed not long ago how this "aesthetics of identity"—inherent in forms of premodern art, in oral poetry, and today in texts transmitted by the *mediats*— functions by assimilation of stereotypes albeit never automatized, floating in the unstable milieu of lived experience (Alatorre 1975, p. xxii; Vassal 1977, p. 94; Lotman 1973, pp. 56–57, 396–99; Gaspar, p. 116). The ordinary voices of the community weave into it and for it a continuous, horizontal, successive weft, from which that of the poets surges forth and is distinguished, as one, and forming (in a temporal dimension particular to it) a vertical continuity.

Like the memory of individuals and groups, vocal poetry makes a homogeneous consciousness out of disparate perceptions. The songs are always given in advance, in the immobile present of memory, said Blanchot. Menendez Pidal spoke of *latency*. He heard it (where it concerned the epic) from that undetermined historical space where the event gives rise to myth and myth emerges in poetry (Menendez Pidal 1959, pp. 49–73; Campos, pp. 20–22). I would extend this concept even to the latter, as it is constantly ready, like the voice of my body, to overturn the probable and even the manifest, from the expected to the real, to the center of the circle that unites us. It is no longer, in this perspective, a past that influences me and informs me when I sing; it is I who gives form to the past, in the same way, it has been said, that each writer creates his precursors. Each new poem is projected on those that preceded it, reorganizes their grouping and confers on it another coherence.

Thus the performance of a poetic work finds the fullness of its meaning in the rapport that connects it to those that have gone before it and to those that will follow it. Its creative force results, in fact, in part from the *mouvance* of the work. Certainly, several genres of oral poetry call for strict memorization of the text and proscribe all variation: Polynesian dance songs, genealogical poems from Rwanda, Native American rituals, perhaps the most ancient Japanese poetry. All appear connected to a particular conception of knowledge and its transmission. Therefore it is a question here of "zero *mouvance*," significant as such (Finnegan 1976, pp. 118, 267, 1977, pp. 156–57, and 1980; Brower and Milner, p. 40; Lapointe, p. 131). In our society, habits developed under the influence of writing push concert organizers to lay out their programs in detail during rehearsals: whatever may be the ultimate goal, this technique contributes to the destruction of effects of *mouvance*. These effects, once attenuated, do not—despite all that—disappear.

The Romantic tradition since Schlegel has treated the written literary work in its *unity*, as the end of an evolving genesis. One would support the idea that it is the same for the oral work, but in its *multiplicity*, manifested by the collective performances; in that, never realized—"context sensitive," as Hymes calls it (Hay, p. 228; Finnegan 1977, pp. 143–51; Hymes 1973, p. 35; Goody 1979, pp. 12–13). Writing engenders the law, establishes restrictions along with order, in speech no less than in the state. At the heart of a society saturated with writing, oral poetry (resisting ambient pressure better than our everyday discourses) tends—because it is oral—to escape the law and to submit only to the most flexible formulas; this accounts for its *mouvance*.

Whence the inexistence of the "authentic" text. From one performance to the next, we glide from nuance to nuance or to sudden mutation; where is there, in this deteriorated state, the demarcation between what is still the "work" and what is already no longer the "work"? Folklorists and ethnologists periodically ask themselves this question: Davenson before, with respect to French songs like "La Pernette" and "Mon père avait cinq cents moutons." The interpreter himself, above all if he is illiterate, is now aware of the modifications that he brings to that which he holds to be an everyday object, something immutable (Davenson, pp. 82–83, 91–94; Menendez-Pidal 1968, I, pp. 39–40; Lacourcière pp. 224–25; Derive, pp. 70–71; Chadwick 1940, pp. 867–99; Lord 1954, p. 241, and 1971, p. 28; Gossman, p. 773). The idea of plagiarism would have as little meaning as that of copyright; both of these are fundamental to the literary institution. If among our singers today we chase the first and claim the second, it is under the marginal influence of writing. I indicated in chapter 12 that this right concerns only the "roles" compromised with writing, that of the text writer and that of the melody composer. To have access to this status, the interpreter must inscribe his voice on a record.

The well-known tradition of English ballads has furnished an excellent testing ground for researchers. Attempts have been made to measure some of its parameters of variability. According to Anders, the volume of variations would be a function of four factors: the span of time separating performances, the length of the text, the breadth of the repertoire of the interpreter, and his familiarity with the work in question. Truisms? The probability of the movement alone is what really counts. Using Sargent and Kittredge's notes, I have made a quick calculation based on two hundred ballads in the Child collection: six pieces (3 percent) have from twenty to twenty-eight different versions inventoried; twenty-eight (14 percent), from ten to nineteen; fifty-two (26 percent), from five to nine, and eighty-five (42.5 percent), from two to four. These figures are valuable only as indicators, as approximative (Anders, p. 223; Buchan, pp. 170–71; Coffin, pp. 2–15; Sargent and Kittredge, pp. 671–74).

More than the number, it is the volume that is important. Finnegan has observed that in Africa work and dance songs demonstrate a rather strong stability; the same holds in general for the oral poetry of peoples in contact with writing, like the Swahili and the Hausa (Finnegan 1976, p. 106). As an example Davenson has set up a comparative table, verse for verse, of four known versions of the French lament of Saint Nicholas, *Il était trois petits enfants*, versions, it is true, that come from various eras (from the sixteenth to the twentieth century) and from different regions: they vary in melody, strophic form, length, in the names and qualities of the characters (except the saint), in the number and the role of these characters (there is or is not a butcher's wife), and in the instruments they use. What remains is the common narrative schema, explicitly referring to Nicholas and reducible to some easily recognizable "functions" and "agents" (Davenson, pp. 265–67). Here we have what is correctly called a "work" that really exists, both as memorial pre-text and as a multiplicity of concrete texts that it is apt to engender.

Most children's songs (at least as long as school does not confiscate them) move in a rather ample poetic space: from one generation to the other, text and melody vary, and we could not speak of any "evolution" in that variation. In Romanian ballads, the formal variations of every type can affect, according to Fochi, up to 54 percent of the text. The songs brought out of Texas prisons by Jackson have scarcely more than a title, a refrain, and some isolated couplets as fixed elements: the singers identify them nevertheless at the center of a poetry that is always in the process of making itself. This textual and musical fecundity, intrinsic to the particular vocal work, can, in historical time, greatly surpass the creative period of new works. Thus, between the 1880s (where Child assembled his five volumes of English ballads) and 1904 (the date of the Sargent and Kittredge collection), several versions of already known texts were collected but did not include any new ballads (Jackson, p. 87; Knorringa 1980, pp. 54–56; Fochi, pp. 104–5; Sargent and Kittredge, p. xiii; Roy 1981, p. 160).

I will group together as *variants* differences of every sort and every size where the *mouvance* of the work manifests itself in the activity of performance. I distinguish between two types (in fact, ones gathered in the operation of the work), depending on whether they are realized between performances due to different interpreters or to the same one.

The first type presupposes the intervention of personal differences, upbringing, age, but sometimes also social constraints imposing on a given class of individuals a certain style or particular tone: thus, in the good old days of Ma Rainey and Bessie Smith, between the male and female blues singers, and at the beginning of jazz, between black and white interpreters (Collier, p. 111–12, 123–30).

The variants of the second type come from either qualitative modifications due to circumstances, or in contrast to a deliberate desire not to repeat itself; sometimes there is with a more subtle intention, namely, the desire to modulate the response to meet audience expectations. The time passed plays a role and greatly increases the import of these effects. Gilferding, who between 1860 and 1880 collected Russian *bylines* in the Lake Onega region, noted that a singer never performed a poem in the same way twice. Rybnikov, while traveling through the region twenty or thirty years later, noted differences so great in the performances of informants already recorded by his predecessor that he hesitated on the identity of several; thus the ballad "Ilya de Murom" in the two versions provided by the renowned singer Trophime Tyabinine varies in length from the simple to the double. Romanian ballads have been the object of several studies of variants. In an excellent little book, Knorringa, in closely examining eleven known versions of the poem *Mogos Vornicul* is led to a transgression of the rather fluid limits of the work, and it is at the level of tradition as such that a specific intertextuality that informs the tradition and gives it its unity is defined (Finnegan 1978, p. 324; Okpewho, p. 248; Bowra 1978, p. 217; Renszi 1961; Knorringa 1978, pp. 66–112).

Several attempts have been made to classify the different types of variants from a poetic perspective. Attempts from a formalist bias that are limited to the verbal apparatus of the tradition appear to me to be of little use, for example, that of Voigt for proverbs (Voigt 1978). I prefer those based on the respective economy of textual, melodic, and rhythmic modifications: traditional French songs have been analyzed several times over from this point of view.

206 □ DURATION AND MEMORY

Some autonomous but correlative variations of the text on the one hand and the melody on the other have been brought forth. The melody is used and renewed more quickly than the text and its borders are all the more uncertain: motifs, entire musical phrases, are dissociated, migrate toward other contexts, are recomposed at the center of the tradition, much like epic formulas. We have been able to write that the melody of oral tradition exists only through its variants. If by chance the work is transferred to a region culturally distant from its original milieu, a more profound transformation is produced, one inevitably adapting it to another musical system. One example is the European lament for the death of the aviator Chavez that a Peruvian Indian sang in strict adherence to his pentatonic scale; another is the blues, whose dissemination paid a dear price: the end of "blue notes" (Davenson, pp. 82–89; Laforte 1976, pp. 34–35; Burke, pp. 121–22; Harcourt, p. 21; Collier, pp. 109–11, 438–39).

Or as well, the same melody carries several songs; sometimes, in the course of its history, it moves from one to the other. Conversely, a single text, one that is almost stable, can be sung using several melodies: for "La Belle Barbière" (no. 44 in Davenson), no less than fourteen have been collected; for the "Beau Déon" (no. 6), twenty-eight. The rhythm of the verse is better maintained, so it seems; in contrast, the strophic form, generally linked with the melody, is scarcely less unstable than the melody.

Musical variants are commonly accompanied by textual variants more often thanks to the freedom of invention prevalent in performance than some causality. Today, the mechanization of transmission has not entirely abolished that freedom. When the authority of the text (imposed by a rite or the model of writing) prohibits any modification of it, the musical interpretation offers the only possible margin for play. Bob Dylan's fans confirm that he never interpreted a song twice in the same way and that he varies his melodies with each recording.

The melodies of textual variants that impinge on vocabulary or syntactic chains can be variously motivated:

(1) by the desire to adapt the work to the particular context of the performance, either by distancing what could be off-key or not understood, or on the contrary by concentrating incongruities or provocations there;

(2) by the need to level off semantic difficulties brought out by the text, especially for an ancient tradition: archaic words, ambiguities stemming from the disappearance of defunct cultural contexts, the apparent arbitrariness of proper names, thus leading to a constant reinterpretation, one rich in reverse meanings;

(3) by the necessities of versification, the rhythms or sonorities of which, by altering themselves over time, often require delicate readjustments, especially in languages that use rhyme.

Other textual variants concern the arranging of discursive masses and the ordering of parts. They probably depend all the more on a deep-rooted dynamism that animates every operation of the voice: this upsurge of speech, so at odds with setting up a program; a surge that no other "poetic art" can ever bring down. This tendency is manifested as well in the distribution of the microtextual schemata, the rhythm of recurrence of formulas, as in the organization of subgroupings: introduction, deletions, exchange of refrains or stanzas. The examination of huge poetic sectors like that of French, English, or Mexican folk songs suggests that the oral poetic unity (where it is identified as such) resides in the stanza more than in the song itself. *Mouvance*, therefore, would have two stages: that of the stanzaic unity and that of the assemblage of these units. This instability is projected, if the poem is narrative, on the structures of the tale; from this comes the additions, subtractions, displacements of episodes or characters, such as one encounters so often in the epic (Buchan, p. 110; Coffin, pp. 5–7; Alatorre 1975, p. xix; Sargent and Kittredge, p. xxix).

We see thus the same mobility, the same slippages in style and composition, the same ephemeral stanzas, the same tonal alterations during the oral existence of the beautiful poem by Jean Cuttat, *Noël d'Ajoie*: composed in 1960 and recorded on tape, this long romance was, over a period of fifteen years of political battles, constantly recited in cafés and public gatherings in Swiss Jura, gradually assuming the role of a national anthem and a freedom song. An unknown number of versions are still circulating, although Cuttat published in 1974 what he considers to be the definitive version. From one to the other of these texts, motifs emerge or disappear; from the epic to intimist poetry, the tone changes; the general theme is inflected in what may be opposite directions. It is finally the function itself of the work in the social group that is more or less modified (lecture given by Mr. Moser-Verrey in my seminar, February 1980).

To errant motifs there correspond couplets, migratory verses, often the debris of forgotten songs, although available, aspiring to be reintroduced into new combinations: the French song "La Pernette" (Davenson's no. 2) has no less than four beginnings and three different endings in its tradition, each one of the differences found elsewhere in some other song. The same mixing is found in English ballads, in children's songs, in a specific Italian folk song in which the bashful lover in one version contemplates the sea, in another the mountain; in the Russian *bylines* Peter the Great, Ivan the Terrible, and Ilya of Murom gingerly exchange names and heroic memories (Davenson, pp. 91–92; Coffin, p. 6; Charpentreau, pp. 120–21; Cirese, p. 39; Burke, p. 144). From this often come extensive modifications touching even the allusive abilities of the text. A given English ballad collected twenty years before from the lips of a young girl who has become the wife of a pastor offers two versions that are narratively identical, but the second glosses over the smaller details concerning food, drink, and love (Buchan, pp. 115–16).

More generally, the technique of *counterfeiting*, practiced widely throughout Europe in the Middle Ages and for which there remain several famous examples, is invoked here. The twelfth-century *Laetabundus* sequence was "counterfeited" some fifty times, in every language and in all registers. Davenson's piece number 122 perhaps originally a Christmas carol, in 1627 parodied a vaudeville that in successive couplets spoke of Alexander, Moses, Gideon, and other heroes; it not only had various onomastic variants but, by a substitution of terms or motifs, gave birth to bacchic songs (I first became familiar with them in this form in 1950), to circumstantial songs (one of which was in honor of the guillotine in 1792), and to several other Christmas carols from the eighteenth century on. Number 138, used by connoisseurs of "pure poetry" in the days of Abbot Bremond (*"Orléans, Beaugency . . . "*), the melody of an Orleanese carol from the sixteenth century, reduced to an enumeration of toponyms, was redone in the seventeenth century to glorify the general from Vendôme. It was provided in the eighteenth century with a couplet addressed to the slowness of the night hours, and in the nineteenth century that which we recognize today, on the Dauphin Charles, which artificially connects this little text to the legend of Joan of Arc (Davenson, pp. 530–32, 579–80; Harcourt, p. 55).

Left to the vagaries of time in this fashion, the oral poetic work floats in the indetermination of a meaning that it never ceases to undo and re-create. The oral text calls for an interpretation that is itself moving. The energy that sustains and informs it recuperates at each performance the lived experience and integrates it into its material. The questions the world asks of it never cease to get modified; for better as much as for worse, the work modifies its responses. I heard in Gangui a song sung for the escape of Bokassa that twenty years earlier had been composed for the death of President Boganda: all that was needed was to change the words a little in order to turn the lament into a mockery. Altering the text is not even essential, provided the historical context is changed. Schiller's *Brigands*, as Gossman noted, shown by Piscator in the revolutionary Berlin of 1926 or in the well-nourished Mannheim of 1957, is not functionally the same play. Were Russian recruiting songs the same songs around 1930 as they were under the czars when a tour of duty lasted twenty years (Gossman, pp. 774–75, 778). Transferred from America to Europe and even preserving its musical identity completely, today's song often gets dulled, leans more to commemoration than to the eruption of values — a result of imitation, probably, but more so of the difference in mentalities and ways of life, attenuating the immediacy of connotations.

It is in this *mouvance* of the poetic function that the "return to sources" is inscribed. The history of oral poetry for two centuries is so much richer than that of written poetry, as if voice, more naturally than the hand, would cede to this nostalgia.

There is a return to emotive themes, to common places, and to the threads of a "popular" poetry, drawn from the vast romantic well: peasant and worker songsters from the end of the nineteenth century, like Gaston Coute, or boulevard singers between the wars, like Charles Tenet. Boris Vian himself in *Cueille la vie* or in *L'école de l'amour* periodically came back, at the risk of some ridicule to cradle his art in this common current. There is a parallel movement in Quebec, facing Gilles Vigneault, Louise Forestier for a while, for the Charlebois of a dislocated America and with the sarcasms of Montreal's Ostid'cho group (Clouzet 1966, p. 83; Millières, pp. 67–78, 103–6).

A return to a folklore felt to be original, the infinitely fertile matrix of songs — as Quebec still provided the example during the twenties with Mother Bolduc and Abbot Gadbois; or Chile, which around 1960 rediscovered the rhythms of the *cachimbo*; or the Argentina of Atahualpa Yupanqui; or the Italy of Giovanna Marini, going back beyond the centuries of musical culture, to the tones of speech and to the bodily inflections of voice. In the United States where learned European music had put less deep roots, the "folkloric renaissance" of the 1940s dug into the mixed riches of popular Anglo-Saxon, Irish, Mediterranean, and African traditions, unleashed on the continent by successive waves of immigration. Linked to the pacifist campaigns of the Vietnam period, but indifferent to ideologies, the "folk," fragile but not very tender, was dreaming of another life and a unanimous recognition within this song whose secret they believed they had found. But it is here that Bill Haley married it to the blues, opened it to black rhythms and launched rock and roll around 1954. It was made up of the idyll; but it appeared suddenly that all the folklores of a superannuated world revived, unrecognizable and sure of themselves, rippling with life and salvatory violence, in this bath of youth (Millières, pp. 17–38; Clouzet 1975, p. 33; Vassal 1977, pp. 127–30; Hoffmann and Leduc, pp. 14–16, 23–27).

Across the span of this blind quest for a lost illusory paradise, the contemporary art of voice has rediscovered, in its manner and its style, that which grounds the social value of oral poetry: a value that the "classical" centuries of our Writing had squelched. At the heart of the group, this singing voice, this voice so ancient and deep, signifies the Law of a parent, but of a reconciled one.

Chapter 15
Rite and Action

Within poetry lies the hope that one day a word will tell all. Song exalts this hope and symbolically fulfills it. This is why oral poetry gives voice its absolute dimension, gives human language its overbrimming measure. From this stem the two functions that, simultaneously or alternatively, it performs in our midst: one, a distraction, arouses knowledge or provokes laughter; the other, an efficacity, sacralizes, specifies, or initiates action (Gaspar, p. 123; Thomas, p. 418; Kristeva 1975, p. 26). The cultural context modalizes them. That is to say, the voice that sings always steals away from the perfect identities of meaning: its echo reverberates in the unexplored shadows of its own space; it reveals them, feigns giving them to us for an instant, then grows silent, having passed beyond all signs.

No more than the storyteller, the singer does not name what he talks about: he prenames it in a preliminary and unique discourse, referring to the incommunicability of a subject. By seizing on a given event or a given object in order to confer existence on it—both poetic and vocal existence—he makes them probable, suitable for stirring up desire or fear, for causing pain or pleasure; but he does not *ex*plicate them; on the contrary, he *im*plicates them.

African civilizations (see chapter 3) consider rhythmic and chanted speech to be the power of life and death, the locus from where emerges all invention: the name makes being, existence is conceived of in terms of rhythm. Such is the key of wisdoms, arts, daily practices, no less than the survival of states. But no culture in the world has been completely ignorant of these values so magnified by Africa (Jahn 1961, pp. 149, 178, 186; Finnegan 1977, p. 239). None among them was unaware of the genetic link connecting poetry to action. "What is it good for?" asks common sense. The question mark applies to *what*, not to *good for*. The poem, animated by voice, is identified with that which it makes exist in the way of perceptions, emotions, intelligence, such that no paraphrase of it would be possible, even if through some aberration, one felt the need for it.

A song evoking childhood, a lost country, or a beloved person, provokes an emotional reaction in most people, one that is much more intense than an ordinary sentence developing the same theme could do. Whence the universality of nostalgic songs and the occasional brutality of their effects on frustrated individuals. It is said that Louis XIV proscribed the song "Ranz des vaches" for the Swiss regiments because this shepherd's lament led mercenaries to desert despite their reputed lack of emotions. The word that the rhythmic or singing voice projects toward the listener agitates or pacifies, separates or mediates. Writing, whatever one may do, attenuates and makes unreal; within voice there erupts and is transmitted without any calming intermediary the No that opposes art to the demands of the Institution, at the moment when the institution is most pressing (Ong 1967, pp. 192–93).

Voice in its spatial depth distances itself from mute order. It naturally leads to scandals. Even as the traditional poet in good conscience submits his words to authority and subjects them to censorship, his very voice, warmly corporeal, raised up from the midst of so many fleeting and weightless discourses signifies something else. It happens that a very closed society recognizes and acknowledges this desire for transgression as a lesser evil in order to defuse it; thus we have traditions of songs intended to defy scatological, sexual, or religious taboos, such as the Aragonese *jotas* studied by Fribourg (Kristeva 1975, p. 13; Fribourg 1978b, pp. 315–18; Coyaud).

Recuperation? The term is ambiguous. The will to subjugate voice and to serve voice is one of the constants in the history of societies. It suffices that this call for pleasure and discomfit, this remixing of blood, resonates hither and yon so that the recuperating effect is voided.

It was not always so. Oral poetry was born from archaic rites—ontologically, if not (who will know?) historically. The rite contained it. One day, it got away; since then . . . The details embellishing this fable are of little importance. What I mean here by *rite* (a term often misused) is that which, inclusive of the social group, defines functional roles at the same time as it ensures a relationship with the divine. A rite is all the more effective when it is actualized in drama: acting out the sacred symbols of lived experience and the unimaginable. A gesture informs it, one that a meterical or chanting voice eventually explains. Myth, another matrix-type form, on the contrary, has for its essence the word that explains the gesture. It gives birth to the story; rite engenders song—one and the other constantly reanimated by the desire carried by voice. Ritual voice utters within an eternalized space-time the secret and imperative word that summons the divinity to be present, to fulfill the empty space in the middle of the group. In time immemorial, an Unknown along the way, a musician angel, Orpheus, taught the formula to our magi from which they derive their powers: the formula is theatricalized to the point of being reabsorbed sometimes in dance, as in the Balinese ritual of Rangda (Gans, pp. 129–30; Ong 1967, pp. 161; Geertz, pp. 112–15).

Rite secures and confirms protective taboos; or it may surpass them and plug into the unconditional. In both of these functionings, its operation is integrated into magic; its agent, sorcerer or shaman, carries the mark of strangeness; yet this mark resides within his voice. It is not completely human; its timbre, range, or articulation distinguishes it from ours. For the Kwakiutl Native Americans, the sorcerer wears a mask intended to modify his voice, so important is it to show how the Spirit intervenes in it. It belongs only instrumentally to this human throat. For this reason myths of the origins of poetry always connect voice to some deity, like the Muses (Bologna 1981, sections 2, 1, 3, 4; Finnegan 1977, pp. 237–38).

Within rite, in fact, the poetic voice speaks a language common to mortals and gods: the "beautiful words" of Guarani seers, in which the memory of a long-ago sojourn and the promise of the "Land without evil" can be heard. Voice bases her prophecy on origins, blended with our history where she reverberates but that she interrupts suddenly, for the sake of another present, that is, as Blanchot magnificently wrote, this presence of men among themselves, poor and naked. A nomadic prophecy, that of the poets of Israel, challenging what is not wandering, announcing the coming of what could never live here and now; more humbly, the mantic poetry of the African diviners: voice always sings, vibrates in theurgic laughter, opening a hiatus in the full disposition of knowledge in the manner of the enigma that the Sphinx, according to Euripides' commentator, "used to sing like an oracle" (Clastres, pp. 105–9; Blanchot, pp. 117–23; Meschonnic 1973, pp. 260–63, 268–71; Bologna 1980, p. 557; Finnegan 1976, pp. 187–91).

Although there is little proof to substantiate it, one may suppose that ritual uses of oral poetry predominate in archaic societies (Winner, pp. 34–45; Chadwick and Zhirmunsky, pp. 238–41; Chadwick 1942, pp. 15–40; Savard 1974, p. 8; Finnegan 1978, p. 124; Burke, p. 176). There are still enough traces to satisfy ethnographic curiosity: shamanic hymns of grief, of departure, of marriage found in the nineteenth century among the Turkish people of central Asia and Polynesia; today still, magic songs of Native American hunters, initiation songs for many African ethnic groups, collective incantations accompanying birth for the Pokot of Kenya (I pointed these survivals out in chapter 4). But as well, just yesterday, pathetic revivals, for example, the hymns of the Zulu prophet Isaiah Shembe, the founder of the "African Church of Nazareth" during the first third of our century, or other derisory relics, little pebbles on the long road of history.

In sixteenth-century Italy and England, certain storytellers or singers would cross themselves or uncover themselves at the beginning of the performance — a final homage to the sacred forces touched by voice. Rite became custom, fixed social habit without motivation.

In what we have thus lost there survives even today, the echo of an obliterated desire, this call for identification that continues to resonate in all vocal poetry. But the initial ritual is socialized; its dramatic force is dulled in the syncretism of religions and the conservatism of social custom. African griots have no part in shamanism. Their function is to appease social rivalries by music and word. The voice of the poet changes abilities and tones. Rite has ceased to contain it. Its dynamism, now liberated, propels it toward the confused horizon of possibilities, avidly seeking action. Perhaps society senses a danger in this emancipation and becomes fearful. It will invent pseudorites to corral this voice, if nothing else to neutralize its perturbing elements — and so, probably, in the darkness of time, writing was invented. Thus, bourgeois society created its literary institution, one today relayed functionally by the televisual Institution (Cazeneuve, pp. 72–75, 79).

As a sonorous figure, the liberated voice, already warm, imprints the trace of future action on the existential fabric. It is this action itself, in one or the other of its modalities: ludic, or "committed," one as real as the other, although opposed to one another in the same way that "do-it-as-if" is opposed to doing, and referring to distinct levels of experience.

Between rite and game there extends the space where the useful seesaws with the gratuitous. The quality of the game is its intensity: its madness, its distance from the ordinary. It is no less ordered than any other action, but ordered differently, as voluntary and free, with marked beginnings and ends, its place and its time, a limited perfection where, when it arises, speech is inscribed — an indisputable reality of "an appearance that is," according to Fink. But *where* is it, if not in speech itself? In fact, in most cultures, it is the rare game that voice does not accompany, in some marked rhythmic form, usually song. For the Inuit of the central Arctic, in a very elaborate ludic system, ten types of games have been counted, nine of which have a vocal activity and eight various forms of song (Huizinga, pp. 2–10; Fink, pp. 76–77; Beaudry, pp. 50–52).

At the time Huizinga was writing his famous work, social development had cut the primitive ties that tethered law, commerce, and war to play, but poetry maintained the contact (Huizinga, pp. 132–34). Poetry plays with the words, enjoys. Huizinga was thinking of written poetry. His proposition holds truer for oral poetry, by itself, thanks to the sonorous articulations, to being able to fulfill the repressed desire to make the body a *plaything*.

Marked by its prehistory, oral poetry thus fulfills a function that is more ludic than aesthetic: it has its part to play in the concert of life, in the cosmic liturgy;

214 OF RITE AND ACTION

it is at once enigma, teaching, diversion, and battle. Historically it never completely loses these characteristics. This is the source of its relative indifference to
the successive canons of beauty as well as, often, its aggressivity, its tendency to
organize itself into forms that are contrastive, provocative, and that stimulate
competition: what the Greek *iambos* at first may have expressed; poetic and
prophesying potlatches to which we owe the most ancient forms of Arabic song
as well as the Germanic, rigorously regimented so as to excite the agonistic pleasure of the voice, plying language for its own exigencies (Huizinga, pp. 66–70,
110–22).

Nothing in the archaeology of poetry allows us to go back to this aspect of the
rite and the game. The ludic song coexists with ritual song in archaic societies
(still today in Africa): in the historian's eyes, one could not be assigned to the
other, but rather, hypothetically, both have a common origin, one so far distant
that it no longer matters to us. Apparently a pure expenditure, a depth of strategy
and investment, the game as rite, like the Freudian *fort-da*, fixes a limit by the
very gesture that breaks it, and vice versa (Finnegan 1977, p. 208; Fink, p. 123;
Huizinga, pp. 46–47; Ong 1967, pp. 28–39; Cazeneuve, p. 81). It manipulates
the subject-object relationship and beyond that problematizes the relations that
for each of us make up the world: a mirror, but one that causes birth, producing
that for which it gives the figure, within its frame; my poem, my song, *symbol* in
the etymological sense of the term, indicator of recognition. The spoken word,
even more so the sung word, is celebration — the transmission of knowledge, initiation, and joy. It is no different today for speech broadcast by the media and,
eminently, for what we could call televised poetry.

Even more radically than theater, performance is therefore *festivity*. It requires
a spontaneous convergence of desires, adhering to common imaginary forms. In
our world, the purely audial *mediats* have caused this characteristic to atrophy.
Television restores it by altering it. For it to be manifested in its primary intensity,
it is enough to gather around a flesh-and-blood singer any half-interested audience. Elsewhere a lavish etiquette arouses and frames the sought-after participation of the audience, as happens for the *pajadas* of the Rio Grande do Sul (Cazeneuve, pp. 80–83; Anido, pp. 167–69). Someone like James Brown, former
gospel singer, who, at some fifty years of age remains one of the strongest figures
of Afro-American song, preserves even in his stage act the passion of black communities in his native Georgia: twenty musicians, dancers, a chorus, actors, however contaminated as one may claim, the James Brown Revue explodes like a
universal celebration. Who in the auditorium would not participate? Leave the
critics until tomorrow.

With lesser means, a group in Brazzaville, deliberately mixing traditional cos-
tumes and three-piece suits, but always barefoot, blends its voice with those of a
public suddenly incited to stand on tables and benches, vibrating with the broken
song that speaks to it about the land, the mother, African unity, another hopeful

celebration. It is here that the villagers in the brush welcome its echoes, return them in their own way, unleashed bazaars in the humid equatorial night, where the life of the neighborhood of the people is recounted in songs, in war cries, in strident drumming by maracas and clinking bottles. These are disparate examples whose ultimate meaning is nothing, if not that across this world bewildered by the end of a century there is being outlined, in dotted lines, tentatively, from place to place, hesitatingly, threatened constantly by commercial powers, a lost Feast, a communal self-celebration of word, voice, and body.

Seasonal or commemorative, public or private, celebration does not necessarily have a joyous connotation: African funeral songs are admirable festive poems. The destruction of precious and rare goods, feasts, the waste of meager riches laboriously collected (as still seen for the most disenfranchised populations from Papua to East Africa), these ostentatious excesses, this denial of daily oppressions—voice can take it on (Huizinga, p. 48; Smith 1972, pp. 161–68; Smith 1980). Unable to abolish these signs materially, the group delegates the immense and devastating task of language to its singers: beyond what the words say, beyond even this body, all the way to the limits of voice.

For this reason (Rousseau already had pointed it out in his *Lettre à d'Alembert*) celebration is opposed to spectacle as a communal action for all the others: all the more reason for the cultural industry that reigns higgledy-piggledy over "national celebrations" and festivals. Song almost always presides over them; but where are *our* festivals? The traditions that nourish them are degraded at the same time and in the same way as our relation to the world and to others has been transformed. Nevertheless, other celebrations come forth, huge savage assemblies that for thirty years have not stopped regrouping themselves around yet another singer, another orchestra, once show biz has assimilated the preceding one.

The game, where it is declared to be such, and the patented celebration, rightly or wrongly seen as institutions, do not seem to allow for the agenda of danger. An apparent innocuousness. In its deeply rooted tendencies, the game lives alongside politicized action; the game suffers the attraction of action, and interferences are produced. The dichotomies that Huizinga set up between the ludic and the useful, between work (or science) and play, no longer resist criticism. Play has its serious side, its effort, its utility (Warning 1979, pp. 327–28; Lotman 1973, pp. 105–10). Neutralizing the fear that stymies efficient action, play spends a refined energy where man believes he has discovered his true, hidden nature, otherwise coded as his social ego. Whence the exemplary force that voice deploys therein. Voice is raised from the bottom of a childhood, to the near side of the reality principle; voice affirms this measured marginality to which the commonality of human beings attaches the mask of freedom.

Thus the playing field is confined to that of politicized action. A moving border area separates them but sometimes also combines them: from there come spoken or sung poems, improvised or not, that arouse through the impact of an experience or of a spectacle, humor, mockery, sarcasm, a numerically considerable part (qualitatively often mediocre) of the oral poetry of our time, all coming from song. But—with the exception perhaps of the most strongly ritualized—there is no culture that does not recognize this form of "art": sharp little ditties that the Voltaic women working the mortar of their courtyard improvise calling back and forth to one another; off-color teasings that the older sisters sing to a Zulu fiancée. Innocent humor; or another that is less so: comic improvisation of Asturian peasants, covering the entire gamut of nuances, from hilarious jokes to the almost blasphemous (Vassal 1977, pp. 10–11; Finnegan 1978, p. 140; Fernandez, pp. 474–76).

Imperceptibly the poem veers from joke to accusation to challenge. The same text, depending on circumstances, will be interpreted in one or the other manner. In many traditional cultures, from Africa to the Pyrenees and to Acadia, there are the songs of reproach that a betrayed lover addresses to the unfaithful woman: at the heart of small isolated communities, such invectives, once absorbed by the group, pass into the local repertoire and take on the role of moralizing discourse, justifying the punishment of misconduct (Finnegan 1978, p. 135; Ravier and Séguy, pp. 94–95; Dupont, pp. 222–23).

Yet (because it is an actual presence and the living community), it is in its openly collective forms that performance claims rather boisterously its passing into "politicized" action. Intimately connected to the tensions that give rise to social energy, it anchors vocal work in the political *agon* or in military violence. The poetic voice—an animating force that either exalts or deplores—thus gives form to already mature passions but ones still seeking themselves, and hurries them to their end.

Hence, the war song (Bowra 1978, p. 413; Camara, pp. 181–82) Most traditional societies support singers whose duty it is to exhort the men to war, to foment their aggressiveness, to excite them to combat: this was a common practice in the High Middle Ages in Europe, as it had been for the Celts and the ancient Germanic peoples, as it still was in 1812 in the Russian cavalry regiments, and up to the end of the nineteenth century in African kingdoms. And what is the "Marseillaise" by Rouget de Lisle, whose original meaning has been muted by years of use?

Or, as well, voice magnifies the common past by conferring on it the weight of its own presence and elicits from it an incitement to battle, a justification, all the more convincing in that the emotion provoked is summary: glorious evocations, commemorations of dead heroes, celebration of the invincible chief, a mythological effervescence whose only product will be the violence it unleashes. Those in power know its effectiveness and exploit it (Brécy, pp. 217–41; *Le Monde* of October 11, 1980; Andrzejewski and Lewis, p. 72): the states of 1914–18 provide rich examples of it—the France of the Montehus and the Botrels is not the least of them! At the beginning of the war against Iran in 1980, Iraqi radio would broadcast songs and poems about the classic victory at Kadisiya as often as news about battles taking place and the president, the standard-bearer of the Arab cause. Or as well, after the fact, voice evokes the past in hopes of multiplying it into the future where voice projects it. The Somalian sheikh, Muhammad Abdille Hasan—great poet and hero of the wars that his people carried on for twenty years against the Ethiopians, the British, and the Italians—having in 1913 exterminated an English expeditionary corps, improvised a long-famous song about this victory.

The weaker, more threatened, and more conscious of dangers the group, the more the poetic voice resonates with force. Song becomes a weapon: partisan songs, during the Second World War, across occupied Europe, from France to the Soviet Union; Latin American guerrilla songs today, such as the Sandinista songs whose text provides the rules for using arms or for making explosives (recording *Guitarra armada*, FSLN, Managua); songs from civil wars. But the horror of this violence is no less a fertile source of poetry. Human beings have never ceased to invest their hatred of war and their desire to escape from its order in the works of their voice, in the name of their simple desire for peace or in a more totalizing resistance movement. The American folk song, it its origins, was bathed in a pacifist tradition carried on from songs dating back to the Civil War: the chagrin of boys enlisted by force, lost fiancées, anger in the face of absurd death. A Tom Paxton, a Phil Ochs, a hundred years later, will find out how to draw the tragically ironic words of their songs about Vietnam from these depths (Vassal 1977, pp. 72–74, 216–22). Penel sent me a series of beautiful songs with an overwhelming laconism, improvised in 1969–71 in the camps of Sudanese refugees, poor devils caught between the northern armies and the black partisans.

A popular antimilitary poetry was developed in like manner in France and in America, starting in the eighteenth century, at the same time as the strength of the armies was growing and war was becoming industrialized. Napoleonic conscription spawned a truly new genre, with epic connotations, the rebel's song, exalting these heroes of modern times. We can find examples of it today still in Breton folklore: among the songs that Ravier recorded in the upper Pyrenees there are five versions of a long ballad about a deserter from the time of Louis-Philippe, a song still alive in the memory of some elderly people. "Le Deserteur" of Boris Vian (the broadcasting of which was prohibited for several years) brought back this tradition in 1954 on a larger scale. Meanwhile, Brel composed "La Colombe" (Coirault, pp. 78, 119; Vassal 1977, pp. 53–54, and 1980, p. 36; Clouzet 1964, pp. 92–93, and 1966, pp. 114–16; Ravier-Séguy, pp. 13–40).

"La Colombe," like "Le Deserteur," was "committed" in an explicit fashion: political songs, strictly speaking, those whose relationship to a possible, desirable, obligatory action is immediately obvious. They are all the more lively in that, being protests, they call for disobedience, for battle, for the desires for a difference where the collective feeling of existence gets reinvigorated.

It is a fact that the majority of political songs are protest songs: less by the message they transmit than by the act of the performance itself, contributing to the destabilization of an order they reject or whose subversion they praise. They form the ill-reputed counterpart of the propaganda song, an old instrument that more or less all states have used since ancient China and the use of which the English of the eighteenth century began to theorize (Neuburg, pp. 117–18).

Articulated upon the event, the political song mimes it figuratively in performance: either by provoking a burst of enthusiasm or revolt within listeners by identification, or by imposing on them the distance of irony or tenderness, which arouse, in the end, the same effects. Physically voice fashions what it says and even more so, what it sings; it reproduces the fact recounted, disperses it in its own space-time. The force of the discourse (the talent of the singer) definitively grounds its reality. The proximity of the event is not even necessary. The very beautiful ballad by Phil Ochs about the assassination of Lou Marsh in Harlem was raised immediately as an outcry. The songs by Woody Guthrie on Sacco and Vanzetti were composed twenty years after the affair, at the request of Folkways Records (Vassal, 1977, pp. 109–10, 222–23).

Coming from urban origins, linked to the development of the industrial society that produced it without wanting it and on which it acts as a parasite, the protest song sinks its roots into the France, England, Germany, and Italy of the fifteenth and sixteenth centuries. Tongues were loosening up in favor of the social and moral crisis that was disrupting Western Europe at that time: "seditious ballads" found in Venice around 1575, French songs from the period of the wars of religion, *mazarinades*. Disdained by the learned but closely watched by the police, rejected into the marginality of the "popular," this poetry unfurled throughout the monarchic seventeenth century. Some songs were circulating around 1615, in Dutch villages, taking sides for or against Oldenbarnevelt; in English cities, in the troubled times of Charles I where street ballads were already denounced and damned to hell by monopolist businessmen. Specialized printers and street singers disseminated satirical opuscules, songs, and prophecies: some 150 openly political works have been found for London alone in a single year, 1641 (Vernillat and Charpentreau, pp. 197–99; Burke, pp. 71–72, 163, 255; Brecy, p. 10).

Throughout eighteenth-century Europe, poems and songs by the thousands narrated daily news, much in the manner of our press. Peddlers' literature was fed in part by them just as it was not long ago in Latin America and Nigeria. But to speak of the event cannot be neutral: no more than today on the part of Victor Jarra singing about the squatters of Puerto Mont or Bob Dylan about the death of the boxer Davey Moore. An ironic reversal doubles the effect by declaring the meaning: in 1892 in French anarchist circles they sang the bravado songs that

Ravachol was supposed to have intoned at the foot of the guillotine. A bit later on, in this same tradition, the softly explosive irony of the Quebecoise romance by Raymond Levesque, "Bozo les culottes," is to be found. Irony introduces doubt into the heart of the event fiction and, by using narrative color, suggests rejection (Zumthor 1982a; Brécy, pp. 146–48; Clouzet 1975, pp. 48–49; Vassal 1977, pp. 160–63, 172; Millières, pp. 57–175).

Within the group to which it addresses itself, the voice of the singer takes on a certain violence. Then, literally, it regurgitates that violence. In most European nations, from the seventeenth to the nineteenth centuries, songs circulated about the crimes of the day, murders, rapes, incest, all that which spectacularly breaks the social contract, or songs about the criminals themselves: poetry where Morality claimed to find its account, since trespasses, atrociously punished in the end, were described there in detail (Neuburg, pp. 83, 86, 127, 137). On the mornings of executions, vendors distributed the text of the song to the crowd, a song composed for the occasion; but, taking part in the violence of the spectacle in which it was integrated, this song signified less the hatred of the crime than the revelation of an oppression.

Along these convoluted paths, a worker's singing poetry, one commemorating conflicts like that of the Angoulême paper workers in 1739 or the revolt of the Lyon silk workers in 1786, found its timid beginnings — in the France of the Encyclopedists, no less. I am thinking here of the lovely album of R. Brecy, which follows this story from 1789 to 1945. C. Pierre has counted no less than two thousand songs of this type between 1789 and 1800, most of them using popular melodies. Over the course of the nineteenth century, all the socializing or anarchic groups took it upon themselves to spread political songs, often extremely violent ones — half washed out in our modern eyes by the pomp of their style. From the 1920s to the war the PCF (French Communist party) reworked this strategy: Vaillant-Couturier and the chorus of his AEAR thus created and spread, much beyond the party, a protest poetry, originals or in translation, one of which at least had some glory years with the Popular Front: "Au-devant de la vie," by Jeanne Perret, using the film score by Shostakovich (Brécy, pp. 7–14, 257–67, 274).

It is the entire history of Europe for the past two centuries that voice has thus *made*: discourse-in-presence, modulated by the rhythms of the body, permeated with warm sensuality, muddled by daily noises, barely nuanced but immediately imperative in the truth of its evidence.

In the course of the years following 1945 and the Nazi trauma, a convergence was produced between this popular tradition and a "literary" poetry coming out of the Resistance: the red line seemed to erase itself, one that for centuries elitist culture had laboriously traced and maintained between poem and song. Vocal poetry reintegrated—in the very heart of the social scene where Leo Ferre began to sing—its native function.

In the United States, events took a different route. The pioneer songs that made poetry out of the westward movement after 1780 kept abreast of a causticity that often implacably belied the legend. But it is rather in the black folklore of the agricultural states of the Deep South that the protest song had its roots; and, if it pushed into the workers' arena, it remained an almost exclusively rural poetry for a long time. Research done by Greenway in 1950 revealed both the relative rarity of the protest song in the factories and the remarkable fact that it was rarely raised except during strikes. Yet, a workers' action par excellence, the strike is the only thing that, in the mechanical conditions of industrial work, can be experienced—or mythified—as disalienating. From 1910 on, thanks to Joe Hill, the singer gunned down in 1915, unions understood from what depths the social existence of the song draws its force. The Great Depression had given them strength: in the beginning of the 1930s several groups were set up in Arkansas, Tennessee, and Kentucky that were devoted to the protest song. In this way, at eighteen years of age, Woody Guthrie discovered the road he was to follow and that would lead him in 1946 to adhere to the association, *People's Song*, the supporter of the unions, of workers groups, of communities seeking a voice (Greenway 1960, p. 303; Vassal 1977, pp. 75–78, 84–92, 111–18; Clarke, pp. 135–45).

In the 1950s, the fight for civil rights once again blended blues and spiritual traditions with those hitherto in possession of white popular song. The golden voice of Joan Baez arose: in English, in Spanish, even in French, hers was the voice of the voiceless, undauntedly coherent (despite the vagaries of her success) with the ideology that sustained her, singing "Le Déserteur" on the parvis of Notre Dame, interpreter of Victor Jarra and Violeta Parra, mastheads for the new Chilean song. This conjuncture was made all the richer because the protest song was developed in Chile from Andean traditions, along a trajectory comparable to that of the folk song; but, beginning with the formation of the Popular Front, several organizations of the masses had supported, enclosed, and directed its dissemination, conferring on it a unique political import for the American continent: that of a cultural fact (Vassal 1977, pp. 47–50, 137–63, 237–46; Clouzet 1975, pp. 45, 51–33, 61).

Here and there the Africa of the independence movements—inasmuch as that, from the beginning of the 1960s, it was plunged into the injustice and misery of an alien form of "development"—reappropriated some of its old poetic traditions, mockery, praise, or blame, and reactivated them in the face of new realities: calling less for a denial than an awakening, by the voice and sound of the instruments, the latent forces that, in each of us as we are torn asunder, grounds the living community. In the singer, according to Camara, the unconscious of the group is at work. The Malian or Voltaic griot, the Kenyan singer, rediscovers the role of mediator in social conflicts that had been theirs before colonization. The Ouagadougou griot Traore Mamadou Balake, the first "modern" singer Upper Volta has produced, cultivates today an original type of song, one that he has created through progressive digression, starting with traditional forms, highlighted with an ironic commentary on current events, whether big or small, public or private: at what moment does this nonconformity become intolerable to the powers and then, to which powers?

But beyond the circumstances and the disintegration of inherited rhetorics, claims of African unity and black identity continue to reverberate in these voices, like an ultimate signification: in a poem recited on radio Mogadishu during the Suez crisis; in the song of the Somali poet Qarshe, about the Berlin Wall, a retort to history at the conference bearing the same name as the city, and that in 1885 had cut Africa into portions; in the improvisation of the Zulu Kunene against missionaries (Finnegan 1978, pp. 99, 115, 117, 141).

Simultaneously, under the influence of Afro-American song, other more aggressive forms are breaking away from local traditions. Today Lagos echoes with enormous loudspeakers playing *Afro-beat* and *juju*, songs by Ebenezer or by Sunny Ade. In this immense, potentially superrich, although currently destitute country, Fela, king of *Afro-beat*, has become for the power structure a threatening enemy; the police hassle him, the army burns down his home, he pays for his colorful personality, denounces scandals, intervenes in electoral campaigns, and parades like a prince in the proletariat areas of Surelers, in the middle of his twenty-seven lovely wives!

One could as easily point out other regions of the world, other peoples in conflict. At the end of the nineteenth century an indigenous oral poetry of protest against white power was formed in line with Maori traditions of New Zealand. For a quarter of a century, until around 1920, Uzbek poetry fed its aggression on political tensions that agitated the people: revolts against the khans, class struggle, calls to the proletariat (Finnegan 1978, pp. 292, 314, 316; Bowra 1978, pp. 426, 473, 513). Nothing radically distinguishes the poetry of a supposedly decolonized Third World and poetries inspired by regionalist movements in old Europe. By taking up long-standing folklorized traditions, they attempt to give them back life by making them espouse a political dimension. Whence the tendency to urbanize, where possible, the publics and the themes; whence the recourse, at least episodic, to local languages or dialects; the replacement, often, of traditional musical accompaniment by modern ones, like the electric guitar.

A small book by Wurm gives a lively analysis of an example taken from Spanish provinces. It is not only at the heart of vast historical and cultural unities, Catalonia, the Basque country, Andalusia, but also at the level of smaller communities, sometimes one inside the first group, Galicia, Asturias, Aragon, Baleares, that this movement of the "lands that want to live" is rooted and takes form in poetry. Desire, sometimes muddled, to break a rigid political framework, to

222 □ RITE AND ACTION

empty the abstraction of state discourse of its meaning, to found a society of concrete human beings. Utopia of our century, conceived and provided by intellectuals? What alone matters here is the taking charge of speech that it has made possible and where, in turn, it finds its solace: the poetry of Gilles Servat or Gweltaz Ar Fur, to take a few Breton examples (Wurm pp. 37–38; Vassal 1980, pp. 82–97, 164).

In the beginning of the 1960s something new was produced in Europe that over the course of time will most probably prove to be of considerable historical importance: rock and roll fell from America onto a youth in black jackets, quasi-marginalized, and fermenting in repressed violence. In the United States, rock, the legitimate heir of the musical renewal of the forties, was already ten years old. In Europe, it promised from the start a radical May '68, totally irresponsible, whose truth when it arrived, was no more than an ephemeral shadow. As song, rock integrated and summarized all the prior protest poetries, but directed its effervescence into an outpouring of pure irrational energies. It broke the sound bubble surrounding and protecting the body; the tender maternal voice, scorned, erupted into furious discord. For this reason rock was received and propagated as music and as collective rhythm: only rarely did it need words to unleash the roaring hurricane. It provided a figure of pure act, arrogant joy, rupture of language invaded by onomatopeias and burps. Violence, sadism, frenzy, blackness, pessimism, cruelty, as Francois Truffaut said of James Dean in 1956; but also modesty of feeling, purity, rigor, a taste for proof and refusal of profitable co-optation. What followed were ten years of liberation festivals, hundreds of millions of fans throughout the world, such a burgeoning of experiences that nothing will ever be the same.

Scandals, familial and police intolerance: we know this short history. The extent of the reaction was proof of the force of these protesting voices. But, more than this counterviolence, more than the bowdlerization of the twist, industry snatched it. When the tally sheet for rock music hits the billions of dollars, voices in the world where we live fall silent (Hoffmann and Leduc, pp. 109–11; Clouzet 1975, p. 80). The Beatles separated, Bob Dylan went away, Brian Jones and Jimi Hendrix died. A few labels and a wiser generation are what remain. At the same time in Latin America festivals of protest songs, enterprises with a good relationship, were multiplying.

Yet, the commercial co-opting is not alone in laying traps for all action poetry. The risk of servility comes in part from the poetry itself and from the ambiguous relationship that conjoins language and praxis. From 1965 on the most radical of the American unionizers rejected protest songs, for being the source of an overactive conscience, suffocating the will to act (Vassal 1977, p. 315). Order itself, object of the protests, plays with this equivocity and with the consequences it entails. It manipulates the singer by interpreting its own plans to his benefit: Elvis

Presley at the start benefited from the racism of those who saw in him the white counterpart to all the black rhythm and blues men (Millières, p. 53). Reaction to the soft anarchism of the hippies, country music, launched under Nixon, reinterprets rock entirely with respect to the rural roots of the "heart of America."

The so-called economic crisis has infected yesterday's rebels with the conservatism of fear. When protest is silenced, it is because there is no more hope. In the Quebec of 1981 (I am writing these lines on December 31), singers seem out of the running: in this privileged land of song, where for twenty years some of the hottest voices of our world have resonated, Ferland today sings about family life and Charlebois about the universal happiness of love. To the south, the voice of Tammy Wynette, queen of Nashville, coddles the dreams of brave people like you and me in her security-blanket folklore: the dreams of those who in this same Nashville stand in line in crowds of pilgrims to go venerate Elvis's solid gold Cadillac or Webb Pierce's guitar-shaped pool. Poetry finally leads back to rite!

Conclusion

We are always at the end of the world. For the seven or eight years of my pilgrimage in Oralia, how many times have I not had the feeling of reaching the end beyond which something irreplaceable would be lost forever? In the voice of the old man Matthieu Mestokosho, a mountain Indian from Mingan, who at ninety-five years of age was still inventing tales and tales upon tales, the last echo of a historic period was resonating, or so it seemed. With Matthieu a wisdom would soon be silenced, an immense knowledge, the fidelity of life (Bouchard, pp. 9–10). What ethnologist has not, one day or another, felt this sadness?

In search of living voices, it was necessary to cover too many ruin-covered fields. The destruction of venerable old cultures strips all of us of humanity, dispossessed of its millenary work, of its memory and its dead; expelled from the warm closeness of communities with a real grip — however uncertain — on the world, whereas ours is certain but more and more unreal. Nothing, however, is ever completely played out. Throughout the Third World, people today are beginning to wake up from this shock, are hanging on to the debris of a broken identity. What else can the present resurgence of Islam, in all its excesses, be? And among us the regionalist movements, still, despite their naïvetés or their aberrations, attest to the fact that Jacobin unitarism has not had the last word (Lafont, pp. 210–50).

Alvin Toffler's "third wave" is already taking form, is ready to unfurl in the direction of a decentralized world, one comprised of the concert of our differences. We would like to believe it. But the ads that make claims about it and the ecologism that prefigures it stem from this recurrent millenarism, studied recently by Worsley, a sudden epidemic, surging forth undauntingly in societies in crisis, at the moment when collective fear is on the point of turning to despair: an imprecatory call, a conjuration of impossible totalities. So it was already around 1660, under the inspired reign of Kimpa Vita—the Dona Beatriz of the Portuguese—in the kingdom of the Congo, a bit after the first contact with whites; for the Xhosa of west Africa, around the prophetess Nonquause, instigator of the great cattle massacre of 1856; for the Sioux of 1870–90, in the ghost dance that led to the slaughter at Wounded Knee; for the Papuans of New Guinea, in the middle of their ransacked villages waiting the saving Cargo; and now in our midst.

And voice in this adventure?

Voice is the instrument of prophecy, in the sense that it makes the prophecy. Voice sounds—or is silent—at the heart (*au coeur*)—in the chorus (*au choeur*)— of the drama. Since the seventeenth century, Europe has spread itself over the world like a cancer: surreptitiously at first, but for a long time now it rampages, an already insane ravaging of forms of life, animals, plants, countrysides, languages. Each day that passes, several languages disappear from the world: repudiated, snuffed out, dead with the last old person, voices never tainted by writing, pure memory with no defenses, windows once thrown wide open upon the real. Without doubt, one of the symptoms of the evil was, from the very start, what we call literature, and literature has taken on consistency, prospered, become what it is—one of the most vast dimensions of human beings—by challenging voice. But, in losing its preponderant position, voice has not been able to be banned from the concert of living powers that determine the destiny of civilizations; in the worst instance, it dissimulated itself there under the pretext of eloquence. It continues to send out signals. The elders of Samoa sing stories of captives drowned en masse, of villages burned by fire from the sky. These are not myths, or perhaps they have become so. But the young people of today, made aware of this servitude, feed their anger on it, a last chance.

It is not a question of deploring what, for better or worse, has become our history, nor what has created the grandeur of our literature, but rather of deciphering the mixed messages they address to us. Five thousand annihilated cultures, the marvelous flowering of humanity, today faded, profaned, struck from our maps, can no longer influence us as such, but rather as the testimony that they have written in this very history, to the advantage of values that we prefer to conceal.

It is not a question of sorting through the density of the temporal duration, nor of reconstituting, if only for the sake of a patrimony, styles of traditional life and thought, warm, but stuffy. It is a question of setting aside a false universalism, it being a confinement—of renouncing (because it is a question of poetry) the privileging of writing.

It is in this sense that it is urgent to supersede ethnocentrism, inspired as it is, along with national naïvetés, by an outdated conception of evolution. For twenty or thirty years, it is true, a new taste for the other, a curiosity about the diverse accompanied the first decolonizations. Ethnology benefited from it, so much the better for it. But neither taste nor curiosity is in question. What alone counts is this appeal to difference—to that which will make it impossible for us to remain *indifferent*. For some centuries now, "one" is in the process of constructing the unitary cultural solitary prison around us where we are held at rest: our technology, our science, our art, our problems. The only hope in the long run is that "one" is in the process: the jail has never been completely built. It is up to us to seize this opportunity to sabotage, however small the enterprise, to slip some sand into the lock being put in, a pipe in drying cement: at least in doing that, the sound of a voice can get to us from outside!

This bit of pipe has been slipped in twice already this century: in the 1920s, then around 1950–60. While they boisterously welcomed the first wave, the second, that of the new Afro-American song, frayed the symbolic system by which the West had lived until then. Our science itself was suspiciously questioning its certainties: order no longer was dissociated from disorder, knowledge demanded another logic, where the third was included (Lyotard, pp. 3–4). But the dominant society, by marginalizing the youthful crowds of the first jazz fans, then the rockers with bike chains, was marginalizing itself with regard to that which in a confused manner they were experiencing: all the rest—provisionally repressed—of knowledge, but that would perhaps return.

For us, the poetic voice is situated at this crossroads of energies: it is the locus of rooting and where it takes up life again. Certainly, in 1982, in the worldwide decline of the record industry, at the still uncertain dawn of the general use of other *mediats*, the megalomania of producers, mass production, suddenly gives the impression of a second failure: this form of orality in its turn, darkens under cultural underdevelopment. Our disenchanted society, tangled up in its diminished measures, its less and less diversified parameters, backs us up to the single issue: to try once more—without quite knowing if this will be the final time—to respond (in terms that one cannot translate into a dead language) to the questions that language asks of the body, that the body asks of language, by the intervention of these reviled voices.

Here and there in the world, ever disparate endeavors are multiplied. Perhaps a great and unfortunate Africa, ruined by our politico-industrial imperialism, finds itself more than other continents close to the end because less gravely touched by writing, warmer than the primary fire by which to forge the new instrument. Yet, for ourselves, in light of history and despite the modern acceleration of time frames, the era of the written word will perhaps have represented only a decisive but brief intermediary.

McLuhan noted that ever since the spread of printing the West has seemed inhabited by nostalgia for a world of touch and hearing—the very one that makes it lose the pure abstract visuality of writing. From the end of the eighteenth century, in France, in England, in Germany, the feeling that there are too many books permeates men and women of letters. Many things have changed. During the past hundred years, the evolution of our sciences like that of poetry was oriented toward the rediscovery of an interiority, toward listening to the primordial voices to which European thought seemed to have beccome deaf. However, bent under the hail of messages that assails us, in our turn we feel almost nauseated by a lassitude of the written: a lassitude shaken by bursts of hope or fear before the new invasion of the computer—pushing to the extreme an abstraction that the user, in the present state of things, not only does not control but is limited to mythifying in order not to perish.

Everything happens as if—episode in a millenary conflict—we are participating today in a return in force of orality: provoked by the inflation of the printed word, since the end of the last century, to the extent that the turning point of modern history seems less to have been, as is generally supposed, the invention of printing than its *mass production*! In North America as throughout Europe, teachers are noting the disaffection of youth for print, their growing inability to master written language: good or bad, and whatever may be the handiest motivations, it is an index. Sherzer was telling me that the Cuma Indians of Panama, workers in the capital and duly made literate, in their eagerness to maintain contact with their village had recently begun to write letters; now they send cassettes, and in recording them find something of the old art of storytellers. In the overproduction of writing, the function of the written word loses all evidence, whereas voice finds its, in a savage way, in an aleatory search for its biological fullness.

For some ten years now, a common ground for the social sciences, more readily perceived as such, is none other than this function of voice. Research centers, research, team projects, theses, scholarly collections, and special issues of periodicals are multiplying on all five continents. Historians, sociologists, and even literary scholars prompted by anthropology: I know of no conference since 1975 that has not had at least one session on the problems of orality. We can no longer count the colloquiums, seminars, and round tables dedicated to it; and already we have left the university ghetto, as a debate on oral literatures bore witness at the Salon du Livre in May 1981, and in March and May 1982 at the conferences on "the work of time" at the Centre Pompidou.

Writing stays put and stagnates; voice flourishes. One belongs to itself and preserves itself; the other pours out its feelings and destroys itself. The first convinces; the second calls. Writing capitalizes what voice dissipates; it rises from the ramparts against the *mouvance* of the other. In its closed space, it compresses time, laminates it, forces it to draw itself out in the direction of the past and the future: from paradise lost and from utopia. Immerged in unlimited space, voice is only present, without a stamp, without a mark of chronological recognition: pure violence. By voice we remain part of the antique and powerful race of nomads. Something in me refuses the city, the house, the security of order: a basic, irrational exigency that one occults easily, but with vengeful awakenings (Duvignaud, pp. 13–16, 26–39).

That is what we are beginning to know; and this cannot be haphazard if this new recognition will have followed the years during which we "problematized" (as we used to call it) the "subject," a potential and immutable operator, invariable center of all our series—or rather, a mass of drives, of lost languages, of silences, of confused propositions sorted through by memory, that administrator of this territory, producer of an *I* about which it folklorizes what its industry does not accept.

Since Artaud, it is in this atomization that an avant-garde theater has taken off to discover the irreducible unity of the body and its gesture. But the quest has led further yet—beyond dramaturgies and narrativities, on the threshold of a "postmodernism" (the prefix of which signifies negation more than consequence), in what we have taken to give the single name of "performance." Having appeared in the United States in the 1960s, in the wake of the Kaprow happenings, musical and choreographic research like Cage's, theatrical ones like Foremena's, questioning of actors like Cantor's, performance is beginning to arouse a bit of critical attention. It is still about seeking its antecedents, inventing an innocent history, and it draws from that elements of memories connected with plastic manipulations rather than those of language, in particular the work of Marcel Duchamp.

As an act, but less action than vital flow, an "allegory of unreadability" (Owens's expression), prior to the emergence of a "theatrical" subject and of a symbolism that permits repetition, multiplication, rhetoric: the "performance" challenges *mimesis* and chooses from the start the part of an *art* severed for us from the ancient representative illusion. A human being *takes place*, here, before me, on stage or on screen where the videodisk projects itself: a place crisscrossed by the current that no meaning immobilizes, a trajectory without characters, corporally designed to the detriment of a subject that it demystifies. In this entirely cathected space, a partial body that has become a sensorial instrument and that *is* performance is decomposed into fragments of libidinal objects by which its simple, unstable, totally objectified presence is unendingly enriched. In Meredith Monk's performances a voice surges forth.

Voice can no longer do anything but prename things, and—we know it today better than before—*that* is the poetic operation par excellence. A first name signifies nothing but a presence: an *ori-gine* ("issue from the mouth," if one goes back to the Latin), outside of affiliations and geneaolgies. The first name tends to reverse the derivations that in the waters of language, pushes names toward meaning, the concrete toward the chosen abstraction.

In the first name an appeal is raised to this polluted, ravaged, but still living and pathetic earth slathered in our barbarities. A candle is lit somewhere: a small light that nonetheless inflames me. Here I am, on the first immemorial morning, and this cry escapes me; a little thing, it is the long history of beings. Since then, everything has been said. I am translating here in metaphors what several of our singers have admitted over the past years. Song is poetic cry, a step ahead of the ready-made banal phrases.

Much the same as today's Africa makes its shoes from our tires, through its genius recuperates and revivifies the debris of our technologies, our literatures, our musics: it is time for us to do fix-up jobs, in the breath of our voices, in the energy of our bodies, the immense and incoherent heritage of these centuries of writing. In the huge marketplace of the ''global village'' of McLuhan, to reestablish an equilibrium between the eye and the ear such that the voice is soon in a state to pierce the opacity around us that we take for reality, with as much power and efficacity as painting did a century ago. Not to start again from zero, which, by definition, does not exist, but to thematize the traditions of vocal poetry, traditions that have been recognized, inventoried, domesticated, reexperienced keeping with day-to-day necessities, for those of us who are camped for just a lifetime on this patch of an ephemeral century.

Bibliography

Bibliography

References in text are given under the name of the author; dates are added when there are several titles for a particular author. Numbers refer to the pertinent pages and volume (by roman numerals) if needed. Group works are found listed under the name of the editor; where there is more than one editor, I have named only the first; where this information is lacking, I cite the work under the first significant word of the title.

In addition to works cited here, readers are referred to bibliographies in Du Berger (1971 and 1973), Finnegan (1976 and 1977), Laforte (1976), Neuburg (1977), and part of Rouget (1980). My citations go through 1981.

Special issues of journals:

Langage 10, 1968
Langue française 42 and 44, 1979
Poétique 39, 1979
Littérature 45, 1979

Abd El-Fattah, K. 1979. "Sur le métalangage métaphorique des poéticiens arabes." *Poetique*, 38, pp. 162–74.
Abrahams, R. D. 1969. "The Complex Relations of Simple Forms." *Genre*, 2, pp. 104–27.
_____. 1972. "Folk Drama." in Dorson, *Folklore and Folklife*. Chicago: University of Chicago Press, 1972, pp. 351–62.
Agblemagnon, F. N. 1969. *Sociologie des sociétés orales d'Afrique*. Paris-The Hauge, Mouton.
Alatorre, M. F., ed. 1975 and 1977. *Cancionero folclórico de México*. Mexico, Colegio de Mexico, 2 vols.
Alexandre, P. 1969. "Langages tambourinés: une écriture sonore?" *Semiotica*, 1, pp. 273–81.

_____. 1976. "De l'oralité à l'écriture: sur un exemple camerounais." *Etudes françaises* (Montréal), 12, pp. 71–78.

Alexandrescu, L. 1976. "Le Bethléem, un mystère paysan contemporain du nord de la Roumanie." *Estudios escenicos* (Barcelona), 21, pp. 149–67.

Alleton, V. 1980. "En Chine: la contagion de l'écrit." *Critique*, 384, pp. 217–27.

Alvarez-Pereyre, F. 1976. *Contes et tradition orale en Roumanie.* Paris, SELAF.

Amzulescu, A. I. 1964. *Balade populare rominesti.* Bucharest, Folklore Institute, 3 vols.

_____. 1970. "Despre stilistica orlitatei cîntelor epice românesti." *Revista de etnografie si folclor* (Bucharest). 15, pp. 461–94.

Anders, W. 1974. *Balladensänger und mündliche Komposition.* Munich, Fink.

Andrzejewski, B. W., and I. M. Lewis. 1964. *Somali Poetry.* Oxford, Clarendon.

Angenot, M. 1973. "Les traités de l'éloquence du corps." *Semiotica*, 7, pp. 60–82.

_____. 1975. *Le roman populaire.* Montreal: Presses de l'université du Québec.

Anido, N. 1980. "Pajadas et desafios dans le Rio Grande do Sul." *Cahiers de littérature orale*, 5, pp. 42–170.

Austin, J. L. 1970. *How to Do Things with Words.* Ed. J. O. Urmson and Marina Sbisa, 2nd ed. Cambridge, Mass., Harvard University Press. 1975.

Awouma, J.-M., and J.-C Noah. 1976. *Contes et fables du Cameroun*, Yaounde, CLE.

Ayissi, L. M. 1972. *Contes et berceuses béti.* Yaounde, CLE.

Bahat, A. 1980. "La poésie hébraïque médiévale." *Cahiers de civilisation médiévale*, 23, pp. 297–322.

Barber, B. 1981. "The Function of Performance in Postmodern Culture." In Pontbriand, *Performance, textes documents*, pp. 32–36.

Barre-Toelken, J. 1969. "The Pretty Language of Yellowman." *Genre*, 2, pp. 211–35.

Barthes, R. 1971. "Ecrivains, intellectuels, professeurs." *Tel quel*, 47, pp. 3–18.

Bastet, N. 1971. "Valéry et la voix poétique." *Annales de la faculté des lettres de Nice*, 15, pp. 41–50.

Baumgarten, M. 1977. "Lyric as Performance." *Comparative Literature* (Eugene,Oreg.), 20, pp. 328–50.

Bäuml, B. and F. 1975. *A Dictionary of Gestures.* Metuchen, N.J., Scarecrow Press.

Bäuml, F. and E. Spielmann. 1975. "From Illiteracy to Literacy: Prolegomena to a Study of the *Nibelungenlied*." In J. J. Duggan, *Oral Literature: Seven Essays.* London: Scottish Academic Press, 1975. pp. 62–73.

Bausinger, H. 1968. *Formen der Volkspoesie.* Berlin, Schmidt.

Beaudry, N. 1978. "Le *Katajjaq*, un jeu inuit traditionnel." *Etudes inuit* (Quebec), 2, pp. 35–53.

Bec, P. 1977. *La lyrique française au moyen age.* Paris, Picard.

Bellemin-Noel, J. 1979. *Vers l'inconscient du texte.* Paris, Presses universitaires françaises.

Ben-Amos, D. 1969. "Analytical Categories and Ethnic Genres." *Genre*, 2, pp. 275–301.

_____. 1976. *Folklore Genres.* Austin, University of Texas Press.

Benson, L. 1966. "The Literary Character of Anglosaxon Formulaic Poetry." *PMLA*, 83, pp. 334–41.

Berger, R. 1976. *La téléfission.* Paris, Castermann.

Bernard, M. 1976. *L'Expressivité du corps.* Paris, Delarge.

_____. 1980. "La Strategie vocale." *Esprit* (July), pp. 55–62.

Berthet, F. 1979. "Eléments de conversation." *Communications*, 30, pp. 109–63.

Bertin, F. 1981. *Chante toujours tu m'intéresses, ou les combines du showbizz.* Paris, Seuil.

Blanchot, M. 1971. *Le livre à venir.* Paris, Gallimard (1st ed., 1959).

Boglioni, P., ed. 1979. *La culture populaire au moyen age.* Montreal, L'Aurore.

Bologna, C. 1980. "Mostro." *Enciclopedia Einaudi*, 9. Turin, Romana.

_____. 1981. "Voce." *Enciclopedia Einaudi*, 14, Turin, Romana.

Bouazis, C. 1977. *Essais de la sémiotique du sujet*. Brussels, Complexes.

Bouchard, S. 1977. *Chroniques de chasse d'un Montagnais de Migan*. Quebec, Ministère des Affaires culturelles.

Boucharlat, A. 1975. *Le commencement de la sagesse: les dévinettes rwandaises*. Paris, SELAF.

Bouissac, P. 1971. "Pour une sémiotique du cirque." *Semiotica*, 3, pp. 93–120.

Bouquiaux, L., and J. Thomas. 1976. *Enquête et description des langues à tradition orale*. Paris, SELAF, 3 vols.

Bourdieu, P. 1980. *Le sens pratique*. Paris, Minuit.

Bouvier, J.-C., ed. 1980. *Tradition orale et identité culturelle*. Paris, CNRS.

Bowra, C. M. 1962. *Primitive Song*. New York, New American Library.

———. 1978. *Heroic Poetry*. New York, Macmillan (1st ed., 1952).

Bragaglia, A. G., ed. 1961. *Andrea Perrucci, dell'arte rappresentative . . . al improviso (1699)*. Florence, Sansoni.

Brassard, F. 1947. "Recordeux de chansons." *Archives du folklore* (Quebec), 2, pp. 191–202.

Brécy, R. 1978. *Florilège de la chanson révolutionnaire*. Paris, Hier & Demain.

Brednich, R., L. Roehrich, and W. Suppan 1973. *Handbuch des Volksliedes*. Munich, Fink.

Bronzin, G. B. 1976. "La drammatica popolare." In *La drammatica popolare*. pp. 3–62.

Brower, R. H., and E. Milner. 1975. *Japanese Court Poetry*. Stanford, Calif., Stanford University Press (1st ed., 1961).

Bruns, G. L. 1974. *Modern Poetry and the Idea of Language*. New Haven, Conn., Yale University Press.

Brunschwig, C., L.-J. Calvet and J.-C. Klein. 1980. *Cent ans de chanson française*. Paris, Seuil (rev. ed.).

Buchan, D. 1972. *The Ballad and the Folk*. London, Routledge-Kegan.

Burgelin, O. 1970. *La communication de masse*. Paris, SGPP.

Burke, P. 1978. *Popular Culture in Early Modern Europe*. New York, New York University Press.

Burness, D. 1976. *Shaka, King of the Zulus, in African Literature*. Washington, D.C., Three Continents Press.

Bynum, D. E., 1969. "The Generic Nature of Oral Epic Poetry." *Genre*, 2, pp. 236–58.

Calame-Griaule, G. 1965. *Ethnologie et langage: La parole chez les Dogon*. Paris, Gallimard.

———. 1976. "Enquête sur le style oral des conteurs traditionels." In L. Bouquiaux and J. Thomas, *Enquête et description des langues à tradition orale*, vol. 3, pp. 915–29.

———. 1980a. "Le temps des contes." *Critique*, 394, pp. 278–87.

———. 1980b. "La gestuelle des conteurs: état d'une recherche." Paper presented at the colloquium, *Oralité, Culture, Discours*, Urbino, July 1980.

———. 1982. "Ce qui donne du goût aux contes." *Littérature*, 45, pp. 45–59.

Camara, S. 1976. *Gens de la parole*. Paris-The Hauge, Mouton.

Campos, H. de. 1976. *A operacao do testo*. São Paulo, Perspectiva.

Caro Baroja, J. 1969. *Ensayo sobre la literatura de cordel*. Madrid, Occidente.

Cazeneuve, J. 1974. *L'Homme téléspectateur*. Paris, Denoël-Gonthier.

Certeau, M. de. 1984. *The Practice of Everyday Life*. Berkeley, University of California Press (orig. 1980 in French, *L'Invention du quotidien: I. Arts de faire*. Paris, Bourgois, 10/18).

Chadwick, H. M., and N. 1932, 1936, 1940. *The Growth of Literature*. Cambridge, Cambridge University Press, 3 vols.

Chadwick, N. 1942. *Poetry and Prophecy*. Cambridge, Cambridge University Press.

Chadwick, N., and V. Zhirmunsky. 1969. *Oral Epics of Central Asia*. Cambridge, Cambridge University Press.

Charles, D. 1981. "Le timbre, la voix, le temps." In C. Pontbriand, *Performance, textes documents*. p. 110–17.

Charles, M. 1977. *Rhétorique de la lecture*. Paris, Seuil.

Charpentreau, S. 1976. *Le livre d'or de la chanson enfantine*. Paris, Ouvrières.

Charron, C.-Y. 1977. "Quelques mythes et récits de tradition orale inuit." Ph.D. thesis, University of Montreal, 2 vols.

———. 1978a. "Le tambour magique." *Etudes inuit* (Quebec), 2, pp. 3–20.

———. 1978b. "Toward a Transcript and Analysis of Inuit Throat Games." *Ethnomusicology*, 22, pp. 245–60.

Chasca, E. de. 1972. *El arte juglaresca en el Cantar de mio Cid*. Madrid, Gredos (1st ed., 1967).

Chevalier, J. and A. Gheerbrandt. 1973-74. *Dictionnaire des symboles*. Paris, Seghers, 4 vols. (1st ed., 1969).

Chopin, H. 1979. *Poésie sonore internationale*. Paris, Place.

Cirese, A. M. 1969. "Il mare come segno polivante." *Uomo e cultura* (Palermo), 2, pp. 26–58.

Cixous, H., and C. Clément. 1986. *The Newly Born Woman*. Minneapolis, University of Minnesota Press (orig. 1975 in French, *La Jeune née*, Paris, Bourgois, 10/18).

Clarke, S. 1980. *Jah Music. The Evolution of Popular Jamaican Song*. London, Heinemann.

Clastres, H. 1975. *La terre sans mal: le prophétisme tupi-guarani*. Paris, Seuil.

Clouzet, J. 1964. *Jacques Brel*. Paris, Seghers.

———. 1966. *Boris Vian*. Paris, Seghers.

———. 1975. *La nouvelle chanson chilienne*. Paris, Seghers.

Coffin, T. P. 1977. *The British Traditional Ballad in North America*. Austin, University of Texas Press (1st ed., 1950).

Coffin, T. P., and H. Cohen. 1966. *Folklore in America*. Garden City, N.Y. Doubleday.

Coirault, P. 1953. *Formation de nos chansons folkloriques*. Paris, Scarabée.

Collier, J. L. 1978. *The Making of Jazz*. Boston, Houghton Mifflin.

Compagnon, A. 1979. "La glossolalie, une affaire sans histoire?" *Critique*, 87, pp. 824–38.

Conroy, P. ed. 1978. *Ballads and Ballad Research*. Seattle, University of Washington Press.

Copans, J., and P. Couty. 1976. *Contes wolof du Baol*. Paris, Bourgois, 10/18.

Coquet, J.-C. 1973. *Sémiotique littéraire*. Paris, Mame.

Corbeau, J.-P. 1979. "Télévision urbaine et imaginaire rural." In A. Suassuna, *Les imaginaires*. Paris, Bourgois, 10/18, vol. 3, pp. 333–44.

Cosnier, J. 1980. "La gestualité dans l'interaction conversationnelle." Paper presented at the colloquium, *Oralité, Culture, Discours*, Urbino, July 1980.

Costa Fontes, M. da. 1979. *Romanceiro português do Canadà*. Coimbre, Coimbre University Press.

Coupez, A., and T. Kamanzi. 1970. *Littérature de cour au Rwanda*. Oxford: Clarendon.

Courlander, H. 1963. *Negro Folk Music USA*. New York, Columbia University Press.

Couty, D., and A. Rey. 1981. *Le théâtre*. Paris, Bordas.

Coyaud, M. 1980. "La transgression des bienséances dans la littérature orale." *Critique*, 394, pp. 325–32.

Cuisenier, J. 1978. "Le théâtre en Indonésie." In *Théâtres*, pp. 223–41.

Dampierre, E. de. 1963. *Poètes nzakara*. Paris, Julliard.

Davenson, H. 1944. *Le livre des chansons*. Neuchâtel, La Baconnière (reprint 1955, Paris, Seuil).

Denisoff, R. G., 1960. "Songs of Persuasion: A Sociological Analysis of Urban Propaganda Songs." *Journal of American Folklore*. 79, pp. 581–89.

Derive, J. 1975. *Collecte et traduction des littératures orales*. Paris, SELAF.

Derrida, J. 1978. *Writing and Difference*. Chicago, University of Chicago Press (orig. 1967 in French, *L'Ecriture et la différence*. Paris, Seuil).

_____. 1976. *Of Grammatology*. Baltimore, Johns Hopkins University Press (orig. 1967 in French, *De la grammatologie*. Paris, Minuit).

_____. 1973. *Speech and Phenomena, and other Essays on Husserl's Theory of Signs*. Evanston, Ill., Northwestern University Press (orig. 1972 in French, *La voix et le phénomène*. Paris, Presses universitaires francaises).

Devereux, G. 1949. "Mohave Voice and Speech Mannerism." *Word*, 5, pp. 268–72.

Dicionário bio-bibliográfica de repentistas e poetas de bancada. 1978. Joao Pessoa (Brazil), Editora Universitaria.

Diény, J.-P. 1977. *Pastourelles et magnanarelles*. Geneva, Droz.

Dieterlen, G. 1965. *Textes sacrés d'Afrique noire*. Paris, Gallimard.

Dolby, W. 1976. *A History of Chinese Drama*. New York, Barnes & Noble.

Dorson, R. M. 1972. "Concepts of Folklore and Folklife Studies." In Dorson, *Folklore and Folklife*. Chicago, University of Chicago Press, pp. 1–47.

Dournes, J. 1976. *Le parler de Jorai et le style oral de leur expression*. Paris, Publications Orientalistes.

_____. 1980. "Aspects de l'oralité dans une culture traditionnelle." Paper presented at the colloquium, *Oralité, Culture, Discours*, Urbino, July, 1980.

Dragonetti, R. 1961. *Aux frontières du langage poétique*. Gand, Romanica Gandensia, vol. 9.

La drammatica popolare nella valle padana: atti del 4 convegno di studi sui folklore padano, Modena 23–26 maggio 1974. 1976. Florence, Olschki.

Du Berger, J. 1971. *Introduction à la littérature orale*. Quebec, Presses de l'université Laval.

Duby, G. 1980. *The Three Orders: Feudal Society Imagined*. Chicago, University of Chicago Press (orig. 1978 in French, *Les trois ordres ou l'imaginaire du féodalisme*. Paris, Gallimard).

Dugast, I. 1975. *Contes, proverbes et devinettes des Banen*. Paris, SELAF.

Duggan, J. J. 1973. *The Song of Roland: Formulaic Style, Poetic Craft*. Berkeley, University of California Press.

_____. 1975. "Formulaic Diction in the Cantar de mio Cid." In Duggan, ed., *Oral Literature: Seven Essays*. London, Scottish Academic Press, pp. 74–83.

Dumont, M. 1982. "Alliances sexuelles et cannibalisme." Ph.D. thesis, University of Montreal.

Dundes, A., ed. 1965. *The Study of Folklore*. Englewood Cliffs, N.J., Prentice-Hall.

Dupont, J.-C. 1977. *Heritage d'Acadie*. Montreal, Lemeac.

Durand, G. 1969. *Les structures anthropologiques de l'imaginaire*. Paris, Bordas (1st ed., 1960).

Durand, R. 1980. "Une nouvelle théâtralité: la *performance*." *Revue française d'études américaines*, 10, pp. 199–207.

_____. 1981. "La performance et les limites de la théâtralité." In Pontbriand, *Performance textes documents*, pp. 48–54.

Duveau, G. 1946. *La vie ouvrière en France sous le second empire*. Paris, Gallimard.

Duvignaud, J. 1975. "Esquisse pour le Nomade." *Cause commmune*,Paris, Bourgois, 10/18, vol. 2, pp. 13–40.

Edmonson, M. S. 1971. *Lore: An Introduction to the Science of Folklore and Literature*. New York, Holt, Rinehart & Winston.

Edson Richmond, W. 1972. "Narrative Folk Poetry." In Dorson, *Folklore and Folklife*, pp. 85–98.

Eliade, M. 1955. "Littératures orales." In Raymond Queneau, *Histoire des littératures*. Paris, Gallimard, pp. 3–26.

Elicegui, E. G. 1972. "Poesía griega de amigo y poesía arabigo-española." *Emerita* (Madrid), 40, pp. 329–96.

Elliott, A. G. 1980. "The Myth of the Hero." *Olifant* (Winnipeg), 7, pp. 235–47.

Eno Belinga, S. M. 1970. *Découverte des chante-fables du Cameroun*. Paris, Klincksieck.

_____. 1978. *La littérature orale africaine*. Issy-les-Moulineaux, Classiques africains.

Etiemble, R. 1974. *Essais de littérature (vraiment) générale*. Paris, Gallimard.

Fabbri, P. 1979. "Champ de manoeuvres didactiques." *Bulletin du GRSL*, 7, pp. 9–14.

Fabre, D., and J. Lacroix. 1974. *La tradition orale du conte occitan*. Paris, Presses universitaires francaises.

Faik-Nzuji, C. 1977. "La voix du cyondo." *Recherche, pedagogie, culture*, 29–30, pp. 19–29.

Favret-Saada, J. 1977. *Les mots, la mort, les sorts*. Paris, Gallimard.

Faye, J.-P., and J. Roubaud, eds. 1975. *Change de forme*. Vol. 1, Paris, Bourgois, 10/18.

Fédry, J. 1976. "De l'expérience du corps comme structure de langage." *L'Homme*, 16, pp. 65–108.

_____. 1977. "L'Afrique entre l'écriture et l'oralité." *Etudes*, 346, pp. 581–600.

Feral, J. 1982. "Performance and Theatricality." *Modern Drama*, 25, pp. 170–81.

Fernandez, J. W. 1977. "Poetry in Motion." *New Literary History*, 8, pp. 459–84.

Fink, E. 1966. *Le jeu comme symbole du monde*. Paris, Minuit (orig. 1960 in German).

Finnegan, R. 1976. *Oral Literature in Africa*. Oxford, Clarendon Press (1st ed. 1970)

_____. 1977. *Oral Poetry: Its Nature, Significance and Social Context*. Cambridge, Cambridge University Press.

_____. 1978. *Oral Poetry: An Anthology*. London, Penguin.

_____. 1980. "Oral Composition and Oral Literature in the Pacific." Paper presented at the colloquium, *Oralité, Culture, Discours*, Urbino, July 1980.

Flahaut, F. 1978. *La parole intermédiaire*. Paris, Seuil.

_____. 1979. "Le fonctionnement de la parole." *Communications*, 30, pp. 73–79.

Fochi, A. 1980. *Estetica oralitatii*. Bucharest, Minerva.

Foerster, D. M. 1962. *The Fortunes of Epic Poetry* Washington, D.C., Catholic University Press.

Fonagy, I. 1970–71. "Les bases pulsionnelles de la phonation." *Revue française de psychanalyse*, 1, pp. 191–36, and 4, pp. 543–91.

Fonagy, I., and K. Magdies. 1963. "Emotional Patterns in Intonation and Music." *Zeitschrift für Phonetik, Sprachwissenschaft and Kommunikationsforschung*, 16, pp. 293–313.

Fonseca dos Santos, I. 1979. "La littérature populaire en vers du Nord-Est brésilien." *Cause commune*. Paris, Bourgois, 10/18, vol. 1, pp. 187–223.

_____. 1981. "Littérature populaire et littérature savante au Bresil. Ph.D. thesis, University of Paris, 3 vols.

Foschi, U. 1976. "La Donna Lombarda." In *Drammatica*, pp. 128–40.

Fowler, R., ed. 1966. *Essays on Style and Language*. New York, Humanities Press.

Freud, S. 1949. "Three Essays on the Theory of Sexuality." *Standard Edition*, vol. 7, London, Hogarth Press.

_____. 1953. "Fragment of an Analysis of a Case of Hysteria (Dora)." *Standard Edition*, vol. 7.

_____. 1955. "Analysis of a Phobia in a Five-Year-Old Boy (Little Hans)." *Standard Edition*, vol. 10.

_____. 1955. "History of an Infantile Neurosis (Wolf Man)." *Standard Edition*, vol. 17.

_____. 1955. "Psychoanalytic Notes on an Autobiographical Account of a Case of Paranoia (Dementia Paranoides) (Schreber)." *Standard Edition*, vol. 12.

_____. 1955. "Notes upon a Case of Obsessional Neurosis (Rat Man)." *Standard Edition*, vol. 10.

Fribourg, J. 1980a. *Fêtes à Saragosse*. Paris, Musée de l'Homme.

_____. 1980b. "Aspects de la littérature populaire en Aragon.' *Critique*, 394, pp. 312–24.

Fry, D. K. 1975. "Caedmon as a Formulaic Poet." In Duggan, *Oral Literature: Seven Essays*, pp. 41–61.

Gaborieau, M. 1974. "Classification des recits chantés." *Poétique*,19, pp. 313–32.

Gans, E. 1981. "Naissance du moi lyrique." *Poétique*, 46, pp. 129–39.

Garnier, P. 1968. *Spatialisme et poésie concrète*. Paris, Gallimard.

Gasarabwe, E. 1978. *Le geste rwandais*. Paris, Bourgois, 10/18.

Gaspar, L. 1978. *Approche de la parole*. Paris, Gallimard.

Gatera, A. 1971. "Les sources de l'histoire africaine: l'exemple du Rwanda." *Presence africaine*, 80, pp. 73–90.

Geertz, C. 1973. *The Interpretation of Cultures*. New York, Basic Books.

Genette, G. 1976. *Mimologiques*. Paris, Seuil.

_____. 1979. *Introduction à l'architexte*. Paris, Seuil.

Georges, R. A. 1972. "Recreations and Games." In Dorson, *Folklore and Folklife*, pp. 173–89.

Giard, L., and P. Mayol. 1980. *L'Invention du quotidien: II. Habiter, cuisiner*. Paris, Bourgois, 10/18.

Gide, A. 1981. *Voyage au Congo and retour du Tchad*. Paris, Gallimard (1st ed. 1927, Paris, Gallimard; Engl. version, 1930, *Travels in the Congo*. New York, Knopf).

Gilles, H. 1979. "Une nouvelle approche de la dynamique du langage." *Diogène*, 106, pp. 119–36.

Gili, J. 1961. "Western and chanson de geste." In H. Agel, ed., *Le western*. Paris, Minard.

Goody, J. 1968. *Literacy in Traditional Societies*. Cambridge, Cambridge University Press.

_____. 1977. *The Domestication of the Savage Mind*. Cambridge, Cambridge University Press.

Goody, J. and I. R. Watt. 1963. "The Consequences of Literacy." *Comparative Studies in History and Society*, 5, pp. 304–45.

Görög-Karady, V. 1976. *Noirs et blancs: leur image dans la littérature orale africaine*. Paris, SELAF.

_____. 1981. *La littérature orale africaine: bibliographie analytique*. Paris, Maisonneuve-Larose.

Gossman, L. 1971. "Literary Education and Democracy." *Modern Language Notes*, 86, pp. 761–89.

Grassin, J.-M. 1980. "La littérature africaine comparée: tradition et modernité." *L'Afrique litteraire*, 54–55, pp. 3–10.

Greenway, J. 1960. *American Folksongs of Protest*. New York, Barnes (1st ed. 1953, Philadelphia, University of Pennsylvania Press).

_____. 1964. *Literature among the Primitives*. Harboro, Pa. Folk Associates.

Greimas, A. J. 1987. *On Meaning: Selected Writings in Semiotic Theory*. Minneapolis, University of Minnesota Press (orig. 1970 in French, *Du sens*. Paris, Seuil).

_____. 1979. "Pour une sémiotique didactique." *Bulletin du GRSL*, 7, pp. 3–8.

Greimas A. J., and J. Courtes. 1982. *Semiotics and Language: An Analytic Dictionary*. Bloomington, Indiana University Press (orig. 1979, *Sémiotique: dictionnaire raisonné de la théorie du langage*. Paris, Hachette).

Grice, P. 1975. "Logic and Conversation." In P. Cole and J. L. Morgan, *Syntax and Semantics*. Vol. 3, *Speech Acts*. New York, Academic Press, pp. 41–58.

Groddeck, G. 1972. "Musique et inconscient." *Musique en jeu*, 9, pp. 3–6.

Guéron, J. 1974. "La métrique des nursery rhymes." *Cahiers de poétique comparée*, 1, pp. 68–93.

_____. 1975. "Langue et poésie: mètre et phonologie." In J.-P. Faye and J. Roubaud, *Change de forme*, pp. 137–57.

Guibert, A. 1962. *Léopold Sedar Senghor*. Paris, Présence africaine.

Guillermaz, P. 1966. *La poésie chinoise des origines à la Révolution*. Paris, Marabout (1st ed., 1957).

Guiraud, P. 1980. *Le langage du corps*. Paris, Presses universitaires françaises.

Haas, R. 1980. *Die mittelenglische Totenklage*. Frankfurt, Lang.

Hall, E. 1950. *The Silent Language*. Greenwich, Conn., Fawcett.

Halle, M., and S. Keyser. 1975. "Sur les bases théoriques d'une poésie métrique." In J.-P. Faye and J. Roubaud, *Change de forme*, pp. 94–134.

Hamori, A. 1975. *On the Art of Medieval Arabic Literature.* Princeton, N.J., Princeton University Press.

Harcourt, M. and R. d' 1956. *Chansons folkloriques françaises au Canada.* Paris, Presses universitaires françaises.

Hauser, M. 1978. "Inuit Songs from Southwest Baffin Island." *Etudes inuit* (Quebec), 2, pp. 55–83.

Havelock, E. A. 1963. *Preface to Plato.* Cambridge, Mass., Harvard University Press.

Hay, L. 1979. "La critique génétique: origine et perspectives." In R. Debray and R. Genette et al., *Essais de critique génétique.* Paris, Flammarion, pp. 227–36.

Haymes, E. R. 1973. *A Bibliography of the Studies Relating to Parry's and Lord's Oral Theory.* Cambridge, Mass., Harvard University Press.

––––––. 1977. *Das mündliche Epos.* Stuttgart, Merzler.

Heidegger, M. 1971a. *Poetry, Language, Thought.* Harper & Row (orig. 1959 in German).

––––––. 1971b. *On the Way to Language.* New York, Harper & Row (orig. 1959 in German).

Helffer, M. 1977. *Les chants dans l'épopée tibétaine de Ge-Sar.* Geneva, Droz.

Hell, V. 1978. *Nathan Katz.* Colmar, Alsatia.

Henry, H. and E. Malleret. 1981. "Traduire en français les rythmes de la poésie russe." *Langue française,* 2, pp. 63–76.

Herkovits, M. J. 1960. *Cultural Anthropology.* New York, Knopf.

Hilger, M. I. 1971. *Together with the Ainu.* Norman, University of Oklahoma Press.

Hoffmann, R., and J.-M. Leduc. 1978. *Rock babies: vingt ans de pop music.* Paris, Seuil.

Houis, M. 1978. "Pour une taxinomie des textes en oralité." *Afrique et langage,* 10, pp. 4–23.

Huizinga, J. *Homo ludens.* London, Routledge-Kegan (orig. 1939 in German).

Husson, R. 1960. *La voix chantée.* Paris, Gauthier-Villars.

Hymes, D. 1973. *Breakthrough into Performance.* Documents du centre de sémiotique d'Urbino, 26–27.

––––––. 1977. "Discovering Oral Performance." *New Literary History,* 8, pp. 431–57.

Ikegami, Y. 1971. "Hand Gestures in Indian Classical Dancing." *Semiotica,* 4, pp. 365–91.

Iser, W. 1978. "Narrative Strategies as Means of Communication." In M. J. Valdes and O. J. Miller, *Interpretation of Narrative.* Toronto, Toronto University Press, pp. 100–17.

Jackson, B., ed. 1972. *Wake Up Dead Man: Afro-American Worksongs from Texas Prisons.* Cambridge, Mass., Harbard University Press.

Jahn, J. 1961. *Muntu: The New African Culture.* New York, Grove Press (orig. 1958 in German).

––––––. 1968. *Neo-African Literature: A History of Black Writing.* New York, Grove Press (orig. 1966 in German).

Jakobson, R. 1963. *Essais de linguistique générale.* Paris, Minuit (orig. 1949–62).

––––––. 1973. *Questions de poétique.* Paris, Seuil (orig. 1919–72).

Jaquetti, P. 1960. "La comptine." In *Atti VIIIᵉ congresso internazionale di studi romanzi.* 3 vols. Florence, Sansoni, vol. 2, pp. 567–99.

Jason, H. 1969. "A Multidimensional Approach to Oral Literature." *Current Anthropology,* 10, pp. 413–26.

––––––. 1977. "A Model for Narrative Structure in Oral Literature." In H. Jason and D. Segal, eds. 1977. *Patterns in Oral Literature.* Paris-The Hague, Mouton, pp. 99–140.

Jauss, H. R. 1977. *Alterität und Modernität der mittelalterlichen Literatur.* Munich, Fink.

––––––. 1982. *Toward an Aesthetic of Reception.* Minneapolis, University of Minnesota Press (orig. 1972–75 in German).

––––––. 1980. "Limites et taches d'une herméneutique littéraire." *Diogène,* 109, pp. 102–33.

Jemie, O. 1980. *Langston Hughes.* New York, Columbia University Press.

Jouve, D., and A. Tomenti. 1981. "Essai sur la culture orale urbaine à Bangui." *Sendayanga ti laso: linguistique actuelle* (Bangui), 4, pp. 16–26.

Jung, C. G. 1959–60. *Collected Works*. 17 vols. New York, Pantheon (orig. in German, 1930–61).

Kellogg, R. 1977. "Literature, Non-Literature and Oral Tradition." *New Literary History*, 8, pp. 531–34.

Kerbrat-Orecchioni, C. 1980. *L'Enonciation*. Paris, Colin.

Kesteloot, L. 1971a. *La poésie traditionnelle*. Paris, Nathan.

———. 1971b. *L'Epopée traditionnelle*. Paris, Nathan.

———. 1980. "Problématique de la littérature orale." *L'Afrique littéraire*, 54, pp. 38–48.

Kibedi-Varga, A. 1977. *Les constates du poéme*. Paris, Picard (1st ed., 1963).

Kindaiti, K. 1941. *Ainu Life and Legend*. Tokyo, Board of Tourist Industry.

Knorringa, R. 1978. *Fonction phatique et tradition orale: constantes et transformations dans un chant narratif roumain*. Amsterdam, Rodopi.

———. 1980. *Het oor wil ook wat*. Assen, Van Gorcum.

Kristeva, J. 1984. *Revolution in Poetic Language*. New York, Columbia University Press (orig. in French, *La Révolution du langage poétique*. Paris, Seuil, 1974).

———. 1975. *La traversée des signes*. Paris, Seuil.

Lacourcière, L. 1966. "La tradition orale au Canada." In C. Galarneau and E. Lavoie, *France et Canada français du XVIe au XXe siècle*, Quebec, University of Laval Press, pp. 223–31.

Lafont, R. 1967. *La révolution régionaliste*. Paris, Gallimard.

Laforte, C. 1976. *Poétiques de la chanson traditionnelle française*. Quebec, University of Laval Press.

———. 1981. *Survivances médiévales dans la chanson folklorique française*. Quebec, University of Laval Press.

Lamy, S. 1979. *D'elles*. Montreal, Hexagone.

Languages. 1976 (*Languages, Literatures in the Formation of National and Cultural Communities*). Adelaide (Australia), Griffin Press.

Lapointe, R. 1977. "Tradition and Language: The Import of Oral Expression." In D. Knight, ed., *Tradition and Theology in Old Testament*. Philadelphia, Fortress Press, pp. 125–42.

Lascaux, G. 1973. *Le monstre dans l'art occidental*. Paris, Klincksieck.

Laya, D. 1972. *La tradition orale: problématique et méthodologie des sources de l'histoire africaine*. Paris, UNESCO.

Laye, C. 1978. *Le maître de la parole*. Paris, Plon.

Leach, M., ed. 1949. *Standard Dictionary of Folklore, Mythology, and Legend*. 2 vols. New York, Funk & Wagnalls.

Le Goff, J. 1980. *Time, Work and Culture in the Middle Ages*. Chicago: University of Chicago Press (French original, *Pour un autre moyan age*. Paris, Gallimard, 1977).

Lejeune, P. 1989. *Je est un autre*. Prais, Seuil.

Lempereur, F. 1976. *Les Wallons d'Amérique du Nord*. Gembloux, Duculot.

Likhatchev, D. 1972. "L'étiquette littéraire." *Poétique*, 9, pp. 118–23 (orig. in Russian, 1967).

Lindenfeld, J. 1971. "Verbal and Non-Verbal Elements in Discourse." *Semiotica*, 3, pp. 223–33.

Literatura. 1973 (*Literatura popular em verso: Estudos*). Rio de Janeiro, Casa Rui Barbosa.

Lohisse, J. 1979. "La société de l'oralité et son langage." *Diogène*, 106, pp. 78–98.

Lomax, A. 1964. "Phonotactique du chant populaire." *L'Homme* 4, pp. 5–55.

———. 1968, *Folksong Style and Culture*. Washington, D.C., American Association for the Advancement of Sciences.

Lomax, A., and A.Halifax. 1971. "Folk Song Texts as Culture Indicators." In P. Maranda and E. Köngäs, eds., *Structural Analysis of Oral Tradition*. Philadelphia, Pennsylvania University Press, pp. 235–67.

Lord, A. B. 1954. *Serbo-Croatian Heroic Songs*. Cambridge, Mass., Harvard University Press.

———. 1959. "The Poetics of Oral Creation." In P Freiderich, ed., *Comparative Literature*. Chapel Hill, University of North Carolina Press, vol. 1, pp. 1–6.

———. 1968. *The Singer of Tales*. New York, Athenaeum (1st ed. 1960).

———. 1975. "Perspectives on Recent Work on Oral Literature." In Duggan, *Oral Literature: Seven Essays*, pp. 1–24.

Lotman, I. 1970. "Le hors-texte." *Change*, 6, pp. 68–81.

———. 1977. *The Structure of the Artistic Text*. Ann Arbor, University of Michigan (original in Russian, 1970).

Lotman, I., and A. Piatigorsky. 1978. "Text and Function." *NHL* 9, pp. 233–44 (French version, 1969, in *Semiotica*, 1, pp. 205–17).

Lusson, P. 1973. "Notes préliminaires sur le rythme." *Cahiers de poétique comparée*, 1, pp. 30–54.

Lyotard, J.-F. 1984. *The Postmodern Condition: A Report on Knowledge*. Minneapolis, University of Minnesota Press (French original 1979, *La Condition post-moderne*. Paris, Minuit).

Mahony, P. 1979. "The Boundaries of Free Association." *Psychoanalysis and Contemporary Thought*, 2, pp. 155–98.

———. 1980. "Towards the Understanding of Translation in Psychoanalysis." *Journal of the American Psychoanalytic Association*, 28, pp. 461–75.

Maquet, J. 1966. *Les civilisations noires*. Paris, Marabout.

Maquiso, E. 1977. *Ulahingan: An Epic of the Southern Philippines*. Dumaguete City (Philippines), Silliman University Press.

Maranda, P. 1978. "Le folklore à l'école. In *Mélanges L. Lacourcière*, Montreal, Leméac, pp. 293–312.

———. 1980. "The Dialectic of Metaphor." In S. R. Suleiman and I. Crosman, eds., *The Reader in the Text*. Princeton, N.J., Princeton University Press, pp. 183–204.

Maranda, P., and E. Köngaš, 1971. *Structural Models in Folklore and Transformational Essays*. Paris-The Hague, Mouton.

Marin, F. M. 1971. *Poesía narrativa árabe y epica hispánica*. Madrid, Gredos.

Massin, B. 1977. *Franz Schubert*. Paris, Fayard.

McLuhan, M. 1962. *The Gutenberg Galaxy*. London, Routledge & Kegan Paul.

———. 1967. *Understanding Media: The Extensions of Man*. London, Sphere Books.

Mendoza, V. T. 1939. *El romance español y el corrido*. Mexico, Universidad nacional.

Menendez Pidal, R. 1959. *La Chanson de Roland y el neotradicionalismo*. Madrid, Espasa Calpe.

———. 1968. *Romancero hispánico*. 2 vols. Madrid, Espasa Calpe (1st ed., 1953).

Meschonnic, H. 1970–73. *Pour la poétique*. Vols. 1 and 2. Paris, Gallimard.

———. 1975. *Le signe et le poème*. Paris, Gallimard.

———. 1978. *Poésie sans réponse*. Paris, Gallimard.

———. 1981. *Jona et le signifiant*. Paris, Gallimard.

Millières, G. 1978. *Quebec, chant des possibles*. Paris, Albin Michel.

Milner, J.-C. 1978. *L'Amour de la langue*. Paris, Seuil.

———. 1982. *Ordres et raisons de langue*. Paris, Seuil.

Montaigne, Michel de. 1962. *Oeuvres complètes*. Ed A. Thibaudet. Paris Pléiade.

Moreno, A., and I. Fonseca dos Santos. 1980. "Creation et transmission de la poésie orale: la chanson d'Alfonso XII." *Arquivos do Centro cultural português*. (Paris), pp. 411–52.

Mounin, G. 1973. "Une analyse du langage par gestes des Indiens." *Semiotica*, 7, pp. 154–62.

Mouralis, B. 1975. *Les contre-littératures*. Paris, PUF.

Mutwa, C. V. 1977. *My People*. London, Penguin (1st ed., 1969).

Nagler, M. 1967. "Towards a Generative View of the Oral Formula." *Transactions of the American Philological Association*, 98, pp. 269–311.

Ndong Ndoutoume, T. 1970 and 1975. *Le Mvett*. 2 vols. Paris, Présence africaine.

Nettl, B. 1956. *Music in Primitive Culture*. Cambridge, Mass., Harvard University Press.

Neuburg, V. 1977. *Popular Literature*. London-New York, Penguin.

Ngal, N. 1977. "Literary Creation in Oral Civilizations." *New Literary History*, 8, pp. 335–44.

Niane, T. 1975a. *Recherches sur l'empire du Mali au moyen age*. Paris, Présence africaine.

———. 1975b. *Le Soudan occidental au temps des grands empires*. Paris, Présence africaine.

———. 1979. *Soundiata, l'épopée mandingue*. Paris, Présence africaine (1st ed., 1969).

Nietzsche, F. 1967. *The Birth of Tragedy and the Case of Wagner*. New York, Vintage Books (original in German, 1871).

Nisard, C. 1968. *Histoire des livres populaires*. 2 vols. Paris, Maisonneuve-Larose (reprint of the 1854 text). 2 vols.

Nyeki, L. 1973. "Le rythme linguistique en français et en hongrois." *Langue française*, 19, pp. 120–42.

Oinas, A. V. 1968. *Heroic Epic and Saga*. Bloomington, Indiana University Press.

Okpewho, I. 1979. *The Epic in Africa*. New York, Columbia University Press.

Ong, W. 1967. *Presence of the Word*. New Haven, Conn., Yale University Press.

———. 1971. *Rhetoric, Romance and Technology*. Ithaca, N.Y., Cornell University Press.

———. 1977a. *Interfaces of the Word*. Ithaca, N.Y., Cornell University Press.

———. 1977b. "African Talking Drums and Oral Poetics." *New Literary History*, 8, pp. 411–30.

———. 1979. "Literacy and Orality in Our Time." In *Profession 79, Publication of the Modern Language Association of America*, pp. 1–7.

Opland J. 1971. " 'Scop' and 'Imbongi' — Anglosaxon and Bantu Oral Poets." *English Studies in Africa*, 14, pp. 161–78.

———. 1975. "Imbongi Nezibongo: The Xhosa Tribal Poet." *Publications of the Modern Languages Association of America*, 90, pp. 185–208.

Oster H. 1969. "The Blues as a Genre." *Genres*, 2, pp. 249–73.

Owens, C. 1981. "The Allegorical Impulse." In Pontbriand, *Performance, textes documents*, pp. 37–47.

Paredes, A. 1958. *"With His Pistol in His Hand": A Border Ballade*. Austin, University of Texas Press.

Paredes, A., and E. Stekert. eds. 1971. *The Urban Experience and Folk Tradition*. Austin, American Folklore Society, University of Texas Press.

Paredes, A., and R. Baumann. 1972. *Toward New Perspectives in Folklore*. Austin, University of Texas Press.

Parisot, H. 1978. *Soixante-treize comptines et chansons*. Paris, Aubier.

Paulme, C. 1961. "Littérature orale et comportements sociaux en Afrique noire." *L'Homme* 1, pp. 37–49.

Penel, J.-D. 1981. "Quelques chants de ronde et de *gbagba*." *Sendayanga ti laso: linguistique actuelle* (Bangui), 4, pp. 22–72.

Pessel, A. 1979. "De la conversation chez les Précieuses." *Communications* 30, pp. 14–30.

Pézard, A. 1965. *Dantes, Oeuvres complètes*. Paris, Gallimard, Pléiade.

Pontbriand, C., ed. 1981. *Performance, textes documents*. Montreal, Parachute.

Pop, M. 1968. "Der formelhafte Charakter der Volksdichtung." *Deutsches Jahrbuch für Volkskunde*, 14, pp. 11-15.

———. 1970. "La poétique du conte populaire." *Semiotica*, 2, pp. 117–27.

Poueigh, J. 1976. *Le folklore des pays d'oc*. Paris, Payot.

Poujol, G., and R. Labourie, eds. 1979. *Les cultures populaires*. Toulouse, Privat.

Quasha, G. 1977. "Dialogos: Between the Written and the Oral in Contemporary Poetry." *New Literary History*, 8, pp. 485–506.

Ravier, X., and J. Séguy. 1978. *Poemes chantés des Pyrénées gasconnes*. Paris, CNRS.

Récanati, F. 1979a. *La transparence de l'énonciation*. Paris, Seuil.

———. 1979b. Insinuations et sous-entendus." *Communications*, 30, pp. 95–106.

Recueil 1980 (Recueil de littérature mandingue). Paris, Agence de coopération culturelle et technique.

Rens, J., and R. Leblanc. 1977. *Acadie expérience: choix de textes acadiens*. Montreal, Partipris.

Renzi, L. 1969. *Canti narrativi tradizionali rumeni*. Florence, Olschki.

———. 1971. "Varianti d'interprete nei canti tradizionali narrativi rumeni." In *Actes du XIIe congrès international de linguistique romane*. Bucharest, Academie, pp. 471–80.

Rey-Hulman, D. 1977. "Règles sociales de recitation des contes en Haute-Volta." *Recherches, pédagogie et culture*, 29–30, pp. 14–16.

———. 1982. "Proces d'énonciation des contes." *Littérature*, 45, pp. 35–44.

Ricard, A. 1977. "Un genre oral nouveau: le *concert*." *Recherches, pédagogie, culture*, 21–30, pp. 30–34.

———. 1980. "Le mythe de la tradition dans la critique littéraire africaniste." *L'Afrique littéraire*. 54–55, pp. 18–23.

Ricoeur, P. 1980. "La grammaire narrative de Greimas." *Documents du GRSL*, 15.

Ringeas, R., and G. Coutant. 1966. *Gaston Coute*. Saint-Ouen, Ed. du vieux Saint-Ouen.

Rondeleux, L.-J. 1980. "La voix, les registres et la sexualité." *Esprit* (July), pp. 46–54.

Rosenberg, B. A. 1970. *The Art of the American Folk Preacher*. New York, Oxford University Press.

Rosolato, G. 1968. *Essais sur le symbolique*. Paris, Gallimard.

———. 1978. "La voix entre corps et langage." In Rosalato, *La relation d'inconnu*. Paris, Gallimard.

Rouget, G. 1980. *La musique et la transe*. Paris, Gallimard.

Roy, C. 1954. *Trésor de la poésie populaire*. Paris, Seghers.

———. 1981. *Littérature orale en Gaspésie*. Montreal, Leméac.

Ruwet, N. 1972. *Langue, musique, poésie*. Paris, Seuil.

———. 1981. *Linguistique et poétique*. Documents du centre de sémiotique. Urbino, p. 100.

Rycroft, D. 1960. "Melodic Features in Zulu Eulogistic Recitation." *African Language Review*, 1, pp. 60–78.

Rytkheou, I. 1978. "Ceux qui ont enjambé les millénaires." *Europe*, 585, pp. 6–16.

Saraiva, A. J. 1974. "*Message et littérature*." *Poetique*, 17, pp. 1–13.

Sargent, H. C., and G. L. Kittredge. 1904. *English and Scottish Popular Ballads*. Boston, Houghton Mifflin.

Sartre, J.-P. 1940. *L'Imaginaire*. Paris, Gallimard.

Savard, R. 1974. *Carcajou et le sens du monde*. Quebec, Ministère des Affaires culturelles.

———. 1976. "La transcription des contes oraux." *Etudes françaises* (Montreal), 12, pp. 51–60.

Scarpetta, G. 1981. "Erotique de la performance." In Pontbriand, *Performance, textes documents*, pp. 138–44.

Scheub, H. 1975. "Oral Narrative Process and the Use of Models." *New Literary History*, 6, pp. 353–68.

———. 1977. "Body and Image in Oral Narrative Performance." *New Literary History*, 8, pp. 345–68.

Schilder, P. 1950. *The Image and Appearance of the Human Body*. New York, International Universities Press (orig. in German, 1923).

Schmitt, J.-C. 1978a. "Techniques du corps et conscience de groupe." Paper presented at the Consciousness and Group Identification Colloquium, Toronto, April 1978.

_____. 1978b. "Gestus, gesticulatio: contribution à l'étude du vocabulaire médiéval des gestes." Paper presented at the colloquium on lexicography, CNRS, Paris, October 1978.

Schneider, M. 1970. "Il significato della voce." In Schneider, *Il significato della musica*. Milan, Rusconi, pp. 151–81 (German original, 1952).

Searle, J. R. 1969. *Speech Acts*. Cambridge, Cambridge University Press.

Sebeok. T. 1978. *Considerazioni sulla semiosi*. Documents du centre de sémiotique d'Urbino, p. 77.

Sébillot, P. 1904–7. *Le Folklore de France*. 4 vols. Paris, Librairie orientale et américaine.

Segre, C. 1979. "Generi." In *Enciclopedia Einaudi*, 6, Turin, Romano.

_____. 1980. "Narrazione/narrativitá." In *Enciclopedia Einaudi*, 9, Turin, Romano.

Serres, M. 1981. *Genèse*. Paris, Grasset.

Seydou, C. 1980. "Poésie pastorale des Peuls du Mâssina (Mali)." Paper presented at the conference *Oralité, Culture, Discours*, Urbino, July 1980.

Sherzer, D. and J. 1972. "Literature in San Blas." *Semiotica*, 6, pp. 182–99.

Sieffert, R. 1978a. *Le cycle épique des Taïra et des Minamoto: le dit de heiké*. Paris, Publications Orientalistes.

_____. 1978b. "Le Théâtre japonais." In *Théâtres*, pp. 133–61.

Slattery-Durley, M. 1972. *Oral Tradition: Study and Select Bibliography*. Montreal, Institut d'Etudes Médiévales.

Smith, P. 1974. "Des genres et des hommes." *Poetique*, 19, pp. 294–312.

_____. 1980. *La fête dans son contexte rituel*. Documents du centre de sémiotique d'Urbino, pp. 92–93.

Smith, R. J. 1972. "Festivals and Celebrations." In Dorson, *Folklore and Folklife*, pp. 159–72.

Stein, R. A. 1959. *Recherches sur le barde et l'épopée au Tibet*. Paris, Presses universitaires françaises.

_____. 1978. "Le théâtre au Tibet." In *Théâtres*, pp. 245–56.

Stern, T. 1957. "Drum and Whistle 'Languages': An Analysis of Speech Surrogates." *American Anthropology*, 59, pp. 487–506.

Stewart, P. 1980. "Il testo teatrale e la questione del doppio destinatario." *Quaderni d'italianistica*, 1, pp. 15–29.

Stierle, K. 1977. "Identité du discours et transgression lyrique." *Poétique*, 32, pp. 422–41.

Stoianova, I. 1978. *Geste, texte, musique*. Paris, Bourgois, 10/18.

Stolz, B., and R. S. Shannon, eds. 1977. *Oral Literature and the Formula* Ann Arbor, University of Michigan Press.

Strauss, L. 1957. "Works of the Mind." Paper presented at a conference at the University of Chicago January 25, 1957, copyright of the Leo Strauss Estate (see French version, 1981, "Sur l'interprétation de la Génèse," *L'Homme*, 21, pp. 21–36).

Taksami, T. 1978. "La littérature des petits peuples du Grand Nord soviétique." *Europe*, 585, pp. 34–44.

Tedlock, D. 1972. *Finding the Center: Narrative Poetry of the Zuni Indians*. New York, Dial Press.

_____. 1977. "Towards an Oral Poetics." *New Literary History*, 8, pp. 507–20.

Terrracini, B. 1959. "Il patrimonio poetico di un commune delle Alpi piemontesi." In *Studi in onore di A. Monteverdi*, Modena, STEM.

Théâtres. 1978. (Les théâtres d'Asie). Paris, CNRS.

Thomas, L.-V. 1978. "Afrique noire: littératures traditionnelles." In *Encyclopaedia universalis*. Paris, Editions universitaires de France, S.A. vol. 1, pp. 413–20.

Thompson, S. 1977. *Motif Index of Folk Literature*. 5 vols. Bloomington, Indiana University Press (1st ed., 1932–36).

Thrasher, A. A. 1978. *Notre silence a déjà trop duré*. Montreal, Bellarmin.

Todorov, T. 1978. *Les genres du discours*. Paris, Seuil.

———. 1984. *Mikhail Bakhtin, The Dialogic Principle*, Minneapolis, University of Minnesota Press (French original, *Mikhail Bakhtine le principe dialogique*. Paris, Seuil, 1981).

Tomatis, A. 1975. *La libération d'Oedipe*. Paris, ESF.

———. 1978. *L'Oreille et le langage*. Paris, Seuil.

Tristani, J.-L. 1978. *Le stade du respir*. Paris, Minuit.

Utley, F. I. 1969. "Oral Genres as Bridge to Written Literature." *Genres*, 2, pp. 91–103.

Valderama, A. Y. 1980. "Le *Harawi*." *Critique*, 394, pp. 303–11.

Valéry, P. 1962. *Variéte. Oeuvres I*. Paris, Gallimard, Pléaide.

Vansina, J. 1965. *Oral Tradition*. London, Routledge-Kegan (original in French, 1961).

———. 1971. "Once upon a Time: Oral Tradition as History in Africa." *Daedalus*, 100, pp. 442–68.

Vassal, J. 1977. *Folksong*. Paris, Albin Michel.

———. 1980. *La chanson bretonne*. Paris, Albin Michel.

Vasse, D. 1974. *L'Ombilic et la Voix*. Paris, Seuil.

———. 1978. "L'Arbre de la voix." *Sémiologiques*, 6, pp. 127–38.

———. 1980. "La voix qui crie dans le désêtre." *Esprit* (July), pp. 63–81.

Vernillat, F., and J. Charpentreau. 1968. *Dictionnaire de la chanson française*. Paris, Larousse.

Vicol, A. 1972. "Aspecte ale relatiilor text-melodie in cintecele epice romanesti." *Rivista de etnografie si folclor* (Bucharest), 17, pp. 107–43.

Vincent, S. 1976. "Les bonnes et les mauvaises alliances." *Recherches amérindiennes au Quebec*, 6.

Voigt, V. 1969. "Structural Definition of Oral Literature." In *Proceedings of the 6th Congress of the International Comparative Literature Association*. Amsterdam, Zweets-Zeitlinger, pp. 461–67.

———. 1973. "Position d'un problème: la hiérarchie des genres dans le folklore." *Semiotica*, 7, pp. 135–41.

———. 1977. "Reduction Possiblities of Recent Folk Tale Research." *Annales de l'université de Budapest*, 8, pp. 225–30.

———. 1978. "Sur les niveaux des variantes des proverbes." In *Strutture e generi delle letterature etniche*. Palermo, Flaccovia, pp. 206–18.

Voltz, M. 1979. "Etnomorphologie des masques bwaba." *Annales de l'ESLSH* (Ouagadougou), 3, pp. 12–51.

Wang, C. H. 1977. "Studies in Chinese Literary Genres." *Comparative Literature* (Eugene, Oreg.), 29, pp. 355–59.

Wardropper, W. B. 1980. "Meaning in Medieval Spanish Folk Song." In W. T. H. Jackson, ed., *The Interpretation of Medieval Lyric Poetry*. New York, Columbia University Press, pp. 176–93.

Warner, A. 1975. *Rezeptionsasthetik*. Munich, Fink.

———. 1979. "Pour une pragmatique du discours fictionnel." *Poétique*, 34, pp. 175–278.

Werner, E. 1960. *The Sacred Bridge*. New York, Columbia University Press.

Wilson, A. 1976. *Traditional Romance and Tale: How Stories Mean*. Ipswich (England), Brewer.

Wilson, E. 1959. *Apologies to the Iroquois*. New York, Vintage Books (Random House).

Winner, T. G. 1958. *The Oral Art and Literature of the Kazakhs of Russian Central Asia*. Durham, N.C., Duke University Press.

Wurm, M. 1977. *Chantez, peuples d'Espagne*. Paris, Albin Michel.

Yates, F. 1969. *The Art of Memory*. London, Penguin.

Yondo, E.-E. 1976. *La place de la littérature orale en Afrique*. Paris, Pensée universelle.

Zadi, B. 1975. "Expérience africaine de la parole." *Revue canadienne des études africaines*, 9, pp. 449–78.

———. 1978. *Césaire entre deux cultures*. Abidjan-Dakar, Nouvelles éditions africaines.

Zavarin, V., and M. Coote. 1979. *Theory of the Formulaic Text*. Documents du centre de sémiotique d'Urbino, p. 89.

Zolkiewski, S. 1973. "Des principes de classement des textes de culture." *Semiotica*, 7, pp. 1–18.

Zumthor, P. 1963. *Langue et technique poétique à l'époque romane*. Paris, Klincksieck.

———. 1972. *Essai de poétique médiévale*. Paris, Seuil.

———. 1978. *Le masque et la lumière: poétique des grands rhétoriqueurs*. Paris, Seuil.

———. 1979. "Pour une poétique de la voix." *Poétique*, 40, pp. 514–24.

———. 1980. "L'Écriture et la voix: d'une littérature populaire brésilienne." *Critique*, 64, pp. 228–39.

———. 1981a. "Paroles de pointe: le *rqakugo* japonais." Nouvelle Revue française, 339, pp. 22–32.

———. 1981b. "Intertextualité et mouvance." *Littérature*, 41, pp. 3–16.

———. 1981c. "Le message poétique oral." *Sendayanga ti laso: linguistique actuelle* (Bangui), 4, pp. 3–15.

———. 1982a. "De l'oralité à la littérature de colportage." *L'Ecrit du temps*, 1, pp. 129–40.

———. 1982b. "Entre l'oral et l'écrit." *Cahiers de Fontenay*, June 1981, pp. 9–33.

———. 1986. *Speaking of the Middle Ages*. Lincoln, University of Nebraska Press (French original, *Parler du moyen age*. Paris, Minuit 1980).

Zwettler, M. 1978. *The Oral Tradition of Classical Arabic Poetry*. Columbus, Ohio State University Press.

Index

Index

Compiled by Hassan Melehy

Literature: and institution, 16; and oral poetry, 27, 32-42, 169-70. *See also* Writing
Lohisse, J., 25, 178
Lomax, Alan, 33, 51, 61, 118, 133, 146
Lomax, John, 51
Lönnrot, Elias, 26, 82
Lorca, Federico García, 156
Lord, A. B., 3, 24, 61, 69, 80, 81, 89, 90, 91, 92, 97, 99, 111, 119, 127, 131, 172-73, 174, 187, 202, 203-4
Lotman, Iouri, 28, 125, 142, 202, 215
Louis XIV, 176, 211
Louis XVI, 108
Louis-Philippe, 217
Lulu, 144
Lusson, P., 131
Lyotard, Jean-François, 21, 23, 113, 132, 183, 226
Lyric: and genre, 76; and narrative, 105-7. *See also* Discourse

Macumba, 66, 134
"Madelon," 48
Maeterlinck, Maurice, 146
Mahabharata, 83
Malinke, 71, 104, 111, 149
Malinowski, B., 22
Mallarmé, Stéphane, 132
Malleret, E., 131
Mallery, Garrick, 154
Mandingo, 54, 85, 122, 198
Manobo, 64, 103, 108, 109, 137, 147; and epic, 84, 87, 94-95; and reception, 186
Maori, 51, 121, 173, 198; and protest song, 221
Maquiso, E., 64, 83, 84, 85, 87, 95, 103, 109, 138, 143, 144, 147, 186
Maranda, P., 23, 29, 37
"Marieke," 109
Marin, F. M., 80, 81, 82, 84, 135
Marini, Giovanna, 209
"Marseillaise," 145, 216
Marsh, Lou, 218
Marx, Karl: and epic, 88
Mask: and gesture, 157. *See also* Theater
Massin, Brigitte, 145, 193
Massin, Jean, 193
Matsushita Electric, 71
Matswa, 73
Mau Mau, 56, 75

Mauss, Marcel, 154
Mayakovski, Vladimir, 131-32
Mayol, P., 65
McLuhan, Marshall, 202, 229; and writing, 24, 227
Meaning: and gesture, 154-55; and performance, 147-48; and speech, 9-10. *See also* Language
Mediat: and epic, 83; and genre, 63; and mass culture, 19; and orality, 25; and oral poetry, 65; and reception, 189, 190-95; and rite, 214; and song, 75; and star, 194; and technology, 18-19; and transmission, 202; and voice, 18-21, 113, 130, 226; and writing, 202. *See also* Communication; Radio; Television
Meier, J., 97
Memory: and blues, 181; and *mouvance*, 180, 202; and orality, 28-29; and performance, 179-81, 196-97; and writing, 197
Mendoza, V. T., 52
Menendez Pidal, R., 15, 52, 80, 97, 98, 133, 137, 138, 161, 199, 200, 202-3
Meschonnic, H., 129, 131, 133, 136, 212
Mestokosho, Matthieu, 224
Metaphor: and speech, 8
Microphone: and reception, 189-90. *See also Mediat*
Millières, G., 50, 109, 209, 219, 223
Milner, J.-C., 28, 44, 45, 103, 118, 129, 135, 203
Milton, John: and blindness, 176; and orality, xi
Mime: and gesture, 157, 158-59
"Mioritsa," 50
Mofolo, Thomas, 26-27
Mogos Vornicul, 205
"Mon père avait cinq cents moutons," 203
Monk, Meredith, 39-42, 228
Monk, Thelonius, 151
Montaigne, Michel de, 15
Montand, Yves, 144
Monteverdi, Claudio, xi, 143
Moore, Davey, 218
Moreno, A., 200
Morin, Edgar, 31
Morse code, 134
Morton, Jelly Roll, 158
Moses, 208
Mouloudji, Marcel, 64

and interpretation, xi; and interpreter, 178;
and irony and parody, 75-76; military, 71-
72; modern era of, 123; and music, x; and
oral poetry, 66, 142-45, 210-11; and
orality, 41-42; and performance, 144; and
poetry, 100; and political action, 215-23;
protest, 219-23; Quebecois, 50, 52, 64,
106, 168, 180, 198, 223; religious, 72-73;
and rite, 213; and sex, 74; and star, 70;
topical, as genre, 74-75; and voice, ix-x,
141-42
Sousa, Soares de, 182
Space: and gesture, 163-64; and performance,
122-25, 197; and voice, 19. *See also* Time
Spectator: and interpreter, 183-87
Speech (*parole*): and gesture, 155; and
language (*langue*), 201; and meaning, 9-
10; and metaphor, 8; and rite, 213; and
voice, 6-8, 47, 141; and woman, 47; and
word, 46-47; and writing, 36
Spielmann, E., 88, 201
Staiger, Emil, 81
Stalin, Joesph, 96
Star: and *mediat*, 194; and song, 70
State: and culture, 14-15; and epic, 94-95
Stein, R. A., 157, 158, 171
Stevens, Wallace: and song, x
Stewart, P., 39
Stierle, Karlheinz, 127
Stivell, Alan, 152, 190
Stolz, B., 97
Strauss, Leo, 30
Stravinsky, Igor, 150
Structuralism: and genre, 37-38
Style: epic, 89-90, 91; and formula, 97; and
oral poetry, 102
Su-nir, 93
Subject: and language, 228; and voice, xii,
6-7, 9, 21-22
Sufism: and reception, 184
Sundiata, 54, 85, 93, 144, 198; and radio, 191

Taksami, T., 49
Tale (*récit*): and narrative, 36-37
Talkings, 130
Tasso, Torquato, 16
Taylor, Vince, 162, 190
"Techniques du corps, Les," 154
Technological civilization: and epic, 95-96;

and oral poetry, 46, 48, 104. *See also*
Mediat
Technology: and *mediat*, 18-19; and memory,
180
Tedlock, D., 27, 30, 31, 80, 132, 133, 136,
180, 187, 188
Telephone: and reception, 189. *See also*
Mediat
Television: and language, 192-93; and
reception, 192-93, 194; and rite, 214; and
the Third World, 20; and voice, xi-xii. *See
also Mediat*
"Temps des cérises, Le," 48
Terracini, B., 50-51
Text: and interpretation, 208; and *mouvance*,
207, 208; and music, 167-68, 206; oral
poetic, and writing, 203-4; and oral poetry,
27-29, 44-45; and performance, 117-19,
197, 206-7, 208; and poet, 167-68; poetic,
and music, 145-47; and reception, 185-86;
and voice, ix-x, 3-4, 41-42; and work, 60-
61. *See also* Discourse; Language; Writing
Theater: and body, 41; and dramatic song, 77;
and oral poetry, 39-42; and performance,
163, 228; and voice, 40; and writing, 41
Theory: and poetics, 3
Third World: and orality, 25, 26, 224; and
protest song, 221; and radio, 20, 191; and
religious song, 72-73; and topical song, 75
Thomas, L.-V., 101, 107, 118, 142, 155, 156,
171, 210
Thompson, S., 9
Thoms, W. J., 13
Timbre: and oral poetry, 148
Time: historical, 121; and oral poetry, 43, 46;
and performance, 119-22, 125, 197. *See
also* Space
Timofeyevich, Yermak, 94
Tito (Josip Broz), 96
Todorov, Tzvetan, 34, 100
Toffler, Alvin, 224
"Tom Joad," 95, 192
Tomatis, A., 5, 10, 129
Tomenti, A., 75, 110
Tone: and language, 133
Toure, Sekou, 71
Townshend, Peter, 163
Tradition: and ethnology, 200; and folklore,
209; and formula, 91-92; and regionalism,
55-56

Theory and History of Literature

Theory and History of Literature

Paul Zumthor retired in 1980 from the University of Montreal, where he was professor of comparative literature. He is well known as a Medievalist and specialist in the field of oral literature. He is author of numerous books, including *La lettre et la voix* (1987), *Parler du moyen âge* (1980), and *Essai de poétique médiévale* (1972).

Walter J. Ong, S.J., Emeritus University Professor of Humanities, William E. Haren Professor of English, and Professor of Humanities in Psychiatry at St. Louis University, is internationally known for his work in Renaissance literary and intellectual history and in contemporary culture as well as for his more wide-ranging work in orality-literacy studies and in the evolution of consciousness. *Orality and Literary* (1982), *The Presence of the Word* (Minnesota, 1981), and *Interfaces of the Word* (1977) are just a few of his many books.

Kathryn Murphy-Judy is assistant professor of French and International Management at the College of St. Thomas. She has taught at the University of Arizona and the University of Minnesota. Murphy-Judy received her Ph.D. in French, specializing in Medieval languages and literature and folklore from the University of Minnesota in 1986.